CADOGANguides

take the kids South of France

ROSIE WHITEHOUSE

Contents

Snapshots of the South of France 01

01

Introduction 29

Preparation 31
Further reading 35

02

History 37

History lesson 38
History in a hurry 44

03

The Riviera 45

ALPES-MARITIMES 48
Nice 48
Around Nice 54
Monaco 56
Special trips from Monaco 60
Around Monaco 61
Cannes 62
Special trips from Cannes 64
Around Cannes 64
VAR 70
Fréjus and St-Raphäel 70
Around Fréjus and St-Raphaël 71
St–Tropez 72
Special trips from St-Tropez 74
Around St-Tropez 75
WHERE TO EAT 80

04

Northern Provence 85

VAUCLUSE
Avignon 89
Special trips from Avignon 92
Around Avignon 96
Carpentras 96
Around Carpentras 97
ALPES-DE-HAUTE-PROVENCE 101
Castellane 101
Special trips from Castellane 102
Around Castellane 102
ALPES-MARITIMES 105
Sospel 105
Around Sospel 106
Valberg 107
Around Valberg 108
WHERE TO EAT 109

05

Western Provence 113

BOUCHES-DU-RHÔNE 116
Aix-en-Provence 116
Special trips from Aix 118
Around Aix 119
Arles 121
Special trips from Arles 124
Around Arles 126
Marseille 129
Special trips from Marseille 132
Around Marseille 134
St-Rémy-de-Provence 135
Around St-Rémy 137
WHERE TO EAT 139

06

Languedoc-Roussillon 143

AUDE 146
Carcassonne 146
Special trips from Carcassonne 149
Around Carcassonne 150
Narbonne 151
Around Narbonne 153
ROUSSILLON 154
Perpignan 154
Special trips from Perpignan 156
Around Perpignan 156
HÉRAULT 161
Agde 161
Around Agde 163
Montpellier 164
Special trips from Montpellier 164
Around Montpellier 167
GARD 170
Nîmes 170
Special trips from Nîmes 172
Around Nîmes 173
WHERE TO EAT 176

07

Corsica 179

CORSE DU SUD 184
Ajaccio 184
Special trips from Ajaccio 188
Around Ajaccio 189
Bonifacio 190
Special trips from Bonifacio 192
Around Bonifacio 193
HAUTE-CORSE 195
Bastia 195
Special trips from Bastia 196
Around Bastia 197
Calvi 199
Special trips from Calvi 202
Around Calvi 202
Corte 203
Around Corte 205
WHERE TO EAT 206

08

Sleep 209

WHERE TO STAY 210
Hotels 210
Holiday villages/ family resorts 213
Youth hostels 214
Self-catering 215
RECOMMENDED ACCOMMODATION 218

09

Eat 241

EATING OUT 242

SOUTH OF FRANCE ON A PLATE 245

EATING IN 247

Some recipes for kids 247

USEFUL PHRASES 249

10

Shop 253

FOOD 254

OTHER SHOPS 255

Markets 255
Small shops 255
Specialist shops 256

CHRISTMAS SHOPPING 258

11

Travel and Practicalities 259

TRAVEL 260

PRACTICAL A–Z 266

FAMILY-FRIENDLY PHRASE BOOK 274

12

Index 277

Maps

Chapter divisions *inside front cover*
Area maps *beginning of each chapter*
Orientation map *inside back cover*

A guide to the guide

In this book we've divided the South of France into five areas. Some of these correspond neatly to their geographical boundaries, like Corsica, but other chapters, like Northern Provence, are more thematic and cover several *départements*.

Each chapter highlights the top towns or cities – the places we think deserve to be singled out either for an overnight stay or as places you'd definitely want to spend a day or two exploring. Some towns may only be places you'll pass through on your journey, but we've included some basics about them should you need to pick up supplies. We've put in as much as we can about the sights, shopping and useful advice for each of these towns/cities, and if there's a decent enough satellite town we've mentioned that too.

After this come the special trips, the must-do excursions within striking distance of your destination town or resort. These are strictly A-list attractions, the ones you won't mind travelling to or devoting an entire day to.

Finally, each chapter also lists sports activities, museums, parks and walks, nature reserves and family friendly beaches.

Advice on specific places to eat is listed at the end of each area chapter.

There are additional chapters at the end of the guide on eating customs, including regional flavours and recipes, plus a list of recommended places to stay, and some general shopping advice. You'll also find a reassuring section offering practical advice on getting to France, getting around, and on how to deal with any problems you may have while you're on holiday.

Inevitably, we haven't listed everything there is to see and do in the South of France. But we have selected those places we think are most suitable for families and that kids will rave about. If you think we've missed something out, please let us know.

About the series

Author

Rosie Whitehouse fell in love with travelling at the age of five when her parents bundled her in the back of the car and drove across Europe. Family travels inspired her to study International History at the London School of Economics and to take up a career at the BBC World Service. She has been travelling with her kids since her son was one month old.

Rosie spent five years in the war-torn Balkans with her young family and now lives in London, where she writes on family matters for newspapers and magazines.

Being married to a Frenchman, Rosie has travelled with their five children all over France. They've taken buses, boats, and trains, as well as trips out in the family car, in order to bring you this book.

Series consultant

Helen Truszkowski is series consultant of Cadogan's *take the kids* series, and author of *take the kids Travelling* and of *take the kids Paris & Disneyland® Resort Paris*. Helen is an established travel writer and photographer. Over the past decade her journeys have taken her around the globe, including six months working in South Africa. Helen's son, George, has accompanied her on her travels since he was a few weeks old.

Series editor

Melanie Dakin is series editor of *take the kids*, having previously acted as consultant editor on the Time Out *London for Children* guide and editor of Time Out's *Kids Out* magazine. Whilst researching this book, Melanie took her eldest child Eve to Corsica to visit her godparents and ride the mountain train.

Cadogan Guides
Highlands House, 165 The Broadway,
London SW19 1NE
info.cadogan@virgin.net
www.cadoganguides.com

The Globe Pequot Press
246 Goose Lane, PO Box 480, Guilford,
Connecticut 06437–0480

Art direction: Sarah Rianhard-Gardner
Cover design: Kicca Tommasi
Series design: Andrew Barker
Original Photography: Mike Clark, Rosie Whitehouse

Managing Editor: Christine Stroyan
Series Editor: Melanie Dakin
Series Consultant: Helen Truszkowski
Author: Rosie Whitehouse

Proofreading: Daphne Trotter
Indexing: Isobel McLean
Production: Book Production Services
Printed and bound in Italy by Legoprint
A catalogue record for this book is available from the British Library
ISBN 1-86011-111-4

Please help us to keep this guide up to date. We have done our best to ensure that information is correct at the time of printing, but places and facilities are constantly changing, and standards and prices fluctuate. We will be delighted to receive your comments concerning existing entries or omissions. Authors of the best letters will receive a copy of the Cadogan Guide of their choice.

Snapshots
of the South of France

Top towns

1 Pont d'Avignon, Avignon p.91
2 Roundabout, Avignon p.89
3 Hotel Negresco, Nice p.52
4 Courtyard, Aix-en-Provence p.116
5 Peillon p.81
6 Harbour, Villefranche-sur-Mer p.55
7 Château
8 Zidane mural, Marseille p.129
9 Fountain, Aix-en-Provence p.116
10 Rooftops, Nîmes p.170
11 Old town, Nice p.51
12 Beach, Fréjus p.70

Look at this!

1 Cathar castle, Peyrepertuse **p.149**
2 Christmas crib figure **p.258**
3 Promenade des Anglais, Nice **p.51**
4 Palais des Papes, Avignon **p.90**
5 Killer whale, Marineland, Antibes **p.64**

6 The walled city of Carcassonne **p.146**
7 Cézanne's workshop, Aix-en-Provence **p.117**
8 Kite festival, Marseille **p.129**
9 Grotte des Demoiselles **p.169**
10 Dinosaur teeth, Aix-en-Provence **p.117**

11
12
13
14

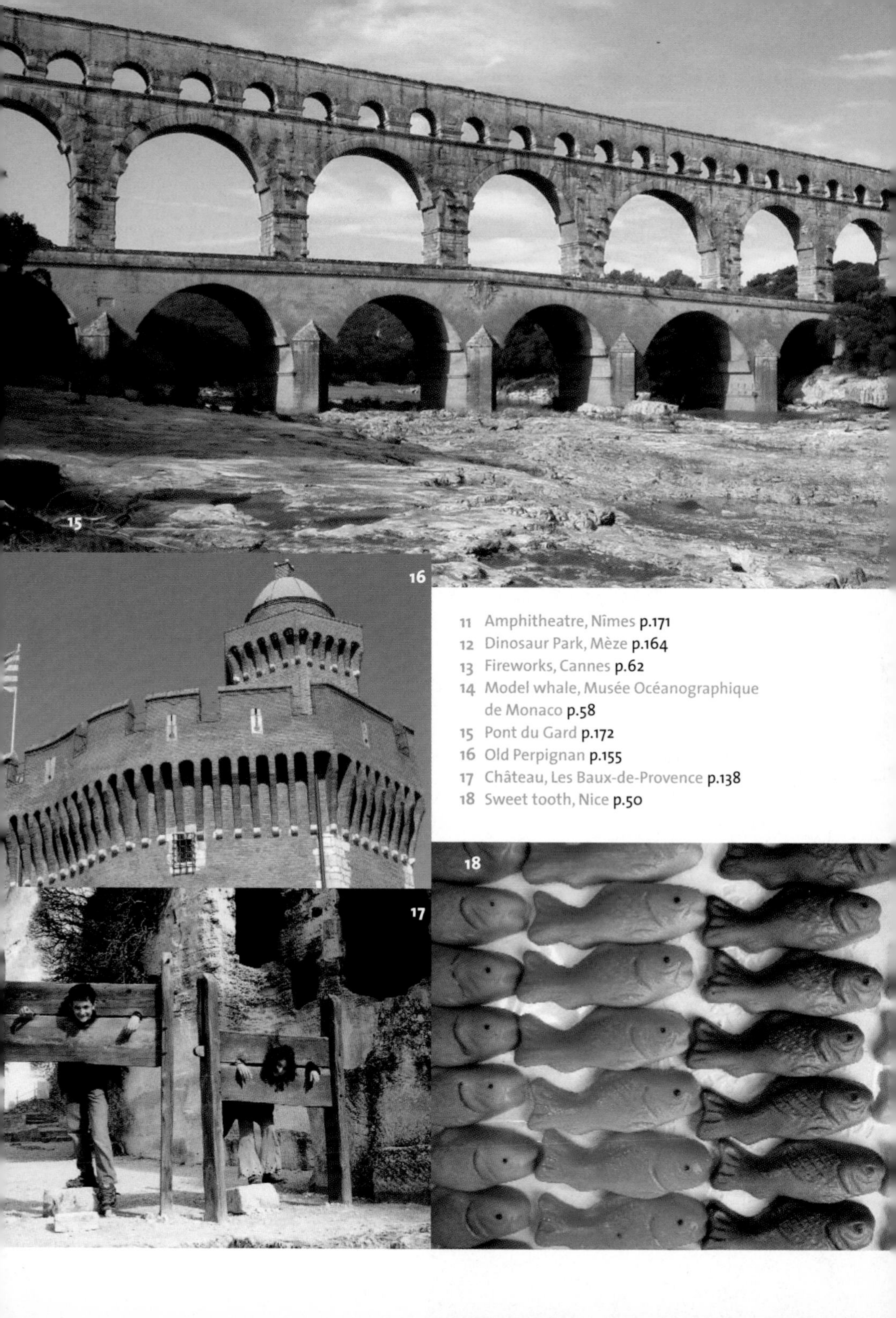

11 Amphitheatre, Nîmes **p.171**
12 Dinosaur Park, Mèze **p.164**
13 Fireworks, Cannes **p.62**
14 Model whale, Musée Océanographique de Monaco **p.58**
15 Pont du Gard **p.172**
16 Old Perpignan **p.155**
17 Château, Les Baux-de-Provence **p.138**
18 Sweet tooth, Nice **p.50**

Buckets and spades

1 Private beach, Juan-les-Pins **p.66**
2 Porto-Vecchio, Corsica **p.193**
3 Rondinara Beach, Corsica **p.194**
4 Beach snack, Antibes **p.68**
5 City beach, Nice **p.53**
6 Fun on the beach, Juan-les-Pins **p.66**
7 Trainee starlet, Cannes **p.62**

7

Animal magic

5

1 Help – a goat! Cap Ferrat Zoo **p.54**
2 Underwater wonders, Musée Océanographique de Monaco **p.58**
3 Riding school, near Corte, Corsica **p.205**
4 Animal buddies, Réserve de Sigean **p.153**
5 Shark pool, Musée Océanographique de Monaco **p.58**
6 Giraffe, Réserve de Sigean **p.153**
7 Bear, Cap Ferrat Zoo **p.54**
8 Flamingos, Cap Ferrat Zoo **p.54**
9 Lioness, Réserve de Sigean **p.153**

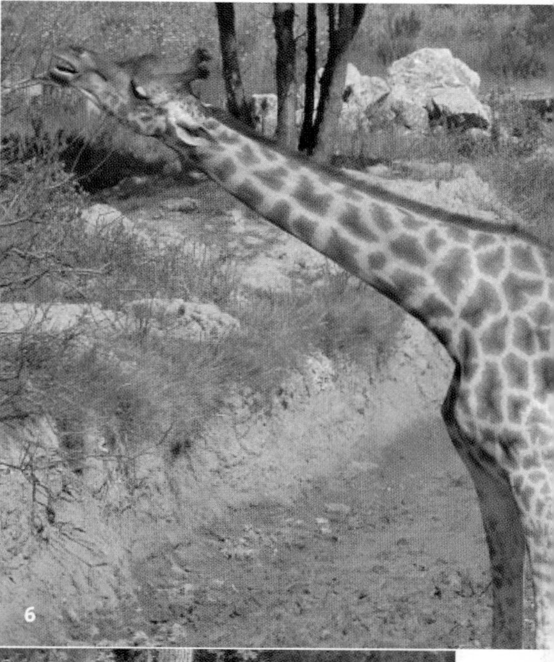
6

8

7

9

Nature lovers

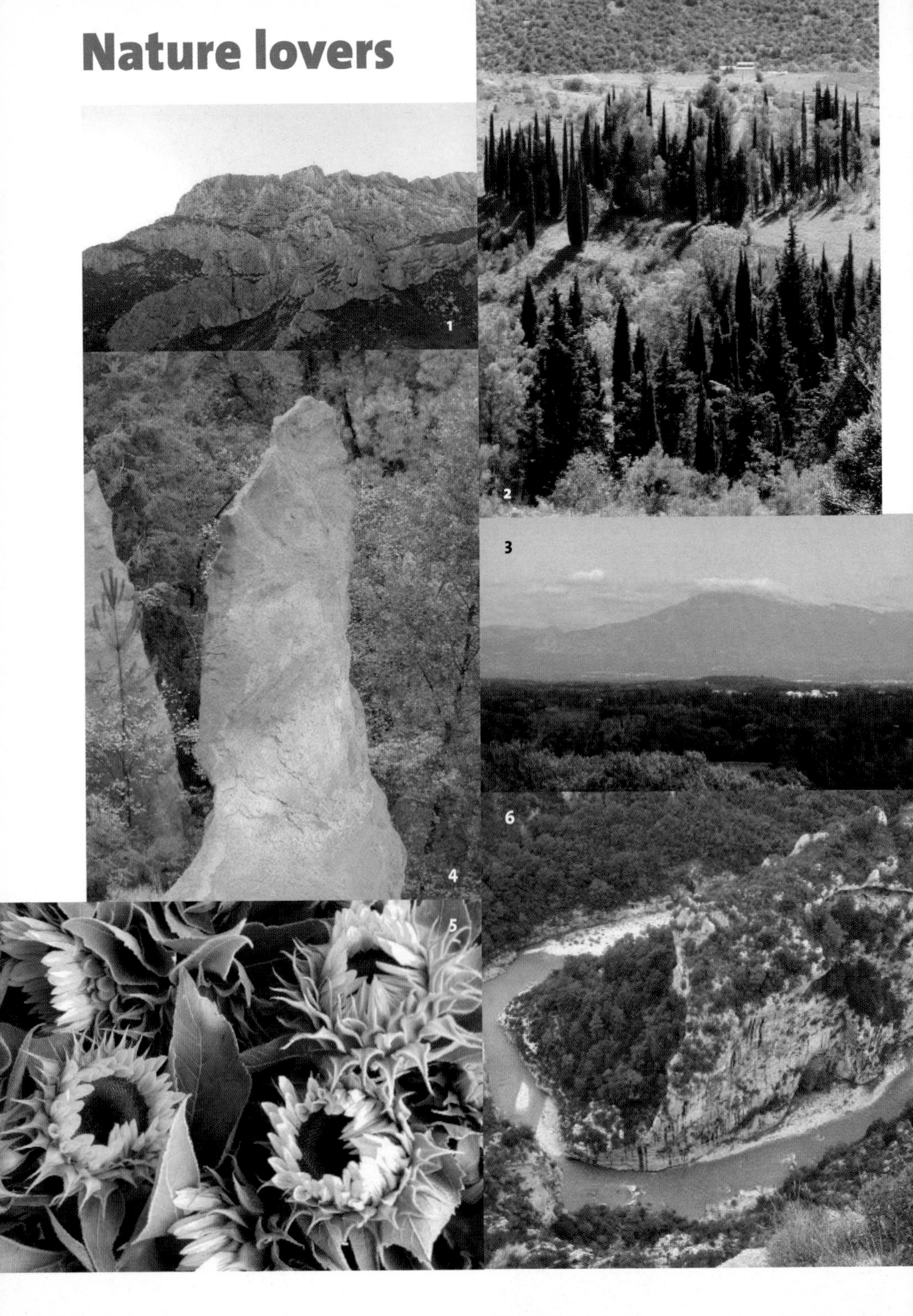

1 Montagne Ste-Victoire p.121
2 Cypress trees, northern Hérault p.168
3 Mont Ventoux p.98
4 Roussillon p.97
5 Sunflowers, St-Rémy-de-Provence p.135
6 Gorges du Verdon p.103
7 Cap Canaille, near Cassis p.133
8 Tautavel p.156
9 Cliffs near Cassis p.133

Trains, planes and automobiles

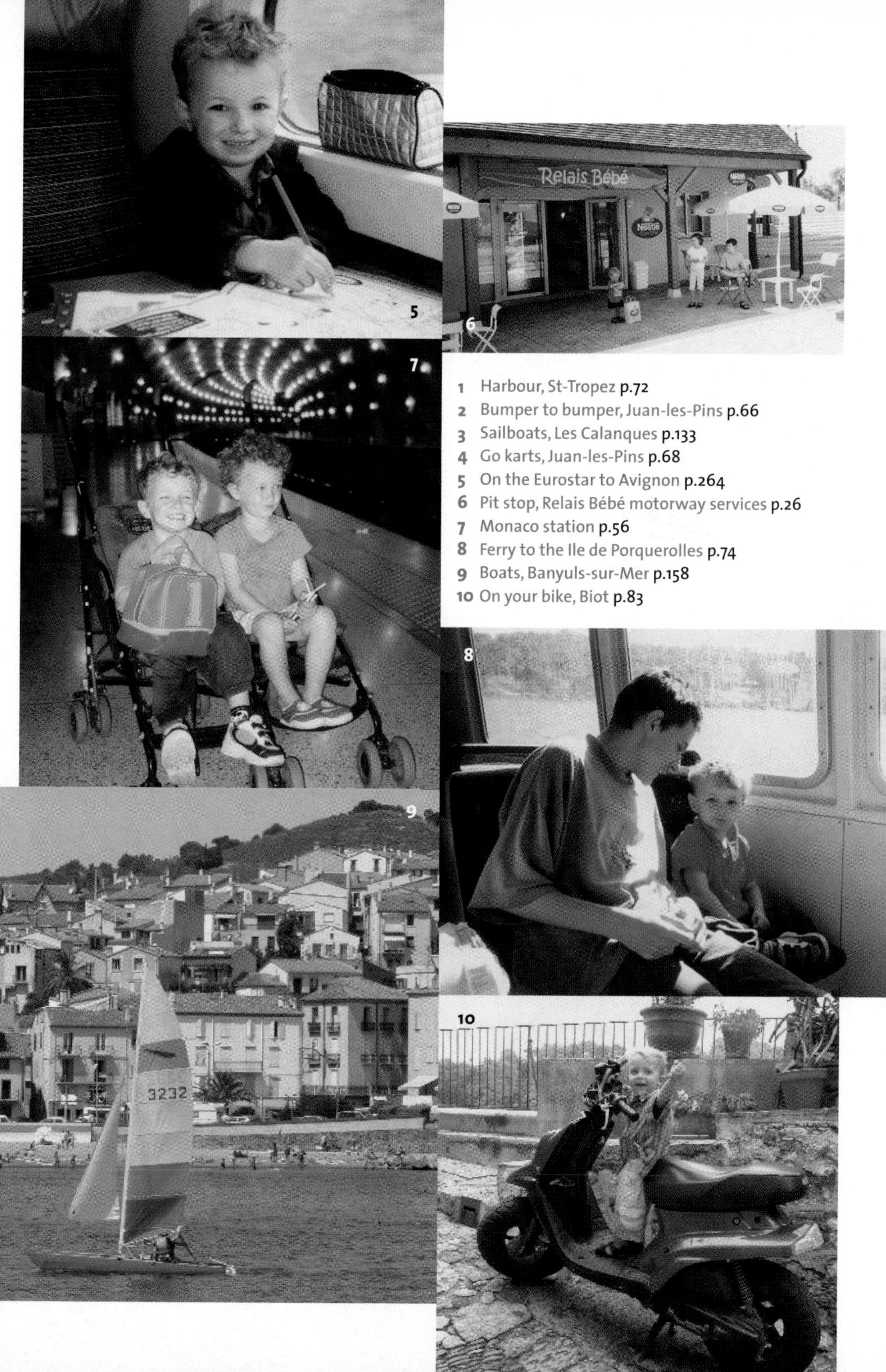

1 Harbour, St-Tropez p.72
2 Bumper to bumper, Juan-les-Pins p.66
3 Sailboats, Les Calanques p.133
4 Go karts, Juan-les-Pins p.68
5 On the Eurostar to Avignon p.264
6 Pit stop, Relais Bébé motorway services p.26
7 Monaco station p.56
8 Ferry to the Ile de Porquerolles p.74
9 Boats, Banyuls-sur-Mer p.158
10 On your bike, Biot p.83

Sporty kids

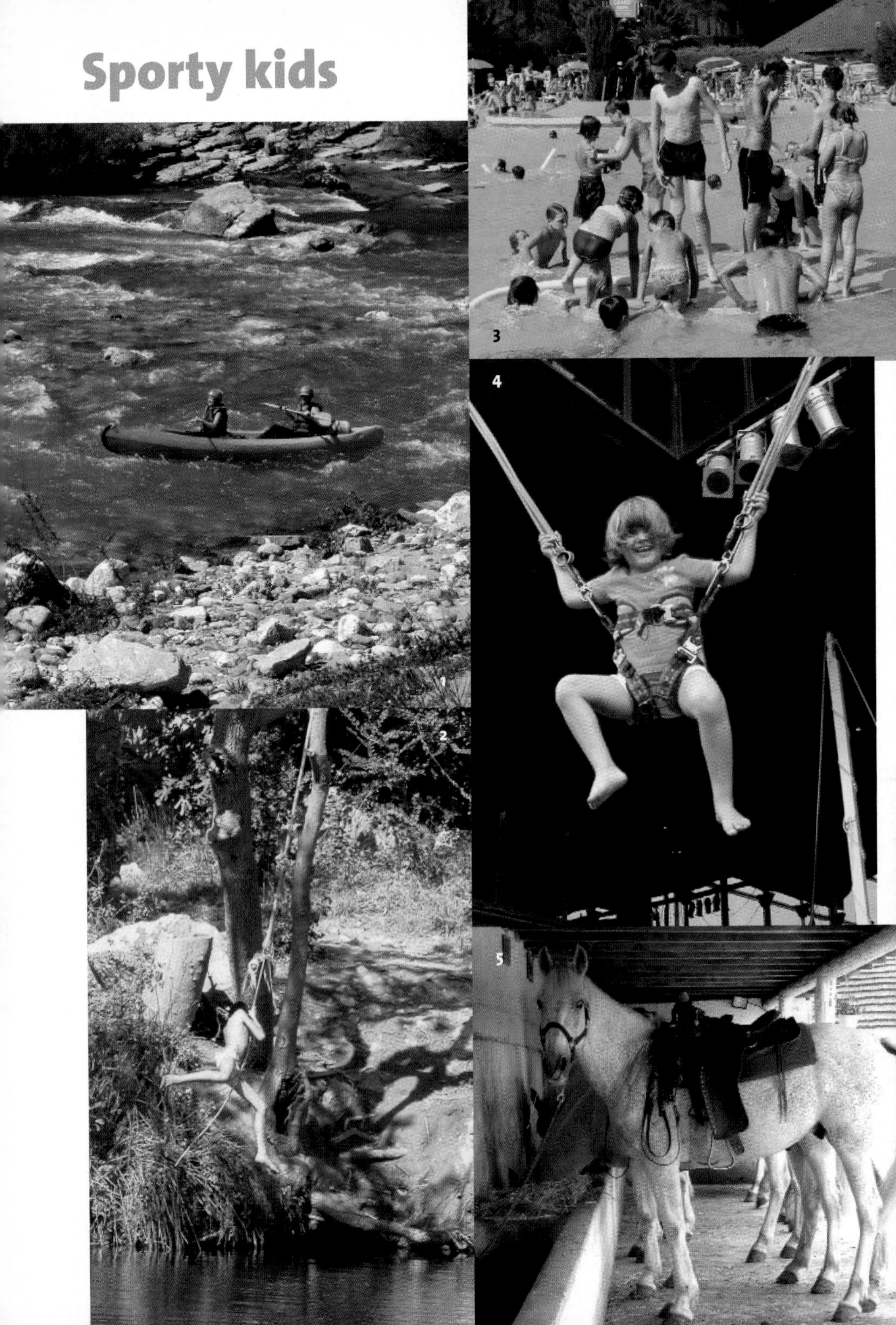

1 Canoeing, near the Pont du Gard **p.172**
2 Junior Tarzan, near Tautavel **p.156**
3 In the pool near Agde **p.163**
4 Bouncey bouncey, Juan-les-Pins **p.66**
5 Stables, the Camargue **p.125**
6 Walking near Roussillon **p.100**
7 Promenade des Anglais, Nice **p.51**
8 Diving, Cap Ferrat **p.55**
9 Sailing, near St-Tropez **p.74**

Eating Out

1 Marzipan wonders, Cours Saleya, Nice p.51
2 Mussels for lunch, Villefranche-sur-Mer p.81
3 Café life, Ste-Maxime p.77
4 Chips at last, Monaco p.82
5 Anyone for melon? Cavaillon market p.99
6 Spiceworld, Antibes market p.66
7 Snack-time, St-Tropez p.73
8 Choosing a picnic, Cours Saleya, Nice p.49
9 Baguette for lunch, Montpellier p.165

Introduction

INTRODUCTION 30

PREPARATION 31
Climate and when to go 31
Planning your break 31
Babies and toddlers 31
School-age kids 31
Teenagers 31
Packing 32
Travelling with kids 32
Boredom-busters 33
Travel games 33
Travel sickness 34
The language barrier 34

FURTHER READING AND VIEWING 35

INTRODUCTION

The South of France is ideal to visit with children, as it's got something for every age group. There are Roman ruins, fairy-tale castles and theme parks; you can kayak, bike and hike your way through some fantastic scenery or simply laze around on the beach. Throughout the area there are child-friendly parks with carousels, hundreds of delicious cake shops and fabulous markets to explore. And although the area is renowned for its luxury villas and overpriced hotels, it is possible to take the kids to the South of France without breaking the bank at Monte Carlo.

France, as a whole, is a good family holiday destination. It is easy to get to, there are excellent facilities and it's genuinely geared up for families. Most French families holiday in France and they expect a good standard of accommodation and top-class food. They also expect that their children will be welcome wherever they choose to stay or eat *en famille* – and their countrymen oblige. So if it's good enough for the French who are we to disagree?

If you're nervous about travelling abroad with kids, France is a good place to start. Unwittingly, I started researching this guide 15 years ago, when I pushed four-week-old Ben along the seafront in Villefranche-sur-Mer. It took 45 minutes to fix the parasol on the buggy and once we got out of the hotel he wouldn't stop yelling. We were besieged by friendly old ladies with offers of help, but since I didn't speak a word of French it only made matters worse. However, since Ben was going to have to learn French, on account of his French granny, I decided I'd better learn too, and quickly.

I also realized that if we were ever going to see anything of the South of France I'd better find out just where Ben wanted to go. If that meant going off the beaten track, so be it. We abandoned the buggy in the hotel and haven't looked back.

This area of France is blessed with acres of sandy beaches and shallow bays that are ideal for little kids. My mother-in-law was checking them out long before I was born and on her advice we've had some fantastic family holidays near St-Tropez and Porto-Vecchio in Corsica. Ben and his three sisters and younger brother have all fallen in love with different parts of France. They've adored the flamingos in the Camargue and the carousels in Avignon. They've fallen head first into the Roman ruins at St-Rémy-de-Provence and spent hours checking out the shops on the Rue d'Antibes in Cannes for the perfect T-shirt. They've even donned their Rollerblades on Nice's Promenade des Anglais and been so taken with Picasso's plates in the museum at Antibes that they wanted to buy one.

There's enough glitz and glamour in St-Tropez to keep junior stargazers happy, but despite the crowds and big spenders it's still possible to get away from it all. We've bumped down plenty of dirt track roads hunting down that perfect B&B. Woeful tales of overbuilding in the area can be taken with a pinch of salt; just 20 minutes from Monaco are some giddy, wild mountain passes and tiny villages. Further down the coast towards Spain, Roussillon enjoys miles of beautiful unspoilt countryside and the best castles in Europe. Yes, some villages have become overrun with tourists, but there are still plenty that haven't, where you can buy ice cream in the local *boulangerie* and listen to the locals discussing everyone else's business.

There's so much on offer in the South of France, that you and the kids can take whatever kind of holiday suits you, whether you want to enjoy a secluded villa, sandy beach, adventure holiday or chic metropolis. But because you're so spoilt for choice you do need to know where to go and what to see: researching this guide we've seen some frankly horrible places and so we hope you can learn from our experience. In this guide we've included only the places that are right for families and where kids can discover the best the South of France has to offer. And if you still need convincing that the South of France is a good place for kids, ask my children; they've had to accompany their mother round the entire region, and they have a long list of places they'd like to see again. I'll get the suitcase...

Climate and when to go

The South of France is great for a family holiday at any time of year. You can swim from May to early October and, in the lower Alps, ski from November to April. You can dig on the beach without catching a chill as early as February and as late as October.

Although many of the hotels close in winter, most of the main attractions are still open. Christmas is a lovely time to visit Provence and the festivities go on for almost a month. The main problem with the winter is the notorious mistral wind, which blows down from the Massif Central to the Mediterranean. It arrives without warning and can last for several days, but if you head east of Toulon you can avoid it. The worst month is November, which tends to see the most rain.

In the summer, on Bastille Day, 14 July, you can join in the celebrations, with live music, fireworks and parades all along the coast from Marseille to Beaulieu. It's a great time of year to catch the night train and see the towns glittering as if decked out with fairy lights.

Summer, of course, is the region's busiest time, and it can be very crowded, but if you go inland in Languedoc and Roussillon or head for Corsica, you'll find a quiet corner even in August. To be sure of avoiding the crowds visit in spring or autumn; May in bloom is simply beautiful, and in autumn the days are long and golden.

Average temperatures in ° centigrade

	Avignon	Corsica	Nice	Perpignan
January	7	12	11	12
February	7	12	12	12
March	11	14	14	13
April	15	16	17	17
May	17	21	20	20
June	21	25	22	23
July	23	28	24	28
August	25	27	26	28
September	23	25	25	26
October	16	21	20	20
November	10	18	16	16
December	8	14	13	14

Planning your break

Before you leave, help the kids find out about where they are going and what they can do while you're there. You can help settle even the smallest toddler with a few pictures and stories about what they can get up to on holiday. Try to involve older children in planning the trip; show them brochures and take account of their ideas. Remember you're not just taking the kids on holiday; you are travelling companions, which means planning a holiday to suit all tastes and meeting each other halfway.

Babies and toddlers

Babies are usually happy to go wherever you take them, as long as it's not too hot. Invest in a pop-up sun tent and protective clothing for them on the beach and a pushchair with built-in sunshade for getting around. With toddlers, you'll be better off planning a trip that doesn't involve too much sightseeing; they're at the ideal age for a bucket-and-spade holiday, perhaps with some kids' club activities thrown in. There are plenty of places in the South of France to unwind on the beach with kids and most also cater for more active types, with a range of waterfront sports activities.

School-age kids

School-age children are far more versatile and enjoy seeing new things. There is plenty to see and do across the region, but endless days sightseeing can take their toll, so be sure to factor in some time for relaxing on the beach or in the countryside. You don't need to see everything to get the best out of southern France; it's not somewhere to race through clocking up tourist attractions, but somewhere to savour slowly.

Teenagers

The region has plenty of small seaside resorts that are ideal for holidays with teenagers. Teens need some freedom and they don't usually like being isolated in a remote place, so small family orientated resorts or campsites are good destinations. You'll find these resorts right along the south coast and in Corsica, and they are usually safe enough for older children to go out alone. It's easy to rent bikes so teens can have more freedom, and in many of the resorts you can hire mobile phones so you can keep tabs on them.

Packing

The key to packing is to keep it simple, especially if you're travelling with a baby. There really is no need to take the entire contents of the nursery; just make sure you have enough nappies, formula and other basics like sun cream and wet wipes to cover the first 48 hours. Unless your final destination is incredibly isolated, you will be able to replenish your supplies once you have arrived.

Take just a few well-chosen toys – you can always buy something extra to entertain the kids while you're away if you need it, and there are some lovely old-fashioned toy shops in this part of France that everyone will enjoy visiting. Take a packet of cards and a travel game or miniature magnetic board game for the journey, and buy disposable cameras so the kids can take their own snaps. Don't forget to bring something to read; finding English-language books for children can be tricky in France, so get the kids to choose a few before you leave. Miniature books are useful as they can be carried in your pocket.

Travellers' checklist

pack a big handbag or a mini-rucksack with:

- **wet wipes and/or tissues**
- **a full change of clothing for tiny tots/underwear and socks for the rest**
- **a few small toys and books**
- **crayons and sheets of paper**
- **drinks and snacks**
- **disposable bags for unforeseen eventualities and rubbish**
- **multiblade pocket knife (If you're travelling by plane, in view of current security concerns, remember to pack it in your main luggage. Do not carry it in your hand baggage or a coat pocket.)**
- **plastic plate or bowl with lid to make sandwiches on or feed the baby**
- **sick bags – take them from the plane or ferry**
- **children's paracetamol**
- **sweets/chewing gum**
- **batteries and film**
- **torch**
- **compass**
- **euros**
- **mobile phone card**

Good to know...baby days

Most hotels in France don't have kettles in the room, so if you are travelling with a baby it pays to invest in a small travel kettle for making up feeds and heating jars of food. To keep feeds fresh, buy a small cool bag with an ice pack; you can use it on the beach and in hotels without minibars.

An electric travel sterilizer is useful, but a large sandwich box with lid and sterilizing tablets can easily substitute for a traditional sterilizer. Look out for a simple cloth attachment, rather like a sling, that fits on all types of chairs and turns them into high chairs. You can buy them online at www.youngexplorers.co.uk.

At night, a favourite cuddly toy will help younger children settle, and if you are sharing a room a personal stereo is helpful, as it keeps older children quiet while you settle the baby. Bring your own audio books along, too, as these are also difficult to find in English.

If your journey will require a stopover, it's easier to pack one small bag with the clothes and other basics you'll need just for the night, especially if you are travelling alone with children in the car. You may also find it handy for flights, too, or if you will be reaching your final destination at night and don't want to go rifling through the suitcase for pyjamas and toothbrushes the minute you arrive. If you don't already have one, invest in a suitcase, or suitcases, on wheels, and remember that a few small suitcases are easier to deal with than one large family one. Finally, when packing, be sure to leave some space for souvenirs.

Travelling with kids

Once you set off, remember that the calmer and happier you are, the less anxious the kids will be. Planning ahead will take some of the anxiety out of the trip, and even if you do feel stressed out by a situation, don't let on. Kids can be just as frightened about flying or taking a ferry as an adult, and even if they weren't to begin with, they can become so if they pick up on your anxiety.

Since the events of September 11, many kids are very aware of the dangers of terrorism and want to talk these things through. Don't dismiss their fears; talk openly with them about their concerns.

They need to know you understand and will do everything you can to keep them safe.

Babies can find new places and a different routine very upsetting at the best of times; on holiday they have the time change (it may only be an hour's difference, but try telling your toddler to wait for dinner) and the hot weather to overcome as well. In the summer, an afternoon siesta is the best way of dealing with the heat. Even if the children don't actually sleep, a quite time cuddled up with a book is just as good.

Travel itself can be exhausting for children of all ages and older kids may miss their friends and the freedoms they have at home. This isn't the time to be tough; it pays to loosen the rules and make allowances – you're on holiday, after all.

Boredom-busters

To stop the kids from going stir-crazy in the car, make regular stops. There are plenty of lay-bys (aires) on French motorways, which nearly always have a small playground. Guides like Michelin's *I-Spy on a Car Journey in France* are useful distractions and hand-held computer games and personal stereos are good ways of letting older children while away the hours.

Don't forget, the gift of the gab can save you if the going gets tough. One of the best ways to keep the kids entertained is to talk to them. It's not often that you get such a long time to chat and there's something special about long journeys and the questions they provoke. If you try to follow the children's line of thought you can learn a lot about them and see how they relate to their new surroundings.

Travel games

Michelin man game

The Michelin man is the symbol of the Michelin tyre company and can be found on maps and guides, cars, lorries, and garages. How many Michelin men can you spot?

Geography game

The first player has to name a place in France. The next player has to name a place that begins with the last letter of the place just named, and so on, until all the players are eliminated.

Numberplate game

Since the Revolution, France has been divided into 95 departments (*départements*), each with its own number. The last two digits of a French numberplate tells you where the car comes from. Tick them off as you spot them, and improve your geography at the same time.

01 Ain **02** Aisne **03** Allier **04** Alpes-de-Haute-Provence **05** Hautes-Alpes **06** Alpes-Maritimes **07** Ardèche **08** Ardennes **09** Ariège **10** Aube **11** Aude **12** Aveyron **13** Bouches-du-Rhône **14** Calvados **15** Cantal **16** Charente **17** Charente-Maritime **18** Cher **19** Corrèze **2A** Corse-du-sud **2B** Haute-Corse **21** Côte-d'Or **22** Côtes d'Armor **23** Creuse **24** Dordogne **25** Doubs **26** Drôme **27** Eure **28** Eure-et-Loir **29** Finistère **30** Gard **31** Haute-Garonne **32** Gers **33** Gironde **34** Hérault **35** Ille-et-Vilaine **36** Indre **37** Indre-et-Loire **38** Isère **39** Jura **40** Landes **41** Loir-et-Cher **42** Loire **43** Haute-Loire **44** Loire-Atlantique **45** Loiret **46** Lot **47** Lot-et-Garonne **48** Lozère **49** Maine-et-Loire **50** Manche **51** Marne **52** Haute-Marne **53** Mayenne **54** Meurthe-et-Moselle **55** Meuse **56** Morbihan **57** Moselle **58** Nièvre **59** Nord **60** Oise **61** Orne **62** Pas-de-Calais **63** Puy-de-Dôme **64** Pyrénées-Atlantiques **65** Hautes-Pyrénées **66** Pyrénées-Orientales **67** Bas-Rhin **68** Haut-Rhin **69** Rhône **70** Haute-Saône **71** Saône-et-Loire **72** Sarthe **73** Savoie **74** Haute-Savoie **75** Ville de Paris **76** Seine-Maritime **77** Seine-et-Marne **78** Yvelines **79** Deux-Sèvres **80** Somme **81** Tarn **82** Tarn-et-Garonne **83** Var **84** Vaucluse **85** Vendée **86** Vienne **87** Haute-Vienne **88** Vosges **89** Yonne **90** Territoires de Belfort **91** Essonne **92** Hauts-de-Seine **93** Seine-St-Denis **94** Val-de-Marne **95** Val-d'Oise

French I-Spy

Teach the kids some new words by playing the game in French.

The euro collector

List the 12 euro zone countries with the kids (as a reminder: Austria, Belgium, Finland, France, Germany, Greece, Ireland, Italy, Luxembourg, Netherlands, Portugal and Spain), and collect a coin from each of the 12 countries, not forgetting Monaco, which has its own euros. It's easier to collect different denominations. They'll be kept happy for hours rifling through your loose change.

Make a scrapbook

A scrapbook makes a great souvenir, and is an on-going project that can be picked up thoughout the holiday. If you have some basic starter pieces, like a map of France, glue, scissors and pens, you can start the scrapbook on the way there. A basic exercise book can be decorated with stickers, articles from newspapers, bits of fabric or street maps. Stick an envelope or flap on the inside back cover to keep all their mementoes – leaflets, tickets, business cards and café receipts. Children who like drawing can keep a sketchbook of the trip.

Travel sickness

Some people are more prone to travel sickness than others, but a queasy travelling companion isn't fun for anyone. The following precautions will help to ensure everyone has as pleasant a journey as possible. Try to ensure the kids get lots of rest before a journey; tiredness is a major factor in making them feel queasy. Make sure they have had something light to eat at least an hour before you leave, but avoid sweets and fizzy drinks. The heat doesn't help in summer, either, so keep the car cool and ventilated. Avoid reading and hand-held computer games and try to take their minds off feeling ill by chatting or listening to cassettes. Motion sickness can be brought on by nerves, so try to keep kids relaxed. If you child suffers regularly from travel sickness, ask your pharmacist for advice, as there are lots of products on the market, many of them homeopathic, which can help.

The language barrier

If you make an effort to speak a few words of French you'll find people will warm to you much more than if you sit in painful silence. That goes for the kids, too, though children can communicate pretty well without language (gestures, sharing toys, smiling and waving) when on holiday. The best way to teach toddlers is to introduce one word at a time and just use it in everyday conversation. For example ask 'Would you like some *pain* (bread)?', 'Do you want a *glace* (ice-cream)?' Flash cards are a good way of building up vocabulary. Make it fun by giving a biscuit or a sweet as a prize for getting a set number right. (This is a good travel game too.)

There are lots of books on the market aimed at helping young children learn French. Usborne publishers (**www.usborne.com**) specialize in language books for the very young, with brightly coloured flash cards and picture and sticker books in French for tiny tots. Usborne's *French for Beginners* comes with a CD or cassette so you can practise on long car journeys. To encourage older children to speak French, it helps if you set a good example by learning alongside them. Usborne also publish an *Essential French Phrasebook & Dictionary* aimed at teens, which will help build up vocabulary for the GCSE. Berlitz produce a language system for kids, *French in Ten Minutes*, which is a colourful cartoon-style language course for ages 11 upwards. Orchard Toys (**www.orchardtoys.com**) have a selection of games, some small enough to slip into a suitcase, for teaching French to under-10s.

FURTHER READING AND VIEWING

Books for toddlers

Babar's Travels, Jean de Brunhoff (Methuen, 1935). Babar sets off in a hot-air balloon for a honeymoon near Marseille but is blown off course and the balloon is wrecked on the Iles d'Hyères. A must if you are holidaying near St-Tropez. There's a useful mini-pocket version available, too.

In France, supermarkets are the best place to buy books for tiny tots. French toddlers are keen on Juliette, a pretty blond-haired girl who has lots of adventures. They love Teletubbies, Spot and Miffy, and popular cartoon characters Leo and Popi.

Books for the under-10s

Asterix in Corsica, R Goscinny and A Uderzo (Hachette, 1973). France's favourite Gallic duo sets off for a trip to Corsica. All the jokes that the French tell about the island are here – the vendettas, the stinky cheese and how you can smell Corsica with your eyes shut.

(Horrible Histories) France, Terry Deary (Scholastic, 2002). An irreverent retelling of French history. The foul famines, terrible terrors and gruesome guillotine are all here.

L'Imagerie de la France (Editions Fleurus, 1994). A great introduction to French lifestyle, history and geography. If you speak some French and want to help your children learn, this book is a good investment. It has lively illustrations and simple French text. It is part of a series and any of the other titles are useful if you're teaching French to the under-10s. It is available from most big bookshops.

The Dancing Bear, Michael Morpurgo (Collins, 1994) An enchanting story about a bear cub and a lonely orphaned girl set in the Pyrenees.

Lettres de mon moulin, Alphonse Daudet (Editions Ouest-France, 1998). Daudet's collection of local tales from the end of the 19th century is a French children's classic. There are some terrible translations for sale in the tourist shops around Fontvieille, so if you can, make a stab at reading them in the original French.

French kids of this age are keen on comic strip books (known as les BDs, short for *les bandes dessinées*). Tintin and Asterix are perennial favourites, but Tom-Tom et Nana, two naughty kids who get up to mischief are very popular too. You'll find them in the magazine *J'aime lire*. The top magazine for this age group is *Astrapi*, a mixture of cartoons and informative text.

Books for pre-teens

Waiting for Anya, Michael Morpurgo (Egmont, 2001). Set in the Second World War, it tells the story of how Jewish children were smuggled over the Pyrenees to Spain.

Le Petit Prince, Antoine de Saint-Exupéry (Harcourt, 2001). The classic story about a pilot who meets a little prince when his plane crashes in the Sahara desert. This short, mystical tale, told in simple language, is suitable for anyone over the age of 8. If your French is up to it, read it in the original, but if not, get a modern translation with colour illustrations. A CD version is also available. The French are crazy about this book: in school textbooks you'll even find sections of it translated into Latin.

Eyewitness Guide: Van Gogh (Dorling Kindersley, 1992). A good investment if you're visiting Arles or St-Rémy with kids who are interested in art.

Les DocuDéments: Napoléon l'empire, c'est moi (Gallimard Jeunesse, 1997). French version of the Horrible Histories series, offering a light-hearted look at the life of Napoleon.

Napoléon, Augustin Drouet (Hachette Junior, 1990). This is a more serious mini biography for kids, with slightly simplified French.

French pre-teens read a lot of English novels in translation. Good novels for this age group are almost non existent in French, although home-grown detective thrillers are popular. There are a lot of good magazines for pre-teens that put English girls' magazines like *Sugar* to shame. *Julie* has the pop star interviews but also runs a politics section, which explains events in the Middle East and other hot spots.

Okapi, for both boys and girls, is similar, and is a good place to find a French pen pal.

Books for teens

L'Etranger (The Outsider), Albert Camus (Vintage, 1989). One of France's most famous modern writers, Camus lived in Vaucluse and although this story is set in North Africa, the themes are relevant to the South of France. This short but powerful book, written in deceptively simple language, is a set text for French A level.

Loser Takes All, Graham Greene (Penguin, 1971). Greene's short story of an unsuccessful accountant who tries to break the bank at Monte Carlo is particularly enjoyable if you're going to Monaco.

The Count of Monte Cristo, Alexandre Dumas (Penguin, 1996). This book is such a powerful evocation of 19th-century Marseille you can almost smell it. Although an enormous tome, as classics go it is surprisingly readable and full of gripping adventure. (Dumas was paid by the word, which accounts for its length, but you can skip the boring bits without losing track of the plot.) Choose a modern translation like this one, rather than an old dusty copy from the library, as the new translations are much better.

Pétain's Crime, Paul Webster (Pan, 2001). Teenagers interested in history will find Webster's account of the Holocaust in France very accessible. It's a horrific story but a surprisingly easy read.

The Xenophobe's Guide to the French (Oval, 2001). A truly tongue-in-cheek look at the French.

The Mystery of the Blue Train, Agatha Christie (Harper Collins, 1995). Murder on the Riviera. Also available on cassette.

Books for you

In this book we've set out to give you the basic background information to deal with questions the kids may ask.

Find out more about the writer Saint-Exupéry in Paul Webster's biography ***Antoine Saint-Exupéry*** (Macmillan, 1993) or in French in ***Saint-Exupéry*** by Nathalie des Vallières (Gallimard, 1998). The best biography of Napoleon is Max Gallo's ***Napoléon*** (Robert Laffont, 1997).

For an easy poolside read, pack ***Paris to the Moon: a Family in France***, by Adam Gopnik (Vintage, 2001). Although the Gopnik family spent five years in Paris, the author's clever observations of family life in France, as seen through American eyes, are as applicable to the south as they are to any other part of the country.

Videos

Videos are a great way of introducing a new place to kids and once the holiday is over they love spotting the places they've visited. Note that French TV uses the SECAM system, so if you bring PAL videos to watch on holiday they'll play in black and white and vice versa.

Some of the best films to look out for are:

Bon Voyage Charlie Brown (1980) Cert U. Snoopy and friends head for France. Not set specifically in the south but gets across some basic ideas to tiny tots. Hours of fun watching Charlie Brown ask for '*un loaf du pain, si vous plait*'.

Crin Blanc (1953) Cert U. Albert Lamorisse's classic about the wildlife of the Camargue region. Crin Blanc is a wild stallion, which refuses to be caught. A young boy dreams of taming him. Watch out for the unhappy ending.

Herbie Goes to Monte Carlo (1977) Cert U. Comedy for kids about a little yellow car.

Taxi (1998) Cert 15. Action-packed comedy about a Marseille pizza deliveryman who becomes a taxi driver and then manages to become a police driver even though he doesn't have a licence. The certificate is for the bad language, which in the original French isn't that strong.

Taxi 2 (2001) Cert 12. The sequel is just as good as the original. In this film the cab driver hero ends up rescuing the Japanese Secretary for Defence. Both films are a huge hit with French teens and only lose a few of the jokes in the translation.

Jean de Florette (1986) Cert PG and ***Manon des Sources*** (1986) Cert PG. These are two riveting tales that focus on the nastier side of peasant life in the villages of Provence. Because of the PG rating, these are films for the over-10s only.

The Man in the Iron Mask (1998) Cert 12. Leonardo Di Caprio takes the lead in this modern retelling of the classic tale of swashbuckling Musketeers. Try to see the 1938 original, too, if you can.

The Count of Monte Cristo (1998) Cert PG. Dumas's classic story starring Gérard Depardieu.

To Catch a Thief (1956) Cert PG. Retro Riviera fun with Grace Kelly and Cary Grant.

In French homes, book characters are also video favourites: toddlers love Babar and Miffy and also watch Teletubbies and the usual Disney characters. Older French children flock to the cinema to watch their cartoon hero Asterix come to life on the big screen. They are also keen on a series of comedies, *Les Visiteurs*, *Les Visiteurs II* and *Les Visiteurs en Amérique*, which are crazy tales of medieval knights who end up by accident in the modern world.

History

HISTORY LESSON 38
Wherever I Rome 38
Dangerous Dark Ages 39
Building France 40
The Hundred Years' War 40
Renaissance and religious wars 41
Le Roi Soleil 41
Revolution 41
Ideology, industrialization and empire 42
The twentieth century 42
Modern France 43
HISTORY IN A HURRY 44

The story begins around 450,000 BC, in a cave in the mountains near Perpignan. France had everything Stone Age man could want; the land teemed with mammoths and there was a fantastic network of caves to provide shelter for the night. In the early 1970s archaeologists made a dramatic find when they unearthed the oldest skull in Europe in the Caune de l'Arago, a cave near Tautavel, Roussillon. Prehistoric man had a number of other firsts in the South of France: he lit his first European fires in Nice and he made one of his first attempts at writing in the Cave of Cosquer in the calanques east of Marseille.

Around 5000 BC, people stopped their nomadic way of life and started to establish settlements and to grow crops. One of the oldest of these farming communities was north of Montpellier in the village of Cambous. Not long after putting down roots, man started putting up menhirs or standing stones, which were of symbolic or astrological importance to these early communities. At Filitosa in Corsica, you can see the first statues made in Europe – huge menhirs carved to look like gigantic warriors. The examples at Filitosa are more numerous and characterful than those found on the mainland, but there are also some strange and unusual carvings on the slopes of Mont Bégo on the Italian border, which were made by Bronze Age shepherds.

From about 1200 BC onwards tribes of Celts and Ligurians began to migrate into France. In the south, these Asterix and Obelix characters were mostly Ligurians, skilled metalworkers and farmers who lived in small walled settlements on craggy outcrops and cliffs, which the Romans called oppida. To this day, a lot of towns in the region refer to their ancient origin with names like Oppedette and Oppéde-le-Vieux.

The Romans named these tribes and the country where they lived 'Gaul' (hence 'Gallic'). Gaul was broadly the same size and shape as modern-day France. The Greeks made an appearance round 600 BC and founded the first city in France – Massalia, which was to become Marseille. They quickly followed with settlements at Nice, Hyères and Agde, bringing with them vines and olive trees – the crucial ingredients of life in the sunny south.

Wherever I Rome

When Rome took control of Spain in the 2nd century BC a safe land route was imperative, which meant taking control of southern Gaul. In 122 BC Roman legions arrived to conquer what is now Provence and Languedoc-Roussillon. The Gauls were divided on the issue of their invaders – some of them were happy to co-operate with the Romans but others fought to the death to defend their territory. Terrible battles at Entremont near

Tell me a story:
A French hero ...Vercingétorix

The Gauls, who were a warlike people and spent most of their time fighting each other, found it quite difficult to unite against the Romans. When all appeared lost, however, they rallied behind a brilliant warrior called Vercingétorix, who was more than a match for Julius Caesar and won a number of battles against him. Vercingétorix was a guerrilla fighter who relied on surprise attacks, but in 52 BC he made a fatal error and tried to attack the Roman army in the field. He and his men were heavily defeated and forced to pull back to the village of Alésia, near Dijon.

The Romans built huge impregnable defences around the village, which were so deep you can still see them today. Vercingétorix was trapped and after a terrible battle he conceded defeat and placed his weapons at Caesar's feet. (These and other details are in Caesar's account of the conquest of Gaul, The Gallic Wars.) After the battle, Caesar toured Gaul with his top prisoner before taking him to Rome, where Vercingétorix was eventually strangled. Over the course of his career Caesar took thousands of Gauls prisoner. He made a small fortune selling them into slavery and used the money to buy his way to the top.

Vercingétorix is a real hero in France, a symbol of resistance like Joan of Arc. He features in the school curriculum and most bookshops carry children's books about his life and times.

As you speed down the motorway through eastern France look out for the huge hoarding with his picture. It's close to the remains of the village of Alésia, which is a good place to break your journey for a stroll. Lots of interesting archaeological finds have been unearthed there and masses of helmets, shields and swords are still being lifted from the battlefield.

Aix-en-Provence followed, but resistance was hopeless. By 118 BC Rome controlled the whole coast and the area was swiftly absorbed into the Roman Empire, becoming Rome's first province, hence the name Provence.

Once the route to Spain had been established, the Romans started to trade further north, travelling up to Brittany to buy salt and taking with them horses and bronze. However, the northern boundaries of Provence weren't secure, and there were frequent raids by Celtic tribes living north of Orange who even managed to defeat the Romans in 105 BC They weren't allowed to get away with it for long, however; Julius Caesar decided it was in his interest to secure these lucrative trade routes by conquering Gaul in 58 BC. His personal fortune and reputation expanded in equal measure to the inexorable spread of Roman dominance.

Life was good under the Romans, and many Gauls were happy to co-operate with them. They brought great prosperity to Gaul, especially to the south, which played a crucial part in the Roman Empire by supplying olive oil, grain and ships. Because of this prosperity, large towns were soon established, which benefited from the Romans' master engineering skills. Among their many feats of technology are the Pont du Gard, the massive aqueduct used to bring fresh water to the city of Nîmes, and the enormous amphitheatres built throughout the region. Because Romans built roads to link their empire, travelling about Gaul was easy for the first time. Remains of these early roads can still be seen all over the south, especially in Narbonne and outside Montpellier.

Dangerous Dark Ages

The collapse of the Roman Empire in 476 left Gaul vulnerable to attacks from outside forces and Germanic tribes swarmed across its borders – Franks, Burgundians and Visigoths arrived, driven off their own lands by the Huns. They had no intention of leaving, and pushed as far south as the Mediterranean.

The Franks were to have the biggest impact; they gave their name to France and their language formed the basis of modern French. In 481 Clovis was crowned king of the Franks, making Paris his capital and conquering huge tracts of land for his people.

Clovis' rule had a lasting influence on France, but unfortunately not a beneficial one. On his death in 511 he had foolishly divided his lands between his four sons, ushering in a period of instability and weakness. The Franks lost huge areas of land to invading tribes, setting a trend that lasted for centuries.

It was up to Charles Martel to turn things around in the 8th century. As King of the Franks he reconquered Aquitaine and Saxony but more important was his resounding success over the Moors who had pushed up from Spain at the Battle of Poitiers in 732. Martel's actions stopped the Moors from an all-out conquest of Europe, although they managed to hang on in parts of the South of France, especially the wild Massif des Maures near St-Tropez. They launched attacks along the coast, terrifying the locals, who fled to fortified hilltop villages for safety.

Charles Martel's grandson, Charlemagne, was an equally fierce warrior, conquering all the lands that comprise modern France and a lot more besides. With an empire that stretched east as far as Munich, Charlemagne has gone down in history as a learned king, with a civilizing influence; he set up the first schools in France and is reported to have been fond of a good Camembert and fine red wine. Yet, upon his death in 814 his empire, too, started to fall apart. It had been divided among his grandsons: the eastern section covered most of modern-day Germany; the central section included most of eastern France and the third section lay east of the River Rhône. This kingdom had little control over the south, where power belonged to local fiefdoms.

Clovis and the vase of Soissons

Despite his conversion to Christianity, Clovis was reputedly a barbarous character, illustrated by the story that all French school children learn about the missing vase of Soissons. Before he became a Christian, Clovis' soldiers sacked the church at Soissons. The spoils were meant to be shared equally, but to his fury, Clovis discovered one of his warriors had kept a vase for himself. Clovis bided his time. One year later, when his troops were gathered for inspection, Clovis took the guilty warrior's axe and shield and threw them to the ground saying they were dirty. As the unfortunate fellow bent down to pick up his things, Clovis lopped off his head, telling the rest of his troops to remember Soissons and who was the boss.

Before long, the Vikings invaded the north and took control of Normandy in 911. Things looked quite dire until a decisive moment in Paris in 987 when Hugues Capet declared himself King of all of France. From a tiny embattled enclave, his descendants would set out to expand and secure the country's borders and would rule until 1789.

Building France

The major problem facing the French kings was that huge areas of western France belonged to the Plantagenets, who were also the kings of England. War raged between the French and English for 30 years until King Philippe Auguste's forces defeated the English at the Battle of Bouvines in 1214. This victory meant Philippe Auguste could begin to unify the country under one ruler, although at this time the country known as France was confined to the north. The south was a different country altogether, with a different language (Occitan), and a people who didn't consider themselves French at all. All this would change under Philippe Auguste.

French knights had participated in the Crusades with enthusiasm and were more than willing to carry out crusades at home. Crusading was an ideal method for bringing enemies into line and, in 1208, when the pope called for a crusade against the Cathars because they didn't adhere to the teachings of the Catholic Church, Philippe Auguste was quick to sign up. He was less concerned with the Cathars' split from the Catholic Church than with the fact that they were under the protection of the local lords of the Languedoc, who were powerful enough to ignore what their king had to say. The papal crusade against the Cathars gave Philippe Auguste a marvellous opportunity to smash the power of the local fiefdoms and bring them firmly under his control. The results were bloody, with an estimated 10,000 people massacred at Béziers alone (*see* also 'A good knight' p.148, 'The sad story of the Cathars', p.147). Philippe Auguste's grandson Louis IX earned the title St Louis for completing the job and Languedoc-Roussillon became part of France in 1271.

The Crusades were equally bad news for the Jews of France, who had been living peacefully in France since Roman times. The Crusaders were virulently anti-Semitic and persecuted the Jews across the country, murdering communities, seizing their property and eventually expelling them altogether in 1394. The Jews fled to areas that were not controlled by the French kings, such as Provence, and eventually to towns like Carpentras that belonged to the pope (*see* p.96).

The south meanwhile, was becoming ever more prosperous because of the Crusades; Aigues-Mortes (*see* p.165), the only city on the Mediterranean under French rule, became an important port under the direction of Louis IX, and Marseille's fortunes were revived.

The Hundred Years' War

In 1328 Charles IV, grandson of Louis IX, died without a direct heir, which prompted a dispute over the succession between Philippe de Valois and Edward III of England. They had virtually equal claims to the throne, with Philippe having the slight edge because he born in France – a more attractive prospect at time when France was beginning to develop a sense of national identity. Such niceties didn't interest Edward, who invaded and smashed the French at the Battle of Crécy in 1346 and almost destroyed the country in the ensuing struggle. Further disasters followed: in 1347 a boat docked in Marseille, carrying the bodies of five sailors who had died of plague (*see* p.131). The Black Death of 1347–8 ravaged the country, killing a a third of the population. The country also saw fierce fighting between local groups siding either with the French or with the English. The fighting was particularly bad in the south at Aigues-Mortes, where so many people were killed in one battle that their bodies were salted and stored in a tower until they could be buried.

The war with England lasted well over 100 years, during which time kings came and went. By 1422, King Charles VII had even lost Paris to his cousin Henry VI of England. Henry declared himself King of France, leaving Charles to run what was left of his kingdom from Berry, an area south of Paris.

It was then that a shepherdess from Lorraine came to the rescue. In 1428, while watching her sheep, Joan of Arc heard heavenly voices telling her to lead an army against the English. She was the first to successfully rally the people together as a nation, convincing the fractious lords of the country to unite behind Charles VII. By 1436 Paris was once more under French control and by 1453 France had regained all its possessions save Calais. In 1481 the king of Provence died without an heir and left his lands to the king of France.

Renaissance and religious wars

The cultured François I (1515–47) began to establish France as a world leader in the arts. Book printing began in Paris, ringing the death knell for the regional languages of the south, which was further emphasized by the declaration in 1539 of French as the official language of the kingdom. However, the country was far from peaceful. The arrival of Protestantism from Geneva plunged France into a bloody religious war, which started in the south where the new religion had taken hold. Thousands of people were massacred, as atrocities were committed by both sides, and many local churches were converted to fortresses. These religious wars tore France apart until Henry IV's Edict of Nantes of 1598, which granted religious tolerance towards Protestants and recognized Protestant control of certain areas in the south. Less than 100 years later the edict was revoked by Louis XIV in 1685. Immediately, thousands of Huguenot craftsmen and manufacturers fled towns like Uzès and Montpellier to settle in Germany and Britain. Those who stayed were likely to find themselves imprisoned in places like the Château d'If (*see* p.132). In the castle at Aigues-Mortes (*see* p.165) you can still see carvings on the wall made by Protestant prisoners.

Le Roi Soleil

Louis XIV came to the throne in 1643 when he was just five years old. He was almost toppled from his throne as a child and grew up determined to make the French monarchy the most powerful in Europe, the head of a strong centralized state with secure borders. As a result he was always pursuing some aggressive war or another along the frontier. He tried to conquer Nice, then part of Savoy, and made Roussillon part of France in 1659. Keep an eye out for the enormous forts he built across the south of France.

On the home front the most important problem for Louis XIV was keeping the nobles under control. His brilliant solution was to build a huge palace at Versailles where his nobles were kept in what was virtually a gilded cage. Louis elevated himself to the position of demi-god, known as the Roi Soleil – the Sun King – and a cult surrounded him at court, with courtiers jostling to watch him get up, eat lunch and attend Mass. When he died in 1715, his extravagance had left the country bankrupt and five years later another plague ravished southern France. Louis XIV's grandson, Louis XVI, wasn't up to the job of reform, preferring to spend his time cavorting with his mistresses rather than running the country. Meanwhile French philosophers and writers began radically to rethink the way the country should be governed.

Can you spot…a French queen?

Not ruling the country in her own right you won't. Women were banned from inheriting the throne in France according to Salic law, a legal code introduced in 508 by King Clovis that was aimed at keeping the peace and stopping clan feuds. It covered everything from inheritance laws to the correct punishment for stealing a chicken.

Revolution

The trigger for the French Revolution happened on the other side of the Atlantic in the Amercan colonies, where the new ideas first dreamt up in France had taken hold. France supported the colonists in their war against Britain, but in so doing was plunged further into debt. Louis XVI was forced to raise already crippling taxes on an impoverished peasantry, but to do so had to call a meeting of the long-neglected French parliament, the Estates General.

It was widely assumed that in return for money the king would initiate some major reforms and delegates from across France came to Paris with huge lists of complaints, creating a sense of national identity that the country had never seen before. When these reforms were blocked the delegates declared a National Assembly and the country rose against the aristocracy. Although the action was centred on the capital, a reign of terror swept the country and thousands of people lost their lives. In the south it was at its worst in Marseille where churches were closed and used as stables. Many of the aristocracy fled to Nice, which was not yet a part of France, but which would be invaded in 1793.

The British took advantage of the chaos of the Revolution to occupy the port of Toulon. It took a young Corsican artillery commander to get rid

Tell me a story:
Who was Charles de Gaulle?

There isn't a town in France that doesn't have a square, street or a school named after Charles de Gaulle. His role as leader of the Free French during the Second World War was crucial in salvaging French pride from the terrible defeat of 1940, and as president of the Fifth Republic in the 1960s he reinforced France's independent role on the world stage. If you drive to the South of France you can stop off en route at Colombey-les-Deux-Eglises where he is buried; it's just off the motorway south of Troyes.

of them and the event catapulted Napoleon Bonaparte to fame.

At home, the Revolution didn't just bring about a sense of national pride, it led to the reorganization of the country. France had been put together like a jigsaw of different regions, all with different laws and taxes. From this point on it was to be divided into *départements* and governed by one set of codified laws, which still exist today. For the south this meant an even stricter crackdown on its own culture and language; it was not in the interests of a newly centralized country to recognize regional differences. In the south the first bridge built across the River Var was to aid the movement of a national French army, rather than in response to any local needs. However, it was an important step in bringing Nice, which had been handed back to Savoy after the Revolution, into easy contact with its French neighbours.

Ideology, industrialization and empire

Once unleashed, it was impossible to stop the revolutionary ideas of 1789 and large parts of Europe were very unstable for most of the 19th century. France saw a cycle of revolutions alternating with conservative and liberal governments, which divided the country for generations.

During this period France also saw great economic growth and expansion, and built up an enormous empire second only to Britain's. The south benefited from these developments along with the rest of the country: the conquest of Algeria in 1830 turned Marseille into a major Mediterranean port and the growth of the railways drew the country closer together as Paris was now hours rather than days away. Tourism on the Riviera began in earnest, as the wealthy, many of them invalids in search of a gentler climate, flocked to the south for winter sun. Many of the most opulent buildings along the Côte d'Azur were built in the 19th century. The decades before the First World War, the *belle époque*, when France became the hub of artistic and scientific life, brought a new influx of devotees to the south. An artistic community gathered there, and many of the painters who set up their easels in the extraordinary southern light were, or would go on to become, some of the most famous in the world: Gaugin, Van Gogh, Renoir, Matisse and Picasso were among those who made their homes here. The lot of the ordinary Frenchman was improved, with better working conditions, new laws on the freedom of the press and legalized trade unions. In 1882 education became free and compulsory, but it was also an important weapon in the government's hand. Education was about bringing up Frenchmen and was used as a way of stamping out regional languages like Provençal. Right up till the 1970s children were punished if they used regional dialects in school.

The twentieth century

Although the battles of the First World War took place in the north, the south suffered as many losses. By 1918 almost 1.4 million Frenchmen had lost their lives and today every village, no matter how small, will have a memorial to its dead.

During the 1920s artistic life blossomed, especially in Paris and on the Riviera. Coco Chanel made the suntan fashionable, and the south became a summer holiday destination instead of just a winter retreat. Anyone who was anyone wanted to be seen on the Riviera and it became the playground of an international beau monde. Later, after the Wall Street Crash, the socialist government of 1936 introduced paid holidays for working men and women, which for the first time brought thousands of ordinary Frenchmen to the Riviera for the summer season. Politics, however, were increasingly polarized between right and left and anti-Semitism was on the rise. When Hitler invaded France in 1940 the right wing took power.

Modern France

The Resistance movement during the Second World War was actually smaller than popular history would have you believe, but thanks to the dogged determination of General de Gaulle to carry on the fight against Germany from London, France was able to emerge into the post-war world with pride. For decades afterwards many of the less heroic episodes of the war were swept under the carpet until events like the trial of Klaus Barbie in 1983 brought them out into the open. Although the death toll was comparatively small, the devastation left by the fighting was enormous, in the south as much as the north. The Allied landings on the beaches of St-Tropez destroyed the area and it took five days of fierce fighting for Allied forces to liberate Marseille alone.

Post-war, economic recovery was rapid with the help of US aid and France played a key role in promoting the European Union. Right up till the oil crisis of the 1970s France enjoyed an economic boom, with industry spreading along the Rhône valley and around Marseille. Mass tourism arrived in force and a government initiative came into play to develop the coast of Languedoc-Roussillon.

Algerian independence in 1962 changed the political balance in the south as thousands of *pieds-noirs* – French settlers born in Algeria – returned to live in Corsica and the south as a whole. This sparked off an independence movement in Corsica and led to a rise in the political right across the region. Thousands of North African immigrants swiftly followed in search of the job opportunities in the rapidly industrializing south. France's immigrant community, however, was still a relatively small one.

The 1990s saw a worrying trend in the continued rise of the extreme right in the south, fuelled by corruption at all levels in politics, recession and growing unemployment. This reached a climax in the presidential elections of 2002 when the extreme right candidate Jean-Marie Le Pen defeated the socialist Lionel Jospin and was able to challenge Jacques Chirac in the final round of the presidential elections. Chirac, who had been tainted with corruption scandals, won by a landslide but the right wing are far from yesterday's men. Watch this space... French history may be complicated but it's never boring.

Tell me a story: September 1943

A more beautiful spot than the Colline du Château in Nice is hard to imagine but hidden among the trees is the Jewish cemetery, where there is a memorial to the Jews of Nice who were murdered in the Holocaust.

During the Second World War many French Jews fled the German-occupied north for the relatively safety of the South of France. The south provided an escape route through the Pyrenees to Spain or across the sea to North Africa, and many hoped they would be safer under the Vichy regime of the south than under direct German rule in the north. Tragically, this was far from the case. The Vichy regime handed the Jews directly to the Nazis – the only territory in Europe not occupied by the Nazis to commit this betrayal.

During this time, thousands of Jews sought refuge in towns like Cannes and Nice. Nice and the border area with Italy were occupied by Italians, who resisted both the German and the Vichy regime's attempts to arrest Jews so they were relatively safe areas. In September 1943, the Italians surrendered to the Allies. The authorities in Rome had tried to organize an escape route for the 25,000 Jews trapped in the Alpes-Maritimes and had struck a deal with the USA to delay the announcement of the Italian surrender until the Jews had left by boat. Tragically the surrender was announced ahead of time and the Jews became trapped. Many went into hiding, or escaped across the border; the unlucky ones were taken to the transit camp of Drancy, outside Paris, before being transported to Auschwitz.

France has not yet shed its anti-Semitic legacy and the number of anti-Semitic attacks has risen dramatically since 11 September 2001. It is a sorry indictment that the cemetery gate in Nice and elsewhere is likely to be guarded by police.

HISTORY IN A HURRY

Just so you know the basics, here's the lowdown on the big events in French history, with particular emphasis on what went on down South.

450,000 BC The first men arrive in Europe and set up camp in Tautavel, Roussillon.

60,000 BC Neanderthal man on Côte d'Azur.

35,000 BC Homo sapiens arrive.

3,500 BC The Neolithic era brings the first settled agriculture in the South.

1,000 BC The local Ligurian tribes start fortifying their villages and the village perché (perched village or mountain stronghold) is born.

600 BC The Greeks arrive and found the city of Massalia, now known as Marseille. They bring with them the crucial ingredients of Mediterranean life – olives and grapes.

125 BC The Romans arrive and reorganize the area into the first province they conquer outside Italy. This provincia gives the area its name – Provence.

476 The Roman Empire collapses. Provence resists being conquered by the Franks and drifts into de facto independence.

700 Arab invasions begin.

879 Provence is proclaimed a kingdom and the South is ruled by different powerful barons and local lords. It's a dangerous time; pirates plague the coast, there are endless invasions, and the locals hide away in their villages perchés.

1095 The first of the Crusades.

1208 The Crusade against the Cathars, a religious sect in Languedoc, begins. The Cathars are massacred and France annexes the whole area in 1271.

1248 Louis IX, St Louis, embarks on the Seventh Crusade from Aigues-Mortes. He sets out to use the Crusades to impose the idea of the divine right of kings and to make himself more powerful than the local barons.

1309 The popes begin their exile in Avignon.

1337–1453 The Hundred Years' War, during which the French and English battle it out to determine who is going to rule the country. The most important development for France is that it unifies the disparate barons, who, by the end of the war, are fighting for France and not just their regions. This idea of France as a nation is instilled in the people's consciousness by a young woman, Joan of Arc.

1347–8 The Black Death enters France by way of Marseille; at its end 1/3 of the country will be dead.

1481 France annexes Provence.

1545 Protestants are massacred in the Luberon. For decades religious wars tear the country apart.

1559 France annexes Roussillon, which up to this point was part of Catalonia.

1638–1715 Louis XIV seeks to build a strong France with secure borders and spends his reign fighting wars to achieve this. This bankrupts the country, and economic stagnation is particularly bad in the South. The middle classes begin to want a say in how the country is run.

1720 A second terrible plague kills tens of thousands of people in Marseille.

1766 The English writer Tobias Smollett takes a trip along the Côte d'Azur and the English aristocracy hear about its beauty for the first time.

1789 The Revolution. This most liberating event is followed by a breakdown in law and order and 'The Terror', when anyone was who was suspected of being against the Revolution is guillotined.

1793 Napoleon breaks the British siege at Toulon and shoots to fame.

1830 Tourism begins in Nice.

1860 Nice and the countryside round it become French (the price the Italians pay for unification).

1869 The opening of the Suez Canal makes Marseille a major port.

1887 Queen Victoria winters on the Côte d'Azur, making the Riviera incredibly popular as a winter destination.

1890s–1910s Artists and writers flock to the South, attracting some of the biggest names of the 20th century.

1914–18 First World War.

1930s Hotels on the Côte d'Azur stay open in the summer for the first time. The countryside is in economic stagnation and many peasants leave.

1942 Nazi Germany occupies the South of France.

1944 Allied troops land on the beaches around St-Tropez.

1946 The first Cannes Film Festival takes place.

1950s The South of France continues to be the place for the in-crowd. The small fishing village of St-Tropez is put on the world map when French starlet Brigitte Bardot holidays there.

1960s Rapid industrialization begins around Marseille. Algerian independence leads to mass immigration of Algerian-born French and other immigrants from North Africa.

1980s Politics in Nice and Marseille become corrupt.

1990s The right-wing National Front Party begin to make headway in local elections in the south.

The Riviera

Alpes-Maritimes · Var

ALPES-MARITIMES 48
Nice 48
Around Nice 54
Monaco 56
Special trips from Monaco 60
Around Monaco 61
Cannes 62
Special trips from Cannes 64
Around Cannes 68

VAR 70
Fréjus and St-Raphaël 70
Around Fréjus and St-Raphaël 71
St-Tropez 72
Special trips from St-Tropez 74
Around St-Tropez 75

WHERE TO EAT 80

03

The Riviera

Highlights

Nibbling your way along Nice's Cours Saleya in the Old Town, p.49
Playing at being part of the jet set in Monaco, p.56
Meeting the killer whales in Marineland, p.64
Catching a boat to the Ile de Porquerolles, p.74
Paddling on Cabasson beach, p.77
Getting lost in the Massif des Maures, p.76

Take the kids to the Riviera – where they can gaze at mountains that plunge into the sea; where they can get a taste for luxurious living in Monaco; where they can see what inspired great painters like Matisse and Picasso; where they can find the true South of France still hidden in the remote valleys of the Massif des Maures, and learn to swim in the shallow waters around Cap de Brégançon.

There are over a hundred miles of coast to choose from, ranging from the built-up, glitzy beaches of the Côte d'Azur all the way to the soft, sandy bays of Var. The area covered in this chapter lies east of the A57 and, with the odd exception, south of the A8 motorway. The Riviera proper runs from Menton to Cannes and is the busiest part of the coast – it's open for business all year round, with lots of

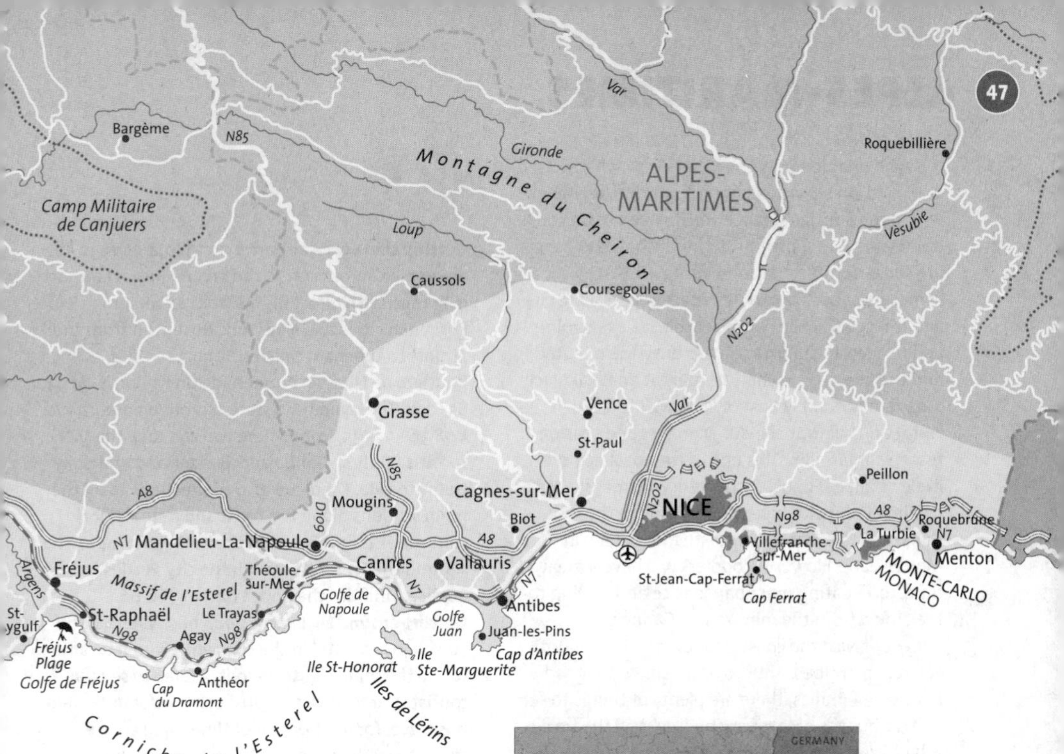

facilities and masses to do. The hairpin bends behind Monaco still look just as good as they did in those 1960s action movies and hidden in the mountains are some of the most beautiful hilltop villages in France. East of Cannes there is a string of family resorts, and throughout the area there are endless sandy beaches and beautiful vineyards.

Such a perfect day

Morning Explore the ancient hilltop village of Grimaud, p.76

Lunch Eat everything made from chestnuts by the river in Collobrières, p.76

Afternoon Make sandcastles on Cabasson beach – a wild half-moon bay with shallow blue water, p.77

Special events

February

Menton: Lemon Festival

Nice: Carnival

July

Throughout the region: Bastille Day celebrations

Eze: Medieval Festival

October

Collobrières: Chestnut Festival

ALPES-MARITIMES

It is fashionable to say the Riviera isn't what it used to be and, on a practical note, more than anywhere else in the South of France you do need to do your homework when planning a family holiday. There are some horrible and some fantastic places – sometimes just a few miles apart. Nice is a big city and it's a good base out of season; it's easy-going and relaxed. In summer it's too busy, too polluted and the beach too pebbly to make it an ideal place for a family holiday. East of Nice, Menton, Cap Ferrat and Villefranche-sur-Mer are good seaside resorts for families. This end of the coast is more likely to appeal to older children, who may want to try their hand at white-water rafting in the mountains behind Menton and taste the highlife in Monte-Carlo. However, toddlers will have a great time, too – eating marzipan in Nice and waving to the crowd from the minitrain in Cannes.

West of Nice the coast is an urban disaster until you reach Antibes. Antibes and Cannes are good towns for families; there are plenty of things to see and do, but the area is very built up and the traffic is bad. West of Cannes are the best beaches in the South of France and a host of family resorts. This is the real Mediterranean France and the best place to come with kids. There are fantastic beaches for toddlers and underwater wonders for snorkelling teens. The Massif des Maures and the Esterel are lovely for walking and picnicking and the Ile de Porquerolles is the prettiest place on the coast – the perfect island hideaway. Despite the glitz and the glamour in resorts like St-Tropez, you can have a relaxed holiday messing about on the beach and you won't need a movie star's salary to pay for it.

Best beaches for kids

Villefranche-sur-Mer – a shallow beach with fine shingle and a good beach café
Antibes – the sandy Plage La Salis
Iles de Lérins – rocky outcrops and tiny coves
Agay – lots of water sports and salty lagoons
St-Aygulf – a long, wide, sandy beach that is safe for little kids
Fréjus/St Raphaël – a huge, wide strip of sand to build castles on
Le Lavandou – lots of sand and roundabouts on the front
Cap de Brégançon – idyllic half-moon bays
Ile de Porquerolles – shallow blue waters that are perfect for learning to swim

NICE

Getting there Nice airport, **t** 00 33 (0)4 93 21 30 30, **www**.nice.aeroport.fr, is the second busiest airport in France, with direct flights from all major European cities and New York. Buses run from the airport to the main coach station, the Gare Routière de Nice, on Promenade du Paillon, **t** 04 93 85 61 81. The main train station is on Avenue Thiers, **t** 08 36 35 35 35, from where you can take the TGV to Paris (5½hrs), Genoa and Switzerland and daily trains to Lille. There are also connections to all the main stations along the coast and a small local commuter train. Nice is on the main autoroute, the A8, and the N7 runs through the city. Ferries to Corsica run from the port, **t** 04 93 13 66 66
Getting around Nice has a good bus system but if you choose a hotel in the city centre you'll be able to see the main sights on foot. There are several tourist tickets – 'Nice by Bus' – that offer unlimited bus travel for a set period of time. You can use trains to explore the coast, the Alps and the Var Valley. For taxis, **t** 04 93 13 78 78
Tourist office 5 Promenade des Anglais **t** 00 33 (0)4 92 14 48 00, **www**.nicetourism.com, **www**.niceandyou.com, **www**.nice-coteazur.org
Special events February: Carnival: lasting 2 weeks, including giant floats and a huge firework display. May: May Day celebrations: every Sun, including parades and maypole dancing. June: Fête des Pêcheurs: held 29 June to honour St Peter, the patron saint of fishermen; a boat is burned on the beach, followed by lots of singing and dancing. July: Bastille Day: huge firework displays on the Promenade des Anglais. September: Nice Military Tattoo: this takes place every 2 years, when over 1,000 military musicians parade through the streets. December: Christmas Market: in Jardin Albert 1er, including a skating rink and Ferris wheel

Nice is a great city to visit with kids of all ages. Its mild climate means you can spend a lot of time outdoors, even in winter, and it's fairly compact so it's easy to get around with kids. There is lots to see and do throughout the city, but to enjoy Nice you don't have to slog round endless museums: it's made to relax in. It isn't a city that makes any demands on you – no official 'must-see' monuments – and kids will love its Mediterranean atmosphere. Life in Nice is about enjoying the sun, the colours, the sweep of the bay and the food.

Did you know...?

The word 'carnival' comes from carne levare, which means 'away with meat'. According to tradition no meat is eaten during the 40 days of Lent, in the run-up to Easter. In the Middle Ages there was always a huge festival just before Lent began, with lots of feasting to eat everything up before the lean days of Lent, and lots of parties and dancing in the streets. The first carnival was held in Nice in 1294.

Nice was part of the Italian state of Savoy until 1860 and is France's fifth largest city. It's a busy, bustling, urban experience – you can sit on the beach and watch the planes landing at the airport at the end of the bay – but it is far from claustrophobic. Despite the heavy traffic, Nice is not a city that makes you feel trapped; it's airy and has plenty of fountains and pretty squares. There are beautiful parks for a peaceful stroll and the beach, though pebbly, is lovely.

Nice is perhaps the best place in France to eat out with children, as the restaurants are easy-going and the local dishes are versions of pasta and pizza. But you won't have to spend all your time in restaurants: Nice is famous for its irresistible market, with mountains of delicious marzipan sweets sitting alongside brightly coloured fruits and vegetables. Pick up some treats for picnics and snacks (*see* below).

Many of the museums, including the Musée Masséna, have small gardens where toddlers can run around while you take it in turns to see the collections. Most museums have children's workshops and activities in the holidays and on Wednesday afternoons during term time. A lot have guided tours for children and their parents, although you'll need to speak French.

Nice is a vibrant city with a definite identity, so it's an excellent destination for older children and teenagers and it's fairly safe, so you can let them explore a bit on their own. Nice is ideal for a short break, a day trip or a stopover with kids, though you'll need at least two nights here to get the best out of the city, and its mild winters make it a good place to head out of season. Nice is not, necessarily, somewhere to spend your entire summer holiday though, mainly because the beach isn't that great for kids and the summer heat makes the pollution levels irritating. If you're planning a longer stay, come at half term or Easter – the attractions are always open and you'll soon find it doesn't rely on tourists to keep it going.

Shopping

You'll find branches of all the main French chain stores in Nice. The main shopping streets are Avenue Jean Médecin and Rue Masséna, which is pedestrianized. For good value, original clothes head for Du Pareil au Même, 44 Rue Pastorelli. The stylish children's clothes store Petit Bateau is on Rue Masséna and is a good place for something smart for the baby of the family. Agnès B at 17 Rue des Ponchettes is where the trendy girls get their clothes; the women's clothes here are cut quite small so teens can fit them if you can afford them.

The big department store Galeries Lafayette is on Avenue Jean Médicin. Here you'll also find the kids' clothes shops Catimini, Kid Cool and Orchestra as well as Pimkie, for a cheap teenage girlie shopping fix. For books, there's a branch of the discount bookshop Maxi Livres, which has a good selection for kids, while teens will want to check out the CDs and computer games in FNAC in the shopping centre Nice Etoile. For sheer, wide-eyed wonder, visit Contesso, 16 Avenue Notre Dame, one of the most famous toyshops in France. If the kids like rummaging around in markets, they might be interested in the flea market in Place Robilante, near the port, which is open Tues–Sat 10–6.

Picnics and snacks

Nice is made for snacking and grazing and a morning walk down Cours Saleya in the old town

Good to know...

You can buy a museum pass from the tourist office or FNAC bookshop, but it may not be the best deal for your family. Nice is full of museums, but with kids you may not want to see them all. Under-7s don't pay an entrance fee and on the first Sunday of every month museums are free, so using a pass card with children may not be necessary. If your children are older, you might consider the *Carte Passe-Musées Ville de Nice*, which gives a discount on the entrance fee and costs €6.10 for 7 days. If you plan to see a lot of museums in the region, you could invest in a *Riviera Pass* to all 62 museums in the area. The pass costs €8.08 per day, €15.24 for 3 days or €25 for 7 days.

Tell me a story:
Why is the Riviera so famous?

Anybody who's anybody has been holidaying on the Riviera for almost 200 years, and it was an Englishman who first put it on the map. Tobias Smollett, the novelist and doctor, came here in the 1760s and took a dip in the Mediterranean as a cure for his consumption. Bathing in the sea was just becoming fashionable in England at this time, but the locals thought he was crazy. Smollet, on the other hand, was very impressed with his experiences and wrote a book about them, which was a runaway bestseller and alerted the rest of England to the delights of the Riviera. When the Napoleonic Wars ended in 1815, everyone in England wanted to flee to the Riviera to escape the rain and soak up the winter sun (in those days, it was a winter destination only). By 1820 over a hundred British families were wintering in Nice and they were soon followed by Germans and Russians; less than 100 years later foreign holidaymakers would number over 100,000.

In the 19th century the Côte d'Azur was definitely an aristocratic destination: it was quite common for British prime ministers to spend weeks on end staying there as it was a good place to do business and meet other influential people. Queen Victoria was a great fan of the region, too, and was especially fond of Cimiez in Nice.

The opening of the Casino in Monte-Carlo in 1863 brought more glamour to the area but the wild side of life really took off after the First World War. The famous authors, actors and painters of the early 20th century either moved in or spent long periods of time on the Riviera. They lived it up in the sumptuous hotels along the coast, like the Eden Roc in Antibes, and drank far too much champagne. The list is too long to mention them all, but among the partying crowd were the writers D. H. Lawrence, Graham Greene and Aldous Huxley; artists such as Matisse and Picasso and the celebrated dancer Isadora Duncan (who met a suitably theatrical end, strangled when her scarf got caught in the wheels of her sports car on the Promenade des Anglais).

In the 1930s the French government introduced an annual summer holiday for workers and soon the locals were able to follow the rich and the famous south for some sun and sea. Today it is fashionable, almost obligatory, to complain that the Riviera isn't what it used to be, and in its heyday it was indeed an exclusive, glamorous playground for hedonistic authors and rich aristocrats. The scenery may have been completely unspoilt by today's holiday developments and tourist shops, but the people who actually lived in the area were poverty stricken and left in droves. Life was tough in those pretty hilltop villages, so don't begrudge the lavender shops and postcard stalls that exist there today.

The rich and famous still come here anyway: some of the world's hottest stars have houses on the Riviera. Elton John has a villa in Nice and Robbie Williams, Lady Victoria Hervey and Geri Halliwell enjoy the buzz in St-Tropez. Keep your autograph book to hand.

will solve all your picnic problems. The best place to picnic is on the beach, but you can literally nibble your way along Cours Saleya and forget lunch.

At Chez Thérésa, which is more of a stall than a restaurant, you can try the local speciality, *socca*, a chickpea pancake. She also sells a good *pissaladière*, a vegetable tart that is the local version of pizza, and other local savouries.

The market is open every day except Monday and Sunday mornings. Pâtisserie Cappa, 7 Place Garibaldi, is the place to try the local speciality, *tourte de blettes*, a Swiss chard and cheese pie.

For standard groceries, there is an Intermarché supermarket on Boulevard Gambetta.

Sweet-toothed kids will love Confiserie Florian, on Quai Papacino, **www**.confiserieflorian.com. The chocolates and crystallized fruit are made from local products, which including fresh flowers. You can watch them being made before you buy some.

The next stop for all things sweet is Auer, the famous *belle époque* sweet shop on Rue St-François-de-Paule, opposite the Opera. Inside there are bowls overflowing with delicious chocolates and candied fruits and some fabulous cakes. Generations of *niçois* spent their childhoods pressing their noses against the glass, admiring the sweets inside.

For more special treats, La Cure Gourmande at 2 Rue St-Réparate is a good place to buy chocolates and sweets to take home.

Things to see and do

Promenade des Anglais

Nice is famous for its seafront, and those familiar with the southeast of England could be forgiven for thinking that at first sight Nice looks like a Mediterranean Brighton. That's no coincidence, because the Promenade was built by an Englishman in the 1820s to allow respectable young ladies to take the air without having to meet the locals down on the beach. Parading up and down the Promenade is still the thing to do for all ages, and trendy kids, young and old, rollerskate and skateboard along here. It's quite safe to let older children out alone along the Promenades des Anglais. One Sunday a month the Promenade is closed to traffic. You can hire rollerblades and mini-scooters at:

Roller Station

49 Quai des Etats-Unis **t** 04 93 62 99 05

Fun'Roll

13 Rue Cassinit **t** 04 93 55 12 32

Nicea Location Rent

9 Av Thiers **t** 04 93 82 42 71

Mini Train

t 06 16 39 53 51
Runs Oct–May 10–5, June–Sept 10–6 and July–Aug 10–7

Little ones will like riding along the seafront on this. It leaves from the Promenade des Anglais, opposite Jardin Albert 1er, for a 40min ride around the Colline du Château and the old town, and along the seafront. In summer there are also pony and trap rides from Jardin Albert 1er.

Colline du Château

Open Daily 7am–8pm
Adm Free

Although it is still called the Colline du Château, or Castle Hill, there isn't a castle up here any more – it was blown up by Louis XIV when he briefly took control of the town. Instead, it's a lovely, shady park with a stunning view of the city and the Bay of Angels and a good café for a rest and a cool drink. Don't miss the enormous waterfall, the Cascade Donjon. You can catch the minitrain from the Promenade des Anglais, but it's more fun to take the lift from the end of Quai des Etats-Unis, which is in use until 8pm during the summer.

Did you hear a cannon...?
Over 100 years ago a rich Scotsman, Sir Thomas Coventry More, installed a cannon on the Colline du Château and ordered it to be fired every day at 12 noon so his young wife, who was a bit forgetful, remembered to turn up for lunch!

Musée Naval

Tour Bellanda t 04 93 80 47 61
Open **Wed–Sat 10–12 noon and 2–5, June–Sept 2–7; closed mid-Nov–mid-Dec**
Adm **Adult €2.29, child €1.37**

This little museum in the park on the Colline du Château has an interesting collection of model boats and organizes events for kids most days between 2–4pm. The classes change regularly so call for details. To get the best out of the workshops you'll need to speak some French.

Vieux Nice

Vieux Nice is the really Italian bit of the city, with buildings that would look at home across the border in Genoa. They're all in rich, warm colours that glow in the sun. Today, it's the trendy corner of town, with a real Latin atmosphere – lots of cafés, shops and young men on scooters, so keep on eye on toddlers in case they stray into the road. It's a good place to visit at any time of day and is especially good for eating out in the evening, as the main street – Cours Saleya – is pedestrianized and full of family restaurants. You'll find toddlers running around until midnight.

Cours Saleya also has one of the best markets in France (*see* above), open every day except Monday and Sunday mornings. The colours are a riot – no wonder the painter Matisse lived here – and the atmosphere is marvellous. It's a showcase of the best of Mediterranean produce and is definitely the place to tempt kids to try something new. The mountains of marzipan fruits and boiled sweets are irresistible and it's the perfect place to stock up for a picnic on the beach.

Musée de Terra Amata

25 Bd Carnot **t** 04 93 55 59 93
Open Tues–Sun 9–12 noon and 2–6
Adm Adult €3.81, child free

This little museum stands on top of one of the most important prehistoric sites in France, but

Did you know...?
The Greeks gave Nice its name. They landed here in the 4th century BC and set up a trading post, called Nikaïa, which is Greek for 'victory'.

you'd never guess, as it's tucked away under a block of flats near the harbour. Over 400,000 years ago, our ancestors took a break from their nomadic life of hunting mammoths across the Alps, and set up camp here, making temporary shelters from sticks, and stone tools for hunting. There was nothing unusual about the huts or tools, but prehistoric man did make a major technical breakthrough in Nice: these people spent their evenings gathered around a campfire, the first time anyone in Europe had lit a fire. One of the members of the camp left a footprint in the muddy earth, 400,000 years ago. It can still be seen today and is eerily reminiscent of the footprints Neil Armstrong left on the moon.

The camp was discovered in 1966 and learning about what happened here is a crucial part of the primary school history syllabus. In term time the museum is always full of school children. The museum organizes children's activities in French in the spring and summer school holidays.

Musée Archéologique

160 Av des Arènes **t** 04 93 81 59 57
Open April–Sept Tues–Sun 10–12 noon and 2–6, Oct–Mar Tues–Sun 10–1 and 2–5
Adm Adult €3.80, child free

The Roman town of Cemenelum was a very important place in its day. In the museum you can see what's left of the baths and the amphitheatre. There are special activities for children ages 7–12 one Wednesday a month. (These are aimed at French kids, who get Wednesday afternoons off school, so it helps if your child has some French.) Next door to the museum is a pretty, peaceful park, which is ideal for a family picnic. Kids have been playing on the ruins for generations.

Musée Matisse

164 Av des Arènes **t** 04 93 81 08 08
www.musee-matisse-nice.org
Open Wed–Mon 10–6 (5 in winter)
Adm Adult €3.80, child free

This is probably the best art gallery for kids to visit. Matisse, who spent a large part of his life in Nice, was one of the most important painters to discover and depict the beauty of the region. His use of bright colours and bold shapes usually appeals to children, and the museum has not only paintings but also lots of photographs of Matisse at work, which helps to bring the collection to life. Kids will like *Storm over Nice*, which gets darker and wetter the further back you step and *The Bees*, with its lively pattern and bright colours. A simple composition, *Still Life with Pomegranates* (Nature morte aux grenades), may also appeal to kids, especially if they like pomegranates.

If the paintings are a hit, you might like to visit the Chapelle du Rosaire in Vence, the church that Matisse designed.

The Russian Orthodox Cathedral

Av Nicolas II **t** 04 93 96 88 02
Open Daily 9.15–12 noon and 2.30–5.30 (5 in winter)
Adm Adult €3, child (under 12) free

The cathedral is a copy of the classic onion-domed churches you'll find in Moscow and is the biggest Russian Orthodox cathedral outside Russia. It looks as if St Basil's in Red Square has decamped to the Riviera for a holiday, and it suits it: the Mediterranean sunshine sets off the gold on the roof perfectly. The cathedral was built by the last tsar, Nicolas II, and was finished in 1912. It's fun to visit with kids because it's something completely different, but watch that little ones who aren't used to Orthodox churches don't try to blow the candles out. There's a shop selling Russian food

Tell me a story: Why are there so many Russians in town?

You may have noticed that many of the restaurant menus in Nice are written in Russian and that most of the expensive shops near and inside the Hôtel Negresco have notices in the window that say the staff speak Russian. Nice has been a popular destination for Russians since the 19th century – royalty and aristocrats, writers and revolutionaries have all found Nice irresistible – and since the fall of Communism Russians have been flocking back to their old haunts. Lenin and Chekhov passed through town, and the famous writer Alexander Herzen is buried here. The Russian Navy used the bay at Villefranche-sur-Mer as a base in the 19th century, when it was part of Savoy.

and goodies by the gate. Make sure you dress appropriately: no shorts or skimpy tops and certainly no hammer-and-sickle or Che Guevara T-shirts! To round off a tour of Russian Nice, try something Russian for supper at Le Transibérian, 1 Rue Bottero, **t** 04 93 96 49 05.

Observatoire de Nice

Bd de l'Observatoire (on the Grand Corniche in the direction of La Turbie) t 04 92 00 30 11
Open Tours Sat at 3pm
Adm Adult €3, child free

This elegant old observatory is set in a large park and offers fantastic views both of its surroundings and the heavens. More than 2,000 stars have been discovered here. On the tour, which is for real star buffs, you'll be shown into the main observatory domes where you can see the telescopes. One of the domes was designed by Gustav Eiffel of Eiffel Tower fame. In August there's a festival of space and stars.

Bowling

Bowling de Nice

5 Esplanade Kennedy t 04 93 55 33 11
Open Daily 11–2.30

A diversion if the weather is bad; good for teens.

Boat trips

Aqua scope

Quai Lunel t 04 92 00 42 30
Open Daily April–Sept 9–7

The boat has a glass bottom for fish spotting. A trip should cost a family of four around €35.

Trans Côte d'Azur

Quai Lunel t 04 92 00 42 30
www.trans-cote-azur.com

This company offers trips along the coast to Villefranche-sur-Mer, St-Tropez and Monaco.

Cinemas

Cinémathèque de Nice

3 Esplanade JF Kennedy t 04 92 04 06 66

Movie World

2 Rue Jacques Offenbach t 04 93 87 25 28

There are lots of cinemas across town and you can find out what's on and where in the newspaper *Nicematin*. Films shown in *version originale* (vo) will be in their original language, so you'll be able to see major Hollywood releases in English. Be aware that film censorship is not as strict in France as it is in the UK.

Dance

Opéra de Nice

Rue de la Terrasse t 04 93 13 98 53 (information); t 04 92 17 40 40 (reservations)

Generations of holidaying families have taken their kids here for a taste of culture. The building looks just like the opera house in *The Story of Babar*.

Parks and playgrounds

Colline du Château is the main park (*see* p.51), but there are lots of small parks and playgrounds around town. In Jardin Albert 1er there's a roundabout and bandstand, and Place Masséna has lovely fountains. You'll find plenty of local families in the playground and the little park of Jardin Alsace Lorraine, off Boulevard Gambetta. The wooded hill of Mont Boron is nice for a picnic.

Parc Floral Phoenix

405 Promenade des Anglais t 04 93 18 03 33
Open Daily 9–5 (7 mid-Mar–mid-Oct)
Adm (incl. greenhouse) Adult €6, child (6–12) €3.80, student €5

If you're in Nice for some time, it's worth a trip to this modern botanical garden, although it's pricey for what it is. The park is divided into five different climatic zones, and there's a large lake and a musical fountain. The gardens are laid out very imaginatively with funny sculptures, stepping stones and waterfalls. There's a huge children's playground where you'll often find local schools. The centrepiece is a greenhouse, called the Green Diamond and shaped like a huge glass tent, which claims to be the biggest in Europe. Just don't expect too much if you've been to Kew Gardens!

Town beaches

Although the Bay of Angels is beautiful, the beach in Nice is pebbly and uncomfortable and is best for watching the planes coming in to land at Nice's busy airport. Public and private beaches alternate along the bay, with most of the private beaches (*see* below) charging per day. The shore drops away quite suddenly, especially at the Colline du Château end of the beach, so watch the kids as they can easily lose their footing. Keep shoes on, too, as there is sometimes broken glass on the public beaches. (Private beaches are cleaned regularly).

If you want an afternoon on the beach, head for Villefranche-sur-Mer, which is just a short hop east along the coast (*see* p.55) by bus or train. There's a lovely beach just below the train station.

Beach clubs in Nice with facilities for kids include:

Bambou

165 Promenade des Anglais t 04 93 80 75 06

Includes children's pool, playground and pedalos, plus restaurant.

Forum

Promenade des Anglais, facing Jardin Albert 1er t 04 93 44 52 38

Houses a playground, children's pool and a restaurant.

Neptune

Promenade des Anglais, opposite Hôtel Negresco t 04 93 87 16 60

There are lots of activities to choose from, including pedalos, a seawater pool, table tennis and children's games supervised by an attendant, plus restaurant.

Water sports

L'Aigle Nautique

50 Bd Franck Pilatte t 04 93 89 23 33

Specializes in water sports for kids.

Cip Nice

2 Ruelle des Moulins t 04 93 55 59 50
Open Mar–Nov daily

Diving for ages 8 and up.

AROUND NICE

Animal lovers

Zoo du Cap Ferrat

St-Jean-Cap-Ferrat t 04 93 76 07 60
www.zoocapferrat.com
Open Daily 9.30–5.30 (7 in summer)
Adm Adult €9.50, child (3–10) €6.50

This is a real Noah's Ark, set in the lush grounds of the villa that once belonged to King Leopold of Belgium. There are over 300 different animals, including panthers, tigers, zebras, llamas, lemurs and crocodiles. Little kids will like the goat enclosure where they can pat the animals, and there's a playground as well. Chimps' tea parties occur regularly, and if that makes your children hungry, there is a lovely café. There's so much to enjoy you can really take your time; allow a good two hours for the visit.

Village hideaways

Eze

Getting there Eze is on the Moyenne Corniche, the N7. Trains and buses stop at Eze-sur-Mer and there's a shuttle up to the village in summer. Buses also go straight to Eze-Village from Nice *gare routière*. It's much too high to walk up from Eze-sur-Mer with kids, and even the walk down can take well over an hour
Tourist office Place Général de Gaulle
t 00 33 (0)4 93 41 26 00 www.eze-riviera.com
Special events End July: Historical pageant

Eze, the archetypal *village perché* (hilltop village), is a charming place to visit, despite the hordes of tourists who also think so. It's a delightful place for a stroll and has a tremendous view along what has to be the most stunning stretch of coast on this part of the Riviera. Hanging vertiginously from its cliff face, it's a natural lookout post. The Romans were the first to spot its potential and part of the village dates from the Roman occupation. After the fall of the Roman Empire, the South of France was plunged into the Dark Ages and villages on the top of craggy outcrops offered locals a degree of safety. Many of these originally had a network of tunnels so that villagers could escape if ever hordes of pirates came ashore.

If you want to avoid the crowds, visit Eze in the morning or for a leisurely stroll in the evening. It's a pleasant place to come for dinner and to buy souvenirs and despite the winding alleys and steps it's negotiable with a single buggy. There's even a flat track so the cobbles won't annoy the baby.

Jardin Exotique

t 04 93 41 10 30
Open July–Aug daily 9–7 (5 rest of the year), closed for lunch
Adm Adult €2.50, child (under 12) free

Don't skimp on the price of the ticket to the garden at Eze's highest point – the view is

Good to know...

Eze has one of the best public toilets on the Riviera. It's in the main car park.

fantastic, but you do need a head for heights. The kids will like the cacti and the climb up to the old ruined castle.

St-Paul-de-Vence

Getting there Buses go from Nice and Cannes.

Just behind Cannes is one of the South of France's most famous villages, the old fortified hilltop village of St-Paul-de-Vence. Its fame is due to the great but impoverished artists who paid for their meals in the local restaurant with paintings. Picasso, Matisse, Braque, Léger and Dufy, among others, all bartered in this way. The pictures are still there but you've got to have deep enough pockets to afford a meal at La Colombe d'Or in order to see them.

St-Paul-de-Vence is a prime spot on the tourist trail, and as such has lost much of its original charm. The area around it is very built-up. For the really lovely *villages perchés*, head further inland toward Peillon, Gorbio, Lucéram and Saorge.

Buckets and spades

Villefranche-sur-Mer

Getting there It's a 10min drive from Nice and there are lots of local trains from Nice, Cannes and Monaco that stop at the station just above the beach. The local bus service is good
Tourist office Jardin François Binon **t** 00 33 (0)4 93 01 73 68 **www**.villefranche-sur-mer.com

Villefranche is a lovely old fishing port that has somehow managed to keep the charm that originally drew the rich and famous to the Riviera. Its apricot-coloured houses, little alleyways and imposing castle make this a delightful place to stay with children. It has one of the best beaches for families on this stretch of coast and in summer, when traffic jams are a problem, you can catch the train to do some sightseeing in Monaco and Nice.

There's nothing specific to see in Villefranche itself but it's a lovely place to unwind. There's an open-air cinema in the citadel in summer, **t** 04 93 01 73 68, and there's a zoo on Cap Ferrat (*see* p.54). Acti'Loisirs, **t** 04 92 47 75 00, **www**.actiloisirs.com, run whale-watching cruises during the summer; tickets cost €40 adult, €29 child.

There are some pleasant family hotels and holiday complexes in the town, but rentals are pricey. The best beach is just below the train station, with fine shingle that is almost sand and although the bay is amazingly deep (the Russian Navy used to drop anchor here), the beach is shallow and safe for children.

Other beaches near Villefranche

Plage Paloma, on Cap Ferrat, is pebbly but family friendly and Plage de Passable is also popular with families and close to the zoo. Tourist trains are usually a hit but, unless your thirst for celebrities knows no bounds and includes stars of yesteryear, it's best to avoid the little train that runs around Cap Ferrat pointing out the villas of the rich and famous – they're stars the children will most probably never have heard of. Save your money to spend elsewhere. The water along this stretch of coast is very clean, as sewage is treated in a new cutting-edge waste-water treatment centre before being released into the sea.

Further along the coast at Cap d'Ail, Plage Mala is a sandy beach with a snack bar, but is a hike up and down stone steps, so is not a good place for babies. The urban sprawl that spreads west of Nice is best avoided; Cagnes-sur-Mer is more Motorway-sur-Mer than anything else, and there's nothing decent until you reach Antibes.

Look at this!

Astrorama

Route de la Revère, Col d'Eze t 04 93 41 23 04
www.astrorama.net
Getting there On the Grande Corniche between Nice and La Turbie
Open Mon–Sat 6pm–10.30pm (11 July–Aug), Sept–June special evening stargazing Fri and Sat 6–10
Adm Adult €6, child €4.50

The French adore observatories and every big town has one. Perched high on the hills above Nice, this one is like a balcony on the night sky. The huge telescopes give you a chance to see the craters on the moon, Jupiter and its moons and even Saturn's rings. The chance to gaze at the stars in such a perfect setting shouldn't be missed. The observatory gets its name from the units that are used to measure distances in astronomy.

Themes of the shows vary depending on the time of year, so call ahead to find out what's on.

Rail power!

If you don't have a car there are three great train rides from Nice:

The Métrazur

Trains run from Nice to Menton via Monaco, leaving from the main SNCF station.

Although this is just a commuter train, it's one of the best train rides in France, allowing you to get a close up look at all those glitzy villas as the train runs behind their back gardens.

Le Chemin de Fer de Provence

Trains run four times a day from the Gare de Nice, t 04 97 03 80 80, on Rue Alfred Binet, which is just up from the main SNCF station www.chemin-de-fer.net

Trains stop at Plan du Var, Puget-Théniers, Entrevaux, Annot, Thorame and St-André-les-Alpes. This journey along the Var valley is great fun and is perfect for Thomas the Tank Engine fans, with steam engines in summer. It's a great way to see the countryside as the trains rattle up the Var Valley close to the Gorges du Verdon (*see* p.102). The best place to break the trip is at the fairytale castle of Entrevaux (*see* p.103).

Le Train des Merveilles

Trains run daily from the main SNCF station in Nice t 08 92 35 35 35 www.traintouristques-ter.com/traindesmerveilles

Trains take a beautiful route up the Alpine valley to Sospel and Tende (*see* p.105–6).

Sospel is a lovely place to get off for lunch (*see* p.105) and there is an interesting museum in Tende, which explains how the mysterious carvings in the Vallée des Merveilles were made (*see* p.106).

MONACO

Getting there Monaco is on the main coastal highway, the A8. There are no customs formalities – just drive in. Depending on the traffic and which road you take, there's no need to budget more than 45mins to get there from Nice. Monaco does not have its own airport, but there's a bus service from Nice airport and taxis from Nice airport should cost around €75 one way. For real glamour there's a helicopter transfer service from Nice, which takes 7mins (Héli Air Monaco, **t** 00 377 92 05 00 50). Expect to pay around €75 one way, with discounts for under-12s and under-2s travel free. Local buses from Nice, and Menton run every 15 mins. Taking the train is by far the best way to get to Monaco. Trains run regularly from Nice and Monaco station is one of the cleanest in Europe, with good connections to all the main towns along the coast. A network of tunnels and lifts take you from the station to the port where you can catch a bus up to the old town

Getting around If you can, avoid driving in Monaco. The town is a confusing system of tunnels and one-way streets, and without local plates you can't drive up to the old town anyway. The bus service is excellent and most of the main attractions are within walking distance of each other. Bus no. 1 or no. 2 will take you up to the old city. For taxis, **t** 00 377 93 15 01 01

Tourist office 2a Bd des Moulins, Monte-Carlo **t** 00 377 92 16 61 16 **www**.monaco-tourism.com **www**.monaco-congres.com **www**.monte-carlo.mc **www**.montecarloresort.com

Special events January: Circus Festival; Monte-Carlo Historic Car Rally. May: Monaco Grand Prix; contact the Automobile Club de Monaco for information and tickets, **t** 00 377 93 15 26 00, www.acm.mc; you'll need to book at least a year ahead. September: Vintage car rally. November: National Holiday and fireworks, 18 and 19 Nov. December: Christmas performances by the Monte-Carlo Ballet, **t** 00 377 92 166 166

Can you spot...a Monégasque euro?
Since Monaco is part of the euro zone it has its own coins. They are collector's items.

***Tell me a story:* How did such a tiny country get so rich?**

The Grimaldis have been in charge in Monaco since 1297, when François Grimaldi entered the town disguised as a monk and seized it for his own. The Grimaldis bought the Rock from Genoa in 1308 and built a mini-empire along the coast, making a living by taxing the lemons and olives that were grown in Menton.

In 1848 Menton rebelled and became part of France, leaving Monaco to fend for itself. Believe it or not, at this time it was the poorest state in Europe. In desperation its ruler, Prince Charles III, decided to build a casino on a rock near the palace, which he called Monte-Carlo after himself. Because gambling was banned in France, the new casino was a runaway success. It made so much money that taxes were abolished for residents and the rest is history.

Today Monaco doesn't survive on gambling alone; it makes its money out of offshore banking and business tourism. It has been a byword for all things glamorous since 1956, when Prince Rainier married the beautiful American movie star Grace Kelly. Since her death in a car crash on the dangerous roads above town in 1982, the junior royals have led soap-opera lives and are rarely out of the gossip columns.

The Principality of Monaco is one of the tiniest, most autocratic countries in Europe, run by the Grimaldi family as their own personal fiefdom. This pocket-sized kingdom – just 2 sq km – with its quite staggering wealth seems to appeal to kids.

Although it is far from beautiful (the surfeit of luxury tower blocks sees to that) it is worth a trip just to experience the sheer weirdness of the place. It is really only worth staying in Monte-Carlo if you have the money to enjoy one of the top-class hotels, otherwise there are much nicer, reasonably priced places to stay nearby. A day trip is adequate to catch all the main sites.

Start at Grimaldi Palace, on the Rock; its towers date from the 19th century, although it was built around a 13th-century Genoese fortress. If Prince Rainier is at home, you'll have to admire it from the outside, but you could time your visit to see the Changing of the Guard at 11.55am. Not far from there is the Musée Océanographique, also well worth a visit, with a small but lovely aquarium in the basement. Then head down to the area newly reclaimed from the sea to the west of the Rock; here you'll find the Grimaldi personal museums and family zoo. Monaco is full of little museums. Some set out to glorify the Grimaldis, and as such are completely ridiculous, and the others are simply the family's private collections, but these self-indulgent mini-museums are likely to make more of an impact on junior imaginations than the big, fancy collections further along the coast. You don't have to visit them all, which is an expensive option anyway. Just pop into a few; you'll get the idea, and it's the best way to see what an odd place Monaco is.

After you've seen the Rock and the museums, catch a bus or the tourist train back into town for a glimpse of the legendary Casino and to cool off in the park before heading home. Don't dare to tread on the grass though, or the police will be down on you in droves. Before you grumble about the police, it's worth remembering that Monaco is very safe (because of the jaw-dropping wealth of the place, security is, unsurprisingly, very tight). If you have teenagers who are champing at the bit for half an hour's freedom, this is a good place to let them do something alone.

Unfortunately, untold riches seem to have gone to the Monégasques' heads; they're not too friendly to small children here, so don't expect the locals to help you with the pushchair. You've got to go over to rough-and-ready Marseille for that kind of welcome.

Shopping

You'll find most of the big names, including FNAC, in Le Métropole Shopping Centre not far from the Casino. For practical shopping, try the

Can you spot...a Monégasque?

There are only 6,000 citizens of Monaco, known as Monégasques. The other 30,000 residents are extremely rich people who don't mind calling a rabbit-hutch-of-a-flat home, because in Monaco they don't have to pay tax. To be resident in Monaco you don't have to live here all year round, though. If you look up at the tower blocks you'll see most of the flats are closed up while their owners are out of town.

Good to know...
If you want to send a postcard you'll need to buy a special Monégasque stamp.

Centre Commercial Fontvieille. It has a huge supermarket that sells absolutely everything. For baby goods there's Bébé Tendresse, which has all the bits and pieces you might need for 0–2 years as well as maternity clothes; there are more good kids' clothes at an even better price at Kid 0/16.

Football fans can kit themselves out in the red and white colours of the local team AS Monaco at their shop on Rue Grimaldi. Further on down the street is the Formula 1 shop where you can buy practically anything you can think of with the image of a racing car on it.

Picnics and snacks

You'll find plenty of sandwich bars and takeaways in the old town near the Palace. The Petit Casino supermarket on the port side also does a good takeaway pizza, and you can buy food for picnics here too. If you need to do some serious shopping the Carrefour supermarket in Fontvieille is one of the best on the Riviera, and if you want to experience local colour, there's a daily market in La Condamine, the area behind the port.

Things to see and do

Azur Express

t 00 377 92 05 64 38
Open **Feb–Dec daily 10.30–6 (11–5 in winter)**
Tour takes 30-min. Return fare €5.64 per person, under-5s travel free

You can catch this little tourist train outside the Oceanographic Museum. The train runs along the port, up to the Casino and then to the Prince's Palace. It's the best way of getting around if you are in a hurry or have tired toddlers.

The Casino

Monaco is famous for its Casino. Its beautiful *belle époque* building is the most famous on the Côte d'Azur, and it has seen countless fortunes won and lost by princes and potentates. In 1891, Charles Deville Wells made his fortune on the gaming tables and inspired the song 'The Man who broke the bank in Monte-Carlo'. Unfortunately for the kids (but less so for you), they'll have to wait until they're 21 to get inside and try their hand. If they start grumbling, maybe they'll feel better if you tell them that Monégasques can't gamble in the Casino either, and that a large part of the interior is full of grannies shovelling money into one-arm bandits. If you want to soak up the atmosphere eat at the legendary Café de Paris in front of the Casino. There's also a pretty park nearby.

Monaco-Ville

The old town is perched on the Rock of Monaco. It's a bit like a toy town these days and it's incredibly clean.

The Palace

t 00 377 93 25 18 31
Open June–Sept daily 9.30–6.20, Oct 10–5
Adm Adult €6, child (8–14 years) €3. Tour takes 40mins

The Changing of the Guard takes place at 11.55am daily – the kids will enjoy it so don't miss out. The Palace has had a picaresque history; it was turned into a home for beggars during the French Revolution when the Grimaldis were driven out and Monaco became part of France. But that's all ancient history – today it's about as sumptuous as you can get. Kids will like gawping at the throne room.

Musée Napoléon

Next to the Palace t 00 377 93 25 18 31
Open Daily June–Sept 9–6.30, Oct–mid-Nov 10–5, mid-Nov–May 10.30–12.30 and 2–5. Closed Mon Nov–May
Adm Adult €4, child (8–14 years) €2

This tiny museum is well worth visiting with school-age children. Kids tend to find Napoleon fascinating and the collection includes a quirky selection of Napoleonic memorabilia and some interesting letters.

Musée Océanographique de Monaco

Av St-Martin t 00 377 93 15 36 00
www.oceano.mc
Open Daily 9–7, 10–6 in winter
Adm Adult €11, child (6–18) €6

Perched above the Mediterranean on the craggy Rock, this is Monaco's main attraction after the Palace, and represents the serious face of museums in the Principality. There's a great view from the restaurant on the top floor, and on a good day you can see Italy. The museum was founded by Prince Albert 1er, who was an explorer, and at one it was one of the biggest of its kind in Europe. It has since been overshadowed, but it still continues to be one of the most important. Jacques Cousteau, the world-famous oceanographer, was its director until 1988. You can watch his films in the museum in the luxurious conference room.

Start in the basement, where there's an interesting little aquarium with lots of multicoloured tropical fish. You can imagine you're Jules Verne in *Twenty Thousand Leagues under the Sea*. Some of the fish on display here are very rare and, as the museum is overly keen to tell you, their water is pumped up from the sea below by a complicated and no doubt highly expensive mechanism.

Upstairs in the main museum the kids will want to see the 20ft whale skeleton. There are still some live whales out there in the sea; take your binoculars to the café on the roof and see if you can spot one. In the height of the season, the best time to visit the museum is in the early morning to avoid the crowds. There's also a small park next door and to the west of the Rock you'll find the wackiest private royal collections (*see* below).

Zoological Terraces

t 00 377 93 25 18 31
Open June–Sept 9–12 noon and 2–7, Mar–May 10–12 noon and 2–6 (5 in winter)
Adm Adult €4, child (8–14 years) €2

Once upon a time Prince Rainier took a trip to Africa and came home with a zoo. If you have any scruples about zoos you'll hate this one. There's a beautiful white tiger in a cage that is probably smaller than Prince Rainier's bedroom. That said, if you have a junior member of the family who is desperate to visit a zoo on holiday, this is a convenient stop off. It takes less than an hour to go round and en route you'll come face to face with some crazy-looking chickens and a guinea pig village with its own school and shops.

Musée de Cires

27 Rue Basse **t** 00 377 93 30 39 05
Open Daily 9.30–6, 11–4 in winter
Adm Adult €4, child (6–12) €1.80

This has to be one of the most naff museums around, but it's worth a visit if you have time – the models are so bad they're funny. The Grimaldis have a personality cult industry in Monaco, so if you thought royal mania was a problem in the UK, you'll think again.

Le Musée des Timbres et des Monnaies

t 00 377 93 15 41 50
Open Daily 10–5 (6 in summer)
Adm Adult €6, child €3

This houses a huge collection of Monégasque stamps and coins as Prince Rainier is an avid collector. The museum is bizarre, if a bit boring. The best bits are the doors, which open automatically and look as if they've been hauled out of a Tintin book.

Collection des Voitures Anciennes

t 00 377 92 05 28 56
Open Daily 10–6
Adm Adult €6, child (8–14) €3

When Prince Rainier isn't collecting stamps he's collecting cars, and here you'll find about 100 of them, the oldest of which dates from 1911. There are Rolls-Royces, Jaguars and even a London taxi that used to belong to his wife, the actress Grace Kelly. There's a small shop with model cars for junior collectors.

Musée Naval

t 00 377 92 05 28 48
www.musee-naval.mc
Open Daily 10–6
Adm Adult €3.80, child (8–14) €2.29

This museum houses 180 scale models of some of the world's most famous ships, including the *Titanic*. Even in miniature the ships are pretty big – the *Nimitz* is 5m long!

Musée National (Poupées et Automates)

t 00 377 93 30 91 26
Open Daily Easter–Sept 10–6.30, Oct–Easter 10–12.15 and 2.30–6.30
Adm Adult €4.57, child (6–14) €3.05

This museum is in the town centre and has a fun collection of dolls from the 18th century through to

Can you spot...a princess?

Keep an eye out for Princess Charlotte, the Principality's new pin-up princess with the long brown hair. If you need to check you've found the right girl her full name is Charlotte Marie Pomeline Casiraghi of Monaco and she was born in 1986.

Princess Caroline's old Barbie dolls. The automata may be a bit unnerving for little ones, but there's a nice Christmas crib.

Louis II Stadium

7 Av des Castelans, Fontvieille **t** 00 377 92 05 40 11
Open Mon, Tues, Thurs, Fri 2.30 and 4
Adm Adult €3.81, child (under 12) €1.91

This is the home ground of AS Monaco, one of the top football teams in the French League. The legendary French goalkeeper Fabien Barthez used to play for AS Monaco before making the move to Manchester United. The joke is that the team are so short on supporters that local school kids are bussed into town to cheer the team if they ever win anything important. There are guided tours in English, which take 45mins.

Boat trips

Aquavision

www.aquavision-monaco.com
Open April–Sept daily, trips take 55mins
Ticket Adult €11, child (3–17) €8

The boat has windows so you can see underwater, and there's an English commentary.

Cinemas

Monte-Carlo Sporting Club

Open-air Cinéma d'Eté **t** 00 377 93 25 86 80
Av Princesse Grace

Shows films in their original language, *version originale* (*v.o.*) under the stars at 9.30pm in the summer.

Le Sporting

Place du Casino **t** 08 36 68 00 72
www.cinemasporting.com

This is the main cinema, with three screens. Films are usually shown in their original language (vo).

Parks and playgrounds

There's a small park in Fontvieille with a duck pond and children's playground, but it's more fun to head up to the observatory gardens if your kids need to run off steam:

Jardin Exotique et Grottes de l'Observatoire

t 00 377 93 15 29 80
Open Daily 9–7, closes earlier in winter
Adm Adult €6, child €3

The garden is high up on the cliff and has great views. There is a network of pretty paths and bridges and some giant cacti. There's a prehistoric cave, too, which has some of the oldest rock carvings in the world. The cave is especially bizarre because it gets warmer the further you go into it. Allow an hour for the visit.

Town beaches

The Monte-Carlo Beach Club

Av Princesse Grace **t** 04 93 28 66 66

This is where the in-crowd cool off and it's quite child-friendly. There is a huge heated seawater pool and plenty of water sports, but you won't get much change out of €150, and that's just to get in with a family!

SPECIAL TRIPS FROM MONACO

Menton

Getting there It's a 45min drive from Nice, off the A8 east of Monaco. There are plenty of trains from Nice, Italy and Switzerland which stop at the Gare Centre on Rue de la Gare and there are local trains along the coast. Buses run every 15mins to Nice from the Gare Routière on Esplanade du Careï, and stop in Roquebrune and Monte-Carlo
Tourist office Palais de l'Europe, 8 Av Boyer **t** 00 33 (0)4 92 41 76 76 **www.**villedementon.com
Special events February: Fête des Citrons (Lemon Festival): celebrate all things lemony, with anything possible made of lemons and lots of parades and fireworks. August: Candlelit procession on 5 August, in which Roquebrune, which has merged with Menton, gives thanks for surviving the plague in 1467. December: Themed Christmas decorations in the public gardens in Menton

Millions of years ago, this is where Italy collided with France and created the Alps. Today, it is the warmest corner of France, with magnificent scenery. The mountains tumble into the sea, and behind Menton are some of the loveliest hilltop villages you'll find in this part of Provence (*see* p.81). All the winter sunshine has made Menton a popular retirement spot, which is good news if you're looking for a family-friendly resort. Many of the town's residents are grandparents whose families come to visit in the school holidays, and there are lots of facilities catering for them. Although teenagers might wish for more nightlife, it is safe for them to go out alone here.

Menton is a good base for exploring Monaco but you can also escape into the Alpine valleys behind the town when you want some peace. There are plenty of sports up in the mountains, like white-water rafting, and some lovely family walks. Since people live here all year round, Menton doesn't have an excessively touristy atmosphere. The town itself isn't overloaded with attractions but it's a cosy place, full of good patisseries like La Cigale on Avenue Carnot, which is a great place for breakfast. There are lots of nice family restaurants, too, and on Rue Saint-Michel you'll find a branch of the lovely sweet shop La Cure Gourmande.

Menton's added attraction is its proximity to Italy. This is where the Italian and French Rivieras merge, and many Italians from Milan come here for the weekend. The main street, Rue Longue, was the old Roman road and the main route to Italy until the Corniches were built in the 19th century. Genoa is 2hrs away by car, but the nicest dip into Italy is up in the mountains (*see* p.105); no doubt you'll want to drive over the border, even if it's just so the kids can say they've been. The coast on the other side of the border is built up and is where the Italians grow lemons and basil in greenhouses.

Things to see and do

Le Musée de la Préhistoire Régionale

Rue Loredan-Larchy **t** 04 93 35 84 64
Open Wed–Mon 10–12 noon and 2–6
Adm Free

This is a nice little museum with some interesting reconstructions and an informative film about the Vallée des Merveilles, which is in the mountains behind Menton. The Vallée is right up in the Alps and hidden among the rocks are some extraordinary prehistoric carvings (*see* p.106). The main exhibit is the skeleton of Menton Man. He lived in 30,000 BC and was found in the Grotte Grimaldi just over the border in Italy.

Cinemas

The Eden

11 Rue de la République **t** 04 92 10 13 52

This cinema is air-conditioned so it's a good place to escape to if the weather is too hot. More fun is the open-air cinema in Lucien Rhein Stadium, which shows a different film every night in summer.

Amusement parks

Koaland

5 Av de la Madone **t** 04 92 10 00 40
Open Wed–Mon 10–12 noon and 2–7 (3–12 midnight in summer)
Adm Free

The kids will love this action-packed adventure park with karting, rides and mini-golf. Don't dismiss these little amusement parks as naff; roundabouts, mini-car circuits and the like are part of the Mediterranean scene.

Boat trips

Bateaux de la French Riviera

Quai Napoleon III **t** 04 93 35 51 72
Tickets Adult from €11, child €5.5

Runs daily trips along the coast from mid-April–end Oct.

Parks and gardens

Menton has lots of parks and gardens. They're very 19th century in style, with palms and fountains, but they are fun to explore with kids. The two most famous parks are Jardin de la Serre de la Madone and the Jardin Exotique. Both charge a small admission fee. Parc du Pian is free.

Town beaches

Menton's small beach is a mixture of pebbles and sand and is pleasant for children.

AROUND MONACO

Bricks and mortar

Trophée des Alpes

La Turbie **t** 04 93 41 20 84
Getting there Off Grande Corniche, A8
Open Tues–Sun 9–8 in summer, 9.30–5 in winter
Adm Adult €4, child (under 18) free

This is the best Roman monument in this corner of Provence. It was built in 6 BC to honour Emperor Augustus's victory over the local Ligurian tribes

Fancy a souvenir...?

In the ticket office you can buy a Roman lamp for €9.90. There are also plastic models of Gauls and Julius Caesar from €4.

Can you spot…an old olive tree?
Try to find the 1,000-year-old olive tree on the Rue de la Fontaine in Roquebrune village.

and it stands on the headland above Monaco, on what was the highest point of the Via Julia Augusta. The monument was a massive political statement and an advertisement for the power of Rome as it was carved with the names of the tribes that had been defeated.

The monument was originally 50m high, but much of it has long since been taken away to construct other buildings. It was partly destroyed by Louis XIV, who briefly occupied this strip of coast in the 17th century and was so angry when he was forced to hand it back to Savoy that he tried to destroy all the castles in the area. At that time, the Trophée was used as a watchtower and castle. What's left is still an impressive 35m high, and there's a small museum on the site where you can see a scale model of the original. The terrace has a fantastic view across the Riviera, and it's worth coming for this alone, even if your children aren't interested in the history.

The Château de Roquebrune

t 04 93 35 07 22
Getting there Off the A8 east of Monaco
Open Daily 10–12 noon and 2–5 (7 in summer)
Adm Adult €3, child €1.5, under-7s free

This is another miniature toy-town type of castle, with lots of armour inside and a 10th-century dungeon. It's good fun to visit and is quite atmospheric, with another great view from the ramparts. The Château has the oldest keep in France (known as a *donjon* in French, which is where the English word for dungeon comes from.)

Buckets and spades

This corner of the Riviera isn't famous for its beaches. The coast is rocky and the beaches are extremely small and made up of pebbles and shingle. Menton (*see* p.60) is the best place for a family holiday by the sea on this stretch of coast.

CANNES

Getting there Cannes airport doesn't cater for normal passenger flights, but there is a shuttle bus service from Nice airport. The train station is on Rue Jean Jaurès and is a short walk from the sea front, and the main bus station is next to the train station. Both bus and train connections are excellent. Cannes is a small town even if it has some imposing hotels; you can walk everywhere or hop on the minitrains if you get tired. The traffic is so bad it's usually quicker to walk, so bring a pushchair, even for older toddlers
Tourist office Palais des Festivals, La Croisette **t** 00 33 (0)4 93 39 01 01 **www**.cannes-on-line.com
Special events March: Board Game Festival. May: Film Festival, **www**.festival-cannes.fr. October: Puppet Festival

Cannes is where you see all the glamour of the Riviera in action and isn't somewhere you would immediately think of as a family destination. There are, however, lots of family hotels and resorts nearby and even the town itself is quite a relaxing place to spend some time with the kids. To do it in style you'll need plenty of money so if you're on a budget base yourself out of town and come into the centre for day trips.

Cannes, the bit you'll want to visit, is actually very small. It's made up of a nice main shopping street, the Rue d'Antibes, the seafront, La Croisette and the old town, Le Suquet. There's one tiny museum.

Do movie stars really come here?

Cannes is famous for its film festival, which takes place in May. All the big names flock to publicize their latest films, all followed around by thousands of staff, journalists and photographers. The big stars stay in the hotels on La Croisette – the Carlton, Noga Hilton, Martinez and Majestic.

At the end of La Croisette near the Palais des Festivals you'll find the handprints of famous film stars; many date from the golden age of film, so kids are unlikely to know who they are. However, some of today's top stars, who they will know, have homes along the Riviera, such as Bono, Elton John, Tina Turner and Joan Collins. St-Tropez is another star-studded spot: pop stars, including Robbie Williams and Geri Halliwell, and lots of top footballers take their summer breaks here.

Did you know…?

It was an Englishman who turned Cannes into a resort. Lord Brougham stopped here in 1834 and was so taken with the little fishing village that he built himself a villa.

Just off the coast are two lovely islands, the Iles de Lérins. If you want to mix a beach holiday with lively nightlife and plenty of activities, Cannes is a good place to choose.

The nicest hotels are along the seafront. These places are used to dealing with fussy film stars and demanding businessmen and, with the emphasis on service at any cost, they're all pretty child-friendly. Money is the name of the game, though, and you'll definitely pay for the privilege of staying. The hotels set back from the front are more reasonably priced, but they aren't as much fun for children and the back streets can become pretty claustrophobic in summer. Be aware, too, that as you head east out of town the railway line begins to run along the coast, so check exactly where your hotel or holiday apartment is. This is a built-up part of the Riviera and even if you have money to burn it is probably more pleasant to base yourself away from the town. West towards the Esterel there are some great places to stay with kids and holiday complexes that cater well for the sporty members of the family.

It isn't all glitz in Cannes – the area around the station is distinctly seedy. Although it's safe for teens to promenade along the front and go shopping in Rue d'Antibes, keep an eye on them in the back streets.

Shopping

Rue d'Antibes is the place for a shopping fix and is great for teens. There's a FNAC for books, CDs and computer games and you can pick up some stylish fashion at Pimkie, a French version of Miss Selfridge. If you want to buy something a bit more special go to Agnès B, on Rue des Frères Casanova. This stylish French designer shop does clothes in small sizes suitable for teens. The main department store, Galeries Lafayette, is on Rue du Maréchal Foch, where you'll also find the children's clothes store Du Pareil au Même. The delicious sweet shop La Cure Gourmande is on Rue Vénizelos.

Picnics and snacks

For basics, try the Monoprix by the station, otherwise, head for Marché Forville, the main market in the old town, which is open daily except Monday (and Tuesday in winter). Near the market you'll also find a selection of bakeries, shops selling roast chickens and pizzerias that sell takeaways. The best places to picnic are on the public section of the beach or on the Iles de Lérins (take a boat from the end of La Croisette).

If you have just popped into town to take a quick look and don't want to break the bank, Cannes has one of the most well-appointed McDonald's in the South of France. It's at the end of La Croisette, close to where the boats leave for the islands and the terrace is right next to a large *belle époque* carousel. If you want something cheap but slightly more authentic you'll find plenty of stalls selling crêpes and baguettes here.

Things to see and do

La Croisette

The Cannes experience takes place on the seafront, along the long promenade called La Croisette. It's the hub of life in the town, the place for strolling up and down to see and be seen; if you want to be really cool do it on Rollerblades. At Alliance Location, 19 Rue des Frères Pradignac, **t** 04 93 38 62 62, you can hire roller blades and children's scooters (*les trottinettes* in French) from €8 a day. They also rent mobile phones if you want to keep tabs on high-speed teens. Anyone under the age of 8 will want a trip on the minitrain (**t** 04 06 14 09 49 39), which starts near the Palais des Festivals. After that, they'll want to ride on the lovely *belle époque* merry-go-round, which is popular with local teenage girls as well.

Musée de la Castre

Pl de la Castre, in the old town t 04 93 38 55 26
Open Wed–Mon 10–12 noon and 2–5
Adm Adult €1.5, child free

This museum is an amusing potpourri of a collection, with bits and pieces from around the world, a

Did you know…?

Cannes gets its name from the canes that grew in the marshes.

> ***Good to know...***
> Unless you're in the film business, avoid Cannes at all costs during the Film Festival. You won't be able to get a room or see any of the films unless you are part of the movie business. The members of staff at most establishments are likely to be much surlier than at other times of the year, and any film stars you might encounter are bound to be even more so.

collection of seascapes and musical instruments. The collection itself may not be that interesting for kids, but they will enjoy climbing up to the top of the Tour Castre for the great view of the bay. The other highlight of the old town is the market, Marché Forville.

Cinemas

What else could you do but catch the latest releases while in Cannes? Tickets to see films during the festival are strictly for the rich and famous only (plus their entourage, PRs and invited press); at other times drop in to the local cinema.

Les Arcades

77 Rue Félix Faure **t** 04 93 39 00 98

Star

98 Rue d'Antibes **t** 04 93 68 81 07

Boat trips

The small islands just off the coast, the Iles de Lérins, are well worth a visit.Boats leave from the Gare Maritime by the Palais des Festivals. The crossing takes 15-mins (*see* p.65). There's also a glass-bottomed boat, the *Nautilus*, **t** 04 93 39 11 82, which leaves from Jetée Albert Edouard.

Go karts

Cannes Formule Kart'in

215 Av Francis Tonner **t** 04 93 47 88 88

This circuit is especially good for 7–12-year-olds.

Town beaches

The beaches in the city centre are disappointing. The sea front at La Croisette is divided into expensive private beaches, so you'll need to add the cost of the beach into your holiday budget – it's upwards of €15 a head for a day on the beach and the clubs have few facilities for small children. They do offer a selection of water sports, however, so are better for older kids. The beaches are covered in imported sand with pebbles underneath, and are not even all that good for making sandcastles, but they are very clean and are raked at night. There's a public beach near the Palais des Festivals and Plage de la Bocca and Plage du Midi are free and run westwards of the old town.

Water sports

Cannes Jeunesse

Quai St-Pierre **t** 04 93 06 31 39

Organizes sports courses for youngsters.

Plongée Club de Cannes

Quai St-Pierre **t** 04 93 38 67 57

www.sylpa.com

Organizes diving courses for children over the age of 8.

SPECIAL TRIPS FROM CANNES

Marineland

306 Av Mozart, Antibes **t** 04 93 33 49 49

www.marineland.fr

Getting there Just off the N7, exit Antibes or Villeneuve-Loubet. It is 200m from the train station at Biot. Bus stop: Gare de Biot

Open Daily 10–4.45 (to 10pm in summer and 12 midnight in July and Aug)

Adm Adult €24, child €16, under-3s free

For most French kids, a trip to Cannes means a trip to Marineland, the biggest theme park in the South of France and a great family day out. Marineland is famous for its spectacular dolphin and killer whale shows; if you buy any French children's magazine there is bound to be an article about them. The park opened in 1970 and many of the dolphins you see performing were born here.

Although the main attractions are the dolphins and killer whales, the site is made up of five different theme parks – in addition to Marineland there is Aqua-Splash, Adventure Golf, La Jungle des Papillons and La Petite Ferme – so you can find something here to please everyone. You pay for each attraction but combination tickets are available. The park attracts more than a million visitors a year, so in the height of the season be prepared to queue.

Good to know...

In July and August you can buy a 2-day pass to all five Marineland attractions. Passes cost €45 for an adult and €25 for children from 3–12, with under-3s free. You can also buy a series of combination tickets (*see* below for prices of the individual attractions). In high season it's best to visit late in the afternoon, when it's cooler, and at any time of year it is worth checking the times of the shows and what time the animals are fed at Marineland and La Petite Ferme, so you can get the best out of your visit. You can eat at the park; children's menus are around €8 and the best food is to be found at La Terrasse.

Marineland has the biggest killer whale pool in the world. It is the size of a football pitch and has glass walls, so you can walk right up to the edge and find yourself eye to eye with a giant, 64m killer whale. There is also a huge shark pool, which you can walk under to look up at the school of hungry sharks in two million litres of water just above your head. If that's a bit scary for the little ones, head for the touch pool where you can stroke the rays. There are all kinds of other sea creatures, including some mysterious jellyfish and playful seals, and there are special events at Easter, Hallowe'en and Christmas.

Aqua-Splash

Open June–early Sept daily from 10
Adm Adult €16, child €13

Cool off in the biggest water park in the Côte d'Azur, with 12 giant slides and a wave pool.

La Petite Ferme

Open Feb–Dec 10–6
Adm Adult €9, child €7

This petting zoo is ideal for the younger ones. Here they can get close to cows, ponies, goats, rabbits and chickens. They can also go on tractor rides, pony rides or boat rides on the enchanted river or have their faces painted. There are special parades at Easter, Hallowe'en, Christmas and during the Carnival season in February.

Adventure Golf

Open 15 June–early Sept daily from 10; rest of year Wed, Sat, Sun and school hols only
Adm Adult €9, child €6

Try out your putting skills on this 18-hole course set in a tropical world of palms and exotic flowers.

La Jungle des Papillons

Open Feb–Dec 10–6
Adm Adult €8, child €5

This is a huge greenhouse full of tropical plants and hundreds of butterflies, as well as bats, iguanas, snakes and crocodiles. Butterfly specialists are on hand to answer questions.

The Iles de Lérins

Getting there Boats leave Cannes from the Gare Maritime in the port, **t** 04 93 39 11 82, and take 15 mins. There are daily departures all year round. Return tickets start from €6.10 for adults and €3.50 for children. There are also boats from Antibes, Nice and La Napoule.

The islands are car free and are ideal for picnics. Buy everything you need before you catch the boat, as there are only a few expensive shops on the islands and hardly any cafés. The islands were once major pilgrimage sites, and are named after two saints who founded religious orders here in the Middle Ages – Ile St-Honorat and Ile Ste-Marguerite. Pilgrims used to cross by boat from the Croisette in Cannes, which is where the seafront promenade gets its name (from *croiser*, 'to cross'). There is still a monastery on St-Honorat surrounded by lavender fields and vineyards.

L'Ile Sainte-Marguerite

This is the larger of the two islands and has some good sandy-cum-pebbly beaches on the southern shores where you can swim from the rocks. You will feel a million miles from glitzy Cannes as you picnic in the pine and eucalyptus forests. There's also a lovely signposted walk, Le Sentier Botanique, which takes you through the forest and highlights trees and plants along the route.

Fort Royal

t 04 93 43 45 47
Open Daily 10.30–12.15 and 2.15–5.30 (6.30 in summer, 4.30 in winter)
Adm Adult €1.5, child free

This fort was built by Louis XIV to protect the coast from the Spanish, but by 1685 it had become a prison. Its most famous resident was the Man in the Iron Mask, who was imprisoned here before being sent to the Bastille. You can visit the state prisons and see the cell where he was held. There's also an aquarium and a museum about the sea.

Tell me a story:
Who was that masked man?

Ask your teenager that question and they are likely to answer 'Leonardo Di Caprio', but the *Man in the Iron Mask* isn't just a Hollywood blockbuster; there really was a mysterious prisoner whose face was hidden from the world.

He was held on the Ile Ste-Marguerite between 1687 and 1690, before being moved to the Bastille prison in Paris, where he later died. In 1711 the king's sister-in-law, the Princess Palatine, mentioned him in a letter to her aunt. The prisoner was treated very well, she said, but two guards stood by him at all times, ready to kill him if he removed his mask. He ate in the mask, slept in the mask, and eventually died in the mask. Even at the royal court his identity remained a mystery and theories abounded as to his identity. The philosopher Voltaire, who was held in the Bastille in 1717, spoke to the men who had guarded the Man in the Iron Mask, and wrote a book about the prisoner. According to Voltaire, the prisoner had the appearance and interests of an aristocrat: he had been tall and very handsome, dressed in the finest lace and linen, and he enjoyed playing the guitar. Voltaire hints that the prisoner was a close relative of Louis XIV, even going as far as to suggest that he was the twin brother of the king, born only minutes after him. This version of the story was made famous by the novelist Alexandre Dumas, who based the third of his books about the Three Musketeers around the tale.

Other stories say that the prisoner was Louis XIV's real father, who wasn't King Louis XIII but the Duc de Beaufort. Other people say it was one of the queen's lovers, the Duke of Buckingham, while still others claim the Man in the Iron Mask was, in fact, a woman – the daughter of Anne of Austria and Louis XIII. Fearing their first child would be their last, and needing a boy child to inherit the throne, the royal couple supposedly swapped their baby girl for someone else's son. The impostor was raised as Louis XIV and the real princess was locked up. An entirely different story claims the prisoner was the playwright Molière. According to this theory, Molière's death of consumption in 1673 was faked and he was imprisoned in the iron mask because his plays had offended religious leaders.

Antibes

Getting there Antibes is moments from the main A8 motorway. It is also on the main Nice–Marseille line, with excellent train connections from Cannes and Nice. The train station is on Place P. Sémard and is a 10-min walk to the town centre. The local bus service is also good. Buses leave from Place Général de Gaulle

Tourist office 11 Place Général de Gaulle, **t** 00 33 (0)4 92 90 53 00 **www.**antibesjuanlespins.com

Special events November: Sugar and Chocolate Fair – what more could a junior gourmet wish for?

Antibes is a delightful town. After driving past the over-built chaos that is Cagnes-sur-Mer it restores your faith in the Riviera. It's a good family resort with plenty of character and beautiful sandy beaches overlooked by Antibes' imposing 16th-century fort. (When Nice was part of Savoy, this was a frontier town and was heavily fortified.) There's a really beautiful view back across the bay to the Alps.

Antibes has merged with two other resorts, Juan-les-Pins and Vallauris. On the positive side this means there is lots to do and some lively nightlife for teens, but don't come here expecting to find a peaceful bolthole. Of the three resorts, Antibes is the more sedate and better for families, Juan-les-Pins is the brashest and Vallauris is so clogged with cars it's best avoided.

If you're renting or looking for a hotel, it pays to do your research carefully (*see* **Sleep**, pp.209–40). This is the urban Mediterranean, with all the ills that go with over-development. At Juan-les-Pins, for example, the railway runs along the beach and you could easily find yourself literally on the wrong side of the tracks. If you can afford to, stay on Cap d'Antibes.

Shopping

There's a charming market in the old town, where you can pick up lots of souvenirs and picnic supplies. For clothes try Bisous de Partout on Avenue Pasteur. For sweets and presents to take home there's a branch of La Cure Gourmande, the region's luxury sweet shop, on Rue de la République.

Things to see and do

Musée Naval et Napoléonien

Av JF Kennedy **t** 04 93 61 45 32
Open Nov–Sept Mon–Fri 9–12 noon and 2.15–6, Sat afternoons only
Adm Adult €3, child €1.5

Napoleon's family lived here during the siege of Toulon, when the British occupied the city in the chaos that followed the French Revolution. It was the breaking of the siege that made Napoleon famous, but during the time his family lived here they were so poor they had to steal figs to keep going. The museum has a collection of models and items relating to Napoleon's connection with the town. After he escaped from Elba, Napoleon landed on the beach at Juan-les-Pins where there is now a monument on the exact spot.

Musée Picasso

Château Grimaldi **t** 04 92 90 54 20
Open Tues–Sun 10–6, closed for lunch out of season
Adm Adult €4.5, child free

Picasso was very happy during his time in Antibes, and the work in this museum reflects it. Small children seem to pick up on this immediately and find the sculptures and paintings amusing.

Picture this...

Pablo Picasso (*see* p.68) made this stretch of coast famous when he moved to Antibes in 1946 and took a studio on the seafront in the Château Grimaldi. In 1947, he started making pots in Vallauris and today there are hundreds of potters jumping on the Picasso bandwagon. Picasso's art seems to provoke as strong a reaction in children as it does in adults. They either love him or they hate him, but his work will get them talking about art and forming opinions, so don't shy away from taking little children to art galleries. In French schools art is taken very seriously and in the *réception* class for 3-year-olds you'll find them painting pictures *à la Kandinsky* and decorating paper plates Picasso-style, so no one will be surprised to see your little ones in the galleries. There are some lovely art books available for small children, particularly in the large FNAC book shops in Cannes or Nice. In the Musée Picasso in Antibes a corner of the shop is dedicated to art books for tinies.

Look out for...

Mes beaux livres à colorier: La Côte d'Azur (Aubéron, €4.95). ***This colouring book is full of pictures of the things you're likely to spot on holiday. It's on sale in most big newsagents.***

There is a whole wall covered in his plates, each with different expressions, and you can while away the time deciding which member of your family would eat dinner off what plate. Be warned, though: little kids like the tactile nature of Picasso's work, and as there are no ropes and no guards, you could end up with small, sticky fingerprints all over a priceless masterpiece. Even if some members of the family aren't all that taken with art, they will probably still enjoy this museum as there's a pretty garden with a great view across the bay.

Musée National Picasso

Pl de la Libération, Vallauris **t** 04 93 64 16 05
Getting there By bus from Antibes
Open Wed–Mon 10–6 in summer, closed for lunch out of season
Adm Adult €2.6, child free

This museum is a deconsecrated chapel, where Picasso painted his series of paintings on plywood, *La Guerre et la Paix*; inside it is dimly lit, just as Picasso requested. This powerful work seems to appeal to children, perhaps because it doesn't pull any punches. What is just as extraordinary is that the paintings were created at great speed – apparently Picasso took as long as it would have done to whitewash the walls.

Boat trips

Visiobulle

Opposite the tourist office, Juan-les-Pins
t 04 93 67 02 11 **www**.visiobulle.com
Open July and Aug 9–6, April–Jun, Sept 11–4.30
Ticket Adult €11, child (2–12) €5, trip takes 1hr

From the big yellow boat with the glass bottom you can see 14m below the surface of the sea. Jules Vernes was so impressed with the sights he was inspired to write *Twenty Thousand Leagues under the Sea* here. Up on deck you can get a good look at the Bay of Millionaires, which is inaccessible by land. You can also see the cliffs of Eden Roc and the luxury hotels and villas along the coast.

Tell me a story: Who was Picasso?

Pablo Picasso was one of the most famous and important painters of the 20th century. He was born in Malaga in Spain in 1881, grew up in the Catalan city of Barcelona, but moved to Paris as a young man in his twenties. The paintings he created in Paris at this time are described as belonging to his Blue Period (1901–4) and Rose Period (1905–6). These are poignant paintings of those on the margins of society such as musicians, beggars and circus performers, with whom, as an artist and foreigner himself, Picasso would have felt an affinity.

Picasso was an extremely original and versatile artist, constantly experimenting and developing new ideas. When an exhibition of African art was shown in Paris, he was fascinated by the angular shapes of the masks and the way in which the human face could be depicted by the simplest of means: a line to represent a mouth or a nose, a round hole for an eye. This interest led him to develop a style of art known as Cubism. In his Cubist paintings you can often see all sides of an object at the same time, or the simplest abstract shape will be used to depict the whole object (the hole and neck of a guitar, for example, rather than the whole guitar). Around this time Picasso began to experiment with collage, and would stick actual objects, such as a piece of newspaper or a bus ticket, to the canvas instead of painting them. This led to experiments in sculpture, but instead of carving the object from wood or stone as in traditional art, Picasso made his sculptures by assembling pieces of junk. One of his most famous sculptures is a bull's head made out of the handle-bars of a bike.

Picasso was energetic and restless, and constantly developing as an artist. He created his masterpiece, *Guernica*, in response to the 1937 bombing of the Spanish town of Guernica during the Spanish Civil War. This powerful allegorical painting evokes the suffering of the village and Picasso's support of the Republicans against General Franco's fascism.

In 1947 Picasso moved to the South of France and helped to make resorts like Juan-les-Pins famous. The dark, ominous pictures he painted during the Second World War were replaced with a lighter, more humorous style, which seems to be infused with the warmth of the southern sun. While here, Picasso became interested in the mythology of the Mediterranean and many of his works feature classical nymphs and centaurs. He continued painting, lithography and making ceramics until his death in 1973 at the age of 91.

You can see his pictures and find out more about the artist at: **www**.picasso.fr.

Go-karts

Circuit Océane

Route de Biot, Antibes, opposite Marineland
t 04 97 21 99 81

Diving

Fabulite

150 Traverse des Nielles, Antibes **t** 04 93 61 47 45

From April to Oct they give introductory lessons to children over 8.

Town beaches

The beaches here are sandy. La Plage de la Salis is one of the nicest beaches on this stretch of coast and it and Plage de la Garoupe are free.

Plage de la Siesta is the best place to go if your children enjoy water sports.

AROUND CANNES

Buckets and spades

If you have a car, head out along the coast road that leads to St-Raphaël. The coastline is made up of rocky red cliffs dotted with tiny sandy coves, which are marked with yellow signs. Agay is the main resort town along this route, and is good for water sports (*see* pp.71–2). The Plage du Dramont saw US forces landing on its shores during the Second World War; now it's a shallow spot ideal for paddling toddlers. Théoule-sur-Mer has nice small beaches, there are pretty coves around Le Trayas, and St-Aygulf and Les Issambres both have long sandy beaches.

Nature lovers

Massif d'Esterel

The N7 from Cannes to St-Raphaël runs through the cork forests of the Esterel; they have been ravaged by fires but are still beautiful. Although these forests throng with tourists in high season, in the early hours of the morning this is a wilderness compared with the hub of activity you'll find on the coast. It used to be notoriously dangerous, a place where highwaymen and escaped prisoners from Toulon preyed on unsuspecting travellers. Even Napoleon was robbed at Pointe de Baumette.

The coast road is magnificent, with the red rock of the region tumbling down into the sea around some lovely little coves. If you're heading out of Cannes, kids who like views should sit on the left and train addicts on the right, as you get a great view of the railway, too.

Every summer part of the South of France goes up in flames and the forests of Provence are especially susceptible. The arid heat of summer dries up the forest foliage, which easily catches fire in the hot sun. Add a strong wind, such as the mistral, and the fire soon fans into an inferno, with flames reaching as much as 100ft high. There's nothing new about forest fires in this region – in 1764 the whole of the Esterel burned down. Today, in order to cut the risk during the summer, large parts of the countryside are closed off to walkers. When you're out walking or picnicking, never light a barbecue or camping stove – it's illegal in many parts of the South of France.

While you're lying on the beach watch out for the planes used to waterbomb the fires. You'll see them swoop down on to the surface of the sea and scoop up seawater to extinguish the blaze.

Look at this!

Musée de l'Automobiliste

Mougins, off the A8, Aire des Bréguières
t 04 93 69 27 80 **www.**musauto.fr.st
Open Dec–Oct 10–6 (7 in summer)
Adm Adult €7, child (12–18) €4

The South of France is famous for the Monaco Grand Prix (and its traffic jams) so it's fitting that it is also home to one of the best collections of cars in Europe. This museum, just off the motorway outside of town, tells the story of the car and has lots of special events and get-togethers for car enthusiasts.

There are over 100 cars on show, including several racing cars, and even one that turns into a boat. There is also a huge collection of model cars and an excellent shop where you can buy everything from car stickers to clothes. If you are feeling flush, hire a vintage car with a driver.

Perfumerie Fragonard

Route de Cannes – Les 4 Chemins, Grasse
t 04 93 77 94 30
Getting there 17km north of Cannes, 2km from Grasse off the N85
Open Daily 9.30–6.30, closed for lunch 12.30–2 and Nov–Jan
Adm Free

Grasse has been the perfume capital of France since the 16th century. The town was originally famous for making gloves but when Queen Catherine de Medici made it fashionable to wear scented gloves, acres of land were turned over to growing flowers to make perfume. Today, the flowers are mostly imported and the town itself has a down-at-heel feel to it.

Parfumerie Fragonard offers tours in English here at their new factory. It is surrounded by a beautiful garden, and the kids will enjoy watching the perfume being made from huge piles of flowers.

FRÉJUS AND ST-RAPHAËL

Getting there The resorts are just off the A8, 35mins from Nice airport, with an airport bus service to both towns. There's also a regular bus service from Cannes. The two towns are well served by trains, with a regular service between the two, and plenty of trains from Nice and Marseille. The TGV goes direct to Paris, Aix, Avignon, Nîmes and Montpellier from St-Raphaël
Tourist offices 325 Rue Jean Jaurès, Fréjus **t** 00 33 (0)4 94 51 83 83 **www.**ville-frejus.fr
Rue Waldeck Rousseau, St-Raphaël **t** 00 33 (0)4 04 19 52 52 **www.**saint-raphael.com

The Var coastline is a beautiful place for a family seaside holiday. On the northern end of the coast are these two seaside towns, Fréjus and St Raphaël, which have virtually merged together and are very popular with families.

The main attraction is the beach, which is huge, sandy and on a bay with a view of the mountains behind. Fréjus was the oldest Roman city in Gaul, and has some interesting Roman ruins, but these are quite small in scale – nothing like the ruins in Arles. The port silted up before the fall of the Roman Empire and took away the town's livelihood, but it did leave that beautiful sandy beach. Fréjus was badly destroyed in the Second World War, and although the old town has been restored, the two towns are essentially modern resorts.

The seafront is especially lovely, with a beautiful view across the bay to St-Tropez. It's very child-friendly, with lots of roundabouts and rides, so remember to factor these in to your holiday budget. Both resorts are great for sporty kids, with plenty of water sports, riding and karting and the Massif d'Esterel is a wonderful mountainous area, perfect for walking and picnicking (*see* p.69).

Because both resorts are so family orientated there are lots of timeshares, retirement properties and family holiday complexes, but Fréjus is also home to France's largest naval air base so it has a year-round, lived-in feel.

Shopping

There's a good toy shop, Maxi-Jouet, on Rue Georges Besse in Fréjus.

Things to see and do

Musée Archéologique

Place de la Vieille Eglise, Fréjus **t** 04 94 51 26 30
Open 9–7 in summer, closed Tues all year and for lunch in winter
Adm Adult €2.20, child free

Divers often found roof tiles and bricks off this stretch of the coast, which led to tales of a mysterious sunken city. The famous French diver, Jacques Cousteau, investigated and found a Roman galleon full of building materials. There's a reconstruction of the boat in the museum.

Amphithéâtre Romaine

Rue Henri Vadon, Fréjus **t** 04 94 51 34 31
Open Wed–Mon 10–1 and 2.30–6.30 (5.30 winter)
Adm Adult €2.20, child free

Fréjus was once an important Roman town, and although there's not much left of Forum Julii, the amphitheatre is worth a visit. These days it's used for bullfighting. Just north of the amphitheatre are the remains of the Roman theatre and aqueduct.

Pagode Hong Hien

13 Rue Henri Giraud, 2km from the centre, off the N7 **t** 04 94 53 25 29
Open Daily 9–12 and 3–6.30
Adm Adult €0.70, child (under 7) free

On the hills above Fréjus stands a pagoda full of statues of Buddha, elephants and dragons, an extraordinary memorial to the 5,000 Vietnamese who died in the First World War. It's a rather surreal visit but a good place to introduce some wider aspects of French history, particularly France's colonial past and its rule over Indo-China, which lasted into the 1950s.

Musée des Troupes de Marine

t 04 94 40 81 75
Getting there On the D4
Open Daily 10–5, closed Tues all year and Sat afternoons in winter
Adm Free

This museum looks at the history of the Marines to the present day. A good outing for those who like playing soldiers.

Cycling

Base Nature

Bd de la Mer **t** 04 94 51 91 10

A huge skate park plus a bike and jogging circuit.

Can you spot...a big top?
There's usually a travelling circus performing along the coast, so look out for the roadside signs. French circuses are very traditional and often include a whole menagerie of animals, from apes to zebras. The ringmaster usually looks as if he has just stepped out of the pages of Babar's Travels.

Water sports

Cip Fréjus
Port Fréjus **t** 04 94 95 27 18
Open All year round
Organizes diving courses for kids aged 8 and up.

Club de Plongée Euro-Plongée Boulouris
Port de Boulouris, 2170 Route de la Corniche, St-Raphaël **t** 04 94 19 03 26 / **t** 06 09 18 53 74
www.eurplongee.com
Open Feb–Dec
Organizes diving courses for kids aged 8 and up.

Slide Water Camp
Ponton Beau Rivage **t** 06 09 84 23 41
Open June–Sept
Water-skiing from the age of 5.

Centre Nautique Municipal
Base Nautique de Santa Lucia, St-Raphaël
t 04 94 83 84 50
Open Easter–end Aug
Organizes sailing courses for kids aged 6 and up. You'll need to speak French.

Boat trips

Boats for the Iles de Lérins, Ile de Port-Cros and St-Tropez leave from the old port in St-Raphaël.

Les Bateaux de Saint-Raphaël
t 04 94 95 17 46
Trips along the coast to St-Tropez and the Iles de Lérins. Also a night cruise along the Esterel.

Le Capitaine Némo
t 04 94 82 71 45
From April to September you can catch a glimpse of life underwater on this glass-bottomed boat.

Go karts

Go Karts
Fréjus Kart Indoor, Zone Industrielle du Capitou
t 04 94 40 83 22

AROUND FRÉJUS AND ST-RAPHAËL

Animal magic

Parc Zoologique de Fréjus
Le Capitou, Fréjus **t** 04 98 11 37 37
www.zoo-frejus.com
Open May–Sept daily 9.30–6, Oct–April 10–5
Adm Adult €10, child (3–10) €6
The zoo is on the hills behind the town and has more than 130 different animal species from five continents, from the smallest, the cotton top tamarin, to the biggest, the Asian elephant. Kids will like the chimpanzee shows, too.

Sporty kids

Aquatica
Fréjus **t** 04 94 51 82 51 **www.parc-aquatica.com**
Getting there On the N98 heading west for Ste-Maxime
Open June–15 Sept daily 10–6
Adm Adult €22, child over 1m and under 12, €18, children under 1m free
A water world of slides and pools in a leafy tropical park, this is one of the biggest water parks on the Côte d'Azur and boasts the largest wave pool in Europe. There are also kids' shows, mini-golf, a funfair and go-kart track, as well as snack bars, shops, ice-cream stalls and restaurants.

Domaine de Barbossi
3300 Av de Fréjus, Mandelieu **t** 04 93 49 42 41
Getting there 32km southwest of Fréjus
Open Daily 10–7
Adm Free, but you pay individually for the rides
Here you can have a go on quad bikes and mini-motorbikes or look round the mini-zoo with llama, chickens, sheep and rabbits to pat.

Wind Club d'Agay
Base Nautique d'Agay, Agay **t** 04 94 82 08 08
Open All year round
Try out windsurfing from the age of 7 in this beautiful bay.

Fun Ski School

Baie d'Agay **t** 06 07 08 17 17

Runs water-skiing courses for children over the age of 5.

Poney-Club de l'Estérel

Le Dramont **t** 06 09 96 25 52 **www**.les3fers.com
Open All year round

Offers riding lessons on small ponies for the very young.

Tell me a story: Who was St Torpès?

Torpès was a Roman soldier who became a Christian. In 89 AD he was punished for this by the Emperor Nero, who had him tortured and beheaded, and then pushed his body out to sea in a boat with a dog and a cockerel for company. Although they were starving, the animals didn't dare nibble at his corpse. The town of St-Tropez was built on the spot where his boat is supposed to have been washed up. You can see the bust of St Torpès in the Eglise de St-Tropez.

ST-TROPEZ

Getting there Driving to St-Tropez can be an ordeal; it's at the end of the D98A, with only one way to get into town, and the traffic is terrible. There is no airport: Nice airport is 90km away and Toulon airport is 50km. If money is no object, there are helicopter connections from Nice, with flights costing €690 for 5 people. St-Tropez has no train station, either: the nearest TGV stop is at Les Arcs, 47km from town and from there a shuttle bus can take you into town in about 45mins, **t** 04 94 54 62 36. There's also a water taxi, **t** 06 09 53 15 47, from St-Raphaël, where there are TGV train connections. Bus connections are poor
Getting around You can catch a boat to and from St-Raphaël or Ste-Maxime, which is a good option in summer when the roads are clogged, but you'll need a car to explore the Massif des Maures and get to the beach. Bus services are poor. For taxi services contact **t** 04 94 97 05 27. Traffic and parking is always a problem, so bikes are a good bet, especially if you are near the beach and the kids are old enough. Holiday Bikes, Rte de Tamaris, Pampelonne et Av Gen Leclerc, **t** 04 94 79 87 75
Tourist offices The most helpful tourist office is just before town, at the junction of the N98/D559 **t** 04 94 55 22 00. In town the main office is on Quai Jean Jaurès **t** 04 94 97 82 66 **www**.nova.fr/saint-tropez. They also produce a useful booklet, *Guide Enfants*, which lists local attractions, play areas and shops
Special events May: Bravade de St Torpès: The saint's relics are paraded through the streets, amidst riotous colour and gunfire June: Bravade des Espagnoles: St Torpès' relics get another outing; this time participants wear 18th-century uniforms and traditional Provençal dress and are accompanied by earsplitting gunfire from blunderbusses. October: Les Voiles de St-Tropez, the end of the season yacht race

No matter what anyone says about it, the jet set still flock to St-Tropez. Film and pop stars, footballers and businessmen all take their holidays in the huge luxury villas dotted on the hills around the town. If you want to, you can spend a small fortune here. Two weeks in one of the more luxurious villas where Fergie had her toes sucked will set you back over £30,000 and that's just for the rental. It's fairly family-friendly luxury, though. Snoop about in these glamorous villas and you'll find boxes of toys and bags of nappies.

St-Tropez was originally a small, sleepy fishing village. In the 1920s it was a bohemian artists' colony, frequented by writers such as Colette and painters such as Paul Signac, but it really came to the attention of the rest of the world in the 1950s when actress Bridget Bardot began holidaying here. Its bohemian reputation was further enhanced when its beaches saw the first topless bathing in the 1960s. Amazingly, just a few

Can you spot…a Star?

To be part of the in-crowd, head for the Bistrot des Lices; in a town full of places to be seen, it is currently the place. Kids will also want to catch a glimpse of the beach restaurant Club 55, which is where stars like Robbie Williams hang out. The other place to star spot is Tahiti Plage, especially in the restaurant Tahiti. Look out for the helicopter parking lot nearby. Nikki Beach is the newest and trendiest club, while down at Cabasson beach you might get a glimpse of the president – the huge castle is his holiday home.

decades before, the whole town had been destroyed in the Second World War and had to be rebuilt from scratch. After the war, the town was reconstructed in exactly the same style, which is unusual for this part of the world. (On a more positive note, if soldiers can wade in along the coast, as US troops did during the war, then it's usually a good indication that the beaches are safe for kids.)

Despite the luxury villas and the lifestyles of the rich and famous you don't have to be a millionaire to go to St-Tropez. Accommodation is more expensive than it is in other parts of the South of France, but that's because it's fairly limited. And although there's a large shopping centre and a McDonald's just on the edge of town, St-Tropez is surprisingly underdeveloped – drive 10 minutes up into the hills and you'll find acres of vineyards and forests of cork and chestnut trees. It's a beautiful place for a family holiday that doesn't have to break the bank.

If you want to enjoy the St-Tropez area in peace, the ideal time to come is May but you can paddle in the sea as late as Hallowe'en. Unlike other parts of the Riviera this part of the coast closes down in winter; St-Tropez faces north and is cold once the wind starts blowing. Although St-Tropez isn't a winter destination, it's actually quite fun at Christmas when there's a skating rink on the Place des Lices and a minitrain that takes you for a tour of the town to see the decorations.

Shopping

Half the fun of visiting St-Tropez is looking at the shops in the town's network of tiny streets. It's easy shopping with kids because each shop usually has a stall outside with a sample of what's on sale within. You'll find any basics that you need in the Géant supermarket just outside town at La Foux. At Gassin on Route du Bourrain there's an old farm, La Maison des Confitures, selling all types of homemade jam. In the town itself, Modo on Avenue Général Leclerc is the place for toys, and for clothes, try Kid Cool on Rue Gambetta or Tropezino in the Passage du Port, which has some stylish designer labels for 0–16-year-olds. Teenage girls will also like Jennifer on the Vieux Port. There's a market on Tuesday and Saturday morning in Place des Lices.

Picnics and snacks

There are plenty of places in town to stock up for picnics and along the coast road you'll see plenty of fruit stalls and places selling roast chicken. Place des Lices is the main market square. It's packed with cafés and is the best place to eat with kids, as they can run around safely. Prices are slightly lower here than on the port side, where they get so many tourists that waiters can't be bothered to be civil.

Those with a sweet tooth will find plenty to tempt them in St-Tropez. Albert Dufresne is the place to buy the local speciality, the *tarte tropézienne*, a sponge cake split and filled with jam and topped with whipped cream. There branches of the shop on Rue Beausoleil and on Avenue des Narcisses. You can buy local biscuits, *croquettes de Maurin des Maures*, at Boulangerie l'Amie du Pain on Boulevard Georges Clemenceau, while Pâtisserie Sénequier on Quai Jean Jaurès sells the best nougat in town and is a nice place for a drink.

Can you spot...a sea fig?

According to local fishermen, giant sea figs are actually a type of squid called Violets. They cling to the rocks and retract when you touch them, disguising themselves as part of the rock. They are considered a delicacy by some; if you cut them open you'll find a grey mass that looks a bit like wobbly scrambled eggs. Connoisseurs scoop this out and eat it.

Things to see and do

Citadelle de St-Tropez

t 04 94 97 59 43
Open Daily in summer 10–12.30 and 1.30–6.30 (5.30 in winter)
Adm Adult €4, child (under 10) €2.50

The view here is not to be missed – you can see all the way to the Alps. The fortress itself is small and compact and only takes moments to see inside but is a good inspiration for sandcastle construction. Inside there's a little museum with scale models of St-Tropez, which children usually enjoy. The souvenir shop has books in English.

Musée de l'Annonciade

Place Grammont **t** 04 94 97 04 01
Open Wed–Mon 10–12 noon and 2–6 (7 in summer)
Adm Adult €4.60, child (12–16) €2.30

This is a really good museum to introduce children to paintings. It's very small, so the number of paintings isn't overwhelming, and there are lots of pictures of St-Tropez, so you can have fun spotting scenes that you recognize. Look out for Paul

Signac's painting of the port, in his trademark pointillist style, in which the image is made up of tiny dots of different colours. Depending on how far away you are, the eye perceives the dots as single blocks of colour. Take time when you go round the museum to show the kids how the pictures change depending on where you are in the room. If the kids know London they may be interested in one of the best pictures in the collection, a painting of the Houses of Parliament by André Derain.

Unfortunately, this is not a great museum to visit with toddlers; the guards stalk you round the gallery and the pictures are hung tantalizingly close to toddler level. Best to take them round when they are tired enough to be carried or taken in a pushchair.

Luna Parc

Carrefour de la Foux **t** 04 94 56 23 97
Open April–Sept 8.30pm–1am

Right next to the supermarket you'll find a selection of activities, from mini-golf to a big wheel. It makes for a fun evening out if you want to treat the kids.

La Maison des Papillons

9 Rue Etienne Berny **t** 04 94 97 63 45
Open Wed–Mon 10–12 noon and 3–6 in summer
Adm Adult €3, child (under 10) €2.50

Don't leave the beach for this museum; it's not a living butterfly experience but a collection of butterflies stuck on to boards with pins.

Cinema

La Renaissance

Place des Lices **t** 08 36 68 03 62

Tennis

Tennis Club

Centre Philippot, Route des Plages **t** 04 94 97 80 76

The club runs tennis courses for kids in the school holidays.

Town beaches

La Fontanette and Plage des Graniers are the closest beaches to the town centre, and although both get busy in summer, they are the place for a quick dip if you are in St-Tropez for a day out.

Plage des Salins is quieter and has a lifeguard in summer.

SPECIAL TRIPS FROM ST-TROPEZ

Iles d'Hyères

t 04 94 58 21 81, **www.tlv-tvm.com**
Getting there There are no cars on the islands. Boats leave daily in summer from La Tour Fondue, on the Giens peninsula, to Porquerolles. Boats also leave from Cavalaire, Le Lavandou and Hyères in season. There's a large car park at La Tour Fondue, which costs €6 a day. Tickets start at €14 return from La Tour Fondue to Porquerolles, but under-4s are free, and it really is money well spent, as the islands are one of the highlights of this part of the South of France

The islands, which include Porquerolles, Port-Cros and Ile du Levant, were a pirate stronghold in the Middle Ages and locals like to claim they inspired Robert Louis Stevenson, who spent a lot of time at nearby Hyères, to write *Treasure Island*. There's certainly a tropical feel to the area, and it's easy to imagine buried pirate treasure in the half-moon bays. The sea is shallow here, so it is perfect for little ones, and the views are glorious.

Porquerolles

Porquerolles, the biggest of the three islands at 8km long and 3km wide, is the best one to head for with children. Come prepared with backpacks because you can't take your car onto the island. There are lots of easy walks, but if you want to explore further you'll need to hire bikes. There are plenty of bike rental shops on the harbour side.

Out of season it's idyllic, with only 300 year-round residents, and beaches are so shallow that the water warms up very quickly so you can swim from the end of April. Make sure to pack snorkel equipment, as the sea is full of attractive and unusual fish.

Can you spot...the Ile d'Or?
Just off Le Dramont is an island with a castle turret on top. It was once the home of a rich but eccentric gentleman, who used to greet his guests in his own throne room. He is supposed to have inspired Hergé to write the Tintin story of The Black Isle.

Tots on tour with Babar

Don't leave home without *Babar's Travels*. At the beginning of the story King Babar and his wife Celeste fly off on honeymoon in a hot-air balloon. The balloon flies over stubbly vines and sleepy farmhouses and, incredibly, the fields they pass over are still there, just south of St-Tropez on the road from town to Pampelonne beach. The honeymooners are heading for the resort of Cassis or La Ciotat, and just off the headland is the huge island fortress, the Château d'If.

Babar and Celeste don't make it to Cassis. A strong wind, the famous Provençal mistral which can appear out of sunny blue skies, suddenly blows them off course. The mistral blows Babar onto a desert island – the Ile de Porquerolles, in fact, between St-Tropez and Toulon. Pack a copy of *The Story of Babar*, too; you'll be struck by how the Opera House in the town where the Old Lady lives looks just like the one in Nice. Notice, too, how the Hotel Hermitage in Monaco looks like Babar's Palace (and maybe even stay there).

Don't worry if you are burdened with pushchairs – there's a beautiful beach, Plage d'Argent, just a few minutes from the port side if you follow the track east along the shoreline. The best beach is Plage de Notre Dame, but it's a 3km hike from the port. Closer, but busier, is Plage de la Courtade, to the right of the port.

There are shops and restaurants in Porquerolles town where you can buy a picnic lunch but they shut at noon sharp, so you may be safer bringing your own supplies. Don't forget, it's forbidden to pick flowers and light campfires. If you want to spend longer on the island there are seven hotels to choose from, but they're pricey and you'll need to book well in advance.

Port-Cros

Port-Cros is the trickiest of the three islands to explore with kids. There is a lot of dense undergrowth and it's a hike to the beach, but it's a great place to go if you have older children who like walking; there are 35km of pathways and beautiful views. If you do go, take a picnic with you, as the few restaurants aren't particularly good.

This island is also the smallest of France's national parks. The water is beautifully clear and great for snorkelling and there's even a scenic swimming route you can follow.

Ile de Levant

This is the easternmost island of the Iles d'Hyères and saw France's first nudist beach in 1931; it's still a popular spot for nudist bathing. A large part of the island is a French military base, and it has been left undeveloped for most of its history; running water and electricity were only installed ten years ago! The island has a sad history: in the 19th century, children were brought here from the capital's prisons and dropped like flies from toiling in what was then an agricultural colony. Moving the children from Paris to the seashore may have been done with good intent but, as with so many other initiatives of the time, it was poorly thought through. It's a downside to what today seems more like paradise.

AROUND ST-TROPEZ

Animal magic

Village des Tortues

Gonfaron **t** 04 94 78 26 41
www.tortues.com
Getting there 40km from Toulon, off A8
Open Mar–Oct 9–7
Adm Adult €8, child €5

The village is in a beautiful setting in the Massif des Maures and is dedicated to the protection of tortoises. The breeding programme has been very successful. So far, 2,500 tortoises have been born here, and they've been reintroduced to the Ile de Levant where they disappeared from 150 years ago. Tortoises live in family groups; the little tortoises are not sent to fend for themselves until they reach the age of 5 or 6. The village also cares for around 200 injured tortoises every year – sadly, many of them have got caught in lawn mowers. In summer the tortoises are fed at 9.30am – they're livelier in the morning and the early evening, so make an early start to see them at their best. There's also a snack bar and a children's play area.

Le Seascope

15 Quai Gabriel-Péri, Le Lavandou **t** 04 94 71 01 02
Open Daily departures, times depend on the weather and the month
Adm Adult €8, child (4–12) €7.50

This special underwater viewer takes up to 24 people at a time to see what life is like under the shimmering blue surface of the Mediterranean. The voyage under the sea takes 45mins.

Village hideaways

Behind St-Tropez are some beautiful hilltop villages, which are nice places to visit either in the morning for a coffee or for an evening meal. If you rent a holiday house or choose a hotel close to, or in, any of these villages you really can't go wrong. They're surrounded by the wild hills of the Massif des Maures and in early or late season you'll have them all to yourselves. If you base yourself in a village you'll be in one of the few parts of the Riviera where you can get a real French experience.

Gassin, a tiny medieval hilltop village, is the closest to St-Tropez and is a great place to eat and drink with kids. Head for Place des Barrys; it's safe for little ones, as there are no cars, and there's a fantastic view across to the Alps. From Gassin the road winds through the hills to **Ramatuelle**; again, the views are stunning, so make time to stop. There are lots of spots for picnics and three ruined windmills along this scenic route. Ramatuelle is a tiny maze of medieval streets with some practical shops, which gives it less of a touristy feel.

Further along the coast is **Bormes-les-Mimosas**, which has surrendered its soul to the tourist lavender shops but is still fun to explore with little kids, who love running around its alleyways and up and down the steep streets. There are some good hotels here, and it's close to the fantastic Cabasson beach.

Hyères

Further on from Bormes-les-Mimosas is **Hyères** – a sizeable medieval hilltop town and a lovely place to go shopping and have a drink but not recommended for staying in as it's too developed. Robert Louis Stevenson wrote *A Child's Garden of Verses* here in the Parc Ste-Claire.

Kiddy Parc

Hyères **t** 04 94 57 68 93
Open April–end Oct 10–7 (11pm in high season)
Adm Adult €4, child over 2 €9.90)

A little theme park.

_Good to know..._Port Grimaud

There's not much to interest kids in this modern, purpose-built harbour resort for the well heeled. There are plenty of cafés, bars and restaurants but most of them are overpriced and of dubious quality. On the plus side, the port is traffic free but then it does get around a million visitors a year. If you decide to visit, it's best to keep a close eye on the kids so they don't get lost.

Grimaud

www.grimaud-provence.com

This is the nicest of all the villages near St-Tropez, with plenty of *chambres d'hôte* nearby to stay in (though you'll need to book well in advance). The village has lots of character and still has a real community feel, with everyone knowing everyone else's business. There are some beautiful old buildings, a windmill and a castle, which you can see for miles. The tourist offices are very helpful and have leaflets outlining easy walks in the area – one takes you past the windmill to the Pont des Fées, the Fairy Bridge. There's also a little tourist train that runs around town in season. If you have a skateboard or micro-scooter bring them with you – the streets are just at the perfect incline for some serious skating and you can join the local kids in front of the church. Market day is Thursday.

Collobrières

Collobrières is the local chestnut capital and here, everything you can imagine is made out of chestnuts, even the ice-cream. Chestnuts have always been important in the rural South of France (*see* **Corsica**, p.179). They're ground up and used in baking as a substitute for flour, among other uses. The chestnut is celebrated in this region with a special market on the last three Sundays in October. You can buy local delicacies at the factory, Confiserie Azuréenne. If you're feeling the strain of holidaying *en famille* you may be interested to know that chestnuts are very good for stress.

Chartreuse de la Verne

t 04 94 43 48 28
Getting there 6km from Grimaud, southeast of Collobrières on the D14/D214. The road is very bendy so allow lots of time
Open Feb–Dec Wed–Mon 11–5
Adm Adult €4.5, child (8–14) €1.5

This ancient monastery, hidden in a valley of cork trees, is the only building for miles. To get there you have a long drive down a dirt track, which at some points is crumbling away. It's great walking country along here, and there are lovely spots to picnic along the way, so bring your own lunch.

The monastery was built in the 12th century and after years of near ruin is now being restored. There's nothing specific for children but it's a beautiful place and the dirt track roads and dense forest will give them a taste of what it's like to explore some of the wilder corners of Europe.

Buckets and spades

St-Tropez is famous for its beaches. These are 5km south of town so you'll need a car to get there with kids. The beach is basically one long stretch of sand, the Plage de Pampelonne, broken up into private and public beaches, all of which have different names. Plage de Tahiti, the closest beach to St-Tropez, is the most famous of the beaches, and the middle part of the beach near Club 55 is the most developed. Behind here is a string of seriously luxurious villas that rent for around £15,000–20,000 a week, but because the building here is very low key, you don't really notice anything from the beach or as you drive along the road. The southern end of the beach is the nicest; backed by vineyards, it has a rural feel. All of the beaches have lifeguards from May–Sept, and all have great cafés and restaurants. (Some of these are very pricey – this isn't fish and chips country!) There's a kids' beach club: Trop Kids (**t** 06 08 06 02 08), **www**.tropkids.fr, open July–Aug for 3–13 year-olds; it's near Club 55.

Good to know....

St-Tropez is surrounded by a string of little family resorts that runs from Ste-Maxime to Hyères, all of which are great spots for a family holiday. The beaches are beautiful and sandy, the sea is shallow and it's a good place for first timers to try their hand at water sports. Cavalaire-sur-Mer is modern and the least attractive of the resorts, while Le Lavandou is the nicest and liveliest (www.lelavandou.com) – Club Med is based here.

You will need to book well in advance, as the area is popular with the French as well as foreigners. With children, you'll want to be as close to the beach as possible, especially if you can't afford a villa or a hotel with a pool. Traffic jams are a problem in summer so bear this in mind when you are making plans.

Le Lavandou

Further out of town, along the coast of the Massif des Maures, can be found some of the best beaches in the South of France There's a lovely walk along the coast to Cavalaire, which runs past some quiet pebbly bays and is suitable for older children. For little ones, Le Lavandou is one of the best resorts on the southern coast of the Massif des Maures. It has a long, huge beach and roundabouts, and a tourist train runs along the front.

Plage de Cabasson

The loveliest beaches in the region can be found below the hilltop village of Bormes-les-Mimosas. Plage de Cabasson, a half-moon bay backed by pine trees, is one of the most beautiful beaches in France. Allied troops landed here in the Second World War and in 1964, when President de Gaulle attended the 20th anniversary of the Allied landings, he was so taken with the area that he made Fort de Brégançon his official holiday home. It is still used by the French president today and, judging by the number of accompanying police, it must be one of the safest places to park your car in the whole area. (The car park is small, however, so it pays to arrive early.) There is a good, inexpensive beach café nearby, where you can hire canoes and jet skis.

Plage du Pellegrin, just along the coast from Cabasson, is wilder and very beautiful; once you've seen these two beaches you won't want to go anywhere else. The view across to the Ile de Porquerolles is incomparable.

Ste-Maxime

Getting there The town is north of St-Tropez on the N98 coast road, and the nearest TGV train station is Les Arcs. You can catch a boat to and from St-Tropez, which is a good option in the summer when the traffic is heavy

Tourist office Promenade Simon Lorière **t** 00 33 (0)4 94 55 75 55 **www.sainte-maxime.com**

Ste-Maxime is the main seaside resort after St-Tropez. It's a real family place with little hotels, a large merry-go-round on the promenade and 6km of golden sandy beaches (the best of which has the unlikely name of Plage des Eléphants). It's a good place to set up your base, as there is a wide choice of accommodation, from luxury villas to family campsites. Although it's slightly less crowded than St-Tropez and more family-orientated, the down-side is that the main coast road runs along the front. However, there are nice shops (including a branch of the toy shop JouéClub on Avenue Jean Jaurès) and cafés, a lovely market on Thursday morning and a daily market on Rue Fernand Berry. In the summer there's a crafts and souvenirs market on Rue Gambetta.

Tell me a story: The true Little Prince

The Little Prince (*Le Petit Prince*) is one of the most famous books ever written in French and its author, Antoine de Saint-Exupéry, is a national hero. The book has been translated into more languages than any other French novel and you'll find images of the Little Prince on everything from pencil sharpeners to the old 50-franc banknote.

Antoine de Saint-Exupéry's mother came from Provence. She was brought up in the Château de la Mole, just behind St-Tropez. The young Saint-Exupéry and his brothers and sisters spent much of their childhood here after their father died. Saint-Exupéry grew up to become a daredevil pilot and adventurer, pioneering the airmail service in North Africa and South America. He wasn't a happy man, remaining nostalgic for his aristocratic childhood, full of self-doubt and torn apart by an unhappy marriage. Although *The Little Prince* is always found in the children's corner of the book-shop, it is as much a novel for adults as it is for children and tells the strange, mystical story of a pilot who crashes in the desert and meets a little golden-haired prince. The prince has left his own planet, Asteroid B612, where he's the only inhabitant, in search of a friend. All the adults that the prince meets mystify him and he worries constantly about the self-centred rose, whom he loves but has left behind. It's a story about how growing old deprives us of innocence and happiness, and Saint-Exupéry, who also had golden curls as a child, is both the prince and the pilot.

Long before he wrote *The Little Prince*, Saint-Exupéry was famous in both France and North America as a journalist and writer. His novels *Southern Mail*, *Night Flight*, *Wind, Sand and Stars* and *Flight to Arras* were all bestsellers. *Night Flight* was turned into a Hollywood movie starring Clark Gable and there was even a perfume named after the book.

Although the illustrations in *The Little Prince* are almost as famous as the prose, Saint-Exupéry was never a professional artist. He did, however, always illustrate his letters and the character of the Little Prince started to take shape in his correspondence to friends in the 1930s.

Saint-Exupéry fought in the battle for France in 1940 before going into exile in America. He left his estranged wife behind in France, rather as the Little Prince leaves his rose on the asteroid. It was in an attempt to mend their relationship after she arrived in New York in 1941 that he wrote *The Little Prince*, and it is important to remember that the novel was written during the Second World War when Saint-Exupéry was isolated, in exile and depressed by the politics around him.

Saint-Exupéry had, like many French people at the time, an ambivalent attitude to the Vichy regime (*see* **History**, p.43), which governed occupied France during the Second World War, and he always refused to join General de Gaulle's Free French in London, believing de Gaulle was a dictator in the making. As a consequence he was attacked as a collaborator by de Gaulle's supporters while being blacklisted by the Vichy regime for his Jewish sympathies – *The Little Prince* is dedicated to his Jewish friend Leon Werth, who he describes as 'needing cheering up'.

In 1943, Saint-Exupéry started flying reconnaissance missions from North Africa for the Allies and in July 1944 his plane mysteriously disappeared over the Mediterranean. Years were spent searching for the wreckage, which was eventually discovered off the coast of Marseille in 1998. Exactly what happened on that summer's day in 1944 is still unknown: German records have no account of the plane being shot down and a rumour has persisted that, depressed by money worries and a bad marriage, Saint-Exupéry committed suicide. It is also possible that the crash was accidental, that the 44-year-old pilot was short of oxygen and suffering from altitude sickness. But we are unlikely to ever know the truth. Just like his Little Prince, Saint-Exupéry simply disappeared...

Tell me a story: Babar's Travels

Gazing out across the bay at Ste-Maxime you'll have a distinct sense of *déjà vu* if you've ever read *Babar's Travels*. Babar's creator, Jean de Brunhoff, holidayed here and, when he painted the Land of the Elephants, this must have been the view he had in mind.

Flamingos often make an appearance in the stories: there's always a flamingo standing by the lake in Celesteville and when Babar meets Father Christmas he tells the elves what colour they should paint the model flamingos. A few hours' drive from Ste-Maxime you'll find thousands of flamingos in the marshes of the Camargue. If you're quiet you can get within a few feet of them.

It was really Brunhoff's wife, Cecile, who invented Babar as a bedtime story for her sons. Her stories became family favourites, which Jean decided to illustrate. In 1931 the first of the books, *The Story of Babar*, was published and two years later, A. A. Milne organized the English translation. The original Babar is a far cry from the trans-atlantic video Babar of today's cartoons. He is the Frenchman's vision of the perfect gentleman – elegant, poised, benevolent, well-educated and widely travelled. He espouses family values, eats *brioche*, skis and lives in a palace that looks like a blend of the Riviera's two most exclusive hotels, the Negresco in Nice and the Hermitage in Monte-Carlo.

Brunhoff wrote six more books before he died of tuberculosis at the age of just 38 and it was only after his death that the books became international bestsellers. Brunhoff's eldest son Laurent made Babar famous when he decided to carry on writing and illustrating the Babar stories after the Second World War. Babar acquired the trans-atlantic twang seen in his later adventures when Laurent de Brunhoff moved to the USA and made his fortune.

Boat trips

Aquascope

t 04 94 49 01 45

Runs daily Mar–Sept, trip takes 30mins

The boat has a glass bottom, so you can see the fish swimming underneath you.

Horse riding

Le Haras d'Azur

Complexe Sportif des Bosquettes, Ste-Maxime **t** 06 07 66 08 61

Les Ecuries de Grimaud

Le Peyrat **t** 04 94 43 24 09

Centre Equestre le Magnan

Route de Grimaud, Plan de la Tour **t** 04 94 43 79 10

Offers lessons for kids on horses and ponies, all year round.

Water sports

Ecole de Voile

Plage du Débarquement, La Croix Valmer **t** 04 94 79 68 01

Organizes sailing and windsurfing courses for kids from April–Oct.

Residence Beach

Parc de Cavalaire, Cavalaire **t** 04 94 64 24 73

Offers a range of sailing and windsurfing courses for kids.

Aqua City

Rte de Muy **t** 04 94 43 96 78

Large water park with slides and pools. There's a skateboard park nearby too.

WHERE TO EAT

The best place to eat with the kids on the Riviera is at a beach restaurant. Many have tables on the sand. Don't assume you'll have to miss out on good cooking, either, as many are top-class restaurants.

Nice

Kids will love the local food, which is a mixture of Italian and French cooking and features child-friendly dishes such as pizzas, ravioli and gnocchi. For evening meals, head towards the old town; Cours Saleya is pedestrianized and has a host of different restaurants. For lunch, there is a pleasant café in the Parc du Château. Skip the restaurants along the Promenades des Anglais.

Chez Thérésa

Cours Saleya

This is just a market-stall café but serves the best *socca* in town, a chickpea pancake which is a local speciality. It's also the best place to try *pissaladière*. It's a fun place to stop because Thérésa is happy to talk to the kids while she cooks on a large open stove that looks like a barrel.

Chez Pipo

13 Rue Bavastro t 04 93 55 88 82

Near the port, this is another place to eat *socca* (chickpea pancake) and *tarte de blettes* (Swiss chard pie), all served up at long wooden tables.

L'Auberge de Theo

52 Av Cap de Croix, Cimiez t 04 93 81 26 19
Open Tues–Sun

The restaurant has a lovely open-air patio and a relaxed and rustic atmosphere, and is a good place to stop for lunch after visiting the Musée Matisse. Menus cost from €20.

Fenocchio

2 Place Rossetti t 04 93 80 72 52
Open daily in season, Feb–Oct

This is a *niçoise* institution; if you come to Nice it is obligatory to try one of their 86 different flavours of ice-cream, from apple to violet.

La Rotonde

Hôtel Négresco, 37 Promenade des Anglais
t 04 93 16 64 00

A meal in here doesn't come cheap, but it's a real experience. It's a magical world of carousel horses and puppets under a ceiling of circus scenes and a chandelier of grapes, and there's no finer place to play at 'Who Wants to be a Millionaire?'. The restaurant is popular with Russians, who have flocked back to the Riviera since the fall of Communism. Good pasta dishes, and menus cost from €23.

Le Pain Quotidien

Cours Saleya, 1 Rue St-François-de-Paule
t 04 93 62 94 32

The Belgian sandwich bar has arrived in the South of France, serving open-top sandwiches and chocolate spread on toast at long wooden tables.

Lafayette

64 Rue Gioffredo t 04 93 80 04 96

This restaurant, based around a movie theatre theme, serves up a menu of grilled meats and pizza. There's a terrace and it's popular with local children but not especially French in flavour.

Don Camillo

8 Place Guynemer t 04 93 89 48 87
Open Tues–Sat

Don Camillo is a byword for good food in Nice. If you want a gourmet experience with older kids, try their new restaurant on the port side. The food is simple and very local – try the home-made ravioli with Swiss chard. Menus from €30.

Le Safari

1 Cours Saleya t 04 93 80 18 44
Open Tues–Mon lunch

This is a great place for people-watching on the Cours Saleya. The waiters are friendly and it's local cooking – lots of pasta, pizza and fresh fish – and is a good place to try regional specialities like gnocchi and ravioli. There's a large terrace but be sure to arrive early, as it's very popular. Menus from €22.

Jungle Arts

6 Rue Lépante t 04 93 92 00 18
Open Mon–Sat

This restaurant is like having a night out with Tarzan, with waitresses prowling around in panther suits and animal skins hanging from the walls. You will find ostrich and kangaroo on the menu, and general world cuisine. Menus cost from €10 at lunchtime and €14 in the evening.

Hippopotamus

16 Av Félix Faure t 04 93 92 42 77

Just on the corner of Place Masséna, this restaurant chain is one of the few in France to embrace the idea of giving kids crayons and entertainment at the table. It's competitively priced and a good place to take unreformed eaters. The kids' menu is €7.50 and everything comes with chips.

Pasta Basta

18 Rue de la Préfecture **t** 04 93 80 03 57

An affordable restaurant for all the family. All the pasta is home-made and you can mix and match the different types of pasta and sauces. Portions are large. Menus cost from €8 to €15.

Salon de Thé Auer

7 Rue St-François-de-Paule **t** 04 93 85 77 98

Come here for an elegant tea experience. It's the kind of place that Babar would frequent.

La Zucca Magica

4bis Quai Papacino **t** 04 93 56 25 27

Open Tues–Sat

By far the best and friendliest vegetarian restaurant in Nice, with imaginative dishes whisked up by a bevy of boisterous cooks in a cosy dining room with wacky decor. The menu features pumpkin – *zucca* is pumpkin in Italian. Menus cost from €13.72.

Plasma Café

11 Rue Offenbach **t** 04 93 16 17 32

This juice and sushi bar has Internet access and is good for teens.

Around Nice

Coursegoules

Auberge de l'Escaou

t 04 93 59 11 28 **www.hotel-escaou.com**

Open Mon (in season), Tues–Sun lunch

It is difficult to find a nicer, more beautifully appointed setting for a family meal out. The restaurant is in the centre of the tiny village and has a terrace with a fantastic view. The menus start from €16, children's menus €8.50.

Eze

Château Eza

Rue de la Pise **t** 04 93 41 12 24

www.chateza.com

Open after Christmas–late Oct

Château Eza is a mini-castle tucked away at the top of the village. The terrace has to have one of the best views on the Riviera and although it's perched precipitously on the top of a crag, it's quite safe for little children. The best time to stop here is mid-morning when you'll find you are virtually the only customers, otherwise the service can be slow and the menu pricey. Lunch dishes such as salads from €10, evening menus start at €45.

Crêperie Le Cactus

La Placette, Eze Village **t** 04 93 41 19 02

Open Mar–Oct

The restaurant is the first one you'll come across as you walk into the old town. If you are with small children it's the best place to have a drink or a snack, as there are fewer precipitous steps immediately by the tables than at the other cafés in town. The crêpes are surprisingly good and start at €5.50, with the most expensive dish €18.

St-Paul-de-Vence

La Fontaine

Place de la Fontaine **t** 04 93 32 74 12

Open Wed–Mon

This is the one venue in the village that seems to have retained some of its original character. It's a relaxed, family-orientated place with a pretty terrace overlooking the fountain. You won't get the best food in St-Paul here but you'll have a happy family meal out. Book in advance in high season. Dish of the day is usually around €13.

Peillon

Auberge de la Madone

t 04 93 79 91 17

Open Tues–Mon in summer

Here you can enjoy a surprisingly good-value gourmet meal just outside the village walls. Meals are served on the terrace among the olive trees, so this is a good choice for eating out *en famille*. Menus start around €30.

Villefranche-sur-Mer

Les Marinières

Promenade des Marinières **t** 04 93 01 72 57

The restaurant is right on the edge of one of the best beaches on this stretch of coast and just minutes from the train station, so it's easy to reach. Servings of *moules* (mussels) are perfect for mini-fish-lovers who like to eat with their fingers, and the risotto is pretty good too. A meal for a family of four should set you back around €50, but you can sit back and enjoy it in peace while the kids dig on the beach at the same time.

La Piazza

Place de la République t 04 93 01 70 69

Good-value pizza in a picturesque square.

Monaco

Café de Paris

Place du Casino t 00 377 92 16 20 20
Open until 2am

This is a good place to stop for a drink or a light meal. You'll pay the price for the surroundings but there's space for the children to run around and it's close to a small park. There's a good mixture of dishes, from fresh oysters to hamburgers, and remember to leave room for dessert. If you want to see inside the Casino the café is a good place to sit the kids with a Coke while you take it in turns to check it out. Menus from €40.

Castleroc

Place du Palais t 00 377 93 30 36 68

It might look a bit touristy since it's right next door to the palace, but local families like it too. It specializes in seafood. Adult meal around €18.

Stars 'N' Bars

6 Quai Antoine Ier t 00 337 97 97 95 95
www.starsnbars.com

This lively American-style bar will appeal to all ages: the waitresses serve you on roller skates, and there is a supervised kids' playroom and a games arcade for teens. It's a popular birthday party venue with surprisingly good food, even if you can hardly call it French cuisine. The terrace has a great view across the port.

Le Texan

4 Rue Suffren Reymond t 00 377 93 30 34 54

Another American-style joint, and part of the international Stars 'N' Bars empire, this is a steak-house that also serves good pizza.

Tony

6 Rue Comte-Félix-Gastaldi t 00 377 93 30 81 37
Open Jan–Oct daily, and Sat in high season

Hidden in the back streets of the old town, this restaurant serves good, generous helpings and is the place to eat *moules-frites* (mussels and chips). Children's menu for €8, adult menus from €14.

Around Monaco

Menton

One of the best places to eat with children in Menton is along the pedestrianized Rue St-Michel in the old town.

Darkoum

23 Rue St-Michel t 04 93 35 44 88
Open Tues–Sun

This small, family-run restaurant at the end of Rue St-Michel serves tasty Moroccan dishes. Couscous is such a staple in France that it's on the school dinner menu; if your kids have never had it before, they might like to try it here. Be prompt – lunch is served strictly between 12 noon–2pm. Menus from €9.

Crêperie St-Michel

5 Rue Piéta t 04 93 28 44 64

This restaurant has lots of character and a funny décor that will intrigue the kids. It's just off the main street in the old town with speedy service.

Le Chaudron

28 Rue St-Michel t 04 93 35 90 25
Open Mon–Wed

A good option for regional cooking. The inside of the restaurant is air-conditioned but with children you are better off eating on the terrace. Children's menus are €9.90, adult menus from €14.

Rikkiki

7 Square Victoria t 04 93 28 27 88

Away from the restaurant fray, this atmospheric and popular place serves authentic Italian dishes.

Oh! Matelot

Place Loredan-Larchey t 04 93 28 45 40
Open for lunch only in summer, Mon–Sat

Have brunch, *bruschetta*, or a buffet in this restaurant/café shaped like the deck of a boat.

Roquebrune

La Grotte

Place des Deux-Frères t 04 93 35 00 04

A really great place to eat out with kids, with delicious pizza and pasta. The restaurant is in the old town and is partly dug out of the rock.

Cannes

La Pizza

3 Quai St-Pierre **t** 04 93 39 22 56

The restaurant serves up good pizza in a congenial atmosphere. Pizzas start at €8.

Planet Hollywood

1 Allée de la Liberté **t** 04 93 06 78 27

Part of the worldwide chain that serves up burgers and chips in a film-star-inspired setting.

La Farfalla

1 Bd de la Croisette **t** 04 93 68 39 00

This coffee-bar-cum-steakhouse has a top-people-watching terrace by the Palais des Festivals and is teeming with starlets during the film festival. The menu covers meals and light snacks.

La Scala

Noga Hilton, 50 Bd de la Croisette **t** 04 92 99 70 00
www.hiltoncannes.com

If you want to feel like a movie star and have a comparable budget, then eat here on the terrace.

Le Jardin

15 Av Isola **t** 04 93 38 17 85
Open Tues–Sun lunch

Popular with locals, with tables in a small garden behind the bar. Menus from €11.

Around Cannes

Antibes

Le Royal Beach Restaurant

Bd Maréchal Leclerc **t** 04 93 34 03 09

The restaurant is right beside a beautiful sandy beach so it's ideal if you want to have a relaxed lunch – the kids can simply slip off and play in the sand. If you want a table at the edge of the terrace, arrive early or book in advance. Even out of season it pays to arrive early as there aren't always enough waiters to go round. The menu is full of local dishes and lots of fish. Menu from €20.

Le Keller

Bd de la Garoupe Cap d'Antibes **t** 04 93 61 33 74
Open April–Oct

On the beach, serving fine local cuisine. Savour ravioli with artichokes, *coquilles St-Jacques* and the house dessert, a mix of fruit sorbets and red berries, while the little ones finish building their sandcastles.

Comic Strip Café

4 Rue James Close **t** 04 93 34 91 40

This is ideal for a quick lunch, with lots of baguettes, salads and cakes. There's a comic strip library downstairs, too.

Biot

Auberge du Jarrier

30 Passage de la Bourgade **t** 04 93 65 11 68
Open Wed eve–Sun

If you want to give a gourmet restaurant a whirl with the kids, this is a good one to try. It has a relaxed atmosphere, friendly staff, a lovely terrace and a chef who will happily serve up children's portions. With menus from €22 this is one of the best-value gastronomic restaurants on the Riviera, but you will need to reserve a table at least a week in advance at the height of the season.

3615 Code Café

44 Impasse St-Sébastien **t** 04 93 65 61 61

A good spot for a speedy lunch, with a large sunny garden at the back for the kids, and an €8 cold buffet – a bargain in this part of the world.

Juan les Pins

Bijou Plage

Bd Charles Guillaumont **t** 04 93 61 39 07

There's sand right under the tables at this beach-side restaurant. The set lunch menu is a €18.50 and is a gastronomic delight, and the nougat ice-cream is dreamy.

Fréjus and St-Raphaël

La Romana

155 Bd de la Libération, Fréjus **t** 04 94 51 53 36

This restaurant is a real find in such a touristy place. It's right on the seafront, with a pizza- and pasta-based menu that will appeal to kids, although there isn't a specific children's menu. The food is surprisingly good and the service is friendly.

Café Galerie du Monde

Place Formigé, Fréjus **t** 04 94 17 01 07

A friendly café/restaurant for a drink or a snack, with tables set out in the picturesque square.

Around Fréjus and St-Raphaël

Anthéor

Les Flots Bleus

On the N98 **t** 04 94 44 80 21
Open April–Oct

This is an ideal choice for kids who like seafood. Meals are served on a terrace with great views of the Esterel and the beach. It's nothing fancy but is relaxing and won't break the bank and there's a free sandy beach across the road.

St-Tropez

Café Sénéquier

Quai Jean Jaurès **t** 04 94 97 00 90

This huge terraced café on the port side is great for a drink or an ice-cream. You can sit and admire the huge luxury boats in the harbour.

Club 55

43 Bld Patch, Rte de Ramatuelle **t** 04 94 79 80 14
Open Christmas, and mid-Feb–Oct

This is the place to spot stars on the beach at Pampelonne. There's a lovely shady terrace but the menus are pricey – budget over €40 a head.

Nikki Beach

Rte d'Epi, Pampelonne **t** 04 94 79 82 04

A trendy new beach club run by Eric Omores, who owns Nikki Beach in Miami. Teens will love bragging that they've been here.

Lei Salins

Plage des Salins, **t** 04 94 97 04 04
www.lei-salins.com
Open April–Oct

This simple and quiet restaurant situated on a small beach serves grills, barbecued fish and Provençal dishes. Simple dishes for kids include salads and omelettes. There are good-value lunch menus; dishes are fancier in the evening. Menus from €25.

Around St-Tropez

Gassin

Hôtel Bello Visto

Place des Barrys **t** 04 94 56 17 30
www.bellovisto.com
Open Easter–end Oct

The view from the shady terrace is one of the best in the South of France, and as Place des Barrys is pedestrianized, it is a great place for kids. The restaurant serves local specialities.

Bormes-les-Mimosas

Pâtes et...Pâtes

Place du Bazar **t** 04 94 64 85 75
Open Jan–Oct

This little Italian restaurant serves up huge portions of pasta (*pâtes*) and is a simple and relaxed place to eat out.

Collobrières

Hotel-Restaurant des Maures

19 Bd Lazare Carnot **t** 04 94 48 07 10

Collobrières is a tiny place and this simple restaurant by the river is a hub of local life. Enjoy good local cuisine, including huge mushroom omelettes and plenty of dishes made out of chestnuts. Prices are reasonable, with omelettes from €8. It can be busy, so to make sure of a table, arrive before one o'clock for lunch.

Cuers

Le Lingousto

Rte de Pierrefeu **t** 04 94 28 69 10
Open Tues–Sun lunch

A real find, this gourmet restaurant not only caters for children, but has a children's menu for €16 as well (adult menus €48). The house specialities are lamb and artichokes. Eat on the terrace.

Northern Provence

Vaucluse · Alpes-de-Haute-Provence · Alpes-Maritimes

VAUCLUSE 88
Avignon 89
  Special trips from Avignon 92
  Around Avignon 96
Carpentras 96
  Around Carpentras 97

ALPES-DE-HAUTE-PROVENCE 101
Castellane 101
  Special trips from Castellane 102
  Around Castellane 102

ALPES-MARITIMES 105
Sospel 105
  Around Sospel 106
Valberg 107
  Around Valberg 108

WHERE TO EAT 109

04

Northern Provence

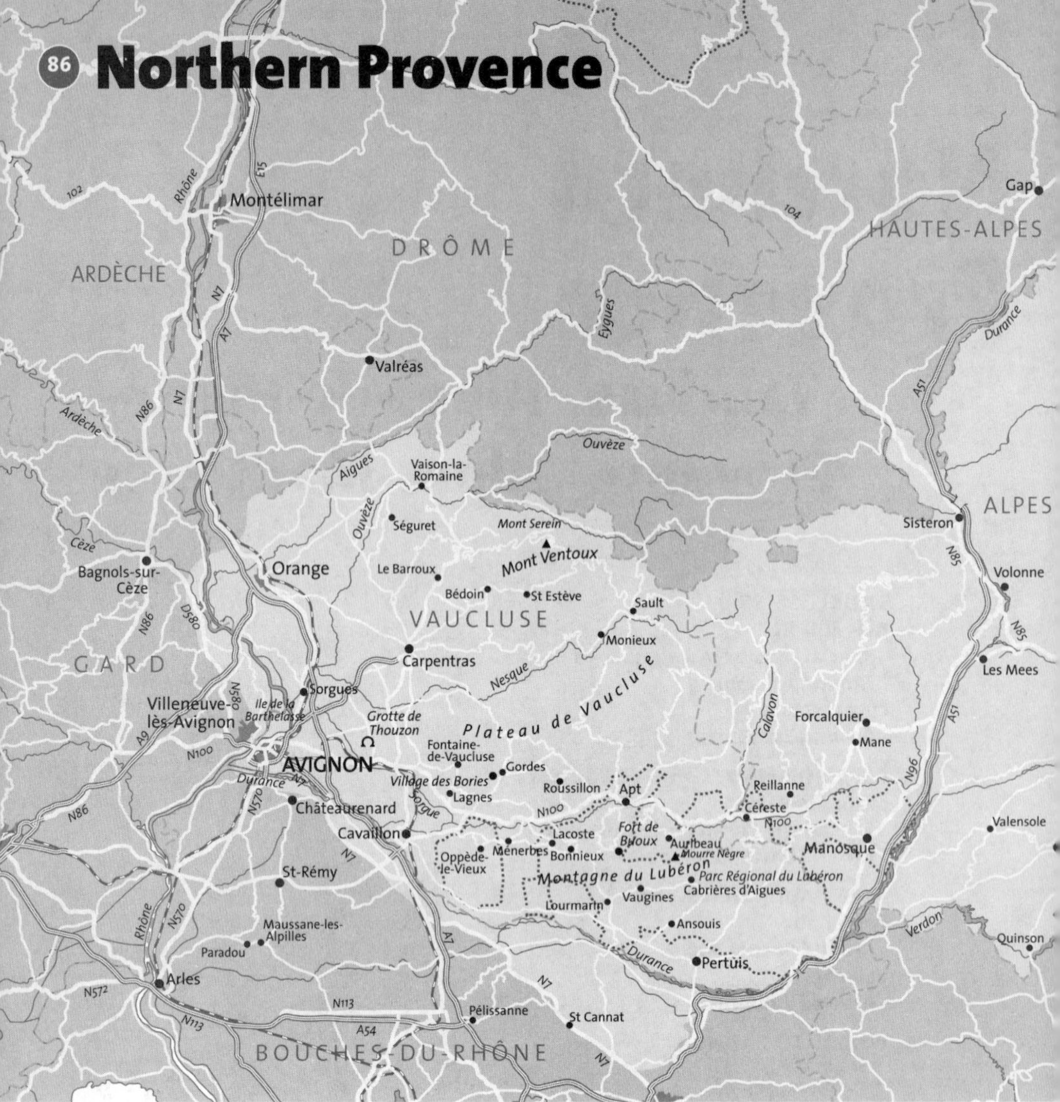

Special events

January

Avignon: Cheval Passion, a horse fair and festival; Poney Passion is the kids' part of the festival

July

Avignon: Theatre Festival

December

Avignon: Christmas Market

Séguret: Live Nativity Scenes

Highlights

Riding on the merry-go-round in Avignon, p.89

Rattling along the Pinecone Railway, p.104

Exploring mountain valleys around Sospel, p.105

Kayaking down the River Sorgue, p.93

Stepping out in the Roman theatre at Orange, p.95

Contemplating the sheer drop at the Gorges du Verdon, p.102

The South of France is full of surprises. One minute you can be sweating in a traffic jam in Juan-les-Pins and the next be eyeball to eyeball with a mountain goat in a rugged Alpine pass. Anyone who tells you that the South of France is built-up and overcrowded has never explored the place fully. Some of the most beautiful and remote countryside in France is within two hours' drive of the Riviera, but you might find that difficult to believe when you're pulling off the motorway on the outskirts of Orange or Avignon to a chorus of 'Oh yuk!' from the back seat. The suburban sprawl around these ancient cities will come as a shock but have faith – this area has always been a major crossroads for travellers. Hannibal waded across the Rhône with his elephants just north of Orange and even today it's still the main gateway to southern Europe.

Such a perfect day

Morning Visit the sweet shop in the ancient city of Carpentras, p.96

Lunch Drive to Fontaine-de-Vaucluse, p.92, and have lunch by the river, p.93

Afternoon Play hide-and-seek in the stone huts at the Village des Bories, p.101, and then refuel with a drink in the square at Gordes, p.97, before taking a stroll along the Fairy Valley in Roussillon, p.97

If you're driving down from the grey and drizzly north, it's almost as though you pass through an invisible door just before Orange. Provence is famous for its clear light, which is why so many painters came here, and even as you whiz along the motorway you can see the colours grow more vivid before your very eyes.

When travelling *en famille* there's always a rush to get to the beach, but in this region take it slowly – this is the perfect place to discover some basic principles of travelling with kids. The beautiful old city of Avignon, for example, is packed with museums, culture and fine restaurants and it can be tempting to rush busily from one attraction to the next before heading home in a whirl, but travelling with kids puts a different spin on things and nowhere more so than in a town like Avignon. Follow the little ones' agenda and you'll learn more about the place just by hanging around in the city's lovely parks and cheap cafés than by clocking up tourist sites. Tourism with kids is all about putting the brakes on and chatting about what you're seeing – it's about taking time to soak up the atmosphere.

East of Avignon is the market garden of France, with lots Roman ruins for history lovers and huge stretches of fabulous countryside where older kids can kayak, hike and gaze at the stars. It's a place to unwind and lose yourself since there's nothing to get stressed out about up here. You don't even have to worry that your children only ever eat pizza since the wild Valleé de Roya, near Auron, was part of Italy until 1947 and nearly everyone in the region eats pizza and pasta all the time.

On a practical note, bear in mind that Avignon can be a very cold place to visit in winter. It may be open all year round because it's a university town but that doesn't mean the kids will be happy there on a freezing cold day in January. When it comes to accommodation, there are some good family hotels in the centre of Avignon, but if you're planning to stay for a week or two it's nicer to find a base in the Luberon hills. The main road from Avignon to Apt is fast and it's possible to explore the city and the countryside round it in one holiday.

Heading east you'll find Peter Mayle country where you can hole up to read *A Year in Provence* at your leisure. Take care when choosing where to stay, however, since some of the less desirable villages have tried to piggyback on the fame his book has brought to the nicer parts of Provence. Avoid renting too close to the main road, the N100, which runs down a flat nondescript valley, and avoid Cavaillon as it's lost in a sea of garden centres and supermarkets. The best places to look for somewhere to rent are in the hills around Gordes, Roussillon and Fontaine-de-Vaucluse and south towards Lourmarin – villages to look out for are Ansouis, Bonnieux, Oppède-le-Vieux, Lacoste and Ménerbes. It was in Ménerbes that Mayle wrote his book and hence rentals are expensive, especially in high season, but there are bargains to be had at half term. It's still pretty warm in spring and autumn so it's a good place to come out of season.

The countryside from Apt to Forcalquier is lovely and the villages have that tumbledown, lived-in feel. Rental prices also drop considerably. You'll find lots of properties in this area listed in catalogues, which usually work out cheaper than holiday firms (*see* pp.216 and 226) and there are lots of great campsites, especially around the Gorges du Verdon. As you travel further east still, the terrain gets even wilder; there aren't any big cities away from the coast so by heading inland you can escape the crowds and hullabaloo and have a quiet break without any fuss. It's definitely the place to head if you like camping and picnicking. You won't find theme parks or attractions up here and the best nightlife you're likely to find is curling up with a good book.

You'll need a car to explore the area properly, but junior train fans will be glad to know that one of the best branch lines in France – Le Chemin de Fer de Provence – rattles effortlessly up the mountain passes from Nice to Digne-les-Bains.

Good to know...

In the summer temperatures soar in this part of France, so avoid sightseeing in the heat of the day, while in the winter the wind is bitterly cold, so you'll need to pack something warm. The name Avignon comes from the Latin *avenio*, which means windy place, and is highly appropriate. When the strong southern mistral wind is up it can blow through air vents in the car and under doors, so don't, by any means, leave the rain cover for the pushchair at home as you'll need it to protect the little ones from the wind. On the plus side, the mistral brings with it pure blue skies and the wonderful clear light characteristic of Provence.

AVIGNON

Getting there By air: There are direct flights from Paris to Avignon-Caumont airport, **t** 00 33 (0)4 90 81 51 51, 8km south of the city centre. Avignon is easy to drive to and is served by both main autoroutes, the A7 and A9. Marseille and Montpellier are both about 1hr away by car. Getting into town can be dispiriting: modern Avignon is a sprawl of shopping centres and business parks. The French love out of town shopping centres so be prepared to see the less than flattering face of modern France as you drive through to the centre. Parking in Avignon can be difficult in the height of the season and theft is also a problem, so choose either the 24hr underground car park under the Palais des Papes (not suitable for people carriers with a roof box) or park just across the Rhône on the Ile de la Barthelasse at Ile Piot, which is free and has a guard. You can take the ferry back across the river or catch the bus. By train: Train connections in general are good; once a week in summer there's a direct Eurostar from Waterloo. The TGV from Paris takes 2hrs 40mins but the TGV station is on the southern outskirts of town, in the Quartier de Courtine, so you'll need to use public transport to reach the centre. Strong winds can disrupt the TGV trains in winter and if you arrive late in the evening you may find it difficult to get a taxi. The regional train station is on Boulevard St-Roch, just outside the city walls near Porte de la République; central bookings, **t** 00 33 (0)8 36 35 35 35

Getting around Even the tiniest people will manage to explore Avignon on foot but a car will help if you want to explore the Ile de la Barthelasse and Villeneuve-lès-Avignon. Car hire is available at ADA, 23 Boulevard St-Ruf, **t** 04 90 86 18 89. You could also explore the area on two wheels. Transhumance, 52 Bd St-Roch, next to the train station, has bikes for hire, **t** 04 90 27 92 61, **e** motovelo@provence.bike.com. For taxis, **t** 04 90 82 20 20. The main bus station is on Av Monclar, near Porte de la République; buses arrive here from all the main local towns

Tourist office 41 Cours Jean Jaurès **t** 00 33 (0)4 32 74 32 74 **www**.avignon-tourisme.com

Special events Cheval Passion: This horse fair and festival held every January is one of the biggest equestrian events in Europe. The streets are filled with stunt riders and dancing horses. Poney Passion is for children, and there's a chance to meet grooms, vets and saddlers and watch a blacksmith at work. Theatre Festival: Avignon is devoted to theatre over 3½ weeks in July, and a whole section of the programme is dedicated to kids. Even without French, there are always circuses and puppet shows to enjoy. If you want to go you'll need to book well in advance and be prepared for crowds. If you're not interested in theatre this isn't the best time to visit the city

Good to know... Avignon Pass

Ask for a pass card when you buy your entrance tickets at the Papal Palace and get up to 50 per cent off the admission price for families at all subsequent major monuments and museums in both Avignon and Villeneuve-lès-Avignon. You'll also get a discount on the little trains and boat trips. The card lasts for 15 days.

Avignon is famous for its enormous papal palace (*see* below), built in the 14th century by Pope Clement V after he fled Rome for the safety of his lands in Vaucluse. He set up home in Avignon and he and his successors lived here for over 70 years. When the papacy finally returned to Rome, the city remained part of their property until the French Revolution. The palace is one of Avignon's main sites, and is really worth a visit.

Avignon is within easy striking distance of some of the area's other top sights, like the Pont du Gard (*see* p.172) and St-Rémy-de-Provence (*see* p.135), so it is good to use as a base for exploring the area. It's an easy city to explore with little kids, as it's quite small and simple to navigate. In the main square there's a huge *belle époque* double-decker merry-go-round that anyone under the age of five will be convinced is the sole reason you've travelled all this way. You can find a carousel in most big towns in France, but the one in Avignon is especially charming. Overall Avignon is a pre-schooler's paradise – there are a couple of little tourist trains that wind through the streets, and some pretty little parks where you can soak up the local atmosphere while they dig in the sandpit. The hotels and restaurants are quite child-friendly too.

Shopping

The main shopping street is Rue de la République, where you'll find branches of the main shops such as Galeries Lafayette and FNAC, where

Tell me a story: What was the pope doing here?

Medieval Rome was a place where plotting and scheming was the name of the game and the pope was one of the most influential men in Europe. For an ambitious king wanting to make an impact on the world stage it was crucial to win the support of the pope. Popes, of course, are elected, so if one pope disliked you there was always a chance that if and when the present one died he could be replaced with someone who might favour your cause. For that reason, being pope was a dangerous job – one that could literally kill you. Political infighting in the Vatican got so out of hand in the 14th century that Pope Clement V – a Frenchman who had the support of the French king – fled Rome for the safety of his lands in Vaucluse. Clement set up his home in Avignon, and he and his successors stayed for 70 years.

When the popes lived here, Avignon was one of the most important cities in Europe, but it was also overcrowded, notoriously filthy, not very holy and ridden with disease. The square in front of the palace was the Piccadilly Circus of medieval Europe and would have been crowded with pilgrims from all over Europe who had walked for weeks just to catch a glimpse of the man. There would have been masses of beggars, too, eagerly awaiting the loaves of bread that were regularly handed out to the city's poor at the palace gates.

Despite the large numbers of poor, Avignon was a very rich city – the pope was an amazingly wealthy man and all the papal profits ended up here. The town was full of artists and craftsman busily creating something new and stylish to please their potentate, including the Papal Palace.

teens can browse through the CDs and computer games. The narrow streets behind Rue de la République have plenty of small boutiques for kids. There's a huge Christmas market in December and a flea market at Place des Carmes on Sunday morning, where you can sometimes pick up interesting souvenirs. A branch of the sweetshop La Cure Gourmande is on Rue des Marchands; they sell the best lollipops (*les sucettes*) that you've ever eaten. Just outside of town is a shopping centre called Mistral 7, where you'll find a supermarket the size of a football pitch, a kids' fashion shop called Orchestra, and plenty of shops for babywear.

Picnics and snacks

Erio Convert, 45 Cours Jean Jaurès, has some of the best bread in the area and a great range of sandwiches. Eat them in the park over the road, which is next to the tourist office and has a small café in summer. The best ice-creams in town are to be found at Le Goëland in Rue St-Agricol, just off Place de l'Horloge; next door is a small Petit Casino supermarket for basics and baby supplies. On the other side of the street is VF Deldon, which has more excellent sandwiches. There's a Shopi supermarket on Rue de la République and a lovely food market at Les Halles on Place Pie, Tues–Sun morns.

Things to see and do

Palais des Papes

t 04 90 27 50 74/73
www.palais-des-papes.com
Open Daily 9.30–5.30, July–Sept 9–7. Last admission 1hr before closing
Adm Adult €9.50 (€7.50 in winter), child €4.30 (€3.50 in winter). English audio tour available

What you see today is an empty shell but in Pope Clement's day the palace was always packed with people, and lucky pilgrims would even have made it into the inner courtyard. Look out for the *fenêtre d'indulgence*, the huge window from where the pope used to bless the crowd. Inside the palace, the walls would have been covered in frescos, while the Great Treasury Hall would have held piles of money and jewels, as taxes collected from all over Europe were processed there. In the other big hall, La Grande Audience, clerks dealt with 8,000 letters and 10,000 petitions a year. This was the high court of the Christian world and a huge fresco of the Last Judgement originally hung on the northern wall to intimidate the populace.

Despite its importance in the Christian world, the palace wasn't a very pious place and comfort was the main priority. Rooms were richly decorated in

Look out for...

The colourful* Histoire de la Provence *– a children's history of Provence. The French is quite easy to understand and anyone studying GCSE French should be able to read it. It's on sale in the shop at the Pont d'Avignon.

Good to know...

Pushchairs aren't allowed in the palace so make this the first stop of the day. It takes about an hour to go round. There are two vending machines inside where you can buy water (both are next to the toilets).

Fancy a souvenir...?

At the end of the tour there's a good shop, which is almost a supermarket for souvenirs. A good investment is the colouring book *Je colorie la Provence*, which is just €4.50.

the most luxurious style, and there were beautiful gardens where exotic birds and lions were kept in cages. Clement VI's study, the Chambre du Cerf, reveals he was interested in more than just prayer: the walls are covered in pictures of hunting scenes. (If you look closely at the one of the frescoes you'll see one of the fishermen doesn't have a rod.)

Much of the pope's time was spent feasting in the Grand Tinel rather than at devotions. In its day the ceiling was covered with a blue fabric studded with gold stars and the pope ate alone on a podium under an even more exotic canopy. The kitchen had a special winch to haul up cattle from below, which were then cooked whole on massive spits. For the coronation of Clement V, the cooks roasted 118 oxen, 1,023 sheep and 60 pigs and served up an astonishing 95,000 loaves of bread.

All this is hard to imagine when you see the palace now, because it is completely empty; it was a prison during the French Revolution and later became a barracks. Look out for the Tour des Latrines where 60 pro-papist counter-revolutionaries were thrown to their deaths.

***Tell me a story:* Who was St Bénézet?**

Although it is known simply as the Pont d'Avignon, its real name is the Pont St-Bénézet, and is named after a medieval shepherd boy called Benoit or Bénézet in Provençal. According to legend, while tending his sheep Bénézet heard the voice of God telling him to build a bridge over the Rhône, followed by an angel who told him to go to Avignon to see the bishop. The bishop refused to take him seriously, but to humour the boy told him that if he could move a huge stone that not even 30 men could shift then he would have all the help he needed. Bénézet miraculously carried the stone to the banks of the river and the bishop, dumbfounded, had to keep his word.

Pont St-Bénézet (Pont d'Avignon)

t 04 90 85 60 16
Open Daily 9.30–5.30, July–Sept 9–7. Last admission 30mins before closing
Adm Adult €3.50 (€3 winter), child €2.50 (€2)

The famous bridge dates from 1185 and was originally half a mile long, with 22 arches. Although its tolls were a good source of income for the town, its upkeep was expensive and the townspeople abandoned it from 1660 – only four arches remain today. If you come to the bridge to 'danse tout en ronde', as in the famous song, keep an eye on the younger ones; the bridge juts into the river and isn't properly fenced, so one mistimed twirl could send them into the swirling waters of the Rhône. If you have toddlers, make sure they're safely housed in the pushchair. If you want to sing the song while you visit, the bridge's shop sells pens that have the words written out in full.

Musée Angladon

5 Rue Laboureur **t** 04 90 82 29 03
www.angladon.com
Open Wed–Sun 1–6, July–Sept daily to 7
Adm Adult €5, child (over 7) €3

There's not a great deal to interest kids in this museum, but it does have the only Van Gogh in Provence (*Les wagons de chemin de fer*) and if you're going to Arles and St-Rémy where Van Gogh painted some of his most famous pictures.

Place de l'Horloge

This will undoubtedly be the kids' favourite place in Avignon. There's a huge double-decker carousel in the centre of the square, plenty of space to run around and a clock tower with models that chime every hour. There are plenty of cafés for a cool drink and during the festival you'll be able to enjoy the street theatre from your café terrace. History buffs will want to know that the square was originally the old Roman forum, while teens will be even more pleased to discover that this is where they'll find the cinema: Cinéma Vox, **t** 08 36 68 03 70.

Les Petits Trains

t 04 90 82 64 44
Runs Mar–Oct daily

Two little tourist trains run every 30mins from 10–7.30 and do a circuit of the old town and the Rocher des Doms park; catch them outside the

Fancy a walk...?

The tourist office has details of four city walks with colour-coded routes throughout the town and even tiny tots will enjoy following the coloured markers along the route. You can also walk along the walls around the town. For a stunning view back along the river, take a cue from local families and take a stroll on the Ile de la Barthelasse along the Chemin des Berges.

Papal Palace or outside the tourist office for sightseeing with little children.

Theatre

Dolphin Blues Peniche

Chemin d'île Piot **t** 04 90 82 46 96

This theatre has shows for kids, many of which are suitable even without understanding French. Ticket prices, times and shows vary so check with the tourist office for details of what's on. Expect to pay around €30 for a family of four. There's also adult comedy and theatre here.

Boat trips

You're spoilt for choice if you want to take a boat trip on the Rhône. There's a free ferry, the Ville d'Avignon, which runs from Pont d'Avignon to Ile de la Barthelasse, April–Jun 10–8, later in July–Aug, Sept 2–6 only. Le Bateau Bus leaves from Allées de l'Oulle for a 1hr 15min return trip to Villeneuve six times a day in July–Aug, adult €6.09, child (under 12) €3.04.

If you feel more adventurous you can also sail down the Rhône to Arles and towards the Camargue from Quai de Ligne. Le Cygne runs cruises to Arles and the Camargue in July–Aug, **t** 04 66 59 35 62. To avoid the infamous mosquitoes of the Camargue, consider an air-conditioned trip with L'Odyssée. Trips run from Villeneuve, **t** 04 90 49 86 08.

Parks and playgrounds

The Rocher des Doms, next to the Papal Palace, is a delightful park with a little playground, a café and a duck pond. It's conveniently situated if some of the group want to visit the museums while the younger ones run around outside. For the benefit of those left in the sandpit, before the Romans arrived the local Celtic–Ligurian tribe had a settlement here and it's easy to understand why they chose the area – you can see for miles. On a windy day Avignon certainly lives up to its name, but when the weather is calm it's a good spot for a picnic lunch.

Next to the tourist office on Cours Jean Jaurès there's another park with a playground and café. It's more popular with locals and is close to a good sandwich shop and bakery (just past the park on the left if you're heading out of town) if you want to pick up a snack. Older kids might want to check out the skateboard park on Ile de la Barthelasse.

SPECIAL TRIPS FROM AVIGNON

Fontaine-de-Vaucluse

Getting there With a family, the only feasible way of getting to the village is by car on the D938/D25. There are plenty of parking spaces in the village and it will cost €3 to park

Tourist office Chemin de la Fontaine **t** 00 33 (0)4 90 20 32 22

This is a great place to come for a family day out, with something that will appeal to everyone. Fontaine-de-Vaucluse gets very busy in summer and is certainly touristy, but it still has bags of charm.

The town is famous for its spring, which is one of the most powerful natural sources in the world. It pumps out more than 630 million cubic metres of water a year and is at its most dramatic in spring when the snow melts on Mont Ventoux. Exactly where the River Sorgue starts is still a mystery, despite countless attempts to locate its source using the most high-tech equipment. According to legend a terrible monster lurks deep inside the grotto, so perhaps he's keeping the source secret.

The village is small and tucked away in a steep little gorge (Vaucluse actually means 'la vallée close' or the closed valley). On a high crag above the town you'll see the ruins of a 16th-century castle but you may want to give it a miss with small children and over-adventurous teens as the battlements are very dangerous.

Shopping

This is a good place to pick up some souvenirs and gifts. Confiserie de la Fontaine in the Galerie Vallis Clausa sells some of the best chocolates, sweets and jam around.

At Cristallerie des Papes, **www**.cristallerie-des-papes.com, you can watch the glass-blowers and buy an example of their work to take home. A tiny glass animal costs just €4.

Things to see and do

La Source

The point where the river bursts out from the rock is a pretty 5-minute walk from the town centre along the riverbank and is suitable for pushchairs. How far you can go depends on the time of year, as the water level is higher in spring than summer. It goes without saying that small children will need supervision. On the way you'll pass the main museums in town and some of the best places to eat with kids (*see* p.110).

L'Ecomusée du Santon

t 04 90 20 20 83
www.musee-du-santon.org
Open Daily 10–12.30 and 2–6.30
Adm Adult €3.80, child €2.30

Fontaine is so small you can't miss the museums; this one is just by the bridge before the road up to the source and is one of the nicest *santon* museums in Provence. *Santons* are traditional Provençal figures, usually made of clay, used to decorate Christmas crèches. This museum has over 1,800 of them. The *santons* in this collection come in all materials – not just clay but also bread-crumbs and wax – and sizes. Don't miss what must be the tiniest crèche in the world, with 39 minute figures inside a walnut shell. For more about *santons*, *see* p.258 and for more on Christmas in Provence, *see* pp.244 and 256.

Moulin de Papier à la Main

t 04 90 20 32 52
Open Daily 9.30–7
Adm free

The source is so strong that it powers water-wheels all the way down the river. The first is at this paper mill, where you can watch paper being made in exactly the same way as it first was in Vaucluse in 1522. Paper continued to be made here until 1968. Once you've seen how it's done you can buy all sorts of notepapers from the shop.

Musée Appel de la Résistance

t 04 90 20 24 00
Open Wed–Mon 10–12 and 2–6
Adm Adult €3, child €1.50

Don't walk past this museum thinking it's a bit too heavy for the kids; although it centres on daily life during the Occupation the museum is surprisingly accessible. The exhibition looks at the Resistance movement, which was very strong in Fontaine-de-Vaucluse and nearby Gordes (the mayor of Fontaine was sent to Buchenwald for his involvement), and also addresses some of the difficult issues of collaboration and anti-Semitism.

Musée de Spéléologie

t 04 90 20 34 13
Open Daily May–Aug 10–12 and 2–6, Sept–April Wed–Sun 10–12 and 2–5
Adm Adult €4.70, child €3.20

Here you can find out more about the underground wonders of Vaucluse, but you'll need to be able to speak French; the museum is by guided tour only. If that isn't a problem, enthusiastic staff will lead you on an hour-long tour suitable for over-8s interested in nature. Find out about attempts to find the source of the Sorgue, see some reconstructions of underground caves and rock formations and look at the different equipment used to explore the world beneath our feet.

Boat trips

The Sorgue here is very shallow and Fontaine is a great place to learn to kayak.

Kayak Vert

Near the tourist office **t** 04 90 20 35 44
www.canoefrance.com
Open Mid-April–Oct
Adult €18, child (under-12) €12

The company will take you on the the 8km stretch from Fontaine-de-Vaucluse to Isle-sur-la-Sorgue and bring you back by minibus. It's an easy trip for over-7s and there are canoes for one or two people. Jackets, paddles and plastic containers for towels are provided and a picnic is included in the price. Wear a tracksuit and pack some sun cream.

Canoë Evasion

Getting there Off the D24 between Fontaine-de-Vaucluse and Lagnes, Pont de Galas **t** 04 90 38 26 22
Price Adult €16.77, child (7–14 years) €10.67, under-7s free

This is another company that organizes trips down the Sorgue, taking a break for lunch at a restaurant. There is room for a small child between two adults in a canoe, so this is a good option for families with younger children.

Vaison-la-Romaine

Getting there By car from Avignon, take the A7 to Orange and then take the D977, 23km from Orange. You can park next to the ruins. There are bus and train connections from Avignon.
Tourist office Place Chanoine Sautel **t** 00 33 (0)4 90 36 02 11
Special events July: Theatre Festival, with plays performed in the Roman theatre. November: Food Festival celebrating local produce

The Roman ruins and old medieval town make Vaison a great place for a day trip with school-age kids. Vaison is packed with history; long before the Romans there was a Celtic settlement on the rocky outcrop above the river. The tribe were called the Vocontii and they named their settlement Vasio. They were followed by the Romans, who arrived in the late 2nd century BC and built a busy and prosperous town called Vasio Vocontiorum, which had a population similar to that of modern Vaison. The modern town is built on top of the Roman one and what you can see of the ruins were only discovered in 1907 when 'la Romaine' was added to the town's name. The ruins are fascinating and are a must for those who enjoy studying the Romans at school; combine the trip with a stop at Orange to see the theatre.

Make time to walk around the medieval city before you leave; many of the more prosaic street names – such as Rue des Fours or Oven Street – date from the Middle Ages and relate to the activities that took place there at the time. Just off the market place you'll see the gateway to the old Jewish ghetto, where the Jews took refuge when the town came under papal rule in the 14th century; they were later expelled in 1563. Accommodation is expensive and not especially good for children; the town isn't too friendly either, so head out of town towards Mont Ventoux and Carpentras to spend the night. There are *chambres d'hôte* and small hotels in the surrounding villages and some expensive but child-friendly hotels towards Orange (*see* p.225). If you want a drink or a snack there are plenty of cafés on the Place de Monfort.

Tell me a story: What was it like to live in a Roman town?

Roman towns were very sophisticated and hygienic, with complex systems for pumping water and removing waste. Sewers ran underground (remember that in Medieval Europe open sewers would have run through the streets) and there was a constant water supply brought from fresh springs via an aquaduct, which was either piped directly into the houses of the very rich or was available to the general public in fountains and public baths. The public baths played an important role in Roman society, and were as important for holding social and business meetings as they were for bathing.

In the centre of every town was the Forum, where you would find find temples and other important public buildings to do with running the town or with commerce. The main marketplace was usually found here, flanked by busy shopping streets. Shops were open-fronted, with goods laid out on tables, and were often on the ground floor of a two-storey building, with apartments above. A lot of the buildings had graffiti on the walls, just like in a modern city.

At Vaison you can see the ruins of some wealthy villas, which show clearly how the house was laid out around an atrium or open hall. There wouldn't have been a full roof; instead something like an awning would have run along the edge of the room, with a small pool in the centre. Furniture was minimal and there were very few windows, but the walls would have been brightly painted, probably in red, which was a symbol of wealth. The poor weren't so lucky and lived in crowded tenements, many several storeys high, which often fell down. For the wealthy, however, life would have been good in a peaceful and prosperous town like Vaison.

Look out for...

The children's guide to Roman Vaison:* Vaison la Romain: A Long Story. *This guidebook is written in English and gives kids insight into the history of the town. It's on sale in the local museum alongside other interesting gifts and souvenirs, including jars of anchovy and olive pastes, which were Roman favourites for tea.

Things to see and do

The Ruins

Pl du Chanoine-Sautel **t** 04 90 36 02 11
Open Daily 10–12 noon and 2–6 (7 in summer, 4.30 in winter)
Adm Adult €6.20, child (under 12) free, reduced price for one teenager per family €2.10

There are two sites and the entrance fee covers both. Watch little children as the Roman ruins can be dangerous – there are lots of little walls to trip over and nothing is fenced off. To get a sense of context, start the visit in the excellent museum in the section of the ruins called the Quartier de Puymin. If you've already seen the theatre in Orange, the ruins of the theatre at Vaison won't seem quite so impressive, so skip them if you are in a hurry and concentrate instead on the Quartier de la Villasse, where you can see the remains of a huge villa, the shopping streets and public toilets.

The Roman Bridge

Cross over the Roman bridge and up into the old town. In 1992 the River Ouvèze burst its banks, killing 37 people and destroying 150 houses and the entire industrial estate. The Roman bridge, however, withstood the torrent of water.

In the old town there are stunning views from the old castle across to Mont Ventoux, but it's a bit precipitous in places so keep an eye on those who aren't that steady on their feet.

Orange

Getting there By car: Orange is off the A7 and A9 motorways; the journey takes 30mins door to door from Avignon. The train station is about 1km from the city centre but there's a bus to the theatre

If you are travelling with school-age children the useful mini-guide, *In the Footsteps of the Romans*, available from the tourist office, will provide a lot of background information.

Did you know...?
Orange gets its name from the Counts of Orange who once ruled the town. One of the best-known members of that family was the Dutch Prince William of Orange, who became William III of England in 1688.

Can you spot...
the supports for the original roof?
Sticking out of the walls of the theatre, above the seating area, you can still see the stones that were used to support the huge awning known as the velum, which protected theatregoers from the sun and rain, and helped the actors to project their voices.

Orange has the best preserved Roman theatre in Europe. Unfortunately, once you have seen the theatre, Orange isn't a place to linger in. It's a stronghold of the extreme-right National Front and has a nasty atmosphere; once you've had a quick look at the ruins the best thing to do is to head out of town. Don't be tempted to take a walk in the St-Eutrope park; it's recommended in lots of guidebooks but it's a seedy and depressing place.

If you have time, it's worth stopping to see the massive Triumphal Arch before you leave; the pictures on the arch show Caesar's army defeating the Gauls. Try to ignore the fact that it's on a busy roundabout and concentrate on the approach road, which is actually the old Roman thoroughfare, the Via Agrippa. If you want to linger there's a small museum opposite the theatre, which has a display of some of the statues and friezes found inside the theatre.

The Roman Theatre

t 04 90 51 17 60
Open 9–12 noon and 1.30–5 in winter, 9–6.30 in summer
Adm Adult €4, child (under 10) free

Built during the reign of Augustus in the 1st century AD, the theatre had capacity for an audience of 10,000, who would squeeze in to watch comedies, tragedies and circus acts, or to attend political meetings. When the Roman Empire collapsed, the theatre in Orange became variously a castle, a slum and then a prison. It was restored in the 19th century and most of the seating that can be seen today dates from this period.

In Roman times the back wall of the theatre would have been decorated with columns and statues and a lean-to wooden roof would have helped to project the actors' voices. Acoustically the theatre was reputed to be the height of sophistication; the audience could have heard a whisper, no matter where they were sitting, which was fortunate for women theatregoers because they weren't allowed to sit in the front rows. The stage would have had a wooden floor with trap doors so the actors could make a quick exit and the curtain, which was about 3m high, was pulled up and down by an ingenious system of pulleys.

AROUND AVIGNON

Animal lovers

Musée Vivant de l'Abeille

Getting there On the D6 east of Manosque
Route de Manosque, Valensole **t** 04 92 74 85 28
Open June–Sept Mon–Fri 8–12 noon and 1.30–5.30
Adm Free

This is only a small wildlife display but it allows an interesting glimpse inside the hives, allowing you to watch the bees at work from behind the safety of a glass window. Wed and Fri afternoons, June–Aug, you can dress in a beekeeper's outfit and look right inside a hive.

Bricks and mortar

Villeneuve-lès-Avignon

If you have a car, pop over to the other side of the River Rhône to the Fort St- André, a surprisingly tranquil area without a postcard- or ice-cream seller in sight. The fort was built by French kings to keep an eye on what was going on, on the other side of the Rhône. Most of that monitoring was done from the two massive towers at the entrance known as the Twin Towers. There's nothing to see inside the fort, but the view is spectacular..

Philippe-le-Bel Tower

Open Daily 10–12 noon and 2–5.30
Adm Adult €1.60, child €0.90

This 14th-century tower has glorious views of Avignon and Mont Ventoux, but there are 176 steps up to the top so it is not an outing to be attempted with toddlers, or on a hot day. If you're up for it, the views are superb, and the visit will inspire some extravagant sandcastle building when you get back to the beach.

CARPENTRAS

Getting there It's on the D950, 25km from Avignon. There's a bus service from Avignon, Marseille and Orange and trains from Orange and Avignon
Tourist office 170 Allée Jean Jaurès **t** 00 33 (0)4 90 63 00 78

Carpentras has a character all its own and is a pleasant place to visit, to browse among its traditional shops and to soak up the atmosphere. Among the most interesting places to shop is the Passage Boyer, an enclosed shopping street, which was built as part of a public works scheme in the mid-18th century.

Carpentras is in the market garden of France and is known for its fruit and vegetables – many of the little shops sell interesting local produce – but as far as the kids will be concerned the most important local products are the little boiled sweets known as *berlingots*, which are mint-flavoured caramels. The sweet shop Clavel on Rue Pont d'Orange is worth a visit. It doesn't appear to have changed since it made the first commercial *berlingot* in 1844 and the window is a kid's dream (and proof you can make anything out of boiled sweets, even a rocket). The biggest *berlingot* ever was made here – it was a massive 56.7kg.

Tell me a story: What is a _berlingot_?

There are different theories about the origins of Carpentras' famous sweet, the mint-flavoured caramels known as *berlingots*. According to one story, in 1313 a local pastry maker had some caramel mixture left over after making a flan for Pope Clement V. He boiled up the extra mixture with lemon juice and mint, dipped little sticks into the mixture and offered it to the pope saying 'Honour to Bertrand de Goth' (the pope's real name). Over the years 'Bertrand de Goth' was corrupted to Ber-Lin-Got.

According to another story, the sweets get their name from the Provençal word *berlingaù*, which means 'knucklebones', and refers to a type of jacks game played by children throughout the region. The 'bones' used to play the game are the same shape as the little hard candies from Carpentras. Traditionally the sweets were red mints but today they come in all colours and in different flavours.

Shopping

Carpentras is a pleasant place to do some shopping and has some good shops for children – and their mums and dads. For baby goods head for Bébé 9 on Place Général de Gaulle. Reynier, 47 Les Halles, and L'Atelier des Jouets, 1 Place de l'Ancien Sénat, both have a great selection of unusual wooden toys. Market day is Friday and in winter is the place to buy truffles.

Things to see and do

The Synagogue

Place Hôtel de Ville **t** 04 90 63 39 97
Open 10–12 noon and 3–5
Adm Free, but it's polite to leave a donation
Men and boys will need to wear a yarmulke to visit; these are in a box by the door.

This is the site of the oldest synagogue in France; it is all that remains of the Jewish ghetto that was once in this part of town. The Jews settled in Carpentras during the 500 years that it was under papal rule, because the pope, hoping ultimately to force them to convert, gave them sanctuary. Those who didn't convert were crowded into the ghetto, where they were forced to pay to leave or enter, and made to identify themselves by wearing a specific type of yellow hat. If you look at the southern side of Carpentras' cathedral you will see a door known as the Porte Juive, where Jews who were forced to convert to Christianity entered the church. The carving above the door shows a more sinister side to Carpentras and depicts a swarm of rats encircling the globe intent on eating it up. Today only around 125 Jews live in Carpentras, but life still isn't easy. The cemetery was desecrated in recent years and the town has a strong National Front following. It can make that *berlingot* taste a bit sour.

The synagogue stands on the site of an even older one and the original ritual baths and bread ovens for making matzo, the unleavened bread eaten at Passover, are currently being restored. When the present synagogue was built in 1741, the local bishop said it couldn't be as high as the nearby Chapel of Penitents, so the rabbi, undaunted, had the ceiling painted with stars so he could see the sky even if he couldn't reach it from the roof.

Security, sadly, has to be extremely tight, so you'll need to ring the bell to enter. Don't bother with the well-meaning but ill-informed English tours organized by the local tourist office; if you are interested, the synagogue itself will find someone who speaks English to guide you around. All faiths, and all ages, are welcome, and toddlers will like gazing up to look at the stars.

AROUND CARPENTRAS

Luberon villages

In the Luberon southeast of Carpentras and Avignon lies a hilly area with some of Provence's most beautiful villages. The most interesting for kids are the three below.

Gordes

Getting there 6km north of the N100, the main road between Avignon and Apt
Tourist office Le Château **t** 00 33 (0)4 90 72 02 75
www.gordes-village.com

The beautiful village of Gordes is popular with wealthy Parisians and as a result it has a lot more style than some of the villages north of here. It's a lovely spot to cool off with a long drink (*see* p.110) or to visit at sunset, when the village glows like gold. It's a great base for a family holiday, and out of season, especially in the February break when the French take to the ski slopes, you'll have the place to yourself.

Buy souvenirs at Marc Peyron in Place du Château and look for locally produced honey sweets and nougat, as honey is a local speciality.

Roussillon

Getting there It's off the N100 on the D4
Tourist office Pl de la Poste **t** 00 33 (0)4 90 05 60 25

Roussillon is known as the Colorado of Europe and is worth the trip even if you've seen the real Colorado. The whole area is a mass of blood-red and ochre cliffs and you can see the great red needles of the Val des Fées – the Valley of the Fairies – from the village just by the car park. These rock formations are actually man-made and are a result of the pigment mines that have been operated here since the French Revolution. This is where

***Tell me a story:* Who was Camus?**

Albert Camus, one of France's greatest writers, was born in Algeria – a French colony at the time – in 1913, where his parents' families had settled from France 50 years before. Camus was brought up in a very poor household; his mother was a cleaner and never learnt to read and his father was killed during the First World War. As a teenager he suffered from tuberculosis and nearly died. He was able to overcome these disadvantages and went on to university and work as a journalist. But his early life would influence his writing: throughout his life he was fascinated by fate and how people deal with their experiences.

His most famous book, *L'Etranger* (*The Outsider*), explores many of the themes that were important to him and that recur throughout his work. This story of a random murder written in a deceptively simple style allowed Camus to explore many of the issues that interested him, including the abolition of the death penalty and the poor treatment by French colonists of the native Algerian population. The book is immensely powerful and full of images of Mediterranean life.

During the Second World War, Camus became a famous Resistance leader, campaigning against the Nazis as well as the French authorities who collaborated with them. His book, *La Peste* (*The Plague*), was a result of these experiences and is all about the horror of dictatorship. Although a radical in his youth (he had been a member of the Communist Party and during the war wrote many articles that supported radical social reform), by the end of the war he had moderated his views, concerned that France could find itself torn apart by civil war.

He won the Nobel Prize for literature in 1957 and bought his house in Lourmarin with the proceeds, but his life was far from content; his marriage was unhappy and he was deeply upset by the war for independence in Algeria. He was just 47 years old when he died.

all those lovely orangey paints that evoke the sunburnt hues of the South of France come from.

The old village is perched on the top of a hill and has some spectacular views across the surrounding countryside. It's a good place to stroll around, write a postcard and enjoy an ice-cream. Even the tiniest members of the family will love walking in the Val des Fées – it's only a short walk of about 30mins and is a good place for a game of Cowboys and Indians. Mix the earth up with a bit of yoghurt and you can make some fantastic war paint.

Lourmarin

Getting there South of Bonnieux on the D943
Tourist office Av Philippe de Giraud **t** 00 33 (0)4 90 68 10 77 **www.lourmarin.com**

Older kids, particularly if they are doing French A level, may be interested to know that Albert Camus moved here after winning the Nobel Prize for literature. He was buried on the left-hand side of the cemetery after his fatal car crash in 1960.

Nature lovers

Collect local herbs, either growing wild or bought in bunches, and dry them as a souvenir of the holiday. Dried lavender, stuffed in little pillows or bags and used to scent clothes in drawers, will be a potent reminder of Provence, and an infusion of rosemary can be used to make hair silky-soft (pour boiling water over rosemary and leave to cool before using).

Mont Ventoux

Getting there **It's an easy drive to the top once the snow has melted. The D974 runs up the mountain.**

Although it's not very high, at only 1,909m, Mont Ventoux is a majestic mountain and aptly named; 'vent' means wind and it's always windy on the summit. There's usually snow up here from December to April; the rest of the year what looks like snow is white rocks on the summit. The mountain was not always so bare: most of the trees that once grew here were cut down to make boats for the French navy over 100 years ago.

It can be cloudy in the middle of the day so, for the best view and in the summer the coolest ride, head up to the summit in the early morning or evening. As you negotiate the tortuous hairpin

Don't forget to pack...
A kite – when the wind blows it's hard to find a better place to fly one.

bends spare a thought for the Tour de France cycle riders who often ascend it on two wheels. Getting to the top of Mont Ventoux can be a bit off-putting: the road is covered in graffiti in support of the extreme right-wing National Front Party and there is a nest of masts and satellite dishes on top of the mountain, but rise above all this, because once you reach the summit the view is fantastic.

The best time to visit is in late spring when the slopes are a riot of wild flowers and you can appreciate the wonderful smell for which Mont Ventoux is known. If you visit in winter you can ski down the mountain. There's a small ski station on the road to Sault, the D164, which hires out equipment, including sleds.

This is great family walking country. In summer there's a fairly easy ascent from the parking lot by the campsite in Mont Serein to the summit; the path is first marked the GR9 and then becomes the GR4. The campsite itself also organizes nature walks for families during the summer. The arrangement is quite informal so pop in for details when you arrive.

There is another good walk from La Font d'Angiou. Take the D974 from Bédoin through St-Estève; 6Km after the village you'll see an information board and a parking place. This path is the start of the walking route GR910, which takes you to one of the main springs on Mont Ventoux and is a particularly pretty walk when the autumn leaves are turning.

For further information about guided walks and other activities for children in the area contact the Maison de l'Environnement et de la Chasse in Sault, **t** 04 90 64 13 96.

Make a botanical scrapbook

Some souvenirs don't cost a thing; children can make a collection of pressed flowers and leaves as a lovely memento of the holiday. Remember that in national parks the picking of wild flowers is illegal so be careful what you pick and where.

Look for **leaves** from the following local plants:

olivier olive tree
cyprès cypress tree
platane plane tree
vigne vine

Local **herbs** to look out for are:

lavande lavender
fenouil fennel
romarin rosemary
thym thyme
basilic basil
sarriette savory
laurier laurel

Tell me a story: **The three Masses of Mont Ventoux**

The imposing, mysterious Mont Ventoux has inspired many local tales, a number of which are about the ruined chapel at the summit. Some people say that at Christmas it glows with a strange luminosity while others claim to have seen ethereal figures filing into the church.

Provence's famous storyteller, Alphonse Daudet, wrote a story based on local tales of the strange goings-on in the chapel. According to his story, there was once a priest who was so keen to enjoy the fantastic food being prepared for Christmas that he rushed through the three Masses observed on Christmas Eve at top speed. So eagerly did he enjoy his Christmas feast that he died of over-eating. When he arrived in heaven St Peter was so angry that he sent him back down to earth to say 300 more Christmas Masses. And so the greedy padre is there to this day, doing his penance every Christmas Eve, up on Mont Ventoux.

Parc Naturel Régional du Luberon

This is the place to bring kids who love the great outdoors and is especially beautiful in the spring and autumn when there are fewer people. Even if you are not keen walkers it's a beautiful area to drive around and there are places to have a picnic.

Maison du Parc

60 Place Jean Jaurès, Apt **t** 04 90 04 42 00
www.parcduluberon.org
Open Mon–Sat 8.30–12 noon and 1.30–7 (6 Oct–Mar)
Adm Adult €1.50, child (under 18) free

This interesting museum traces the geological history of the park, but to get the best out of it you need to speak French. The centre has leaflets on walking and hiking in the surrounding countryside and has cycling itineraries from the Cavaillon plain to the Forcalquier hills. There are signs in English along the routes giving details of key sights, shopping and accommodation.

Can you spot...a cyclist?
The Tour de France often passes this way when the race takes place in July. Check the route on www.letour.fr

La Ferme de Gerbaud

3km north of Lourmarin **t** 04 90 68 11 83
Open Daily in summer 9–5 (shop closes 8pm), winter weekends only 9–3.30
Adm Adult €4.75, child (under 12) free. Guided tour in English takes 1½hrs

This farm tour is all about Provençal plants and explains how herbs such as thyme, sage, bay and lavender were all used in the past to make perfumes, medicines and dyes. You can buy lavender oil and dried herbs from the little shop afterwards.

Fancy a walk...?

You're spoilt for choice for family walks in the area. From the abbey at Sénanque, north of Gordes on the D177, there is a pretty walk along the river-bank, which is particularly lovely when the lavender is in bloom. Take time to unwind and enjoy the scenery. There's another good family walk at the cliffs of Rocques des Bancs; drive from Lourmarin to Bonnieux and just before the village, take the path marked '*route de la forêt des cèdres*'. The path runs through a forest and under the cliff side; follow it for about 5km until you come to a car park.

You could also take a stroll around the Mourre Nègre: take the D48 to Auribeau from Apt and look for the village car park. The path runs in a circuit from the car park and is indicated by blue arrows. It takes about 2hrs to walk the circuit and there are some beautiful views.

There are several good picnicking spots in the area too. If you want to picnic and swim head for the banks of the Etang de la Bonde, 3km south of Cabrières d'Aigues on the D9, or for Lac du Paty, 15km north of Carpentras, off the D13. It's sign-posted off the road. There is a really easy walk around the pretty Lac du Paty to a small chapel.

For picnics with older kids, go to Lac de Monieux. Take the D1 from Sault in the direction of Carpentras then take the D942 to Monieux. There, take a left turn to the lake just past Monieux. The path, the GR9, runs along the gorge and is a bit precipitous, so isn't suitable for the younger ones.

Horse riding

Kids who like riding will enjoy exploring the park on horseback. These have horses for hire:

Centre Equestre

Lourmarin **t** 04 90 68 38 59

L'Ecole du Cheval

Apt **t** 04 90 74 37 47

Bikes

In the spring and summer, the Luberon is a great place to explore by bike, although both you and the kids will have to be pretty fit as the terrain is reasonably challenging.

Mountainbike Luberon

Rue Marceau, Bonnieux **t** 04 90 75 89 96
www.luberon-news.com/mountainbike-luberon

Here you can hire bikes for children, bikes with baby seats and children's trailers. They'll deliver if you are staying locally.

Grottoes and caves

Kids like the excitement of exploring caves and a trip underground can be a good way of escaping the summer heat. Bring a fleece or a jumper if you're going underground.

Grotte de Thouzon

Le Thor **t** 04 90 33 93 65
www.grottes-de-thouzon.com
Getting there On the N7 towards Cavaillon, 15mins south of Avignon
Open April–Oct daily 10–12 noon and 2–6, July–Aug 10–7, Sun only in Mar 2–6, closed Nov–Feb
Adm Adult €6, child (5–12 years) €4
Last admission 30mins before closing time

Did you know...?
Lavender was used by Romans for washing (the name comes from the same Latin root as laver – to wash), but it has many other uses: lavender is an antiseptic, is good for promoting calm and aiding sleep and soothes sore throats, sunburn and blisters. Forty-three per cent of all French lavender is produced in Vaucluse.

The 45-min tour takes you along the course of an underground river that was only discovered in 1902. The path follows the bed of a fossilized stream and there are long, thin stalactites that look like golden icicles. This is a good grotto to visit with little ones as the walk is fairly level.

Look at this!

Aptunion

Rte d'Avignon, 2km out of Apt heading west
t 04 90 76 31 43
www.kerryaptunion.com
Open Mon–Sat 10–12 noon and 2–6
Adm Free

Sitting on a deck chair by the pool, it's easy to forget that Provence wasn't always a sun-drenched land of plenty. Life here was hard, and preserving the abundant varieties of fruit for the harsh winter was a necessity, not just a quaint hobby. Today in Apt it's still a major concern and is big business – the town is the crystallized fruit capital of Provence. At Aptunion you can tour the factory and buy some candied fruit to take home. Prices start at €4.

Village des Bories

4km east of Gordes, off the D2 **t** 04 90 72 03 48
Open Daily 9–dusk
Adm Adult €6, child €3, under-10s free

This village is made up of dry-stone huts, known locally as *bories*, that are similar to the Neolithic huts found in Ireland but here are believed to date from the 18th century. Huts like this appear across the Midi and Provence, and were often used by shepherds for shelter. The village here was believed to have been built as refuge from the plague that ravaged Marseille in the 18th century. If you go to the village of Cabrières you will see a stone wall built to keep people fleeing Marseille from travelling any further and endangering other communities.

ALPES-DE-HAUTE-PROVENCE

CASTELLANE

Getting there On the N85, 71 km from Nice and 27km from Digne-les-Bains. It's at the eastern end of the D952 if you are coming from the Gorges du Verdon
Tourist office Rue Nationale **t** 00 33 (0)4 92 83 61 14
Special events January: Fireworks on 31 January to celebrate the lifting of a siege in 1586. October: Marathon along the Gorges du Verdon

Castellane is a lively little town with plenty of hotels and restaurants, set around a town square that is typical of the South, full of plane trees and people playing *boules*. In this corner of Provence there aren't many towns, which is one reason why Napoleon stopped here on his way to Paris once he had escaped from Elba. Today, it's the ideal place to base yourself if you want to explore the Gorges du Verdon (*see* p.102). This isn't the place to come for a wild nightlife but is ideal for families, and if you like camping there are some pleasant campsites in the surrounding countryside.

Things to see and do

Notre Dame du Roc

The town nestles beneath a huge craggy outcrop, sliced out of the surrounding rock like a slab of cake. A 40-minute climb will bring you to the little chapel of Notre Dame du Roc on the top. With older children it's worth the effort for the stunning views down the valley.

Maison des Sirènes

Pl Marcel Sauvaire **t** 04 92 83 19 23
Open Daily 9–12 noon and 2–6
Adm Adult €2.30, child €1.50

You may be a long way from the sea but just 6km from town is the Col des Léques, where hundreds of fossilized sirenians, a type of marine mammal and early relative of the manatee, have been found. *Sirène* is French for mermaid and these extinct creatures may be the origin of the mermaid myth.

Aboard Rafting

Pl de l'Eglise **t** 04 92 83 76 11
www.aboard-rafting.com

Active kids will be in their element in this part of France and Aboard Rafting organizes all kinds of outdoor activities. There are bikes for hire, canoeing for over-8s who can swim and adventure courses in the forest, including an assault course by the River Verdon. For the adventure courses kids must be over 1.20m high and need to bring their own sports gear. Courses run April–Oct; 1½hr course costs €12.

SPECIAL TRIPS FROM CASTELLANE

The Grand Canyon du Verdon

Getting there Castellane is at the eastern end of the Gorges du Verdon. Road connections from the coast are good and its just 2hrs' drive from St-Tropez or Nice.

The Grand Canyon du Verdon is Europe's largest canyon and it is definitely worth dragging protesting children off the beach to see it. It's dizzyingly high cliffs plunge down to the bluey-green waters of the River Verdon and at points, the canyon as much as ½km wide. Around the canyon there is some extremely wild and remote countryside – out of season you won't see another soul. What's really extraordinary is that the canyon was ignored until 1905; the locals knew it was there but it was useless for agriculture so no one really bothered with it. In the 1950s there was even a plan to flood the whole thing and turn it into a huge hydroelectric dam; it was only lack of money that prevented the scheme.

You'll need a car to see the area; you can get a map of driving itineraries from the tourist office in Castellane. Fill up with petrol and bring a picnic, as there are few garages and shops along the way. There is a road running along each side of the canyon – the D71 is known as the Corniche Sublime although, if you're behind the wheel with a bunch of overexcited kids in the back, you may not feel so sublime driving along it. If you're not one for driving on the edge choose the road that runs along the southern side. In summer, if you just want to drive along and admire the view, go in the evening when there is less traffic. Out of season you'll have the road to yourself.

Fancy a walk...?

Unfortunately, a lot of walks in the Gorges du Verdon aren't suitable for little children either, but there is plenty to enjoy in admiring the view. Even if you are an experienced walker it's best to take a guide as the area is unpredictable; storms can be violent and spring form nowhere and the level of the river can change dramatically because of the dams. Older kids could try the 2-hr hike from Point Sublime through the Samson corridor, which follows a series of tunnels to Chaos de Trescaïre. Ask at the tourist office in Castellane for details.

Les Lacs du Verdon

The lakes around the Gorges du Verdon are part of the hydroelectric system but are lovely places for a picnic. Lac de Ste-Croix is the biggest and has little boats for hire, but no swimming. If you want a dip you'll need to go to the Lac du Castillon, north of Castellane; boats are also available for hire there, on its southwestern tip.

There are pedal boats and canoes suitable for kids at the Pont du Galetas, but canoeing along the length of the gorge isn't feasible for inexperienced canoers or small children as the current is very dangerous.

AROUND CASTELLANE

Castles and forts

Colmars

Getting there On the D955 north of Castellane
Tourist office Porte de la Lance **t** 00 33 (0)4 92 83 41 92

Colmars is a beautiful fortified town, full of ramparts and towers. If you are wishing you had time to see everything in the South of France and wanted above all to see Carcassonne, forget it – this is much better. It's totally unspoilt and much more likely to feed the kids' imaginations. The town is surrounded by acres of woodland where you can walk and picnic and there's a good campsite on the edge of town.

Entrevaux

Getting there The Pinecone Railway (*see* p.104) runs just below the castle; it's a terrific ride and is the best mode of transport to use if you are coming from Nice or Digne-les-Bains. By car take the N202 from Nice

Entrevaux has a real fairytale castle, which you'll see if you approach by train. It was once one of the strongest castles in the area – it had to be because the border between France and Piedmont was once only a few miles away. Everything east of here only became French about 150 years ago. A rocky zigzag path takes you to the top, but it's hard going, so take it slowly; the climb will take a good 20mins. If it's too hot you can escape to the crumbling dungeons and a network of tunnels instead. If all those ruins become too much, there's a motorbike museum, the Musée de la Moto, in the town centre, **t** 04 93 79 12 70. It's open every day in summer and is free.

Nature lovers

Gorges du Loup

The drive starts at Pré-du-Loup, east of Grasse. Follow the D3 up the gorge and then take the D6 back. There are beautiful waterfalls along the route but, if you do decide to explore on foot, look out for the slippery steps under the Cascade de Courmes.

Grottoes and caves

In this part of France the ground beneath your feet is riddled with caves and the porous rock of the region means water can easily soak through, creating amazing stalactites and stalagmites.

Grottes des Audides

Rte de Cabris, St-Vallier-de-Thiey **t** 04 93 42 64 15
Getting there 9km from Grasse
Open Daily 10–6 in summer, otherwise times vary
Adm Adult €5, child (4–11 years) €3

The cave is 60m deep and was only discovered in 1988. The open-air prehistory museum explaining what it was like when the cave was inhabited in prehistoric times makes this an especially interesting trip for kids. However, it's not an ideal destination for the very small: you can't take a pushchair or carry a baby in a backpack and you'll need a free hand for the guardrail, so you'll need help if you have more than one small child. For the right age group, it's fascinating; the guides speak English, and Cabris itself is a lovely village to stop off in for a drink and a stroll.

Grottes de St-Cézaire

St-Cézaire-sur-Siagne **t** 04 93 60 22 35
Open June–Sept daily 10.30–6, July–Aug 10.30–6.30, Feb–May and Oct 2.30–5, Nov–mid-Feb Sun only 2.30–5
Adm Adult €4.57, child €1.98

This is a beautiful cave, 40m underground, with red stalactites and stalagmites in the shape of flowers, animals and toadstools. There's a shady picnic spot too.

Souterroscope de Baume Obscure

t 04 93 42 61 63
Getting there 10km from Grasse on the N85
Open 10–5 (7 in summer)
Adm Adult €7.62, child (4–12 years) €3.81

A guided walk, with English commentary along an underwater river, but expensive for what it is.

Sporty kids

Fun Kart

Plateau de la Sarée, Rte de Gourdon, Grasse
t 04 93 42 48 08

Kart racing on a large circuit for adults and kids.

Look at this!

Musée de Préhistoire des Gorges du Verdon

Rte de Montmeyan **t** 04 92 74 09 59
Getting there Quinson, south of Riez on the D11
www.museeprehistoire.com
Open Daily 10–6, closed last two weeks in Dec and Tues mid-Sept–mid-June
Adm Adult €5.80, child (6–18 years) €3.10; family ticket 2+2 €14.50, extra child €2.30

If getting history off to a good start is a bit of a challenge in your house, you couldn't make a better investment than a trip to this new museum. Designed by British architect Norman Foster, it has everything you need to bring the past to life –

films, reconstructions and stylish exhibits. After you have visited the cave where the actual discoveries were made, you can see a reconstruction of a prehistoric village, learn how to be an archaeologist and find out how to cut flint and light a fire without matches.

Musée Nature en Provence

4 Allée Louis Gardiol, Riez
Open Daily Mon–Sat 10.30–12.30 and 2.30–5, July–Aug times vary
Adm Adult €1.50, child free

This little private museum has over 3,000 fossils and a remarkably well-preserved skeleton of a wader bird that is over 35 million years old. This is certainly not a high-tech museum experience but junior fossil hunters will enjoy it, and the museum itself is charming.

Confiserie Florian

Les Ateliers de Tourettes-sur-Loup, Le Pont du Loup
t 04 93 59 32 91
www.confiserieflorian.com
Open Daily 9–12 noon and 2–6.30
Adm Free

Here you can watch sweets being made for the famous shop in Nice. It's an old-fashioned place, where men in white hats and blue aprons mix up delicious concoctions, some of which use crystallized flowers from the area (Tourettes-sur-Loup is the violet capital of France and they grow more violets here than anywhere else in the country). The best part of the tour, though, is the free sweet-tasting session at the end, and if that's all too much, it's a nice place just to stop for an ice-cream.

Rail power!

The Pinecone Railway

Le Chemin de Fer de Provence
Ticket costs depend on the journey: adult, Nice–Annot return €24.40, child €19.50; adult Nice–Digne one way €17.95, under-4s €8, 4–12 €14. If you have a big family it's worth asking if they will give you a reduction for a *'famille nombreuse'*; depending who is on duty you may not have to have any official documentation or railcards. Trains run 4 times a day; the journey between Nice and Digne-les-Bains takes 3hrs 10mins
Trains leave from the Gare de Nice, **t** 04 97 03 80 80, on Rue Alfred Binet, just up from the main SNCF station and in Digne-les-Bains from the station on Av Pierre Sémard, **t** 04 92 31 01 58. Trains stop at Plan du Var, Puget-Théniers, Entrevaux (*see* p.103), Annot, Thorame and St-André-les-Alpes (This is the stop for Castellane, *see* p.101). There are steam trains in summer between Puget-Théniers and Annot

This is a great trip to take with little children. From Digne-les-Bains in the north of Provence, the Train des Pignes – the Pinecone Railway – rattles across the Gorges du Verdon on the way to Nice. At some points along the way the track runs at 3,000ft above sea level. It's a great journey and for fans of Thomas the Tank Engine, a dream outing. (Thomas mania is rife in France too; you can stock up on his adventures in the kids' section of most big bookshops.) Older children and teens may be less thrilled with the train, but the scenery is spectacular and there are lots of stops along the route so you can get off to walk or spend the night in any of the delightful towns along the way. If you don't have a car, it really is the best way to see the countryside and even if you do, it means you can relax and enjoy the view.

The Pinecone Railway is so called because, when it opened, the train ran so slowly you could jump off and pick up pine-cones from the side of the track. Today the carriages go at such a pace it's hard to stand up on board; keep hold of the little ones when the train pulls out of the station. Take your own food and drink but don't try to make sandwiches on board as the train shakes so much it's virtually impossible to put them together.

SOSPEL

Getting there There is a train from Nice that runs up the Vallée de la Roya and is one of the best ways of seeing the scenery, or there's a bus from Menton. By car it's 40km northeast of Nice on the A8 to junction 55, then the D2204. It's 5km from Menton on the A8 to junction 59, then the D2566
Tourist office Pont Vieux **t** 00 33 (0)4 93 04 15 80

This is a good place to base yourself or to stop for the night if you want to explore the Alps. From here you can drive into the Parc du Mercantour and the pretty villages of Lucéram and Saorge, where kids will have fun exploring the ancient alleyways. If you've been left disillusioned by the hilltop villages (*villages perchés*) close to the coast, the villages up here will revive your spirits.

No doubt you'll be chugging along in second gear to get to Sospel. The roads are steep but it's a popular area for biking holidays and the Monte-Carlo Rally roars round the hairpin bends in January. Think twice about bringing anyone who suffers from motion sickness.

The Vallée de la Roya only became part of France in 1947 and still feels more Italian than French; if you listen carefully you'll hear people speaking an Italian dialect and the local cuisine features excellent pizzas. The train journey up to the Italian border is one of the great rides in France and, by car, the D93 and N204 will take you straight to Italy.

Sospel is close enough to the coast for you to enjoy a quick dip in the sea or the bright lights of the Riviera. The town was badly damaged during the Second World War, but has been completely restored and has lots of character.

Stargazing

The air in Haute-Provence is the cleanest in France and here you'll find the least amount of clouds and fog in the country. The sky above the Gorges du Verdon, west of Digne-les-Bains and north of Castellane especially, is among the clearest in Europe. It's ideal if you want to put up your telescope and study the night stars and it is one place that you can see that all stars aren't necessarily the same colour: when you look at the stars in Orion here, for example, they burn blue, red and orange. Even without a telescope you can see an amazing amount with the naked eye, so pack a guide to the night sky. You may spot a shooting star or, depending on the time of year, a meteor shower.

If you are in the Alpes-Maritimes you could visit Astrorama at Eze, near Nice (*see* p.55) for more stargazing. For specialist astronomy shops, try Parsec in Nice, at 18 Avenue Maréchal Foch, **t** 04 93 85 85 58, which specializes in astronomical supplies, or Nature et Découvertes in the Centre Bourse shopping centre in Marseille (*see* p.129), which stocks telescopes and star guides for children. Other places you can visit with young astronomers are:

Centre d'Astronomie

St-Michel l'Observatoire, off the road from Forcalquier to Apt on the D5 **t** 04 92 76 69 09
www.astrosurf.com/centre.astro
Open Times vary according to activity
Adm Prices vary according to activity
This is by far the best place to come with young astronomers, as the centre organizes a range of different events and activities for children, including stargazing evenings. Themes change according to the time of year, so ring ahead to find out what's on.

Parc d'Astronomie du Soleil et du Cosmos

Av Charles de Gaulle, Les Angles, just outside Avignon **t** 04 90 25 66 82
Open Jan–Nov Tues–Sun 9.30–530. If you are in the area for a long time, keen junior astronomers who speak French might like to sign up for the Wed afternoon workshops aimed at 9–12-year-olds. Tours at 2.30 and 4
Adm Adult €6.10, child (5–12 years) €4.57
This is an astronomy theme park aimed at younger kids interested in space rather than science buffs, which includes, among other exhibits, mini-versions of the famous French Arianne rocket.

Observatoire de Haute-Provence

Near the Centre d'Astronomie **t** 04 92 70 64 00
www.obs-hp.fr
Open April–Sept Wed only 2–4, winter tour at 3 only
Adm Adult €2.30, child €1.50
This is for serious astronomy buffs with close-up looks at the telescopes.

Things to see and do

Fort St-Roch

t 04 93 04 00 70
Open July–Aug Wed–Mon 2–6, otherwise weekends only
Adm Adult €4, child €1.50

The fort was built in 1932 as part of the defences to keep the Italians at bay that included the Maginot Line. Eventually the Germans besieged the fort in 1944 and held out here until the end of the war. There's a small museum inside that explains what it was like to serve as a soldier in the fortress.

The Orient Express

Some of the coaches from the original train are in Sospel station. To visit, make an appointment on **t** 04 93 04 00 17.

AROUND SOSPEL

Nature lovers

Le Vallée des Merveilles

Hidden up in the Alps are some extraordinary pictures carved into the rocks thousands of years ago by the Bronze Age shepherds who grazed their sheep here. Carved over a period of centuries, they number in the tens of thousands, and include images of people, animals and tools, as well as abstract symbols such as spirals, circles and ladders. Why they are there has never been proven conclusively, but many archaeologists believe they mark the way to the summit of Mont Bégo, which was at that time regarded as a holy mountain.

The etchings can only be seen in the summer months, and to visit them you need to be fit and capable of hiking, so this is an expedition for sturdy teens. The best way to see these *merveilles* is with a guided tour, otherwise walking alone this high up can be dangerous. Tours are organized from the Bureau des Guides du Vallée des Merveilles, 11 Av du 16 Septembre 1947, Tende, **t** 04 93 04 77 73. Before you set off it's worth knowing that vandalism is a problem and that some of the originals carvings have had to be moved to a museum (*see* below) and have been replaced by copies.

Teenagers will also manage the 4hr walk from Coaraze to the abandoned village of Roccasparvière. According to a local story the village was abandoned because of a curse by Queen Jeanne of Provence. She had been forced to hide in the village from her enemies and while she was there someone in the village killed her twin sons and served them up for dinner. She vowed the day would come when no cocks would crow in the place, which is indeed the case today, although that is probably due to the well drying up. If you do hike up here, rent the film *Jean de Florette* when you get home; it's all about a feuding village and a well that mysteriously runs dry (*see* p.36).

Le Musée des Merveilles

Av 16 Septembre, Tende t 04 93 04 32 50
www.museedesmerveilles.com
Open Wed–Mon 10.30–6.30 (Sat until 9)
Adm Adult €4.57, child €2.29, under-7s free and to all on first Sun of the month

Sadly, the Vallée des Merveilles (*see* above) has suffered from vandalism in parts, and many of the images have been moved for safe keeping to this new museum. It has some excellent interactive exhibits and children's workshops, and will give smaller children, who might not be up for the invigorating climb in the valley, the chance to see the drawings.

Sporty kids

Breil-sur-Roya

There are two companies in the area that organize all sorts of outdoor activities. Water sports here are only suitable for older kids, as the current is very strong:

A E T Nature

Quartier Foussa t 04 93 04 47 64
e infos@aetcanyoning.com
www.aetcanyoning.com

Roya Evasion

t 04 93 04 91 46 e Roya.evasion@wanadoo.fr
www.royaevasion.com

Rail power!

Le Train des Merveilles

t 08 92 35 35 35

Driving can be heavy going along what must be some of the most winding roads in Europe, so if you can't face sick bags and grinding along in first gear, catch the train from Nice to Tende. It's a great ride and the best way to appreciate the scenery. Trains run daily from the main SNCF station in Nice and stop at Sospel and Tende.

VALBERG

Getting there It's 80 km from Nice on the N202 and then the D28, at an altitude of 1,610–2,100m. There's also a coach service from Nice bus station.
Tourist office Place du Quartier
t 00 33 (0)4 93 23 24 25 **www**.valberg.com

Of the 15 ski resorts in the Alpes-Maritimes the charming resort of Valberg is probably the best choice for a trip with children. It has been a resort since the 1930s, the only one to be given the label 'P'tits Montagnards', which means it has extensive family facilities and is well geared up for children of all ages. It is considered to be the place most locals would choose to spend the weekend.

Snowfall has been unreliable in recent years and the snow, when it comes, isn't as good for skiing as it is further north. For that reason there aren't any package deals to the Alpes-Maritimes from the UK and USA; it's somewhere to visit for a day or a long weekend.

The skiing season is from late December to early March but these days snow in the region can be somewhat scant, and all the main resorts are equipped with snow cannons if the heavens don't oblige. Not surprisingly the town is keen to promote itself as a summer resort, too, with walks, cycling and other outdoor pursuits.

Things to see and do

The slopes

There is a toboggan run and a ski school, Les Orsons (Bear Cubs), for children from the age of 3. The children's club Petits Poucets can cater for kids 14 months–6 years for the whole day (10–5). Weekend Enfants 'Ski Plus Evasion', ***t*** 04 93 02 51 20, has a Sunday club for ages 7 and upwards. They offer 6hrs of nonstop skiing, including lunch. Longer courses are available in the school holidays.

Espace Adventure

t 04 93 23 24 25

This is a huge forest climbing frame, or outdoor adventure playground, for anyone over 4 years old. It takes around 2hrs to do the circuit and tickets cost €10. There are also mountaineering workshops for kids that last 1hr 30mins and cost €14.

Essential items for skiing with kids

Generally, in French resorts, children who have not skied before can take lessons from the age of 5; younger children who can ski may also be able to take lessons. Nonskiers can toboggan, ice-skate, go on sleigh rides, make snowmen or ice sculptures or just enjoy a good old-fashioned snowball fight.

If you're planning on skiing you'll need to pack some non-woollen zip-up tops and body warmers in breathable materials, plus thermals and waterproofs. It's best to hire your equipment the first time you ski, but do pay particular attention to boot fittings and make sure your child is happy before they set off for the slopes; staff at the resorts will be able to advise on fit. Toddlers are unlikely to be able to communicate discomfort in cold conditions; let them run around and play rather than be cooped up in a pushchair for too long. If your child seems listless pick them up and go indoors; a warm bath and a hot drink should soon revive their spirits.

Include the following in their kitbag, with all items of clothing clearly labelled with their name:

- snowsuit/ski trousers and jacket
- waterproofs
- gloves (not wool)
- ski hat/bandana (not wool)
- ski socks (not wool)
- thermals
- a scarf or neck warmer
- ski helmet (also for hire on-site)
- snow boots
- lip balm
- sun cream (factor 25+, reapplied regularly)
- sunglasses
- goggles

Young Explorers, **t** 01789 414791, **www**.youngexplorers.co.uk, is a UK mail order company that specializes in stylish and affordable kids' skiwear.

Luge d'Eté

Télésiège du Garibeuil
Open July–Aug daily
Adm Ten rides cost €22.60

A *luge* is French for sledge, and this is a dry-ski-slope version of sledging, with separate circuits for adults and children.

AROUND VALBERG

Nature lovers

Parc National du Mercantour

Getting there The D2205 crosses the park

The park is in the highest part of the mountains along the border with Italy. It was founded in 1979 and is home to some of the most exciting wildlife in this part of France – chamois, mouflons, ibex, eagles, falcons and marmots. There are even a few wolves – the last in France. Bring some binoculars to spot the birds of prey.

The park is enormous and criss-crossed with trails, stretching 120km from the Col de Tende to Ubaye and including the mysterious Vallée des Merveilles (*see* p.106). It's a beautiful spot for walking and picnicking with a pretty waterfall, the Cascade de Lance, just 30mins' walk from town. It's clearly signposted in the town centre.

You can hire bikes and go riding at the Ratery ski station, **t** 04 92 83 40 92, on the D78 6km from town.

Mercantour National Park Office

23 Rue d'Italie, Nice **t** 04 93 16 78 88

The park headquarters are in Nice and the helpful staff can advise you on walks or sporting activities for children on offer in the park.

Can you spot...a chamois?

There are around 50,000 of these mountain goats out there somewhere in the Parc de Mercantour, though don't expect them to be friendly. After all, you do use one of their relatives to clean the windscreen on your car.

Good to know...tips for walkers

The French are keen on walking and you'll find plenty of walker's guides aimed at families. Most bookshops, newsagents and tourist shops will carry at least one title. Look out for the series *Les Sentiers d'Emilie* and *Balades en Famille*; both have easy-to-follow maps and prices are usually around €8.

Randoxygène is an annual guidebook published by the tourist office in Alpes-Maritimes, which lists services for walkers and is full of practical advice and tips. They also publish a useful book, *The Guide to Mountain Bike Excursions*, which has suggestions for family outings as well as the more serious stuff. Both books are available free of charge from the tourist office in Nice.

There are two useful websites, **www**.parcsnationaux-fr.com, which has a lot of information on walking, riding and biking in the national parks, and the website of the French ramblers' association, Fédération Française de la Randonnée Pédestre, **www**.ffrp.asso.fr.

Guidebooks and websites will make clear what you can and cannot do in the parks: for example, it's forbidden to pick flowers and collect fossils or rocks and access to woodlands is regulated in summer and in high winds due to fire risk.

If you are hiking in July and August, be sure to book space in the mountain refuges. Club Alpin Français in Nice has list of refuges that can be booked in advance, **t** 04 93 62 59 99.

Finally, it's important to pace whatever walk you plan to suit your children; ½km stroll can be enough for a four-year-old, especially if you factor in the amount of time spent looking at things en route. With little children walks are more about discovery than the challenge of actually getting somewhere.

Neige et Merveilles

t 04 93 04 62 40 **e** Neige.merveilles@wanadoo.fr

One of the few companies in the area that offer special walking holidays for families in the Alpes-Maritimes.

Gorges du Cians

This is a beautiful deep-red gorge carved out by the River Cians, between Valberg and Entrevaux on the N202 from Nice. At the church in Touët you can see the river rush by through a grill in the floor.

Sporty kids

You can try out the slopes at:

Auron

Getting there It's 97km from Nice; take the N202, then the D2205

Tourist office La Grange Cossa **t** 04 93 23 02 66

Auron is an unsophisticated, family-orientated resort suitable for beginners, with lots of kid-friendly restaurants and hotels. There are ski schools for all ages: Ecole de Ski Français has a mini-club with purpose-built facilities for kids aged 4–7 and a crèche for kids aged 2–5. Team Ecole de Ski Français Multiglisse offers courses at the weekend and during the school holidays for kids over 8. Kids over 5 can also try their hand at riding baby scooters and play in the snow garden. Prices are around €35 per day, **t** 04 93 23 02 53. When all that skiing palls, there are pony and sled rides and a big skating rink in the town centre.

Isola 2000

Getting there 76km from Nice **t** 04 93 23 28 00

Tourist office t 04 93 23 15 15

Isola was built by British architects and has a distinctly grey 1960s-concrete aura. It has good skiing and facilities but not a lot of charm. There's a children's ski club, Les Pious Pious, for kids from 4–7, which costs €47 per day.

Aquavallée

Isola **t** 04 93 02 16 49

Open Mon–Fri 11–8, Sat–Sun 10–8

Adm Adult €4, child €3

This may essentially be a ski resort but there's also a big water park where children can exhaust themselves in all manner of chutes, flumes and big waves.

WHERE TO EAT

There are plenty of inexpensive restaurants across the region. In large cities like Avignon, restaurants are open all year round, but in other places opening times will be more seasonal. In good weather, you can't beat eating in the open air, so bring a picnic basket. Remember, though, that in many parts of the South of France it's illegal to build a campfire or use a camping stove. Look out for signs and park regulations.

Avignon

Le St Louis

20 Rue du Portail Boquier **t** 04 90 27 55 55

Open Mar–Jan

Classy, Provençal cooking in one of Avignon's chicest new restaurants, where the chef will happily prepare something simple for the children. The restaurant is built into the arches of a 16th-century cloister where the kids can run around while you finish your meal in peace, and meals are served in the large walled garden in summer. In a bustling little city this is an oasis of calm.

Les Brantes

2 Rue Petite Fusterie **t** 04 90 86 35 14

This is an excellent value-for-money restaurant just off the Place de l'Horloge, popular with locals as well as tourists and with very friendly staff. The restaurant is air-conditioned but also has tables in a courtyard. There is a kids' menu (pizza, pasta, ham or steak *hachée*, plus drink and ice-cream) for €5.30.

Simple Simon

26 Rue Petite Fusterie **t** 04 90 86 62 70

Tearooms are the height of chic in Avignon. After seeing the sights, enjoy a cup of one of 15 different varieties of tea, with a scone or a Bakewell tart for a change from *pains au chocolat*. The restaurant is small, so large pushchairs and double buggies are tricky to manoeuvre.

Jusqu'à la Lune

9 Place du Cloître St-Pierre **t** 04 90 85 34 63

Tucked away in one of Avignon's prettiest squares, this restaurant serves basic crêpes and good salads at competitive prices. You can choose your own ingredients to put inside the crêpes – a must for fussy eaters.

Le Bercail

Ile de la Barthelasse, near Avignon t 04 0 82 20 22

This is a pleasant riverside restaurant with a good view of the Palais des Papes. There's a children's menu for €7.

Woolloomooloo

16 Rue des Tienturiers t 04 90 85 28 44

This curiously named eaterie is a fun restaurant to go to with the kids. The eclectic décor reflects the global cuisine and there's a children's menu, takeaway service and even home delivery. It's the place for a chicken tandoori fix and there's often live music.

Around Avignon

Le Mas des Aigras

Chemin des Aigras, Russamp Est t 04 90 34 05 66

Open Jan–Nov

Just north of Orange off the N7, this hotel-restaurant has some of the friendliest staff around and is popular with families. The gourmet chef is bubbling over with enthusiasm and happy to modify anything on the menu to suit junior taste buds, whipping up scrambled eggs if necessary. There's a large fenced garden and pool.

Fontaine-de-Vaucluse

Les Terrasses

Chemin de la Fontaine t 04 90 20 20 75

Good-value café on the banks of the river where you can watch the trout swimming by. There's a great view of the water wheel and the large terrace is quite safe for toddlers. The service is both speedy and friendly and the restaurant serves nonstop in season. The kids' menu (sausages, steak *hachée* or ham with chips, drink and ice-cream) costs €6.1 or there is a kids' pizza for €5.30.

Vaison-la-Romaine

The town isn't great for eating out but there are some good child-friendly restaurants in the area.

Hôtel les Géraniums

Pl de la Croix, Le Barroux t 04 90 62 41 08

Open April–Oct

Tucked away in a tiny hilltop village near Vaison-la-Romaine, this hotel has a great restaurant, with English-speaking staff. Meals are served outside in the summer on one of the two large terraces. Children's menu €7.75.

La Maison

Malaucene, Hameau de Piolon, just outside Beaumont du Ventoux t 04 90 65 15 50

Open Wed eve–Sun and April–Oct

A friendly restaurant with good food and a wide selection of child-friendly dishes.

Le Mas de Bouveau

Violes, Rte de Cairanne, just west of Gigondas t 04 90 70 94 08

Family-run hotel–restaurant serving local specialities.

Manosque

Le Petit Pascal

17 Promenade Aubert Millot t 04 92 87 62 01

Closed Sun and Mon eve

This hole-in-the-wall restaurant serves delicious Provençal cooking in a relaxed atmosphere.

Luberon villages

Bonnieux

Pizzeria la Flambée

2 Pl 4 Septembre t 04 90 75 82 20

Serves a good choice of dishes, from truffles to pizza, with wonderful views from the first-floor terrace.

Le Pont Julien

N100 north of Bonnieux t 04 90 74 48 44

This restaurant serves up local specialities at affordable prices, with plenty of lamb dishes, a speciality of the Luberon, and a children's menu for €8. There's a shady terrace as well. Main course from €11.

Gordes

Auberge de Carcarille

Rte d'Apt par D2 t 04 90 72 02 63

e carcaril@club-internet.fr

www.auberge-carcarille.com

Top-class cuisine in a relaxed atmosphere, with large garden and fantastic views of Gordes, one of Provence's most famous hilltop villages. Children's menu €9.50, adult menus from €15–35.

Le Bouquet de Basilic
Rte de Murs **t** 04 90 72 06 98
Open Fri–Wed, except Christmas–Jan

Fresh, organic and veggie-oriented food, good for lunch and dessert.

Le Renaissance
Pl du Château **t** 04 90 72 02 02

Good, basic food, consisting of pizzas, salads and omelettes. The bonus of eating here isn't so much the food as the beautiful setting. The café is set well back from the road so the kids can run around the fountain while you eat.

Roussillon

Bar Le Castrum
Pl de la Mairie

A friendly place to have a drink and an ice-cream. It's on the village square so kids can run about.

Mincka's
Pl de la Mairie **t** 04 90 05 66 22
Open Fri–Wed and April–Oct

Next door to Le Castrum, with a terrace overlooking the village square where the children can wander if they get bored. The restaurant serves good local dishes in a relaxed and friendly atmosphere. Best to book in advance. Menus from €15.

Castellane

Le Grilladin
26 Rte de Grasse, on the N85 **t** 04 92 83 72 04
Open June–Sept

Something to suit everyone, from local dishes to salads and pizzas, all served on a shady terrace.

Ma Petite Auberge
Pl Central **t** 04 92 83 62 06

Traditional food presented in a simple fashion in a beautiful setting just under Notre Dame du Roc. There's a large terrace and a big garden with huge, shady lime trees where you can eat out in summer. Local lamb chops a speciality. Menus from €14.

La Main à la Pâte
Rue de la Fontaine **t** 04 92 83 61 16
Open Wed–Mon and Feb–Dec

This is a simple restaurant serving good pizza.

Around Castellane

Le Moulin de la Salaou
Rte des Gorges du Verdon **t** 04 92 83 78 97

This fine old 17th-century mill has been converted into a hotel–restaurant with a romantic, leafy courtyard. The food is good and basic, the staff are friendly and there's a children's menu. Try the lamb if it's available. Menus from €9–22.

Sospel

L'Escargot d'Or
3 Bd de Verdun **t** 04 93 04 00 43

Sospel is a charming, relaxed town and a good place to escape the crowds along the coast. This restaurant serves first-class meals, most of which are regional specialities, on a terrace by the river. Booking essential in season. Menus from €10.

Around Sospel

Saorge

Lou Pountin
Rue Revelli **t** 04 93 04 54 90
Open daily except Wed in winter

If you're exploring the mountains along the Italian border this is a good place to stop for lunch. The village is spectacular and the restaurant serves up some great fresh pasta, ravioli, savoury flans and pizza. Menus from €8.

Le Bellevue
5 Rue Louis Périssol **t** 04 93 04 51 37

The big draw of this cheerful brasserie-cum-tearoom is the view from the panoramic windows.

Tende

La Margarita
Av de 16 Septembre **t** 04 93 04 60 53

Tende is so close to the Italian border it's no surprise that the pizza is excellent and this pizzeria is very popular with locals.

Valberg

Le Chalet Suisse

Av de Valberg **t** 04 93 03 62 62

If you're checking out the ski action this is a good place for fondue or a tasty pizza. There's a large, sunny terrace at the end of the slopes where you can watch the 007-wannabees do their turns. Children's menu €9.50; adult menu €19–21.

Around Valberg

Isola

Au Café d'Isola

Pl Jean Gaïssa **t** 04 93 02 17 03

Reasonably priced pizza and salad.

St Martin Vésubie

La Treille Rue Dr Cagnol **t** 04 93 03 21 06

Excellent pizza and pasta, served at weekends only in winter.

Western Provence

Bouches-du-Rhône

BOUCHES-DU-RHÔNE 116
Aix-en-Provence 116
Special trips from Aix 118
Around Aix 119
Arles 121
Special trips from Arles 124
Around Arles 126
Marseille 129
Special trips from Marseille 132
Around Marseille 134
St-Rémy-de-Provence 135
Around St-Rémy-de-Provence 137
WHERE TO EAT 139

Western Provence

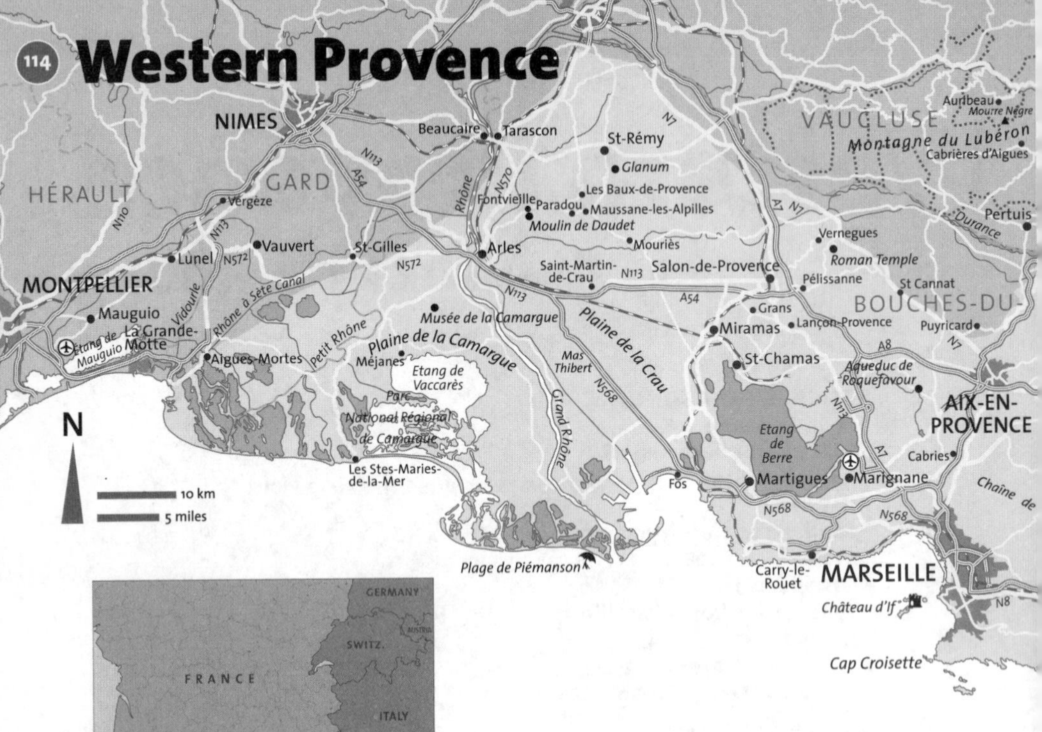

Although this is one of the more built-up and industrialized corners of the South of France it has beautiful countryside and fantastic sites to visit; in fact, there's so much to do, you'll be hard pressed to fit it all in on a single visit.

Among the many attractions are Aix-en-Provence, the perfect Provençal town; Arles, bursting with history; and the Camargue, with its flocks of flamingos and empty beaches. This is one corner of the South of France where it's possible to keep everyone happy.

There are lots of activities and attractions to enjoy, from sipping Roman drinking water and walking with dinosaurs to exploring the region's many interesting museums and wild open spaces. Nature lovers are spoilt for choice, with horse riding in the Camargue, walking in the Alpilles or sailing around the *calanques*, the dramatic coves east of Marseille. When planning your holiday, bear in mind that spring is the best time to see the Camargue – in summer it can be very hot and infested with mosquitoes. You can get the best out of Western Provence as a whole if you avoid the peak season entirely, but since the big towns are open for business all year round you won't be missing a thing and so it's an ideal choice for a short break at half term. If you plan to come in summer, try to book a hotel or villa with a swimming pool, as it's a long, hot drive to the beach.

Although this region has some of the best France has to offer, be prepared to encounter the worst as well. West of Marseille the main motorway runs through some of the most hideous industrial wasteland in Europe. The smell of petrol wafts through the air from the huge Fos oil refinery, creating a surreal backdrop to flamingo watching in the eastern Camargue, while to the north of St-Rémy the landscape is dominated by suburban market gardens.

It pays to be careful about location when you're booking your holiday. If you're planning a self-catering holiday, the best areas to rent a house are

Highlights

Reliving history in the Roman Ruins in Arles, p.121
Munching your way through the market in Aix-en-Provence, p.116
Watching pink flamingos in the Camargue, p.124
Hi-tech heaven – the Cathédrale des Images at Les Baux, p.137
Bobbing on a boat around the *calanques*, p.133
Picnicking in the Alpilles, p.129

either between St-Rémy-en-Provence and Arles, or in the beautiful countryside around Montagne Ste-Victoire near Aix-en-Provence. Hotels are good value here, and some of France's most family-friendly hotels are found in and around Arles (*see* p.227). For a seaside holiday, Stes-Maries-de-la-Mer or the famous cordial capital, Cassis, are both good family resorts to use as a base.

Such a perfect day

Morning Pay a visit to the Cathédrale des Images in Les Baux, p.136, then drive on to Arles, p.121, to see the amphitheatre
Lunch Eat at Le Calendal in Arles, p.140, the most child-friendly restaurant in France
Afternoon Admire the flamingos and take a dip in the sea in the Camargue, p.124

Special Events

May
Stes-Maries-de-la-Mer: Gypsy Festival
June
Tarascon: Tarasque Festival. A model of a terrible dragon – the '*tarasque*' – parades through the streets
December
Throughout the region: Christmas Markets selling all kinds of gifts, local festive sweets and mouthwatering pastries

AIX-EN-PROVENCE

Getting there The nearest airport is Marseille-Provence, **t** 00 33 (0)4 42 14 14 14, 25km from Aix. Air France flies daily to Aix from Paris Orly and there are direct flights from London. From the airport take a shuttle, **t** 00 33 (0)4 42 14 21 14, or taxi, **t** 00 33 (0)4 42 78 24 24. By car, if you're coming from the west or east you'll need to follow the A8, from the north the A51 and from the south the A52. It's 175km from Nice, 150km from Montpellier and 80km from Arles. The main bus and SNCF train stations are just a few minutes from the main centre and there are hourly train connections from Marseille. The TGV from Paris takes 2hrs 50mins and arrives at the station outside town, the Arbois Europôle. The bus station, with connections to local towns, is on Boulevard de l'Europe, **t** 00 33 (0)4 42 91 26 80
Getting around Aix is a small town and you can cover the sites easily on foot
Tourist office 2 Pl du Général de Gaulle **t** 00 33 (0)4 42 16 11 61 **www**.aixenprovencetourism.com
The tourist office website has a special children's page, which is useful if you're here for more than just a short holiday.
Special events March: Carnival, with huge parade through the streets. July: Dance Festival. December: Christmas Market and Fair, where you can buy santons, the traditional Provençal figures made to decorate the Christmas *crèche* (crib)

Aix is beautiful , the archetype of the southern French town and the sort of place you probably had in mind when you first thought of heading to the South of France for a holiday. It's a pleasure just to wander around the old streets and nibble your way through the market, followed by a drink in one of the cafés along Cours Mirabeau, perhaps the celebrated Deux Garçons, favourite of Emile Zola and Cézanne. Later, look at the old forum in Place des Cardeurs and stop for a snack at the child-friendly Chez Roger or one of the other restaurant terraces, and simply watch the world go by.

Aix is perfect for visiting with children. It's an easy town to explore and to relax in, as it's largely pedestrianized and very compact; the squares are as safe for toddlers to run in as the parks and gardens; and the university gives it a vibrant buzz that will appeal to teenagers.

Whether you choose to stay in the town itself or in the surrounding countryside, Aix is a great base for a family holiday. There are some beautiful, tranquil spots out towards Montagne Ste-Victoire and Aix is well situated for touring as it's close to the main east–west highway.

Shopping

Aix is full of gorgeous shops. Children will be interested to know there's a branch of La Cure Gourmande on 16 Rue Vauvenargues, where you can buy some delicious chocolates and sweets to take home. If you want to pick up local guidebooks or buy books in French, the best place to look is Goulard on Cours Mirabeau. Espace Tintin, also on Cours Mirabeau, is the place to pick up cartoon magazines and trinkets.

For accessories and all things sparkly, Kazana, at 29 Rue Maréchal Foch has an unusual selection of earrings, bracelets and necklaces that won't break the piggy bank. There's a good children's shoe shop Cendrillon (French for Cinderella) on Rue Thiers, which is also where you'll find the catalogue shop 3 Suisse, which is hugely popular with French girls.

Stylish kids will enjoy the T-shirts on sale in the market, but unfortunately they're not cheap. For good-value children's clothes try Du Pareil au Même on Rue Maréchal Foch, and for teenage girls there's Pimkie on Rue Bagniers.

If you want to buy *santons*, Santon Fouque at 65 Cours Gambetta is the place to go; they've been making them here since 1934. For toys, the best toyshop is JouéClub on Place Capeliers, but for something cheap and cheerful, buy toys in the market. There's a flea market in Place Verdun on Tuesday, Thursday and Saturday, and on Saturday nights in summer there's an evening market too.

Picnics and snacks

The market is Aix's main attraction. It's one of the best in France and is bursting with ready-to-eat picnic goodies, so skip breakfast and graze among the stalls here. You can buy home-made biscuits, cakes and masses of beautiful fruit. There's a market every morning but it's at its biggest and

Can you spot...Le Palais de Justice?
It's on Place Verdun. Things weren't always peaceful and civilized in Aix – witches were burnt on this spot in the Middle Ages.

Can you spot...a calisson?

These tiny marzipan biscuits have been made here since 1473 and today the local bakers make 200 tons of them a year. You can see calissons being made at Les Calissons du Roi René, La Pioline, t 04 42 39 29 89.

best Tuesday, Thursday and Saturday mornings. Aix is heaven if you have a sweet tooth: the local marzipan sweets – *calissons d'Aix* – are available at Calissons du Roi René, 7 Rue Papassaudi, and you'll find delicious handmade chocolates at Puyricard on Rue Rifle-Rafle. They're beautifully presented and make good presents to take home. If you've time, pay a visit to the factory, Chocolaterie Puyricard, **t** 04 42 96 11 21, on Route du Puy-Ste-Réparate in the village of Puyricard. It's just north of Aix off the N7.

For bread, Le Pain Quotidien on Place Richelme is a good place to buy crusty loaves and chocolate spreads for picnics; for more basic supplies there's a Monoprix supermarket on Cours Mirabeau.

Things to see and do

Cézanne's Studio

9 Av Paul Cézanne **t** 04 42 21 06 53
www.atelier.cezanne.fr
Open 10–12 noon daily and 2–5, April–Sept 2–6
Adm Adult €5.30, child €3.80

Cézanne was born in Aix in 1839 and painted many of his most celebrated works in his home town. The studio has been left exactly as it was when he last walked out, but in those days it was in the countryside instead of on the edge of a housing development, and was chosen for its clear views of Montagne Ste-Victoire, the subject of many of his paintings. All the everyday objects that appear in his still lifes are still lying around the studio where he left them, which, given that Cézanne was an intensely private person, can feel a bit voyeuristic, but there's a good audio-visual display and artistic kids will love it. You can pick up a leaflet, *In the Footsteps of Cézanne*, from the tourist office.

Musée d'Histoire Naturelle

6 Rue Espariat **t** 04 42 26 23 67
www.museumaix.fr.st
Open Daily 10–12 noon and 2–6
Adm Adult €3, child free

Most of the museums in Aix focus on fine art and are not that great for kids, so this makes a refreshing change. It's housed in a beautiful 17th-century mansion with fantastic doors and ceilings and is wonderfully old-fashioned, with exhibits displayed in elegant glass cases, including the plastic dinosaurs on sale at the ticket desk. As a nod to modernity, there is an interesting computer corner. The area around Montagne Ste-Victoire is known as the land of the dinosaurs and some of the oldest fossils in France have been found here, including a nest of eggs 60 million years old. You'll see some of the local finds here, as well as a reconstruction of a ferocious *Variraptor mechinorum* with terrifying talons.

French-speakers may be able to join palaeontologists from the museum on a local dig; call **t** 04 42 27 91 27 for details.

The Roman Baths

55 Cours Sextius **t** 04 42 23 81 82
www.thermos.sextiu.fr
Open Times vary, telephone in advance
Adm Free

The Romans founded Aix and built their town around this mystical hot spring. (Caius Sextus, the consul general who defeated the local Ligurian tribe at Montagne Ste-Victoire, built the baths in 122 BC and the city is, in part, named after him since the 'x' in Aix-en-Provence is in his honour.) But long

Dinosaur hunting

The South of France is full of tales of dragons and fierce beasts who hid in caves or on the banks of the River Rhône, so it will come as no surprise that the region is a dinosaur-hunter's paradise and home to some of the most important fossil finds in Europe.

In 1848 the first dinosaur bones to be found in France were unearthed on Mont Ventoux in Vaucluse. They were bones of a sauropod, a dinosaur similar to a diplodocus. This prompted intensive scientific study in the area, which established that 65 million years ago herds of dinosaurs roamed the forests and laid their eggs here. The best places to see fossils are in the rocks and cliffs near Sanary-sur-Mer and in the Haute-Provence Geological Reserve near Digne, where there's an extraordinary collection of ammonites.

Remember that it's illegal to collect fossils in national parks, so don't be tempted to disturb any rocks along the way.

Tell me a story: What was life like before the Romans arrived?

The Ligurians, a Gaulish tribe, lived here prior to the arrival of the Romans; the locals were known as Salyens and, like other tribes in the South of France, lived in fortified villages on the top of a hill, known to the Romans as *oppida*.

These houses were dug at least half a metre into the soil so that the floors were just below ground level. The interior consisted of just one room with a central fire that was constantly lit and was used for cooking, light and heat. The family would sleep on benches along the wall.

Their diet consisted mainly of stews and bread, and they drank beer and would already have been making wine by the time the Romans began their conquest of Gaul. In times of siege the village was self-sufficient; there would always be a spring and some fields inside the village walls, and in times of war the people from smaller nearby settlements would seek refuge within.

The Gauls were a warlike people and fought very fiercely in battle. In 52 BC their leader, Vercingétorix, a hero in France to this day (*see* **History** p.38) was defeated at Alésia, after which the whole of Gaul fell under Roman control.

before the arrival of the Romans, the local Celto-Ligurian women used to bathe here and believed the water aided fertility.

The baths are still popular with the ladies of Aix and are now a luxury spa. Unfortunately children aren't allowed in the modern baths but you can still see the ruins of the Roman baths in the foyer and have a quick swig of the water. It's a foul 36°C and is not dissimilar to drinking bath water.

Cinemas

Le Cézanne

Rue Marcel Guillaume **t** 04 36 68 72 70
www.lecezanne.com

This is the biggest cinema in the area, with 12 screens, so you're likely to find something for everyone here. Aix is quite a safe town, so teenagers should be fine going on their own.

Oppidum of Entremont

t 04 42 63 13 20
Getting there Off the D14, 4km north of Aix
Open Wed–Mon 9–12 noon and 2–6
Adm Free

Here you can visit the Salyens' settlement, which was a fortified town as early as 2000 BC. In its heyday up to 5,000 people lived here and you can still see the outline of their houses, but a visit here is more about getting the feel of the place and letting your imagination run riot.

Look out for... Je Colorie la Provence
This colouring book is full of pictures of the region's main sights. It costs €4.50 and is on sale in most tourist shops and newsagents.

Musée Granet

Pl St-Jean-de-Malte **t** 04 42 38 14 70
Open Wed–Sun 10–12 noon and 2–6
Adm Adult €1.50, child free

Here you can see the finds that were excavated at Entremont.

SPECIAL TRIPS FROM AIX

Salon de Provence

Getting there It's on the E80, 50km from Marseille and 41km from Avignon. The main bus station is on Place Morgan and there are train connections to all the main cities
Tourist office 55 Cours Gimon **t** 00 33 (0)4 90 56 27 60

Salon is a pretty town, even if it has something of a suburban atmosphere. Teens may find it a bit tame, but there is enough to see and do to warrant a day trip, although it's not somewhere you'd stay the night or base yourself. After all, Aix-en-Provence is just up the road.

Shopping

Salon has lots of good shops. For kids' clothes head for Orchestra on Cours Victor Hugo; Jouéclub on the same street is the place to go for toys.

Picnics and snacks

There's a Petit Casino on Rue Lafayette opposite the tourist office and a lively market on Wednesday mornings.

Château de l'Emperi

t 04 90 56 22 36
Open Tues–Sun 10–12noon and 2–6 (all day June–Sept)
Adm Adult €3, child €2.30

This château houses one of the best collections of military memorabilia in France and is the biggest of its kind in Europe. Two brothers are responsible for amassing the impressive collection, and it's enough to get toy soldier fans into a state of rapture. A whole army is arrayed across the length of the museum, which covers the period of French military history from Louis XIV to the First World War, including a fascinating collection of Napoleonic bits and pieces. Families with pushchairs will not find it that easy to get around.

Maison de Nostradamus

11 Rue Nostradamus **t** 04 90 56 64 31
Open 9–12 noon and 2–6, closed on Sat and Sun am
Adm Adult €4, child €2

This is the house in which the famous astrologer wrote his predictions, although you won't see anything of the original house, as today it belongs to the Grévin empire, the French version of Madame Tussaud's. Each room features instead a waxwork scene and the tour of the house takes you through stages of Nostradamus' life. There are tours in English and the audio tour plays automatically in each room. It's a tricky visit with little children; pushchairs need to be left downstairs and you have to go at the pace of the tour, so there's no rushing through if small people get restless. For older children with more patience it's an informative experience.

***Tell me a story:* Who was Nostradamus?**

He started life as Michael de Notredame in St-Rémy-de-Provence in 1503 but became Nostradamus when his father, a Jewish lawyer, converted to Christianity and adopted the Latin version of his name. Nostradamus trained as a doctor in Montpellier and, like many doctors at the time, became interested in astrology and began publishing his predictions in a yearly almanac. His most famous work is *Les Centuries*, first published in 1555, and he rocketed to international fame when the Queen of France became his main fan. In 1566 Nostradamus died of gout sitting in his chair – just as he had predicted.

Can you spot...a fighter jet?

Salon is famous for its Ecole de l'Air, where France's crack fighter pilots come to train. You'll see the planes screeching overhead and the cadets in all the bars in town. Flight training sessions are usually on Tuesday lunch times.

Musée Grévin de la Provence

Pl des Centuries **t** 04 90 56 36 30
Open Mon–Sat 9–1 and 2–7, Sun 10am–12 midnight July–Aug
Adm Adult €4, child €2.50

This is another Grévin venture, but is actually a very pleasant museum. There are waxwork scenes of all the main events and legends in the history of Provence, from the founding of Marseille to the films of Marcel Pagnol. There's an undeniably kitsch element, but the models are very good quality and it's worth visiting the museum in order to introduce some local history to the kids. There's an excellent audio tour in English.

Village des Automates

St-Cannat, 16km northeast of Salon
t 04 42 57 30 30
Open April–Sept daily 10–6; Oct–Mar Wed, Sat, Sun and school and bank hols 10–5
Adm Adult €7.50, child (3–14 years) €4.50

In the heart of the pine forest you'll find all your favourite fairytale characters come to life, from Aladdin to Gulliver. There are over 500 animated figures, a fairy-tale castle and a circus plus a playground, picnic area, café and shop. It's not worth driving miles out of your way for, but it's a fun outing if you are in the area.

AROUND AIX

Animal magic

Zoo de la Barben

t 04 90 55 19 12
Getting there It's 6km east of Salon; follow the D572 for Pélissanne and then St-Cannat
www.zoolabarben.com
Open Daily 10–6

Can you spot...Copain de la Provence?
This children's guide to Provence, Copain de la Provence by Sandrine Moirenc, might help children learning French to pick up a few new words on holiday. It's aimed at the over-8s and costs €22.56.

Adm Adult €9.20, child (3–12 years) €4.60; ask for a reduction if you have more than four kids over 3 – the youngest may get in free

This medium-sized zoo, perched on a hill just outside Salon, has a good selection of animals from around the world. If you want an outing to treat the junior members of the family this is the place to come, as all the animals they would expect to see are here. The views are great and you can look down on the Château de la Barben, where one of Provence's famous kings, René, used to live. If you're lucky, you'll also get to see the local fighter pilots in training. Rest assured the animals seem accustomed to the jets.

In the summer you can ride to the top of the hill on a small train. If you're visiting with a buggy, follow the route recommended for pushchairs (*les poussettes*) and you won't miss anything. There are plenty of picnic areas en route and a small café should the kids need refuelling.

Bricks and mortar

Abbaye de Thoronet

Draguignan **t** 04 94 60 43 90
Getting there Just off the N7
Open Daily 9–7 (5 in winter), except Sun lunch and in winter
Adm Adult €3.50, child free

The drive to Thoronet takes you over the border into Var; if you take the quiet D-roads avoiding the motorway it's a lovely journey. The abbey itself is in a beautiful valley full of lush vines, and if you're on your way to the coast, it's a good stopoff point because the motorway is nearby. There's nothing directed specifically at children here but the spot is delightful and if the kids are studying the Middle Ages at school, it's a good place to come and explain how an abbey worked. If you speak French the shop has some good books for kids too.

Thoronet was a Cistercian abbey, built in the 12th century, and around 20 monks and a dozen lay brothers once lived here. The highlight of the trip is just to sit quietly in the cloister; it's so relaxing that you can even manage this with tiny ones. Older children who like drawing will find it's a good place for sketching.

It is still in use as a religious building so make that clear before you go in.

Town life

St-Maximin-la-Ste-Baume

Getting there Just off the A8
Tourist office Hôtel de Ville **t** 00 33 (0)4 94 59 84 59
www.stmaximin.com

Although technically over the border in Var, this is a pleasant town to stop in for coffee and to buy a few croissants. It has lots of atmosphere, isn't too touristy and is just 2mins' drive from the motorway. In summer there's a weekly evening market on Saturdays. In the Middle Ages this was a

Fancy a walk...?

The Maison de la Nature et de l'Environnement, 2 Place Jeanne d'Arc, t 04 42 93 15 80, can advise you on walking near Aix. There are some easy walks around the Aqueduc du Roquefavour, west of Aix on the D64 and it's also fun to wander in the pine forests past the Château de Tholonet, off the D17; Cézanne painted Montagne Ste-Victoire from there. East of Aix, off the D10, you can walk by the Lac de Bimont – park either at the dam before the lake or after at Les Cabassols.

There's another good walk to the Grotte Ste-Marie-Madeleine at St-Maximin, which is an important pilgrimage site and is signposted from the town. According to legend Mary Magdalene landed in the Camargue and spent 30 years living in the cave just above the town. Her tears are cited as the source of the spring that starts in the cave. The walk is especially pretty in the autumn when the leaves are turning, but since it isn't on the main tourist agenda, it makes for a lovely summer outing, too. There are plenty more walks in *52 Balades en Famille autour d'Aix-en-Provence* by Jean Reynaud, available in bookshops.

busy place, where anyone who was anyone – kings, popes and the like – made a pilgrimage to see the relics of St Mary Magdalene in the convent. The holy objects are still paraded about in July.

Nature lovers

This may be a built-up corner of the South of France, but if you drive out along the road towards Montagne Ste-Victoire, you'll see why Cézanne was so captivated. On a sunny day the view is unbeatable. There's parking, toilets and a little café at the information centre, La Maison de Ste-Victoire, at the foot of the mountain.

ARLES

Getting there Nîmes/Arles airport is 25km from town; Marseille airport is 70km. By car Arles is on the A54 and is 30km from Nîmes. You won't be able to park in the town centre in summer but there are car parks around the city and a bus service to take you into town. There is a TGV from Paris daily, which takes just over 4hrs. Arles SNCF station is just a few moments' walk from the amphitheatre and there are plenty of local services. The bus station is on Avenue Paulin Talabot, **t** 04 90 49 38 01
Getting around Arles is a small town and everything except the Musée de l'Arles Antique is within easy walking distance
Tourist office Bd des Lices **t** 00 33 (0)4 90 18 41 20
www.ville-arles.fr www.arles.com
Special events March/April: At Easter there's a special festival, the *Feria*, with bullfights. May: Parade by the local Camargue cowboys, *les guardians*, on 1 May. June: St John's Day, 24 June, has dances with people dressed in traditional costume. September: Rice Festival, with more local music and traditions

Arles is a great town to take the kids with loads of atmosphere and plenty to see and do. You can use it as a base for exploring the Camargue and Les Alpilles or just visit for a fantastic day out.

Arles is packed out with top-class Roman remains incorporated right into the town rather than excavated and displayed in museums, which gives a sense of living alongside history. The best place to see this is in the old Forum and the amphitheatre, which is still used for bullfighting.

Good to know...Arles museum pass
It will save you money if you intend seeing all the main sites. Adult passes cost €12, children's €10. Passes are available from the tourist office, Bd des Lices **t** 04 90 18 41 20.

Arles is easy to get around on foot, and has lots of good family hotels, including the most child-friendly hotel in France, Le Calendal (*see* p.140).

Julius Caesar founded Arles as a garrison town; he called it Arelate, which means 'the town in the middle of a marsh' and he made sure there was plenty to keep the troops happy, including a theatre, an amphitheatre and a huge racetrack.

Arles soon became a very important Roman town. It was strategically positioned on the main road between Italy and Spain and at the mouth of the Rhône, and the three main Roman roads met here – the Via Aurelia, the Via Agrippa and the Via Regordane. Even now the main motorway still shoots past the southern suburbs of town following the Roman example.

Arles was a bustling trading city with a busy port and olive mills. Goods from remote parts of the Roman Empire were brought here and shipped across the Mediterranean.

Shopping

The main shopping streets are Rue de la République and Rue de l'Hôtel de Ville.

Marie Coquine on Rue de l'Hôtel de Ville has an unusual collection of toys and clothes, as well as the more usual cuddly Babars and plastic Asterix models. Les Bébés Troqueurs on 27 Rue du 4 Septembre has some stylish baby gear, some of which is second-hand.

Picnics and snacks

Boitel, 4 Rue de la Liberté, has a good selection of pizza, quiche and sandwiches to take away.

Did you know...?
Until recently Arles was home to France's oldest citizen. The longest-serving resident of the town, Jeanne Calment, died in Arles in 1997, at the extraordinary age of 120.

Can you spot...
the ruins of the aqueducts?
They're in the middle of the roundabouts on the outskirts of town. Originally they were used to bring fresh water into Arles for the public lavatories the Romans built in the town centre.

Eat them in the Jardin d'Eté. For basics, the Select garage on Boulevard Georges Clemenceau has everything you'll need. If you are looking for Provençal products, Les Délices de Mon Enfance, 22 Rue Copernic, sells delicious nougat and Provençal biscuits, and you shouldn't miss Charcuterie La Farandole, 11 Rue des Porcelets; they've been making donkey sausages, a regional speciality, since 1877. Even if you don't want to buy them it's worth the look on your children's faces when they realize what they're made of. On Saturday morning there's a great market on Boulevard des Lices, where you'll also find a McDonald's disguised as a French café. There are plenty of cafés in Place du Forum, including the Café du Nuit, made famous by Van Gogh.

Things to see and do

Les Arènes

Rond-Point des Arènes **t** 04 90 49 36 74
Open May–Sept daily 9–6, Oct, Mar–April 9–5.30, Nov–Feb 10–4.30
Adm Adult €4, child €3

Like much of the Roman architecture in Arles, the amphitheatre is still in use and bullfights are still held here. These are not Spanish-style fights to the death, but are known as 'course á la cocarde', where a ribbon is tied to the bull's horns, which the bullfighter must try to remove. It's still a dangerous business and a number of modern-day gladiators have been killed here; the seats for the ambulance crew are handily situated just above the main gate. If you want to take the children to a bullfight double-check that it isn't one of the occasional Spanish-style corridas where the bull is killed.

The amphitheatre was built in 90 AD and could seat 20,000 people. In the 8th century, when the Arabs invaded southern France, the amphitheatre became a fortress and people built their homes inside the walls – at one time it gave shelter to three churches and 212 houses. The castle-style towers were added in the Middle Ages.

The Roman Theatre

Rue de la Calade **t** 04 90 49 36 74
Open May–Sept daily 9–6.30; Oct, Mar–April 9–11.30 and 2–5.30; Nov–Feb 10–11.30 and 2–4.30
Adm Adult €3, child €2.20

The Emperor Augustus, who ruled immediately after Julius Caesar, had this 10,000-seater theatre built in the 1st century AD. After the fall of the Roman Empire it was used as a quarry. If you've already been to Orange you can save the entrance fee as you can see nearly everything from the road. For more about Roman theatres *see* p.171.

Thermes de Constantine

Pl de la République **t** 04 90 49 36 74
Open May–Sept daily 9–6.30; Oct, Mar–April 9–11.30 and 2–5.30; Nov–Feb 10–11.30 and 2–4.30
Adm Adult €3, child €2.20

These were once the biggest Roman baths in Provence. Originally, there would have been a furnace under the floor to heat the bath water and warm the rooms. In the excavations you can get a good view of the hypocaust heating system, a series of hollow bricks that sent a current of hot air under the floor and into the walls. It warmed the water at the bottom of the bath and the cooler water then sank to the bottom, creating an even temperature.

Keep a close eye on toddlers, as it can be very dangerous exploring the ruins.

Les Alyscamps

Av des Alyscamps (across the Bd de Lices, near the theatre) **t** 04 90 49 36 74
Open May–Sept daily 9–6.30; Oct, Mar–April 9–11.30 and 2–5.30; Nov–Feb 10–11.30 and 2–4.30
Adm Adult €3.50, child €2.60

Roman law forbade burials within the town walls, so cemeteries like this grew up outside the city. Then, as now, the more prosperous families built large tombs as an indication of their status. If you are travelling with toddlers who need to let

Did you know...?
The Romans were responsible for calling this part of France 'Provence', see History p.38. After they conquered the South of France, it was absorbed into the Roman Empire and given the rather unimaginative name of Provincia.

off steam but you don't want to miss out on the sightseeing, this is a good place to head. It's a shady and mystical place – just as it is in the eponymous painting by Van Gogh – and it was used as a cemetery right up to medieval times.

Cryptoportiques du Forum

Rue Balze **t** 04 90 49 36 74
Open May–Sept daily 9–6.30; Oct, Mar–April 9–11.30 and 2–5.30; Nov–Feb 10–11.30 and 2–4.30
Adm Adult €3.50, child €2.60

This eerie underground cellar is much like a church crypt in style, yet is believed to be where the Romans stored their food. It gives a good indication of how sophisticated Roman towns were, with their tall buildings and cellars.

Musée d l'Arles Antique

Presqu'île du Cirque Romain **t** 04 90 18 89 08
Open Daily 9–7, Nov–Feb 10–5
Adm Adult €5.35, child (12+) €3.80, under-12s free

Although the museum is a bit of a walk from the centre, don't miss it out. It is on the site of the old Roman circus, which was a huge racetrack, and inside you'll see some great models of Roman Arles: there's a reconstruction of the town as it would have been in the 4th century and a model of the circus where 20,000 people would crowd in to watch the chariot races. Visit it after you've seen the ruins; it really helps to bring monuments such as the theatre to life. Don't miss the model of the Barbegal mills, where tons of flour were ground every day. (If you've got a car, you can drive up into hills and see the real thing, *see* p.128.) There's also an interesting collection of jewellery, sculptures, mosaics and pots.

Who were the gladiators?

The first gladiators were prisoners of war and slaves but by the time of the Roman emperors they included freemen and professional fighters – there were even a few female gladiators. Before they fought in the arena they trained at a special school. The crowds were very active in these gladiatorial contests. For example, if a gladiator was wounded and could not continue the fight he could appeal for mercy; but if he got the 'thumbs down', decided by the emperor, often egged on by the crowd, he would be put to death. As well as each other, gladiators fought all manner of wild animals, such as lions, elephants and crocodiles.

Tell me a story: Who was Frédéric Mistral?

One of the reasons French governments have placed so much emphasis on centralization is that France is at heart a very decentralized place. Just over 150 years ago, people in this part of France even spoke a different language – Provençal. That was not considered good for national unity and French was decreed the official language for schools, the government, the military and the media. Frédéric Mistral, a poet from the area, determined to dedicate his life to preserving his mother tongue and local traditions. According to legend, this was prompted by his mother's tears at not being able to understand his poems in the French language, so he decided from then on to write in Provençal. He and five other poets set up a literary movement to promote the Provençal language, and their efforts were finally recognized in 1904 when Mistral won the Nobel Prize for Literature. Look out for his statue in the Place du Forum – the inscription is in Provençal.

Museon Arlaten

29 Rue de la République **t** 04 90 93 58 11
Open Oct–March daily 9.30–12.30 and 2–5; June–Aug 9.30–1 and 2–6; April–May and Sept 9.30–6
Adm Adult €4, child €3

This is a really old-fashioned museum where the floorboards creak and the blinds are drawn to keep out the summer sun. It is housed in a 15th-century palace built on top of and into the remains of the old Roman forum. It was founded by the poet Frédéric Mistral, who dedicated his life to preserving and promoting local Provençal customs. Among the collections are many intriguing little artefacts that will catch the children's attention, especially if you're staying in an old farmhouse and may have come across them before. There are also some interesting life-size scenes showing how people used to live in Arles. Look out for the reconstruction of the traditional Christmas Eve feast and the famous Tarasque monster (*see* p.128).

This is also the one place you're guaranteed to see women wearing the traditional lace shawls and headdresses of Arles. Mistral specified that the attendants dress up like the heroine of his poem 'Mireille' (*see* p.126).

Need to let off steam?

The Jardin d'Eté, just behind the theatre on Bd des Lices, has a good playground and is the best place to have a quick picnic.

Planète Crèche

10 Pl Louis Blanc **t** 04 90 93 05 91
Open Daily 10–7
Adm Adult €3, child €2

You'd be forgiven for thinking that the Christmas nativity crib or *crèche* was unique to Provence; in fact, 79 countries worldwide also have cribs at Christmas. You'll find 100 of them in this museum. Tiny tots who are thoroughly fed up with the Romans will love it.

Le Petit Train d'Arles

t 04 90 18 41 20
Runs June–Sept from Bd des Lices, ride lasts 40mins

If you are pressed for time, the best way to catch all of the monuments in town is to ride on the tourist train.

Boat trips

A fun outing is to take a boat down river to the Camargue. Trips are organized by Bateau Odyssée, **t** 04 90 49 86 08. If boats aren't your thing, Camargue Safaris Gallon Organisation, 38 Avenue Edouard Herriot, **t** 04 90 93 60 31, run trips in 4-wheel-drive vehicles, **www**.camargue.com.fr.

SPECIAL TRIPS FROM ARLES

The Camargue

Getting there The Camargue is just south of Arles. Follow the D570; the road splits as you arrive in the Camargue. The D36 takes you down to the salt capital of France, Salin-de-Giraud, and the D570 carries on to Stes-Maries-de-la-Mer

You'll need a car to explore the area properly with children, but even the most travel-weary kid will sit up and take notice of the Camargue. It's absolutely unique, with flocks of flamingos rising up from the reeds like pink clouds.

There are about 10,000 flamingos in the Camargue, so this won't be one of those bird-watching experiences that demands hours of patience – you can't miss them. Even in autumn when they fly off for warmer climes, at least 2,000 stay in the marshes all year round. The best place to see them is at the Etang du Fangassier. In winter you can ski in the Alps in the morning and watch the flamingos flying before you go to bed. It's a truly extraordinary experience.

Among the other animals in the area, you may see the Camargue's white horses (which are, in fact, born brown but turn white when they are four years old). For French children they're immortalized in the classic film *Crin Blanc*, a real tear-jerker about a peasant boy and his affinity with a wild Camargue horse.

Keep an eye out for bulls, too – they're raised for bullfighting and a lot are exported to Spain, while the meat is a local speciality which you'll see on all the restaurant menus in the area. The animals live semi-wild and are cared for by local cowboys, who are called *gardians*.

Parc Ornithologique du Pont de Gau

Getting there 4km before Stes-Maries-de-la-Mer on the D570, **t** 04 90 97 82 62
Open Daily 9 (10 in winter) until sunset
Adm Adult €7.50, child (under 10) €4 with guided tour; adult €4.25, child €2.50 without

This park cares for lots of sick and injured birds. Most of them are returned to the wild but those that are too weak are kept and form part of a breeding programme. If your French is up to it, it really is worth taking the guided tour, but even if not, this is a great place to bring the kids face to face with nature, with pathways that wind their way through the marshes (*marais*).

Good to know...

The climate in the Camargue is harsh, with freezing winter winds and tortuous summer heat, so when exploring, don't forget to pack a sunhat in summer and wrap up warm in winter. Whatever time of year you come, be prepared for mosquitoes and make sure you lock your car, as theft is a major problem. There are very few shops, so bring some basic supplies and make sure you have a full tank of petrol. A pair of binoculars for bird spotting will also be useful.

Fancy a walk...?

There are organized walks from Le Domaine de la Palissade, on the D36 near Salin-de-Giraud, **t** 04 42 86 81 28, open daily 9–5.

At the Marais de Pont-de-Gau you can see swans, ducks, geese and flocks of flamingos and at the Marais de Ginès you can watch the birds from special lookouts. In the height of summer it's best to visit in the early morning or evening, as there aren't any trees and the sun can be fierce. Bring a bottle of water and come prepared for mosquitoes, whatever the time of year.

The visit takes about 2hrs and there's a pleasant café to relax in afterwards.

Horse riding

The best way to explore the Camargue is on horseback and there are numerous farms that hire out horses and give guided tours. Most farms, however, only let over-7s ride.

The Association Camarguaise de Tourisme Equestre, at the Centre des Ginés, Pont de Gau in Stes-Maries-de-la-Mer, **t** 04 90 97 86 32, will be able to advise you on horse riding in the area.

Les Cabanes de Cacharel

Rte de Cacharel **t** 04 90 97 84 10
www.camarguecheval.com
Getting there Just outside Ste-Maries-de-la-Mer on the D85A

Horses for hire, plus pony and trap rides for those who can't ride or who are too small. Trips last anything from 1hr to a whole day, starting at €10 per person for the pony and trap and €13 for a horse only.

Did you know...?

If sea levels rise just 50cm, at least half of the Camargue is likely to disappear. If you climb up to the top of the church tower in Stes-Maries-de-la-Mer you'll see it's just a stone's throw from the beach, but in the Middle Ages it was 2km away from the sea! Some scientists predict the Camargue could disappear in the next 100 years, so see it while you still can.

Other ways to explore the Camargue

As well as the suggestions below, you could also try hiring a bike or taking a boat trip from Stes-Maries-de-la-Mer, *see* p.126.

Domaine de Méjanes

Etang de Vaccarès **t** 04 90 97 10 10
Open Mar–Sept 9–6, Oct–Nov 10–4

If horse riding isn't your thing you can jump on the little train that runs around the lake. Sundays and bank hols from Easter–July you can watch the *guardians* show off their skills in the *ferrades*, where the bulls are branded.

Les Marais du Vigueirat

Mas Thibert, on eastern edge of the Camargue
t 04 90 98 70 91

If you can't ride you can explore the countryside from the back of a horse and cart. Trips run May–Aug and last 2hrs; adult €8 and child (under 12) €6.

Stes-Maries-de-la-Mer

Getting there It's on the D570, 40km south of Arles. There's a regular bus service from Arles
Tourist office 5 Av Van Gogh **t** 00 33 (0)4 90 97 82 55 **www**.saintesmariesdelamer.com
Special events May: Gypsy Festival (you'll hear a lot of Gypsy music around here; the Gypsy Kings are from Arles). July: Fiesta Vierginenco, with traditional costumes

Stes-Maries-de-la-Mer itself is a busy resort with a lot of choice for activities – shops, boat rides, bullfights, horse rides and water sports – but it's all fairly low key and family orientated. It's a good place to be based for exploring the area, with plenty of accommodation (elsewhere in the Camargue accommodation is limited). The nicest hotels are out of town on the edge of the marshes.

Picnics and snacks

There's a Petit Casino supermarket on Rue Victor Hugo, where you can stock up on picnic supplies. Pâtisserie Feline, on the same street, has nice cakes.

Things to see and do

The Church

Pl d'Eglise **t** 04 90 97 87 60
Open Crypt: daily 8–12 noon and 2–6 (closed during services)
Adm Free; small charge to climb the tower

Tell me a story: The Gypsy Pilgrimage

Legend has it that the aunt of Jesus, Mary Jacob, along with Mary Magdalene and Mary Salome, the mother of the apostles James and John, landed on the beach at Stes-Maries-de-la-Mer after fleeing Palestine in a tiny boat, which is how the village got its name. Their servant Sarah became patron saint of the Gypsies and every May Gypsies from all over Europe descend on the town to see the statue of Sarah and her relics, which normally reside in the church, carried down to the sea to be blessed. It's a colourful event with plenty of Gypsy music and costumes but, unfortunately, it's now heavily policed and sometimes resentment between the townsfolk and Gypsies can get somewhat out of hand.

One of the first things you'll notice about the church is its lack of windows. This is because churches here had to double up as fortresses for the whole village to take refuge in when pirates were spotted along the coast. In the crypt you'll find a statue of St Sarah and her relics – she's the patron saint of the Gypsies and every year in May the statue is carried down to the sea and blessed by the bishop of Arles (*see* Gypsy Pilgrimage, box). Climb the tower for stunning views.

Bikes

Le Vélo Saintois

19 Av de la République **t** 04 90 97 74 56

The whole of the Carmargue is accessible by bike and since it's quite small, the distances are manageable with kids. This company can arrange to deliver bikes to your hotel; prices are around €15 a day. The tourist office (**t** 04 90 97 82 55, open daily 9–8) has a list of itineraries and can advise on which are suitable for different age groups.

Boat trips

One of the best ways to see the Camargue is from a boat. There are lots of companies operating tours:

Tiki III

t 04 90 97 81 68 **www.**tiki3.fr

Getting there Route d'Aigues-Mortes, follow the D38 west out of Stes-Maries-de-la-Mer and take the turning for the Camping Le Clos du Rhône,

Open Mid-March–mid Nov daily, sailings at 10am, 2.30pm and 4.15pm (11.15am during school holidays, 6pm July–Aug)

Tickets Adult €10, child €5

This trip aboard an atmospheric paddle steamer heads into the Camargue up the Petit Rhône and as far as the Bac du Sauvage. Halfway through the trip the boat stops so you can get a close-up look at the horses and bulls and meet a real Camargue *guardian*. The boat has toilets and a buffet. The trip lasts 1 ½hrs, which should be about right for kids.

Kayak Vert Camargue

Stes-Maries-de-la-Mer **t** 04 66 73 57 17

Hires out canoes for one or two people, with room to pop a little one in between the adults in a two-person canoe. Jackets, paddles and a plastic container for storage are included. Wear a tracksuit and pack some sun cream, a picnic and bring lots of bottled water.

Can you spot...Mireille?

Her statue is in the main square north of the church. The poet Mistral once saw a young girl from Beaucaire throw herself on the altar of the church, praying for the return of the lover who had abandoned her. It inspired him to write his famous poem 'Mireille' about a well-off farmer's daughter who fell in love with a basket-weaver. Her father refused to let her see him so she ran away to Stes-Maries-de-la-Mer to ask the saints for help. Her lover found her there, exhausted by the arduous journey, and she died in his arms.

AROUND ARLES

Bricks and mortar

Château du Roi René

Bd du Roy René, Tarascon, **t** 04 90 91 01 93

www.monuments-france.fr

Getting there It's on the D99, just off the N570 south of Avignon. There are train and bus connections from Avignon.

Open April–Sept daily 9–7, Oct–Mar Wed–Mon, 9–12 noon and 2–5

Adm Adult €5.50, child free

When Provence was a kingdom of its own, this was a frontier town and the two giant castles on either side of the River Rhône are proof that it wasn't that friendly with its neighbours.

The castle at Tarascon is one of the best medieval castles in France. It was the home of the Provençal King René and looks just like the Bastille prison in Paris did before it was destroyed during the French Revolution. There's a great view from the castle roof across the Rhône, although today, unfortunately, it takes in a lot of industrial sites.

The inside may look a bit tame but that wasn't always the case – during the French Revolution both revolutionaries and counter-revolutionaries were thrown to their deaths from the battlements. After that the castle was a prison from the 18th century right up till 1926.

Buckets and spades

The Camargue has some beautiful, wild beaches, with among the best at the seaside resort of Stes-Maries-de-la-Mer. If you drive on past the salt works at Salin-de-Giraud, you'll find lagoons full of flamingos and a large beach, the Plage de Piémanson, which is a good spot to have a picnic and run around but isn't safe for swimming. From here you can see the whole of this corner of France summed up in one ironic image, as the majestic flamingos fly against the backdrop of the distant oil refinery at Fos. Keep and eye out too for distinctive yellow camomile flowers.

Look at this!

La Petite Provence du Paradou

75 Av Vallée des Baux, Paradou **t** 04 90 54 35 75
Getting there Off the road from Arles to Salon on the D78E
Open June–Oct daily 10–7, Nov–May 2–7
Adm Adult €4.50, child €2.50

This model village is a replica of rural Provence at the beginning of the 20th century, with over 300 little figures going about their Provençal business in the school, in the marketplace and at work on the farm. It's a good stop off once you've done a few of the sights – even the junior members of the family will recognize the models of the local attractions like the waterwheel at Fontaine-de-Vaucluse – but watch out for the raised platforms designed to help the kids see better . They're too narrow and can be dangerous. The tour takes about 30mins.

Fancy a souvenir...?
You can pick up a free sticker at the ticket desk.

Musée des Santons Animés

Getting there On the D5, 4km from Baux, direction Mausanne **t** 04 90 54 39 00
Open April–Sept daily 10–7, Oct–Mar 1.30–7
Adm Adult € 3, child € 1.50

Santons are the traditional clay figures made to decorate the Christmas crib, but in this part of the world they make them in the form of local characters too. Look out for Van Gogh and Daudet among the more usual nativity figures.

The museum is smaller but more accessible than La Petite Provence du Paradou (*see* above), and little ones will enjoy pressing the buttons to activate the models. There's a child-friendly gift shop where you can buy the tiny bits and pieces that go with the *santons* – rolling pins, pots, pans, etc – that make great additions to a dolls' house.

***Tell me a story:* Blanquette**

All over this corner of Provence you'll see tiny plastic model goats in the souvenir shops. That's because one of Daudet's most famous stories is about a little goat called Blanquette. She's as famous as Peter Rabbit but unfortunately she had about as much luck as Peter's father. Blanquette was one of seven goats belonging to Monsieur Seguin; each of the previous six had run away and were eaten by the local wolf. Seguin was very proud of Blanquette, a beautiful little white goat, and tried to keep her from running away. When she began chewing on her rope he locked her in the barn, but she escaped by jumping out of the window. At first she was very happy drinking from the mountain stream and nibbling at the bushes, but when darkness fell she encountered the wolf and things turned nasty. Blanquette was very brave and fought off the wolf all night long, but as the sun rose she fell down exhausted and the wolf ate her up.

Fancy a souvenir...?

The shop in the Moulin d'Alphonse Daudet is tiny but it sells copies of Daudet's tales in translation as well as in French. You can also buy a model of Blanquette (*see* p.127). If you're interested in Daudet head over to Tarascon to visit the museums there, as well.

Moulin d'Alphonse Daudet

Getting there Just outside Fontvieille off the D17
t 04 90 54 60 78
Open 9–12 noon and 1.30–6, (10–5 in winter)
Adm Adult €2, child €1

There isn't a Frenchman who hasn't heard of Alphonse Daudet. At school you can't escape his famous stories *Lettres de mon moulin* (Letters from My Windmill), which were published in 1866. Daudet was born in Nîmes in 1840 and although he loved Provence his stories often make fun of the locals, especially their Walter Mitty-like imaginations and their love of food. He was like a French fusion of Beatrix Potter and Thomas Hardy.

Some sticklers complain that this isn't the actual windmill that Daudet wrote about – it was in fact just round the corner – but it doesn't make any difference: he never lived in a windmill anyway but in a large château.

This is a nice place for a stroll, with clear views from the top of the window, especially of the industrial suburbs of Beaucaire. That doesn't matter, either, as the industrialization of rural Provence was exactly what Daudet was writing about and he probably would have seen the funny side of modern-day Provence, too.

Maison de Tartarin de Tarascon

55 Bd Itam **t** 04 90 05 08
Open April–Oct Mon–Sat 10–12 noon and 2–7, Nov–Mar 10–12 noon and 1.30–5
Adm Adult €1.50, child €0.80

After the Tarasque, the most famous resident of Tarascon is Tartarin – a character invented by Daudet. He's the caricature of a Provençal man who loves telling tall tales.

Le Monde Merveilleux de Daudet

Av des Arènes **t** 04 90 91 07 70
Open 22 Mar–31 Oct daily 2–6; July–Aug and school hols 10–12 noon and 2–6
Adm Adult €6.10, child (5–12 years) €4.50, under-5s free

This is a good place to bring the kids to explore the world of Daudet's tales. Little ones will love it because just behind the museum you'll find the live versions of the farm animals in the stories.

Barbegal

Just up the road from Daudet's windmill off the D82 you'll see the sign 'Meunerie Romaine', which leads to the remains of a 4th-century industrial flourmill. Water would have poured into mill on the south side and activated eight successive mills, grinding 300kg of flour an hour and showing just how close the Romans were to an industrial revolution. You can see a model of the mill in the museum in Arles (*see* p.123).

Tell me a story: A monster tale

Local legends tell of the monstrous Tarasque, who lived on the banks of the River Rhône many years ago. According to the stories, the Tarasque was massive – as big as 12 elephants – with the head of a lion, the body of a gigantic crocodile , six legs and a long spiky tail. Its claws were long and terrible and it had skin like iron and teeth like swords. It destroyed all the bridges across the river, and ate up anyone who dared to swim or sail across, and was especially fond of eating children. All the daring feats and plans the locals dreamt up to snare the monster were unsuccessful; even brave knights who travelled from afar could not kill it. The villagers became so desperate that they thought they would have to abandon their homes.

Then one day Saint Martha happened to pass through the area. The villagers begged her to stop and help, so without hesitation she walked down to the riverside. She was a beautiful young woman and very brave. Barefoot and armed only with a jug of holy water she went up to the very edge of the river. She began to sing and soon the riverbank started to shudder and the beast appeared, but instead of gobbling up the saint, the monster fell down at her feet, wriggling like a puppy. Saint Martha put a belt around his neck and led him into the town, where he was duly despatched by the populace. When his stomach was cut open out jumped the chivalrous knights who had tried to kill him. The people named the town Tarascon after the monster and every year in June they parade an effigy of him round the streets. It isn't that scary these days, though – the effigy is full of sweets. For more information see **www**.tarascon.org

Town life

Salin-de-Giraud

Getting there Follow the D36 south of Arles
Tourist office Next to the town hall (Hôtel de Ville) **t** 04 42 86 80 87

The town is on the other side of the Camargue from Stes-Maries-de-la-Mer and is the industrial face of the Camargue, but it's actually far more interesting than appearances would have you believe. Salin is a town that lives off its saltworks and just on the outskirts there are huge mountains of the stuff, harvested by a process of evaporation. The Romans were the first to harvest salt here and today the Camargue is the most important salt-producing area in Europe. To see the salt mountains close up catch the Petit Train des Salins, **t** 04 42 48 81 87. It runs tours of the saltworks April–Oct, every 30mins from 10–12 noon and 2–7.

Musée du Riz

Rue de Salin Giraud, Le Sambuc **t** 04 90 97 20 29
Open Daily 8.30–12 noon and 1.30–5
Adm Adult €3.80, child Free

Rice-growing is the other big business around here, with red rice the local speciality. After the Second World War part of the northern marshes of the Camargue were drained and the water replaced with fresh water, so rice could be planted. This museum is a slightly curious, one-man-band type of affair, so if you can, get chatting with the owner, who's a very interesting character. There are good rice cakes on sale in the shop.

Rail power!

Le Train des Alpilles

17 Av de Hongrie **t** 04 90 18 81 31
Runs from Arles to Fontvieille, trip takes 40mins Mid-April–Sept Wed and Sat, rest of year Wed only
Departs 10, 1.30 and 3.10 from Arles, 10.50, 2.20 and 4 from Fontvieille

The journey isn't particularly outstanding, but if the kids like trains this is a fun way to get out into the countryside, particularly if you need a break from the car. The adventure of riding on a real diesel engine will enchant Thomas fans.

MARSEILLE

Getting there All the main autoroutes in the South of France lead to Marseille. The city is accessed via the A7, A55 and A50. You can park at the Centre Bourse near the Vieux Port. The airport is 22km out of town at Marignane, **t** 00 33 (0)4 42 14 14 14, **www**.marseille.aeroport.fr. The TGV from Paris takes 3hrs, and arrives at the main station, the Gare St-Charles, t 04 91 54 42 61. From there the metro will take you directly to the old port, or there is a shuttle bus from the station every 20mins during the day and early evening. For a taxi call, **t** 04 91 02 20 20. The bus station is on Place Victor Hugo, **t** 04 91 08 16 40. Ferries sail to Algeria, Corsica, Sardinia and Tunisia; contact SNCM, **t** 08 36 67 95 00
Getting around The metro has two lines and runs from 5am–9pm. This is the quickest way of getting around and is perfectly safe but not very accessible for pushchairs. Metro tickets last one hour and are also valid for the bus
Tourist office 4 La Canebière **t** 00 33 (0)4 91 13 89 00 **www**.marseille-tourisme.com
Special events September: Kite Flying Festival on the Plage du Prado. October: Folklore Festival December: Santon Fair; Christmas Parade

Marseille's reputation is such that you might think it has little to offer children.

It's dirty, dusty and busy, with one of the biggest ports in the Med but you'll learn a lot more about France here than you will encounter lounging on the beach in the Riviera. If you're used to big cities like New York or London there's nothing going on in Marseille that will surprise you.

Zinedine Zidane – a football legend

Zidane is Marseille's native son, born here in 1972 to Algerian parents who had come to the city as part of the large influx of Algerians who arrived in the 1960s in search of work. When France won the World Cup in 1998 he became a national hero and even though he now plays for Italy he is adored in his native city. Zidane's achievement was particularly welcome in a country that suffers from racial tensions and he became a great role model for the country. There's a huge mural of him at 82b Corniche President JF Kennedy. Find out more on his official website, **www**.zidane.fr

Tell me a story: Gyptis and Protis

This story relates to the founding of Marseille by the Greeks over 2,600 years ago. The Celtic king of Provence was looking for a husband for his daughter Gyptis. According to local tradition, a huge banquet was arranged during which Gyptis was to offer a drink of water to the man she had chosen to marry. By chance, a Greek ship landed on the coast a few days before the feast, so the king invited the Greeks and their leader Protis to join them. To everyone's surprise, during the banquet Gyptis chose Protis as her future husband. As a wedding present, the king gave the happy couple a piece of land along the coast, where they later founded a new city called Massalia. The remains of the ancient Greek city of Massalia were found in modern-day Marseille when the Centre Bourse shopping centre was being built. There's a small museum in the basement (*see* p.132).

It's certainly not somewhere you'd spend the whole of a family holiday, but it is worth scheduling in some time here to see the sights and it's usually worth a stopover. Teens tend to enjoy Marseille's easy-going atmosphere and buzz, and because a lot of the budget airlines now fly here it has become quite a hip holiday destination. People are friendly and genuinely like children, it's not too touristy and if you don't mind the litter it makes a refreshing change from the glitz further down the coast. The downside is there's plenty of racial tension, although there was a huge demonstration against the extreme right during the 2002 presidential elections.

Marseille is France's oldest city, so there's lots of history to soak up and a wide variety of things to do. Originally founded by the Greeks, it was later ravaged by Caesar because it sided with his great enemy, Pompey. Once the French conquered Algeria and the Suez Canal was built, it became one of the key ports in the Mediterranean.

If you have a child studying for English A Level they might recognize Marseille from Charles Dickens' *Little Dorrit*. The story starts here in the heat of an August day, when there isn't a breathe of wind to make a ripple on the foul water in the harbour. For Dickens, Marseille was like the tower of Babel, a melting pot of Indians, Russians, Chinese, Spaniards, Portuguese, Englishmen, Frenchmen, Genoese, Neapolitans, Venetians, Greeks and Turks. Today the harbour is cleaner but Marseille is still just about as cosmopolitan as cities come. Dickens felt it was less a place to be looked at than to be smelt and tasted. You'll either love it or hate it and the same goes for the junior members of the family.

Safety first

As with any big city, you'll need to watch your valuables here. Don't leave handbags hanging on the back of the pushchair or on the back of your chair at a café. It isn't somewhere to let teens out alone, either: it's a rough and ready port and if you don't know which areas are safe to go to it can be dangerous to just wander around aimlessly.

However, if you stick to the town centre, which is where you're likely to want to be anyway, you are unlikely to encounter any problems.

Shopping

As you'd expect in a big city there are masses of good shops. Rue St-Ferréol has a branch of up-to-the-minute and affordable Pimkie, for teenage girls' clothes, plus a branch of the Disney Store, a newly renovated Galeries Lafayette and a Virgin Megastore. For more CDs, computer games and books go to FNAC in the Centre Bourse shopping centre, where there's also a branch of the chain Nature et Découvertes. It has a great selection of toys for kids interested in nature and is the place for astronomy supplies. For more toys try Alcalay Jouets, 3 Rue de la République. For *santons*, head for Marcel Carbonel, Rue Neuve-Ste-Catherine.
www.carbonel.com

Figures start at €9 and there's also a small museum and workshop on site where you can see the santons being made. Gilbert Orsini, 6 Rue du Pilon, also makes *santons* in the traditional way; he's been making them since he was eight.

Football fans will want to check out the Olympique Marseille shop at 100 La Canebière. If anyone in the family is a keen stamp collector there's a stamp market on Cours Julien on Sunday, similar to the one in Paris on the Champs Elysées.

Did you know...?

The French national anthem, the 'Marseillaise', was so called because revolutionaries from Marseille sang it on their way to Paris in 1789.

Did you know...?
It may look a bit grubby round the edges, but Marseille is famous for its soap. It's made from lavender and olive oil and you'll see it on sale in all the tourist shops.

Picnics and snacks

The local biscuits are called *navettes* and, as the name implies, are shaped like little boats. They've been baking them since 1781 at Four des Navettes, 136 Rue St-Marseille. Expect to pay around €6 for 12. Stock up on basics at Monoprix on La Canebière, and for fruit and vegetables head for the Marché des Capucins. Marseille has a huge Corsican population of over 300,000 and there are plenty of Corsican bakeries around town, which are good places to stop if the kids need refuelling. You'll find one near the old port on Rue de la République. For more cakes and sweet treats, Boulangerie Michel, 33 Rue Vacon, is the place to buy the traditional 13 desserts served at Christmas (*see* p.244).

If you want to relax and have a drink, Cours Julien is a large pedestrianized square south of La Canebière with lots of cafés to choose from, and if you want to snack on your goodies you can picnic at the Parc du Pharo or, if you have more time, take a boat trip to the islands.

Things to see and do

One of the pleasantest ways to spend time in Marseille is simply to stroll around the old port. Although there are lots of museums in Marseille, only a handful of them are suitable for visiting with kids on holiday. The best of the bunch are mentioned below.

Vieux Port

The old port is a great place to wander around soaking up the atmosphere. Today it's just a pleasure port and the main business of shipping and ferry companies goes on round the corner. Two forts stand at the mouth of the harbour, built by Louis XIV as much to keep an eye on Marseille as defend it, but unfortunately they're not open to the public. Every morning at 8 there's a fish market on the dockside; get there early enough to have a look at the day's catch, which often includes seahorses and other strange creatures, but keep an eye out for the seagulls diving overhead.

You can catch boats to the *calanques* and Château d'If from here, and the minitrains also leave from the port side. To the right of the port is Le Panier (the Basket), the oldest part of Marseille, where the original Greek settlement was. You can see immediately that it was rebuilt in the 1950s.

During the Second World War, thousands of Jews came to Marseille in the hope of catching a boat across the Mediterranean. At that time, the puppet pro-Nazi Vichy government had the administration for the southern part of France, but it was still a safer place for Jews and resistance workers to live than in the north. In 1943, the Nazis became aware that the area was attracting Jews and resistance fighters, so they occupied the area and blew the whole of Le Panier sky-high. The 20,000 residents were given a day to evacuate and underwent a screening process by the French police, who then dispatched 3,500 of them to concentration camps. Out of 700 children rounded up, only 68 returned.

The Great Plague of 1720

On 25 May 1720, the *Grand St-Antoine* docked in the port at Marseille. On board were the bodies of five sailors who had died of the plague. By 10 June hundreds of people had fallen ill and within days a quarter of the town was infected. In August the plague really took hold and 1,000 people a day were dying. People were so ill that they died in the streets where they fell. By the time the plague had run its course, 38,000 people had been killed in Provence, 15,000 of them in Toulon alone.

Can you spot...?
The Bronze marker on the port side which shows where the Greeks first set foot in France.

Mini Trains

t 04 91 40 17 75
Runs From the old port April–Sept

Once you've had a stroll around the old port and orientated yourselves you can catch one or other of the two mini trains, which are invaluable for getting around the town and seeing the sights. One takes in the old town, while the other goes up to Notre-Dame-de-la-Garde (*see* below) on an hour-long round trip. Getting up there on foot is quite a hassle, so it pays to take the mini train.

Good to know...Wednesday afternoons

Many French schools are closed Wednesdays (children are expected to attend class on Saturday mornings instead), which means many museums and tourist attractions, especially those that have limited opening hours out of season, may be open on Wednesday afternoon. Bigger museums often have special children's activities and cinemas and theatres sometimes have special shows for children on a Wednesday too.

Musée des Docks Romains

Pl des Vivaux **t** 04 91 91 24 62
Open 10–5
Adm Adult €1.80, child under 10 free, Sun am free

When the area was rebuilt after the war the remains of the old Roman docks were revealed. The museum houses a large collection of Roman amphora and jars for storing wine and oil that look as if they've come straight from Ali Baba's cave.

Notre-Dame-de-la-Garde

t 04 91 13 40 80
Open 7am–7.30pm (9 July–Aug)
Adm Free

Notre-Dame-de-la-Garde is the must-see monument of Marseille – it's the symbol of the city. It can be quite a trek to get there, so it's best to catch the mini train from the old port. Originally this was more than just a church, it was a lookout post and place to hide in time of danger; today you'll get great views of the city when you've reached the top of the hill. The interior is a bit kitsch and full of plaques offering up specific prayers – one of which is for Olympique Marseille, the local football team.

Le Stade Vélodrome

Getting there Via metro to Rond-Point du Prado
www.olympiquedemarseille.com

This is Marseille's other place of worship. The city is crazy about *le foot* and the city's team, Olympique Marseille, is one of the top teams in Europe. In the early 1990s they were dogged by allegations of match fixing and corruption but that has all since been put behind them. The stadium was done up for the World Cup in 1998 and can hold 60,000 people, making it France's second biggest stadium. Tickets for matches can be bought at the Virgin Megastore (*see* p.130).

Need to let off steam?

Parc Borély has a duck pond and small botanical garden and you can watch the locals playing _boules_ in the summer. Nearby is the town's sandy beach, Plage du Prado. There are children's playgrounds along the Promenade de Plage and there's a skate park and plenty of space to play football on the edge of Plage Borély, if Zidane has inspired you.

Galerie des Transports

Pl du Marché-des-Capucins Metro Noailles
t 04 91 54 15 15
Open Wed–Sat 10–6
Adm Free

This old tram station houses a collection of omnibuses and steam trains and makes for a good outing if you can spare the time.

Jardin des Vestiges

Centre Bourse **t** 04 91 90 42 22
Open Mon–Sat 12 noon–7
Adm Adult €1.80, child free

This museum houses the remains of the Greek city Massalia, including the eastern ramparts and city gates as well as models, mosaics and the remains of a Roman ship. Although it doesn't merit a special trip it's well worth a visit if you have time and are in the Centre Bourse for some shopping.

SPECIAL TRIPS FROM MARSEILLE

Château d'If

t 04 91 59 02 30
Getting there Boats leave from Quai des Belges in good weather only, 9.30–6.30 daily. Tickets cost €8 and the crossing takes 20mins. Boats also sail to the Iles du Frioul, an archipelago made up of two main islands and several small ones, where you can swim from the rocks
Open April–Sept Tues–Sun 9–7, Oct–Mar 9–5
Adm Adult €4, child €2.50

The island served as a prison from the 16th century until the First World War. Its most famous prisoner was the fictional Count of Monte Cristo (*see* box) and even though he never existed, you can visit his cell. (Just to make it all the more surreal, in the novel, the hero Dantès, the Count of Monte Cristo, returns to the Château d'If to find

Tell me a story: The Count of Monte Cristo

Edmond Dantès, the Count of Monte Cristo, is the hero of Alexandre Dumas' novel of the same name. *The Count of Monte Cristo* was one of the first really popular novels and was a runaway success on both sides of the Atlantic, responsible for putting Marseille on the tourist map. The novel is a real rollicking yarn, full of intrigue and adventure. Young readers who are not intimidated by its length will enjoy it (Dumas was paid by the line and was short of money at the time, so didn't stint on words). Dantès is a young sailor who becomes embroiled unwittingly in Napoleon's plot to return to power in 1815. He is betrayed by jealous friends and his own family as a Bonapartist spy and is imprisoned in the Château d'If. After years in solitary confinement, Dantès meets and befriends an Italian priest, Abbé Faria, who has dug a tunnel to link the two cells. Faria tells him how to find the fortune that he has hidden on the island of Monte Cristo.

After many adventures, escapes and much derring-do, Dantès avenges himself on those who betrayed him and sails off into the sunset with his beautiful fiancée. Amazingly, Dumas based his tale on a true story – the real Dantès was a young man called Picaud who was denounced as an English spy and imprisoned in a castle with an Italian cleric who died leaving him a fortune. After he escaped, Picaud later returned to murder those who had betrayed him, just like in the book.

that his cell has been turned into a tourist attraction since he was the only person ever to escape.) Like the fictional Dantès, most of the people who wound up in the Château d'If were political prisoners although none of them was ever fortunate enough to escape. Equally unfortunate was the first rhinoceros ever to set foot in Europe, who was brought ashore here in 1516 en route to Rome as a gift for the pope, but sadly it died in transit.

Cassis

Getting there The train station is 3.5km from town so you'll need a car to get about. Cassis is off the main A50, less than 30mins from Marseille
Tourist office Quai des Moulins **t** 00 33 (0)4 42 01 71 17

Cassis is a charming family resort and still retains the feeling of a small fishing port. It has a delightful harbour and is famous for its cliffs – a rarity in France. A sizeable year-round population means it doesn't have the slightly artificial feel of some other Mediterranean resorts.

Although there are masses of places to eat along the port side, you may want to head for one of the two restaurants on the main town beach, the Plage de la Grande Mer, where the children can run around safely. If you're on a budget, there are masses of sandwich shops and snack bars so it's easy to picnic on the beach.

Shopping

The shopping in Cassis is excellent, especially if you're looking for presents and souvenirs. The main shopping street is Av Victor Hugo, where there's a branch of the luxury sweet shop La Cure Gourmande. Behind the harbour are some tiny alleyways full of interesting little shops and cafés.

After Cassis there are a series of uninteresting resorts and the naval base of Toulon, which is a mini-version of Marseille and is pleasant enough, but isn't somewhere to spend a family holiday or even much time sightseeing.

Petit Train de la Calanque de Port Miou

t 04 42 01 09 98
Departs daily, afternoons only May–Nov
Adult €5, child (5–12 years) €2.50

The tourist train takes a 40min tour of the old town and then makes a brief stop in Port Miou, which is the first of a series of dramatic coves.

Les Calanques

Getting there Boats run from Marseille's Quai des Belges and from Cassis
Fares Various prices according to the type of trip. A return mini-trip from Cassis to En-Vau is €10 per person, but there are longer trips that allow you to disembark and enjoy a night-time *son et lumière*. From Cassis you can hire a boat to make the trip on your own. A boat for about 8 people with a captain costs from €155 for 2hrs to €400, **t** 06 85 55 67 48

The *calanques* are steep coves with dramatic white rocky cliff sides. They look like fjords but they're not; fjords were cut by glaciers but the *calanques* are submerged valleys, formed 10 thousand years ago when the water level rose dramatically and flooded the steep valleys along the coast. The *calanques* are full of hidden secrets. In 1991 a diver discovered a cave in the Calanque de

Sormiou covered with prehistoric paintings of bison, deer, fish and even penguins and seals. There are also strange hand paintings that may be a form of early writing. At the end of the last Ice Age the cave would have been accessible from dry land, but unfortunately today it's well below sea level and is not open to the public.

Kids will enjoy a boat trip that allows them to get off the boat in one of the tiny coves between Cassis and Marseille – in the summer the boat is the only feasible way of getting to the *calanques* anyway, as large stretches of the cliff path are closed. Don't attempt the trip if it's windy; the journey will be too rough for anyone to enjoy. Out of season you can walk to the *calanques* but it's quite perilous; the cliffs are very steep and there is nothing to keep little ones away from the edge.

En-Vau is the most stunning *calanque*. It has a small beach and some boat trips will stop long enough for a paddle.

AROUND MARSEILLE

Animal magic

Zoo et Jardin Exotique

Sanary sur Mer **t** 04 94 29 40 38
Open Daily 8–12 noon and 2–6 (7 in summer)
Adm Adult €6.50, child €5

This small zoo is set in a lush park planted with cacti and exotic plants, so you can stroll among the bougainvillea while the little ones enjoy the Vietnamese pigs, wallabies, monkeys and multi-coloured birds. There are flamingos if you can't make it to the Camargue to see them in the wild.

Institut Océanographique Paul-Ricard

Ile des Embiez **t** 04 94 34 02 49
www.institut-paul-ricard.org
Getting there There's a regular ferry service from early morning to midnight in the summer from Six-Four-les-Plages on the N559, east of Marseille,
Open May–Aug daily 10.30–12.30 and 1.30–5.30; Sept–April 10–12 noon and 1.30–5.30; Aquascope runs every 40mins April–Sept
Adm Adult €4, child €2

You may have trouble getting them out of the water but a trip here will show the kids that there's more to the Mediterranean than paddling. You can see the fish that live here in a series of aquariums and then a contraption called the Aquascope will take you to the bottom of the sea to observe them in the wild. This is a very popular attraction in high season, so to be sure of a place you'll need to reserve a seat. There's also a little train that tours the island, go-karts and pony rides.

This is a research centre as well as a museum and belongs to the drinks magnate Paul Ricard. It was set up to study pollution in the sea and to find ways of dealing with accidents like the Exxon Valdez oil spill.

Planet Aquarium

Plan de Campagne, Cabriès
Getting there Northwest of Marseille off the A51
Open Oct–Mar Tues–Sun 10–7; April–June and Sept 10–8, July–Aug 10–11pm, closed Mon, last admission 1hr before closing
Adm Adult €8, child €6

This is a swanky new aquarium and is fairly predictable, but fun if you haven't seen too many similar attractions. You can stroke the ray fish and walk through a glass tunnel to see the sharks swimming overhead – some of them are over a metre long. There's also a discovery space where you can learn about how the aquarium functions, a section devoted to the fish of the Carmargue and an incredible 3-D cinema where you can explore a wreck at the bottom of the sea. It's air-conditioned so is a good spot to escape from the afternoon sun and is ideal for little ones who have never heard of Julius Caesar.

Buckets and spades

The best beach in the centre of Marseille is along Bd Kennedy. Plage du David has lots of sports activities and Clos des Plages, a quiet beach north of the town, is the best place for families. For a nicer beach you'll have to head out of town towards Cassis. Forty minutes along the coast is Six-Fours-Les-Plages, a family resort on the edge of Toulon. The resort itself is nothing special but the Plage de Bonnegrace, more commonly known as Brutal Beach, is good for windsurfers.

Sporty kids

You can spend the day swimming, sliding down the water shoots, jumping in the waves and shooting the rapids.

Aquacity

t 04 91 51 54 08 **www.aqua-city.com**
Getting there It's off the A51 between Aix and Marseille, exit Plan de Campagne, direction Septemes-les-Vallons
Open Daily June–Sept 10–7.30
Adm Adult €15, child (under 12) €12, family €12.96, free entry on birthdays

You can even stay the night in an Indian tepee (each tepee can sleep two adults and four children and has a toilet, shower and washbasin). The park gets half a million visitors a year so expect to have to queue in high season. There are restaurants, shops, a playground, a picnic area and baby-changing facilities.

***Good to know...*Aubagne**

If you're a fan of Marcel Pagnol, don't destroy your illusions by taking a trip to his home town of Aubagne, just outside Marseille. It's an uninspiring suburb and isn't worth the trip, whatever the leaflets might say.

Theme parks

There are two big theme parks near Marseille and although they're nothing out of the ordinary they make a good day out.

Eldorado City

Châteauneuf-les-Martigues **t** 04 42 79 86 90
www.eldoradocity.fr
Open Mar–Nov 10–6 (till 7 July–Aug)
Adm Adult €12, child (3–12 years) €9, birthday parties available

Eldorado City is a vast amusement park built around four themes: the Wild West; Mexico; a Native American village; and the Canadian outback. Among the attractions are mechanical bucking bulls, a mini-farm and a huge children's playground. There are Wild West-style shows every day from 11.30. Expect to queue in summer and bring your own food if you're on a budget.

OK Corral

N8 Cuges-les-Pins **t** 04 42 73 80 05
www.okcorral.fr
Open Daily 10–6, closed Nov–Jan
Adm Adult €14.50, child (under 140cm) €12, free for children under 1m

Another Wild West theme park and the biggest park in the South of France. You'll be spoilt for choice between the Colorado Rapids, the Ghost Town and the Lasso Loop. There are height restrictions on some of the rides but there is still plenty for little ones – a mini-canoe ride, animals and an Indian café.

ST-RÉMY-DE-PROVENCE

Getting there It's 8km from Avignon on the D99. There are bus connections from Avignon and Arles
Getting around If you don't have a car you'll need a bike; contact Cycles Ferri, 35 Av de la Libération, **t** 00 33 (0)4 90 92 10 88, open daily 7.30–7.30. They also have baby seats and helmets for hire. This is great biking country, so make the most of it
Tourist office Place Jean Jaurès **t** 00 33 (0)4 90 92 05 22 **www.**saintremy-de-provence.com
Special events May: Fête de la Transhumance, during which shepherds drive thousands of sheep through the streets along with goats, donkeys and carts. August: Fête de la Charrette, 15 August. A huge cart decorated with fruit and vegetables is pulled around town by 50 carthorses. The *Feria* is also in August, with lots of bullfights

For such a tiny place, St-Rémy has a lot of history. Nostradamus was born here and Van Gogh painted some of his best pictures while he was in the asylum on the edge of town. But long before Van Gogh put St-Rémy on the map, it was an important Roman settlement. The remains of the Roman city of Glanum are next to Van Gogh's hospital, although these were only discovered after he died.

The countryside to the south of the village is some of the most beautiful in Provence, with rocky

Tell me a story: Vincent Van Gogh

Van Gogh grew up in Holland, the oldest of six children. He was very close to his younger brother, Theo, who supported him throughout his troubled life and helped him financially.

In 1886 he moved into his brother's flat in Paris. It was here that his life as an artist really took off; he met fellow artists Toulouse-Lautrec and Pissarro and became interested in Japanese art, which would have a major influence on his style.

In 1888, he left Paris for the South of France and settled in Arles, where he persuaded his friend, the artist Gauguin, to follow him. His friendship with Gauguin was a fiery one and it was during this troubled period that Van Gogh cut off his ear. The locals found this artistic behaviour incomprehensible and nicknamed him '*fou roux*' ('red-headed madman') and eventually hounded him out of town.

Exactly why Van Gogh went mad is unclear. He suffered from syphilis, which causes mental problems in its later stages, but there was also a history of mental instability in his family. His brother, Theo, suffered from it and his younger brother, Cornelius, killed himself. There were many events in his life that contributed to his instability: he had been fervently religious in his youth, but later lost his faith, which caused him great distress; he was very unlucky in his love affairs; and although he was a friend of Gauguin he felt Gauguin regarded him as an inferior. It was Gauguin's decision to leave Arles that finally pushed him over the brink. In May 1889 he became a voluntary patient in the hospital in St-Rémy and a year later Theo persuaded him to leave St-Rémy for Anvers near Paris. It was there that he shot himself.

Some of his most extraordinary paintings were created in Arles and St-Rémy (*see* above), but unfortunately none of these are in Provence; they're all in collections in Amsterdam, Paris, London and the USA. Although his paintings now sell for millions (his *Sunflowers* set a record), he sold only one painting in his lifetime, and that was to his brother, Theo.

landscapes typical of the Mediterranean at its best. Take time to breathe in the scents and admire the eagles soaring overhead.

St-Rémy makes a good base for a family holiday; the town itself is pretty and, out of season, not too touristy, there are lots of hotels, and houses to rent, and it's within easy reach of Avignon, Arles and the Camargue.

Even if you're just passing through make time to take a walk among its medieval streets or have a picnic. St-Rémy has lots of great shops, but as they do so well in the height of season many are closed in the winter. Just before Christmas the Petit Marché du Gros Souper is the place to buy ingredients for the traditional Christmas Eve meal (*see* p.244).

Centre d'Art Présence Van Gogh

8 Rue Estrine **t** 04 90 92 34 72
Open Tues–Sun 10.30–12.30 and 2.30–6.30
Adm Adult €3, child €2

The centre has a permanent exhibition of Van Gogh reproductions and an excellent audio-visual show that tells the story of his life. It's also a good place to pick up some postcards.

The hospital where Van Gogh was cared for, St-Paul-de-Mausole, is south of the town centre, next to the Roman city of Glanum. The tourist office has a special bicycle/walking trail to help you discover the sites where Van Gogh painted some of his most famous works. Unfortunately vandalism is a problem in St-Rémy and you'll be lucky to find the signs still up. *Les Paveurs* was painted in Boulevard Nirabeau, *Les Oliviers* was painted at the end of Allée Saint-Paul and *Les Coquelicots, La Montagne de St-Rémy*, *Les Deux Trous* and *La Carrière* were painted in the fields in front of the hospital.

Invest in a pocket guide to the life of Van Gogh, *Van Gogh in Provence*. You'll find it on sale in the museum and all the local newsagents. The booklet has pictures of the paintings Van Gogh made locally, so you can interest the kids in the works by showing the place and the picture at the same time. For those who are particularly keen, pack a copy of the *Eyewitness Guide: Van Gogh* (Dorling Kindersley, 1992).

Roman City of Glanum

Av Van Gogh **t** 04 90 92 23 79
Open April–Sept daily 9–7; Oct–Mar 9–12 noon and 2–5
Adm Adult €5, child free

Fancy a souvenir...?

There's an interesting shop at Glanum. Look out for the kids' guide – it may lack something in translation but it has great pictures. There are also pocket money replica Roman coins and model Roman soldiers for sale.

Before the arrival of the Romans, the Greeks had already had a small settlement here around a sacred spring. The Romans re-dedicated the spring to the god Glan, who gave the town its name; you can find the site of the shrine at the top of the ruins. The town was only discovered in 1921 so when Van Gogh sat down to paint the olive trees next door this was just another grove.

Archaeologists believe the original settlement was up to seven times bigger than the ruins you can see and it's still being excavated. Some of the finds from the site can be seen in the Hôtel de Sade in the town centre, but for Roman remains it's better to head for the archaeology museum in Arles (*see* p.123).

Most Roman towns were laid out on a grid system, but the main road in Glanum is unusual because it is curved; this was the only way that water could be channelled out of the town centre after a heavy Provençal downpour. Part of the columns of the temple have been reconstructed using the same techniques as Roman builders. It's a stunning sight against the blue sky and gives you an idea of how impressive Glanum must have been when it was first built.

The Mausolée des Jules and the Triumphal Arch, once the main entrance to the town, are free and outside the main site. If you're visiting in high season it's worth coming to see them in the evening, when the main site is closed and there are fewer tourists. The mausoleum isn't actually a tomb but a memorial to one of the early founders of the town; the images around its sides are of important battles against the Gauls and the eastern side reads like a cartoon strip. In the actual site, keep an eye on toddlers – the dangerous parts of the ruins aren't fenced off. Before you go, don't miss out on tasting some Roman delicacies at the Taberna Romana in the summer months.

AROUND ST-RÉMY-DE-PROVENCE

Nature lovers

The countryside around St-Rémy and Les Baux is beautiful and the tourist office in St-Rémy has exceptionally helpful staff and plenty of leaflets on walking, cycling and hiking in the area. There's an idyllic picnic spot not far from St-Rémy: turn right on the way out of town towards Glanum. There should be a sign but either ask in the tourist office or in the shop opposite if you're unsure. You can drive right up to the lakeside, so it's a good option if you're burdened with pushchairs.

Town life

Les Baux-de-Provence

Getting there **It's off the D5, south of St-Rémy-de-Provence. Les Baux is 15 km from Arles, 25km from Avignon, 40km from Nîmes and 60 km from Aix-en-Provence. If coming by car you'll have to park outside the city walls and walk into town or you can catch a bus from Arles**
Tourist office t 00 33 (0)4 90 54 34 39
www.lesbauxdeprovence.com

The small town looks down on the Val d'Enfer (Valley of Hell), which is supposed to have inspired the writer Dante. There are lots of local legends about witches and fairies living in the valley, and from a distance Les Baux itself resembles a giant skull. The castle was a stronghold during the Middle Ages and became quite powerful in Provence, but the town went into decline when France finally took control of the region; French troops smashed the local warlords and the town was razed to the ground in the 17th century. It was only saved by the discovery of bauxite aluminium ore – named after the town but no longer mined here – in 1822.

Today it's a tourist hot spot though still a very beautiful place. The countryside around is a sleepy mixture of vineyards and olive groves, with plenty of farms where you can stop and taste the olive oil. You couldn't find a more idyllic spot to rent a house or base yourself in a hotel.

Unfortunately, in the summer the crowds in the village can be unbearable and so it's better to save your visit for the evening, even though the castle will be shut. You can get a wonderful view down into the Val d'Enfer by the Musée des Santons. If you care to brave the crowds, it is a good place to pick up souvenirs. You can see *santons* being made at Santons d'Art: J Peyron-Campagna on Rue de l'Orme.

Things to see and do

Château des Baux

t 04 90 54 55 56 **www**.chateau-baux-provence.com
Open July–Aug daily 9–8.45; May–June 9–7.30; Sept–Oct 9–6.30, Nov–Feb 9–5
Adm Adult €6.50, child (7–17 years) €3.50, third child free

Anyone who enjoys playing with toy soldiers will love this castle. In the courtyard you'll find reconstructed medieval siege weapons and inside there's an exhibition explaining the turbulent history of the village. The towers are wonderful for exploring, offering bird's-eye views across the horizon so the knights could keep an eye out for their enemies. The visit takes about 30mins and there's an audio guide in English. Keep a close eye on toddlers – it's dangerous up on the battlements.

Musée des Santons

Pl Louis Jou **t** 00 33 490 54 34 39
Open Daily 8–7
Adm Free

If *santon* museums that are extensions of *santon* shops are getting you down, this is the place to go. It's completely non-commercial, the models are all traditional and there's not a sprig of lavender in sight. *Santons* were originally made to decorate the Christmas crib (*see* p.258) and although Les Baux can be as touristy as it gets, the village has one of the nicest Christmas festivals around. Maybe that's why this is one of the few *santon* displays that actually feels genuine. On Christmas Eve there's a special procession of shepherds to the church in Les Baux, where the smallest lamb is carried into the church to be blessed.

Look at this!

La Cathédrale d'Images

t 04 90 54 38 65 **www**.cathedrale-images.com
Getting there Take the Route de Maillane, just below the old town of Les Baux-en-Provence
Open Feb–Oct daily 10–6
Adm Adult €7, child €4.10

Don't miss this awe-inspiring audio visual show, which takes place inside an old limestone quarry built like an Egyptian temple. Over 2,500 images are used in the displays and projected on to the walls and ceilings, accompanied by music and a light show. Themes change every year, so ring ahead to find out what's on this year. The play of images and light appeals as much to the very young as older kids – babies and toddlers enjoy watching the changing pictures. It gets quite chilly inside so bring a sweater even if it's hot outside, and bring drinks and biscuits for babies as you'll find you'll want to linger. The site is perfectly accessible with a pushchair and shows usually last about 30mins, but you are free to stay as long as you want.

WHERE TO EAT

Restaurants in this part of France are open all year round. Large cities like Marseille and Aix have a life beyond tourism, so there's a lot of choice. They are both good places to try some local gourmet cooking but you will also find plenty of inexpensive pizza and pasta joints.

Local markets, bakers and delicatessens are full of gorgeous picnic supplies and there are some delightful spots to picnic in the Camargue, around St-Rémy and Aix.

Aix-en-Provence

Café Bastide du Cours

43 Cours Mirabeau **t** 04 42 26 10 06
www.cafebastideducours.com

This café is one of the mainstays of this famous street and has been serving up coffee and absinthe since 1807. It's a great place to sit and soak up the atmosphere, with friendly waiters who enjoy serving up Cokes to kids. There are plenty of ice-creams and crêpes to boost blood sugar levels too.

Le Démodé

5 Rue Campra **t** 04 42 23 30 66
Open Sept–July Tues–Sat, except Christmas

This is an old-fashioned restaurant serving crêpes and other basic dishes. Children's menus €7, adult menus from €13.

Le Pain Quotidien

5 Pl Richelme **t** 04 42 23 48 57

The Belgian sandwich chain has arrived in France. This is a popular family café and is a good place for a quick snack and a restorative coffee. Salads cost around €10, sandwiches and chocolate spread on toast served at big wooden tables from around €4.

Laurane et sa Maison

16 Rue Victor Leydet **t** 04 42 93 02 03
Open Tues–Sat, and Mon lunch

If you feel like putting on the Ritz this is a good option for a fancy meal with older children. Prices are moderate considering this is Provençal cuisine at its best, and the atmosphere is cosy. It's popular with locals so book ahead, especially at lunchtime.

L'Hacienda

7 Rue Mérindol **t** 04 42 27 00 35
Open Tues–Sat

Not to be confused with a former, once famous Manchester nightclub, this restaurant is just off Place des Cardeurs. Provençal food is served at lunch time and Tex-Mex dishes in the evening. It's popular with local youngsters and has a relaxed atmosphere. You can eat outdoors in summer.

Around Aix

Salon de Provence

Graffiti Café

Pl des Centuries **t** 04 90 56 42 61

This pleasant brasserie is situated in a pedestrianized square, just below the castle and near the exit of the waxworks museum. The kids can run around safely while you relax, then they can tuck into the kids' menu with staples like ham and chips followed by ice-cream for €6. The café is open daily and operates nonstop, which is quite a bonus if you're running late.

Cotignac

Les Trois Marches

11 Cours Gambetta **t** 04 94 04 65 99
Open Mar–Dec

This restaurant is in a pretty rural setting and serves moderately priced, fresh and simple fare.

Le Temps du Pose

11 Pl de la Marine **t** 04 94 77 72 07

Tucked away in a picturesque square between the cliffs and the centre of town, this gallery–café serves good milkshakes, teas and snacks, as well as lunch menus.

Le Tholonet

Chez Thome

La Plantation **t** 04 42 66 90 43
Open Tues–Sun, all year

A short drive out of Aix, this restaurant serves good country fare outdoors in a wooded setting or inside if it's too cold. There are some vegetarian dishes and divine desserts.

Arles

Café La Nuit

11 Pl du Forum t 04 90 96 44 56

This is the famous café from Van Gogh's painting, and is a nice place to have a drink or an ice-cream, but it isn't worth eating here – the food is expensive and substandard.

Café P Boitel

4 Rue de la Liberté t 04 90 96 03 72

This small café is tucked away in the best bakery in town. It's a good place for a savoury snack or a mid-afternoon cake.

Hôtel Le Calendal

5 Rue Porte de Laure t 04 90 96 11 89
e contact@lecalendal.com
www.lecalendal.com

This is the most child-friendly restaurant in Arles – perhaps in the whole of the South of France – and serves great food. There's a children's corner with books, toys and videos, a proper changing area in the toilet, and potties. Outside there's a large, leafy garden with a giant chess set. If you're eating out with little ones, you couldn't find a better place.

Le Grillon

Rond-Point des Arénes t 04 90 96 70 97
Open Thurs–Tues, except Sun eve

This is a good place for a speedy lunch, a crêpe or an ice-cream and the terrace has a great view of the amphitheatre. Menus from €9.

L'Aqua Café

Quai St-Pierre, situated on the other side of the river to the main town. Access is via the Pont de Trinquetaille t 06 08 45 91 66
Open mid-Jan–mid-Dec Mon eve–Sat

This restaurant on a riverboat is great fun for dinner if your children are no longer toddlers. Meals are good value, with lots of salads and menus from around €12.

Cargo de Nuit

7 Av Sadi Carnot t 04 90 49 55 99
Open Mon–Sat, except Mon eve

This lively tapas bar is great to visit with teens. There's live blues or salsa at weekends, the food is good value, and the place stays open till dawn.

Vitamine

16 Rue du Doctor-Fanton t 04 90 93 77 36

This well-known vegetarian restaurant is just off the Forum. There's pasta and salads at reasonable prices and you can eat outside in summer.

Around Arles

The Camargue

Chez Bob

Mas Petite Antonelle, Rte du Sambuc Gageron t 04 90 97 00 29 31
Open Wed–Sun

This restaurant was founded by a well-known Resistance fighter, Robert Boyer, who had famous friends like Picasso to dine here. Bull steaks are a speciality of the menu, and the bull theme is continued through to the décor with bullfighting notices hanging everywhere. Robert has been dead a few years now and his restaurant is now run by a friend. Menus are around €31, so it's more of a place for a treat with older kids than a family diner.

Longo Mai

Le Sambuc t 04 90 97 21 91

The restaurant in the hotel is child-friendly and popular with local families. The owner, a former cancan dancer, serves up some tasty regional cooking.

La Pirate

2 Pl Mireille Stes-Maries-de-la-Mer t 04 90 97 83 53

Small, reasonably priced, family-run pizza joint where they're happy to heat up the baby's bottle and chat to the kids. If you can't face another pizza there are *moules* and omelettes, or lots of chips if you just want a snack. It's one of the few places in town that's open all year round, so is less touristy than most of the other eateries in town and is set well back from the road on a small square where the kids can run around.

The Delta

1 Pl Mireille Stes-Maries-de-la-Mer t 04 90 97 81 12

This popular place serves up local fish dishes like bouillabaisse and *bourride*. There's a terrace in summer. Children's menu €6, adult menu from €15.

Fontvieille

Le Chat Gourmand

14 Rte du Nord **t** 04 90 54 73 17
Open Thurs–Tues lunch, Wed in season

This restaurant serves top-class local food on a pretty terrace in summer. There's even a children's menu, so it's a must for junior gourmets. The restaurant is small so is not ideal for toddlers.

La Peiriero

Av des Baux **t** 04 90 54 76 10
e info@hotel peiriero.com
www.hotel-peiriero.com
Open late Mar–Oct.

If there were a competition for the most family-friendly restaurants in France, La Peiriero and its sister Le Calendal in Arles would win hands down. Both have relaxed atmospheres and are popular with French and Belgian families. Near the restaurant there's a kids corner with toys and videos in French and English. The hotel has a large garden with swimming pool, table tennis and a giant chess set. The kids' menu makes a welcome relief from spaghetti or steak *haché* and changes daily. Booking essential in summer.

Marseille

There are plenty of cafés and bars on the Quai de Rive Neuve side of the old port. Cours d'Estienne d'Orves has cafés and small restaurants and is a good place to head with children. Another good place to eat with kids is Escale Borély on Avenue Pierre Mendès-France.

Marseille is famous for its fish dishes but the pizzas are excellent too, due to the city's large Italian population. The city's cosmopolitan ethnic mix means it is one of the few parts of the South of France where you can also find international cuisine. The city isn't overrun with tourists either, so you won't find surly waiters who can't be bothered to help, and in general people are friendly and helpful.

Café l'Art et les Thés

Centre de la Vieille Charité, Le Panier **t** 04 91 56 28 38

Relaxed café serving sandwiches, snacks and cakes, and a good place to head for a coffee break.

Café Parisien

1 Pl Sadi Carnot **t** 04 91 90 05 77

If you want the kids to see a classic French café with traditional décor, this is it. It's popular with locals and is not as touristy as the bars on the port side.

Hippopotamus Vieux Port

33 Quai des Belges **t** 04 91 59 91 40

Part of the family-orientated French chain, this branch is conveniently situated on the edge of the old port and serves kebabs, steaks, salads and lots of chips. Kids get pens and colouring books, you get value for money. Children's menu €7.50, adult menus from €12.90–€24.20.

Pizzeria au Feu de Bois

10 Rue d'Aubagne **t** 04 91 54 33 96
Open Mon–Sat

Just off the Rue de Rome, you'll find some of the best pizzas in town at excellent prices, with menus from €8. There's also a takeaway service from the counter outside.

Pizzeria Jeannot

Vallon des Auffes **t** 04 91 51 11 28
Open Wed–Sun, except Fri lunch

This is where to come for a pizza in a nice setting. The terrace is just on the water's edge and there are loads of children playing around the harbour. You'll need to budget about €18 a head for adults.

Le Roi du Couscous

63 Rue de la République **t** 04 91 91 45 46

Couscous is a French staple and this place serves up the best in town.

La Pâte Fraîche et Ravioli

150 Rue Jean Mermoz, Metro Rond-Point du Prado **t** 04 91 76 18 85

Lovely pasta dishes are served up in a little restaurant behind the kitchen. You should budget €45 for a good family meal.

Around Marseille

La Grotte

Calanque de Callelongue **t** 04 91 73 17 79

Splash out at this terrace by the sea where you can eat some excellent pizza and fish dishes. It's a big restaurant and can get very busy at lunchtime, so be sure to arrive early or book ahead. It's a lovely spot in the evening too.

Chez Bernard

Calanque de Magaud **t** 04 94 27 20 62
Open April–Sept

Yes, it is possible to have a romantic lunch with the kids in tow. This restaurant is right on the beach so they'll be happy to go off and play while you have a moment together. The restaurant specializes in fish and menus cost from €7–€36. To find the restaurant you need to follow the corniche in the direction of Le Pradet-Carqueiranne until you reach Pont-de-Suve. Park the car at the Parking Sté Marguerite and follow the path down to the beach, where you'll find the restaurant.

St-Rémy-de-Provence

There are lots of brasseries and restaurants to choose from in St-Rémy. In the height of season, they'll be packed, so arrive early and book ahead.

Le Bistrot des Alpilles

15 Bd Mirabeau **t** 04 90 92 09 17
Open Dec–Oct Mon–Sat

This lively and popular spot serves up good pasta dishes and tasty deserts on an attractive terrace.

La Gousse d'Ail

25 Rue Carnot **t** 04 90 92 16 87

This restaurant serves gorgeous Provençal dishes, using fresh pasta, lots of vegetables and *bouillabaisse*. Kids' menu €11.50, adults from €14.

La Manège

6 Bd Marceau **t** 04 90 92 65 95

Lovely cooking in a restaurant decorated with old buses and eccentric knick-knacks. Menus from €15.

Auberge Sant Roumierenco

Route de Noves **t** 04 90 92 12 53
e santroumierenco@net-up.com
www.aubergesantroumierenco.com

This is an idyllic spot for unwinding, away from the crowds, and enjoying good Provençal food while the kids explore the garden. Meals are served under the trees in summer.

Around St–Rémy

Les Baux-de-Provence

Hostellerie de la Reine Jeanne

t 04 90 54 32 06

Just inside the village, this restaurant has a terrace and is your best bet if you want a proper sit-down lunch, with good local dishes on offer.

Crêperie Jardin des Délices

Rue du Trencat **t** 04 90 54 48 38

Popular with holidaying French families, the food here features pizzas, salads and crêpe dishes. The service is speedy and friendly and there's a kids' menu (dish of the day, drink and dessert) for €5.50.

Languedoc-Roussillon

Aude · Roussillon · Hérault · Gard

AUDE 146
Carcassonne 146
Special trips from Carcassonne 149
Around Carcassonne 150
Narbonne 151
Around Narbonne 153

ROUSSILLON 154
Perpignan 154
Special trips from Perpignan 156
Around Perpignan 156

HÉRAULT 161
Agde 161
Around Agde 163
Montpellier 164
Special trips from Montpellier 165
Around Montpellier 167

GARD 170
Nîmes 170
Special trips from Nîmes 172
Around Nîmes 173

WHERE TO EAT 176

06

Languedoc-Roussillon

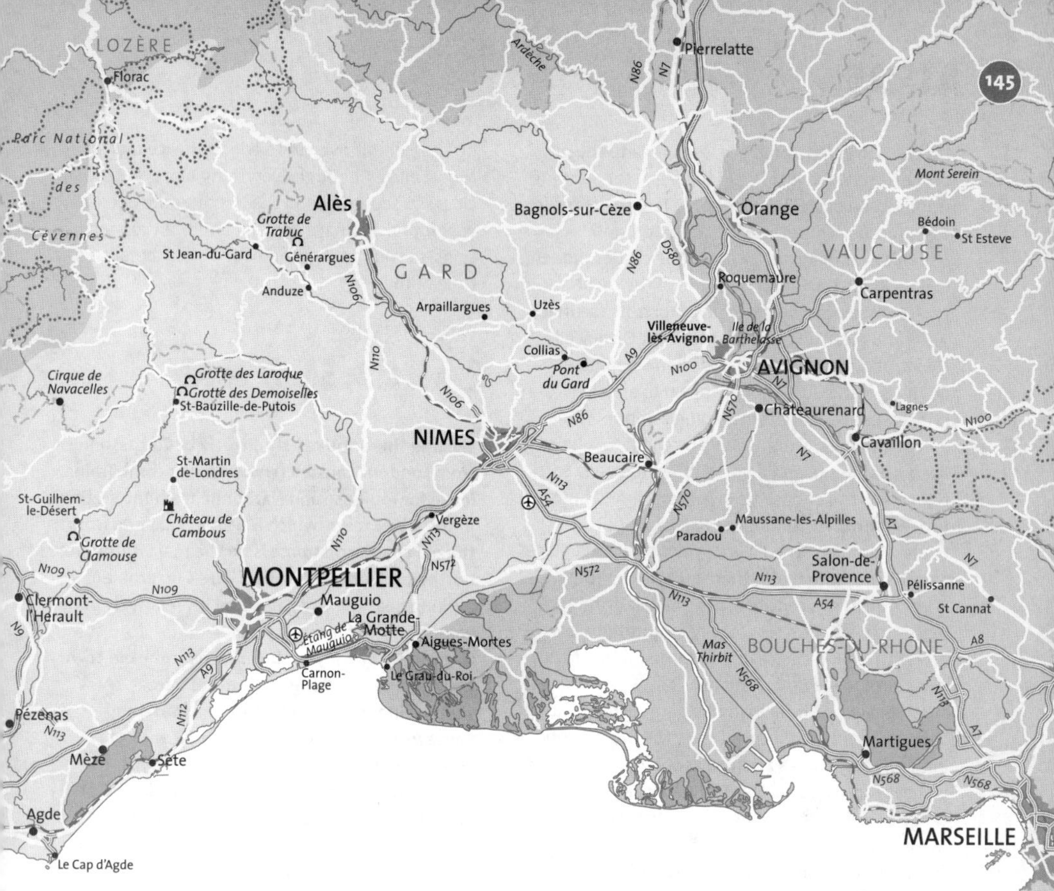

Such a perfect day

Morning Breakfast in Place de la République in Perpignan, then gawp at the live snails on sale in the marketplace, pp.154–5. Drive up into the hills to visit the museum at Tautavel, p.156

Lunch Have a relaxing lunch by the river at Au Vieux Moulin in the Gorge de Galamus, p.159

Afternoon Either kayak on the river or head up to the ruined Château de Quéribus, p.149

Special events

July

Carcassonne: Bastille Day celebrations, including fireworks reputed to be the best in France and dances across the region

July and August

Tautavel: Prehistoric Festival

August

Carcassonne: Medieval Festival

Aigues-Mortes: Fête de St-Louis

December

Perpignan: Christmas Market

Highlights

Imagining you're a knight in a fairy tale defending castles in the air, p.149

Digging on the beach at Collioure, p.158

Playing hide-and-seek in the medieval streets of St-Guilhem-le-Désert, p.168

Kayaking under the Pont du Gard, p.172

Being 21st-century citizens in Montpellier, p.164

Exploring the magical underground world of the Grotte de Clamouse, p.169

Languedoc-Roussillon is the Cinderella to the glitz of the Riviera. Yet, just like in the fairy story, it is far from second best. There are some real treasures to be found, both natural and man-made, and perhaps best of all are the fairy-tale castles hidden in the clouds. Carcassonne is one of the most perfect medieval towns left in Europe. Its fortified walls and gleaming turrets gave Walt Disney all the inspiration he needed to design Sleeping Beauty's castle, so it should appeal to all fairy princesses and knights in shining armour.

In a huge area like this you'll be spoilt for choice as to what to see and do first. When it comes to towns, you can choose from Roman Nîmes, high-tech Montpellier, traditional Narbonne or the Spanish atmosphere of Perpignan. It's a good place to get away from it all – there are wild remote gorges, acres of sandy beaches and beautiful places to walk. It's a very family-orientated area, too, with a huge choice of accommodation, from campsites to elegant châteaux.

Borders get a bit fuzzy in this part of the world and this chapter concentrates on the main towns and the coast. That's because as you move north you head into Central France, technically part of Languedoc-Roussillon but no longer part of Mediterranean France. When it rains in the wild countryside of the northern borders it can look more like Scotland than the South of France – so we've left it to one side for another book.

There are lots of sandy beaches along the coast but the best place for a seaside holiday is west of Narbonne. To the east, the coast is flat and tends to be built up. Languedoc-Roussillon is a good destination for all the family: toddlers will like digging on the beach and meeting the animals down on the farm; school-age kids will love the Roman ruins and the hands-on museum at the Pont du Gard; and teens will enjoy the thrill of kayaking on the Hérault river and a trip to the ice rink in Montpellier. Although everything along the coast closes in September, all the big cities are open all year round and have good air and train connections, so you can visit them for a short break at any time of the year.

Did you know...?

Languedoc takes its name from the Langue d'Oc, which was what all the regional dialects of the south (like Provençal) were called in the Middle Ages. It was based more closely on Latin than the French that was spoken in the north at that time. You won't find anyone speaking these dialects any more but you may come across some of the words in place names.

CARCASSONNE

Getting there You can fly directly to Carcassonne from London Stansted (**www.**ryanair.com). Trains leave for Toulouse and Narbonne from the station in the lower town, which is a short taxi ride from the old city. Carcassonne is on the main *autoroute* northwest from Narbonne. There's no problem parking near the city gates and it's relatively good value at €3.50 for the day

Getting around If you stay in or near the old town you can do everything on foot. For a treat, try sightseeing from the comfort of a horse and carriage: Calèches de la Cité, **t** 04 68 71 54 57. Rides run April–Sept 10–6 and last 20mins. Alternatively hop on the Petit Train de la Cité at Porte Narbonnaise, **t** 04 68 24 45 70. Trains run May–Sept 10–12 noon and 2–6

Tourist office 32 Rue Aimé Ramond **t** 00 33 (0)4 68 77 71 11 **www.**carcassonne.org

Special events July: Bastille Day fireworks. August: Medieval Festival

Carcassonne is a perfect medieval town, and it is like stepping into the pages of a fairy tale. It's a great place to visit with children, especially the under-10s, who won't be aware of all the tourists and won't care that the whole place was restored in the 19th century. For children who like playing forts and castles or dressing up as princesses, the whole town is a make-believe world come to life.

Walking into the city through the Porte Narbonnaise is something you never forget, even if you are only five when you do it and it is like stepping back in time. Today the narrow streets are like an Aladdin's cave for souvenir hunters, so be sure to fix the budget before you get out of the car. The number of shops selling plastic swords and shields is quite overwhelming, but for kids this only adds to the excitement.

Carcassonne was founded by the Romans, who called their town Carcaso. In the Middle Ages it had one of the most important castles in Europe – this

Tell me a story:
The sad tale of the Cathars

In the Middle Ages, a group of Christians in southwest France broke away from the Catholic Church and developed their own style of Christianity. They were known as Cathars. Some of their ideas were radically different to the pope's idea of Christian teaching, believing, for example, that men and woman were equal and that it was as bad to kill an animal as it was to kill a person. More importantly, and worryingly for the pope, they believed the earth was created by the Devil not God, and that man was condemned to be born again until he learned goodness – only then would he go to heaven.

Pope Innocent III didn't accept this challenge to his authority and in 1208 he ordered a crusade against the Cathars. The French king, Philip II, was only too happy to oblige, as the local lords in the south were far too independent for his liking. It was a bloody affair, and the Cathars were killed without mercy. In Béziers alone, it was reported that 20,000 people were put to death (although today historians think it was more like 10,000 people). After a long siege, the leader of the crusade, Simon de Montfort, made Carcassonne his base of operations. He was eventually killed in action in Toulouse but is buried in the cathedral in Carcassonne. Find out more on **www.cathars.org**.

was the frontline with Spain, then one of the most powerful countries around. After the annexation of Roussillon in 1659, Carcassonne lost strategic importance and fell into disrepair. The city was eventually restored in the 19th century by Viollet-le-Duc, who has to have been the busiest architect in France. It's difficult to find a historic building he didn't manage to tart up and we have him to thank for giving Carcassonne its fairy-tale feel.

Carcassonne is a great town for a weekend break, since you can fly directly from London Stansted. Book a hotel in the old town, as the lower town is nothing special. If you're holidaying for a week or so in Languedoc, Carcassonne is an essential stopover or perfect for a big day out. It's not somewhere to base yourself for a longer trip; for that you're better heading off into the hills, where there are some even more impressive castles.

There is some lovely countryside to the north. Take the road to Mazamet (D118) to reach the wild peaks of the Black Mountain. There are pretty villages, especially Roquefère and Mas-Cabardès, and plenty of *chambres d'hôte*. If you're heading in the other direction, stay to the south of Rennes-les-Bains, where it's beautiful and remote and you're close to castles literally built in the clouds, like Quéribus and Termes. Avoid Limoux, which is nothing to write home about.

Shopping

Carcassonne is a great place for kids to spend their pocket money, with endless souvenir shops full of plastic swords and toy soldiers. Access to the old town is free and since you can spend a pleasant time strolling about the streets without paying to go into anything, it isn't necessarily an expensive outing, which leaves some money for souvenirs.

Loubatières, 2 Rue Cros Mayrevieille has a good selection of guides and children's books in both French and English. It stocks a number of books for children on local history – look out for the series of mini-stories for the under-10s, *Famous Figures of the Occitan Lands* (Editions Loubatières), available in English and French and costing €5 each. *Trencavel* is the true story of a young knight and viscount of Carcassonne who defended his city during the anti-Cathar crusade. If you speak French and like fairy tales keep an eye open for *Contes Traditionnels du Languedoc* (Editions Milan). French children read a lot of fairy tales and the art of writing a good fairy tale is part of the national curriculum.

In the lower town you'll find plenty of the main chains. There's a Monoprix department store on Rue Georges Clemenceau and most of the main shops are here, too. For clothes, check out Du Pareil au Même or, for teenage girls, Jennifer. For littler ones, Bébé 9 on Rue de l'Aigle d'Or and New Baby on Place Carnot are the places for children's and maternity clothes and, of course, baby equipment.

If you are looking for toys, JouéClub has a good selection, while video games addicts will like Difinitel Micro on Rue du 4 Septembre.

Can you spot…a rugby player?
Carcassonne is as famous for its rugby team as it is for its ramparts. It has one of the top teams in the country and the locals are crazy about rugby.

Picnics and snacks

While you're doing the sights don't forget to pop into one of the town's cake shops to try the local speciality, *boulets de Carcassonne*, made with peanuts and honey. Skip dessert and head for La Cure Gourmande on Rue St-Louis, which is a sweet-eater's paradise. Epicerie de la Cité on Avenue Arthur-Mullot is open until 3am in summer if you run out of picnic supplies or milk. Market days are Tuesday, Thursday and Saturday morning.

The lake of La Cavayère on the edge of town is the place to eat your picnic, with sandy beaches and plenty of space for kids to run around.

Things to see and do

Les Lices

Walk between the inner and outer walls, where the knights used to train in the Middle Ages. If you look carefully at the bottom of the inner wall you can see where the brickwork changes – that's all that's left of Roman Carcassonne. Simon de Montfort, who led the anti-Cathar crusade in the 13th century (*see* p.147) only captured it by trickery. There's jousting here during the Medieval Festival in August. Tickets cost €10 for adults and €5 for a child.

Tell me a story: A good knight

Ramon Roger Trencavel was just what a knight should be – honest, brave and fair. He was lord of Carcassonne at the time of the crusade against the Cathars, and although he was very young, just 24, his city looked to him for leadership in this time of hardship. Although he was not a Cathar himself, he felt it was his duty to protect all his people, and he offered the Cathars refuge within the city walls. When the crusade began in earnest, hundreds of refugees fled the surrounding countryside for the safety of Carcassonne. It was perhaps this generosity that led to Trencavel's downfall: before long the city was besieged, and with the intense summer heat and the large numbers of people there was not enough water to go round. With his people dying of thirst, Trencavel knew he had no choice but to talk to the enemy, and offered himself as hostage so that the people could flee the city unharmed. The crusaders accepted but did not keep their word, and Trencavel was never released from prison. He died there a few months later, most probably murdered by the crusaders.

Fancy a souvenir...?

The castle shop has excellent souvenirs. There's a wooden toy siege machine for €8 and plastic knights cost from €4. There is also a wide selection of puzzles and board games, even computerized ones, all on the theme of knights and castles.

Le Château

t 04 68 11 70 72 **www**.monuments.fr
Open Daily 9.30–5; April, May and Sept 9.30–6; 7 June–Aug 9.30–7.30
Adm Adult €5.50, child free

This is the castle inside the castle and was the stronghold of the Trencavel family. They weren't Cathars themselves, but they protected the Cathars during the crusade and it cost them the city. There's an interesting exhibition that shows what the castle was like before Viollet-le-Duc set to work, but it won't ruin your day out if you miss it. There's a drinks-vending machine in the shop.

Im@ginarium

Rue St Jean, La Cité **t** 04 68 47 78 78
www.cathars.org
Open Daily 11–6, July–Aug 11–8
Adm Adult €7, child €4.50

This is a sound and light show that tells the story of the crusade against the Cathars, with a small, computerized exhibition upstairs. The show is very interesting for older children, especially if you're intending to explore the Cathar castles around Carcassonne. The presentation starts with a helpful English-speaking guide answering questions about the Cathars. However, the English translation of the commentary that goes with the actual show is a hilarious mixture of French meets Elvis Presley and leaves something to be desired. Don't bring very small children, as the show starts with Simon de Montfort rising from the grave and is enough to make a grown man shudder.

Mémoires du Moyen Age

Espace Pont Levis **t** 04 68 71 08 65
Open 10–7.30
Adm Adult €4, child €2.50

The visit takes about 30mins and includes a film and some extremely fine models. The exhibition brings the castle to life and gives the kids an idea of what it was like to live in Carcassonne during a siege. It's well worth a visit – don't dismiss it just because it's in the car park.

Les Aigles de la Cité

Colline de Pech Mary **t** 04 68 47 88 99
Open Easter–Hallowe'en; flying displays July–Aug 3–7, show lasts 45mins, call for flight times out of season
Adm Adult €7, child (under 12) €5

Kids usually enjoy watching huge birds of prey, and here you can see them swoop overhead in an appropriately medieval setting. Choose a late afternoon show in summer, as it can be very hot, especially for babies. If you're lucky you may actually get to hold an eagle on your hand.

Le Parc Australien

t 04 68 25 05 07
Getting there On the A61
Open Daily in school holidays 2–12 midnight, otherwise Weds and weekends only
Adm Adult €4, child €2.50

If all this medieval tourism is getting to be too much, head here to sample a little bit of the outback. You can even buy a boomerang to take home with you.

SPECIAL TRIPS FROM CARCASSONNE

Les Cinq Fils de Carcassonne: The Cathar Castles

These are some of the most dramatic castles in the world, so high up they're in the clouds. They feature in lots of local fairy tales (read about them in *Contes Traditionnels du Languedoc*, Editions Milan), but their real claim to fame is for being the last strongholds of the Cathars. The sect didn't build the castles themselves; they belonged to the local lords who gave them sanctuary. If you are planning to visit the castles pack a few books on what it was like to live in a medieval castle. These places fire up the children's imaginations and they'll be full of questions.

The castles are hidden away in some of the most beautiful countryside in France. Getting up to them is tricky with little children, but just admiring them from a distance is a fantastic experience. The surrounding countryside is a stunning place to visit, so pack a picnic and enjoy the drive. You'll pass through some of the sleepiest villages in the country, such as Bugarach, and if you want to really take your time, there are plenty of *chambres d'hôte* to stay in. Scrabbling over the ruins can be very hot in summer, so pack sunhats and plenty of water.

Château d'Aguilar

t 04 68 45 51 00
Getting there 4km east of Tuchan
Open Daily June–Sept 10–12 noon and 3–7
Adm Adult €2.30, child €1

This castle has seen plenty of sieges. It's one of the easier castles to get up to with kids, as there's just a short climb up to the entrance.

Château de Quéribus

t 04 68 45 03 69
Getting there 2.5km east of Tuchan
Open May and Oct 9.30–6.30; June and Sept 9–7, July–Aug 9–8. Weekends and school holidays only in winter 10–5, closed first three weeks of Jan
Adm Adult €4, child (6–15 years) €2

This is the most stunning of the Cathar castles and the last stronghold to fall to the crusaders after a brief siege in 1255. How anyone ever had the guts to attack it is mind-boggling – it's 728m up a mountain. It's a 15-min hike up to the castle and if it's windy don't attempt the climb – the wind can be so strong it can cause the smaller ones to lose their balance. Fans of the hit French comedy *Les Visiteurs* will love this castle as it looks just like the one in the film (*see* p.36).

Château de Termes

t 04 6 8 70 09 20
Getting there 12km west of Villerouge
Open May–Sept 10.30–6.30; July–Aug 10.30–7.30
Adm Adult €3.50, child €1.50

It's hard to imagine a more romantic setting than the green valley that surrounds this castle. There was a 4-month siege here and when the castle finally fell it was a turning point in the war against the Cathars.

Château de Peyrepertuse

t 04 68 45 03 26 **www.chateau-peyrepertuse.com**
Getting there Near the village of Duilhac
Open Daily summer 10–7 in summer (9 July–Aug), winter 10–6
Adm Adult €4, child €2

This is the largest castle in the area and the most impressive – it's up 900m high, and on a good day you can see Quéribus and beyond to the sea from its dizzy ramparts. It's a tough 20-min climb from the car park up a perilous staircase carved out of the rock. Be aware that nothing is fenced off and there are some very dangerous drops, so best to make the trip with older children.

Château de Puilaurens
t 04 68 20 65 26
Getting there From Axat take the D117 towards St-Paul-de-Fenouillet, then the D22 towards Gincla
Open Daily 10–6 (5 in winter), July–Aug 9–8; closed Jan
Adm Adult €3.50, child (6–12 years) €1.50

This castle is rumoured to be haunted, and when you see the outline looming high up on the mountain top, it's easy to believe it.

The Canal du Midi

Started in 1666, the Canal du Midi is one of the oldest in Europe. It stretches 240km from the Atlantic to the Mediterranean and took 12,000 men 15 years to build. Explore it by boat, bike or on foot. The nicest stretch is west of Béziers, where it passes through some very pretty villages and where you can have fun negotiating the seven locks at Fonsèranes. Pack a picnic and unwind on the towpath, or hire a bike for a shady cycle ride. You can hire boats in any of the villages along the canal.

Cruise boat hire

The Barge Company
12 Orchard Close, Felton, Bristol BS40 9YS
t (01275) 474034 (toll free from US: **t** 800 688 0245)
www.bargecompany.com

Organizes holidays afloat for families on the Canal du Midi.

Shorter boat trips

Boats leave from the port of Carcassonne and trips last from 30mins to half a day. Ticket prices depend on the length of the trip and start at €3.50 for an adult, €2.50 for a child.

Lou Gabaret
Carcassonne Harbour **t** 04 68 71 61 26
Trip takes 1hr 30mins
Ticket Adult €6.86, child €5.34

AROUND CARCASSONNE

Bricks and mortar

Château Chalabre
t 04 68 69 37 85 **www**.chateau-chalabre.com
Open Daily 10–6.30
Adm Adult €12, child €4, in the afternoon adults are charged half price

This is a mini-medieval theme park in an old château, with horse riding, medieval shows, entertainments and games. You can even try your hand at archery. Kids who spend their days dressing up as knights and princesses will love it here. There's a picnic area and teashop.

Nature lovers

Grottoes and caves

Gouffre de Cabrespine
Caunes-Minervois **t** 04 68 26 14 22
Getting there 18 km north of Carcassonne
Open Daily Mar–Nov 10–12 noon and 2–6; July–Aug 10–7
Adm Adult €6.71, child €3.05, visit takes 45mins

Grottos are a great way to escape the heat of the midday sun, and this is one of the best to visit with kids; there is a huge underground cavern and a

***Good to know...*visiting farms**

In this part of the world you'll see lots of leaflets and roadside notices advertising farms that are open to the public. Goat farms (*ferme des chèvres*) are especially fun to visit with kids and most French kids will be taken to one on a school outing. You'll also see other farms that raise deer (*élevage des biches*) and even ostriches (*autruches*). Although all these are fun to visit, be prepared for some questions about the harsh realities of farming – the French aren't softies when it comes to the end use of the animals they breed and meat products are often for sale on the farm (that's the whole point of visiting for most French people). Some children might find it upsetting.

Fancy a walk... ?

There is beautiful walking country north of Carcassonne. From the village of Minerve, off the main road to Béziers on the D5, follow the green signposts labelled 'Chemin de ronde, Ponts naturels'. From here, pick up the path opposite Rue des Martyrs, which follows the banks of the River Cesse.

For a walk through the woods of the Black Mountain, start from the village of Laviale, which is off the D620 on the D9 in the direction of Castans. Take the path that runs from the parking lot in the cemetery and is labelled '*Sentier des ruisseaux*'. The hamlet of Cupserviès has a pleasant walk that starts at the waterfall and leads along a path up to the dolmen on the hill. Cupserviès is past Lastours off the D101 on the road for Roquefère.

More walks in the region are listed in *Les Sentiers d'Emilie en Pays Cathare* (Rando Editions, €8); even it you don't speak French the book is useful since the maps are self-explanatory.

natural feature called the Devil's Balcony, which is higher than the second story of the Eiffel Tower. Grottos are a big feature of southern France and it's worth making time to visit at least one. There's easy access to this one and it's pushchair friendly – just don't forget to bring sweaters.

Grotte de Limousis

Conques sur Orbiel **t** 04 68 77 50 26
Getting there 15km north of Carcassonne on the D118
Open Daily Mar–Sept 10–12 noon and 2–6; July–Aug 10–6; school holidays 2–6
Adm Adult €6.10, child (6–13 years) €3.05

Although not as spectacular, there are some lovely crystal formations. Look out for the scratches made by bears on the cave wall.

Look at this!

Dinosauria

Av de la Gare, Espéraza **t** 04 68 74 26 88
www.dinosauria.org
Open Daily July–Aug 10–7, rest of the year 10–12 noon and 2–6
Adm Adult €4.50, child (6–12 years) €3.50, workshop €4

Esperaza is rich dinosaur-hunting country and important finds are made here every year, so there is always a lot to see. The exhibition covers both local dinosaurs and those from other parts of the world, and there's a good collection of dinosaur eggs. You can visit the dig and watch palaeontologists at work on their finds. There are children's workshops in the summer for kids aged 6–12, with different themes.

NARBONNE

Getting there Narbonne is just off the main A9 motorway. The railway station is north of the town centre, on Boulevard Mistral. There are train connections to Toulouse, Paris and Perpignan
Getting around You can explore the city centre on foot, but you'll need a car to explore the surrounding areas. There is, however, a bus to the beach and a small tourist train, branch line, L'Autorail Touristique du Minervois, **t** 04 68 27 05 94, that runs from Narbonne into the countryside. Trains leave from Rue Paul Vieu on weekends in July and August and Sundays in September. Tickets: adult €9.30, child €6.14
Tourist office Place Salengro **t** 04 68 65 15 60

Narbonne is a leafy, pleasant town with a fascinating medieval centre. It's divided in two by the Canal de la Robine, which is surrounded by a lovely park. One of the best things to do with kids is take a trip on the canal. There are a number of companies in the city centre offering boat trips; hire motorboats for a quick ride or take a longer trip to the coastal lagoons. Boats leave from the Pont des Marchands.

The heart of the town is in front of the Hôtel de Ville, which is a great place to stop for a drink. The Pont des Marchands, a lovely covered market, is behind the Hôtel de Ville and is a good place to shop with children.

The museums in Narbonne won't be of great interest to kids, but they will enjoy the atmosphere of the town, which is very different from those of Provence and Roussillon and feels as though it should belong in central France. It's only a short drive to the beach, a huge strip of sand that goes on for miles. The coast is far more interesting here than it is further east and is backed by the rocky

Tell me a story: The witches of Gruissan

There are lots of fairy tales set in Gruissan. This one tells the story of a young fisherman who lived in the region. One day he began to suspect that someone was using his fishing boat at night. Every morning when he arrived with his nets to start the day's work, he found the boat's deck was already wet, as if it had recently returned from the ocean. One evening he hid behind a dune to keep watch over the boat and there in the moonlight he saw seven women climb aboard and sail away. The young fisherman kept watch all night, waiting for them to return. Eventually, at dawn, he saw them come back, but before he could say anything, they had disappeared in the direction of the village.

The next night he hid himself on the boat and waited for the mysterious women. When they arrived to set sail as before, they didn't notice they had a stowaway and sailed away with him on board. Just like the 12 dancing princesses in another fairy tale who danced every night at a secret ball, these women were heading heading for a party, and were sailing across the Mediterranean all the way to Egypt. The young fisherman could not believe his eyes when he saw where he was, and he knew that no one else would believe that he had sailed so far so quickly, so he stealthily brought a palm leaf back on board with him to prove where he had been.

When he returned he showed the leaf to the village priest, who said the mysterious women must be witches to be able to carry out such magic. He told the fisherman to put salt across the entrance of the church the following Sunday, because anyone who was a witch would be too scared to step over the salt on the threshold. Sure enough, the following Sunday seven women from the town refused to go into the church. When they realized their secret had been discovered, they didn't wait to find out what would happen next and fled the town.

hills of the Massif de la Clape. You can see the Pyrenees in the distance and watch the flamingos on the lagoons. More exotic animals are on view at the zoo in Sigean.

Things to see and do

St-Just Cathedral

Cours St-Eutrope
t 04 68 33 70 18
Open Daily 10–7, closes for lunch Oct–June; treasury open July–Sept Mon–Sat 11–6, Oct–June Mon–Sat 2–6
Adm Free

Just like Narbonne itself, St-Just looks as though it would be more at home further north. Work started on the cathedral in 1272 when Narbonne was a prosperous town but by the end of the 14th century it had fallen on hard times; its harbour had silted up and the River Aude had changed course, leaving the town a backwater. Lack of money and a row over knocking down part of the city wall to make space for the cathedral meant that St-Just was never finished. Inside the cathedral, the treasury is worth a visit. Look out for the astonishing tapesty of the Creation, which will intrigue children with its amazing detail, and see if they can spot the elephant.

Horreum

Rue Rouget de Lisle
Open Daily 9–12.15 and 2–6, closed Mon mid-Oct–end May
Adm Adult €5, child €2.50

Narbonne was an important trading town on the road between Italy and Spain. This excavation has unearthed the remains of an old Roman warehouse – the only complete one in the world. It's a maze of tiny chambers and there's a great frieze of trained bears and their trainers on one wall.

Shopping

L'Echiquier d'Oc on Rue Droite is interesting to browse in; it specializes not only in chess sets but also plenty of interesting wooden toys and knickknacks. Librairie St-Just, 35 Rue Droite, is an old-fashioned bookshop with helpful staff. It has a good selection of local guidebooks and is especially good if you are looking for advice on family walks with kids. Here you'll find the series *Les Sentiers d'Emilie*, which lists easy walks that take less than 2hrs. There is also a branch of the discount bookshop Maxi Livres on the Pont des Marchands, which is the best place to buy books for kids in French. Also on the Pont des Marchands is Le Club des Petits, for children's clothes.

AROUND NARBONNE

Animal lovers

Réserve de Sigean

Sigean **t** 04 68 48 20 20
www.reserveafricainesigean.fr
Getting there On the N9, 15km south of Narbonne
Open May–Aug daily 9–6.30; April and Sept 9–6; Nov–Dec 9–4; Mar and Oct 9–5
Adm Adult €18, child (4–14 years) €14

The visit takes 3hrs, one of which is spent touring in a bus. It's best to come first thing in the morning or late afternoon to avoid the heat of the sun; most of the animals will be sleeping in the shade during the hottest part of the day. Although the ticket office closes at around 6pm, it depends on who's on duty if they'll let you in after about 5.45pm – if you do get in you can stay in the park another hour and a half but you won't get to go on the tour.

In the sunniest corner of France, a little bit of Africa doesn't look out of place, and this wildlife park is a big attraction and gets very busy. There are 3,800 animals, including antelopes, chimpanzees, elephants, lions, rhinos and bears, and there's a lovely lagoon full of flamingos. This is the main zoo experience in the South of France so it's the best place to come if your kids equate holidays with a trip to see the animals.

You can visit the zoo either on foot or in a car – there's 6km of road. In the car tour you'll see lions, Tibetan bears, zebras, ostriches and white rhinos and on foot you'll see elephants, giraffes, wolves and chimpanzees. There's a picnic area and a panoramic restaurant in the centre of the park.

Buckets and spades

Narbonne Plage and Gruissan

www.narbonne-plage.com
Special events Fishermen's Festival: On 29 June there's a special procession with lots of local colour

These two busy resorts are within minutes of Narbonne and they both have plenty of facilities and sports activities – volleyball and football on the beach, water sports, mini-golf, quad bikes and go-karts – so they are a good base if you have a family who needs a lot of organized entertainment laid on.

Gruissan, with its castle and old streets, is the prettier option of the two. The old town is between a lagoon full of pink flamingos and a stretch of long sandy beaches. The Plage de Pilotis is lined with old fisherman's cottages built on stilts and is one of the nicest seaside resorts in Languedoc. If you have a car it's possible to make day trips from here to the main tourist attractions in the region, like Carcassonne.

Fancy a souvenir...?

Mes Beaux Livres à colorier: Le Languedoc (Aubéron €4.95). It's on sale in most big newsagents and has pictures of all the main attractions to colour in.

Water sports

La Nautique

Narbonne Ville **t** 04 68 65 17 53

Organizes windsurfing courses for over-10s – all equipment provided – from €98 a week. There are also sailing courses for over-6s.

Base Nautique Navalia

Narbonne Plage **t** 04 68 49 70 5

Specializes in sailing lessons for children.

Club Sub-Aquatic Narbonnais

Narbonne Plage **t** 04 68 90 76 47

Has special diving courses for kids.

Aquajet

Narbonne Plage **t** 04 68 49 92 25
Open Easter–Oct

This is a big water park with three slides, boats, train rides and roundabouts.

Club Mickey

Narbonne Plage
Open July and Aug 9–12.30 and 3–6.30
Adm Half day €7, full day €12

Beach club with activities specially designed for 5–13-year-olds, both in and out of the water.

Tennis

L'Ecole de Tennis

Narbonne Plage **t** 04 68 75 00 28

Tennis courses for 5–7-year-olds.

Fancy a walk...?

There are lots of easy walks around Narbonne Plage. From Peyriac de Mer on the D105, you can walk around the lagoon, l'Étang de Doul. The path starts from the car park near the tennis courts. There's also an easy stroll around the Ile Ste-Lucie, at Porte-la-Nouvelle, which is on the main N139. The Parc Naturel Régional de la Narbonnaise in Narbonne, **t** 04 68 42 23 70, organizes accompanied walks for families.

Bikes

This is great cycling country; you can hire bikes at:

Pub-cycles

Narbonne Plage **t** 04 68 49 85 72.

They also have junior cycling equipment and baby seats, Rollerblades for adults and children and go-karts. The owners speak English.

Mini train

Petit Train des Lagunes, Port-la-Nouvelle
t 04 68 48 14 93
Runs mid-June–Sept

Little kids love the tourist train that runs past the beach at La Franqui and the Ile Ste-Lucie, the small wild island in the lagoon.

Le Musée de la Baleine

t 04 68 48 00 39.
Open Daily 10–6
Adm Free

This is on the train route, and inside you'll find the skeleton of a huge whale (*la baleine*), which was washed ashore in 1989. The museum is really a wine warehouse and the owner, a keen naturalist, brought the skeleton here in his 2-CV car and cleaned up the bones himself.

ROUSSILLON

PERPIGNAN

Getting there Perpignan is on the A9 autoroute. There are direct flights from London Stansted (**www**.ryanair.com) and daily flights from Paris with Air Littoral (**www**.airlittoral.com). The airport, **t** 04 68 52 60 70, is 5km north of the city centre. From there you can hire a car or take the shuttle bus to the town centre. Get a city map before you set off – Perpignan is one of the most confusing towns to find your way around after dark. The town is well connected by rail, with high-speed TGVs from Paris via Montpellier and direct trains daily from Brussels, Frankfurt, Geneva and Milan. If you arrive by train you can clock up one of the sights immediately: the somewhat unprepossesing train station was declared the centre of the world by Salvador Dalí, and surrealists have been making the pilgrimage ever since. You'll have to hop on another train to see his painting of the station, though – it's in Cologne

Tourist office Palais des Congrès, Place Armand-Lanoux **t** 00 33 (0)4 68 66 30 30 **www**.perpignan tourisme.com

Special events February: Carnival: Mayhem and merriment as revellers throw flour at passers-by. March/April: Good Friday Procession: Red-robed penitents progress through the town. June: Medieval Market for the Feast of St Jean. July/August: Tautavel Prehistoric Festival. December: Christmas Market: Look out for the '*Caga Tio*', a local speciality filled with sweets and small gifts, rather like a Mexican *piñata*

Perpignan is something else – a French town with a Spanish atmosphere. It is Catalan before it's French, despite the fact that it has belonged to France since 1659. Back then, the French had to fight long and hard to take control of Perpignan, and they besieged the city many times before they were able to take it for good. Today it is happy to be part of modern France but culturally it's still close

Did you know...?

Hannibal and his elephants passed near to Perpignan on their way to attack Rome in 218 BC. They stopped at Elne, which is just 13km south of the town.

to Spain. The town is just 30km from the border and the architecture and palm trees feel as though they belong much further south. It's a good place to head for a short break with the kids and a great base for exploring Roussillon, one of the loveliest and sunniest parts of France. It's less than half an hour to the mountains and the coast is only 10 minutes away.

Kids will like the old medieval town, with its rabbit warren of streets, and as it's virtually pedestrianized they can run around safely. Perpignan is not over run with tourists, and its attractions are simple; sunshine, colourful market stalls, good food and a lively café atmosphere more than make up for the fact there isn't a great deal of specific sites to visit. The old town is small and is a good place to let teenagers spend some time on their own.

In the 1970s Perpignan had a bad reputation as thousands of Spaniards flocked over the border from Franco's repressive Spain to live it up in the city's fleshpots. But now that there's plenty of that on offer back in Barcelona, the city has cleaned itself up.

Shopping

Perpignan has all the major chains: the big department store Galeries Lafayette is on Place de la Résistance and there's a Monoprix on Rue de la Barre. For children's clothes, try Cendrillon on Rue St-Jean, Du Pareil au Même for stylish bargains, and Mod 8 for shoes on Rue des Trois-Journées, or Pimkie on Rue de Marchands, which will appeal to teenage girls. Le Club des Petits on Rue des Augustins has good-value kids' clothes, too. Also on Rue des Trois-Journées look out for the shop run by former French rugby captain Serge Blanco. It's named after him and is full of rugby regalia. Perpignan is passionate about its rugby, and rugby kit is seen as a fashion item.

For children's books, there's an especially good branch of the discount bookshop Maxi Livres on Rue de l'Ange. Mané Récréation, on Rue Voltaire, is a good traditional toy shop. If you need a puzzle or a board game for something quiet to do during the heat of the day this is where you'll find it.

Picnics and snacks

Most kids dream of somewhere like Mangez-moi on Rue Petite-la-Monnaie – a sweet shop with child-sized chairs and music, serving whole plates of sweets like sugar-coated hors d'oeuvres.

Can you spot...the Catalan Flag?
It has red and yellow stripes. You'll see it hanging everywhere.

There are literally thousands of sweets to choose from and, depending on your age, you may be glad to know the shop opens at 7am.

You can graze your way around the old town, which is full of excellent delicatessens and bakeries. For last-minute staples, try Patrick, a late-night grocer on Rue Petite-la-Réal. There is great picnicking potential, with beautiful countryside just 20mins from town, so stock up on picnic supplies in the market place on Place République (open daily except Sunday). You can buy roast chickens here and then browse among the specialist food shops off the main square. Place République is a good place to stop for a coffee and Coke to watch the passing scene. Try Le Petit Moka, a lovely café (next to a shop where they sell live snails); teenagers might enjoy Net and Games on Rambla du Vallespir, a little cybercafé that's popular with students.

Things to see and do

Le Castillet

t 04 68 35 42 05
Open Daily 10–7, winter 11.30–5.30
Adm Adult €3.80, child €1.50

This is a little museum of Catalan art and traditions, housed in the 14th-century fortified gate used as the symbol for the town. Depending on their temperament kids will shudder deliciously at or be horrified by the building's mysterious past: the body of an unidentified child was discovered here in 1946 when the tower was being restored. It had been walled up in the tower in the 18th century and once exposed to the air the bones turned to dust.

Look out for...

The Balades en Pays Catalan **is a French paperback book packed full of games to help kids aged 8 and above to discover the region. It costs €9.90 and is on sale in most tourist shops and newsagents. The tourist board also has a leaflet,** ***Visites Contées*****, which lists storytelling events for children in the region's main tourist attractions.**

Place de la Loge

This is the heart of the old town and a good place to stop for a drink. In summer you can sometimes see local dancers perform *La Sardane*, a traditional Catalan folkdance.

Palais des Rois de Majorque

Rue des Archers **t** 04 68 34 48 29
Open Daily 10–6 (5 in winter)
Adm Adult €3, child €2

This huge and imposing citadel is the oldest royal palace in France, and is a good place to visit with kids because you can explore as much or as little of it as you like. There are breathtaking views from the ramparts across to the mountains and lots of space in the gardens for little ones to let off steam. It's often used as a gallery for local modernist exhibitions, which might appeal to older kids.

Cinemas

Le Castillet

1 Bd Wilson **t** 04 68 51 25 47

Opened in 1911, this is the oldest cinema in town, and it is still more convenient than the out-of-town multiplex.

Parks and playgrounds

There's a children's playground on Bd Jean Bourrat. For a walk or picnic try Le Serrat d'en Vanquer, an old fort-cum-park, which is 3km out of town on the N9 on the way to Spain. It is open until 8pm in summer and is closed on Mondays. Admission is free.

SPECIAL TRIPS FROM PERPIGNAN

Centre Européen de Préhistoire de Tautavel

t 04 68 29 07 76
Getting there 30km north of Perpignan off the D117
Open Daily Oct–Mar 10–12.30 and 2–6; April–June and Sept 10–6; July–Aug 9–9
Adm Adult €6, child (7–14) €3, under-7s free

The study of Tautavel man is a major part of the French primary school curriculum, but outside of France few people have heard of the Caune de l'Arago, which is astonishing: it was there in 1971 that archaeologists found the remains of the first men ever to set foot in Europe, the skull of a man who died 455,000 years ago. After careful excavation the cave also revealed large numbers of milk teeth, suggesting that children lived there too. The cave itself is 2km from town and open to the public in the summer. Here at the museum you can find out what life was like for Tautavel man. The upper floor of the museum is a bit tedious, with collections of bones and fossils, but downstairs is fascinating, with reconstructions of life in Tautavel, a reconstruction of the cave and a clever film projected onto the walls to give you the impression you've stepped back in time. There is also an excellent but bloodthirsty film – which might be either too strong for some children or the best part of their holiday – featuring the butchering of a horse and Tautavel man tearing raw liver with his teeth. Hurry past it if it's not your thing. Next door, in the adjacent Palais de Congrès, the exhibition continues with a 3-D display. If you're visiting in the summer look out for events connected with the Prehistoric Festival in July and August.

Fancy a souvenir...?

The museum has an excellent shop, containing prehistoric-themed paraphernalia like pieces of flint or miniature plastic prehistoric men and animals. Slightly more learned is *Noune, Child of Prehistory*, a storybook in English.

AROUND PERPIGNAN

Animal magic

Parc Animalier des Angles

t 04 68 04 17 20
Getting there Off the D118 for Axat at Les Angles
Open Sept–June daily 9–6, July–Aug 9–7
Adm Adult €8, child (4–14 years) €6.50

This is more of a reserve than a zoo and is a wonderful visit. The animals here are indigenous to the Pyrenees and wander freely in the open countryside within the boundaries of the park. This is home to all kinds of mountain animals – deer, bears, mouflon, ibex, wolves and bison – and to see them you'll need patience and quiet as the animals aren't on display as in a zoo; all the creatures here are living in the wild.

There are two circuits round the park: the longer route is 3.5km and takes you past the bison and the wolves; the shorter is 1.5km. There are some regular picnic spots along the route where you can stop and catch glimpses of bison flitting through the forest. The park is open all year round and is as exciting in the snow as it is in the summer sun.

Le Tropique du Papillon

Elne **t** 04 68 37 83 77
Getting there On the N114 between Elne and Argelès
Open July–Aug daily 10–7; April–June and Sept 10–12.30 and 2.30–7
Adm Adults €4.57, child €2.29

This is a series of large greenhouses where the butterflies fly freely; some might even land on your hand. There's also a playground and a very nice souvenir shop.

Les Aigles de Valmy

Château de Valmy, Argelès-sur-Mer **t** 04 68 81 67 32
Open Flying displays daily 2.30, 3.30 and 4.30, plus evening shows 9.30 July–Aug
Adm Adult €7.50 (evening show €9), child €6 (evening show €7)

Watch a display of giant birds of prey in the evocative surroundings of a château with a beautiful park.

Bricks and mortar

Fortresse de Salses

t 04 68 38 60 13
Getting there 16km north of town on the N9
Open Daily 9.30–7 in summer, winter times vary
Adm Adult €5.50, child (under 17) free, visit takes 45mins

After his marriage to Isabelle of Castille, Ferdinand of Aragon decided to beef up his new country's defences and built this fortress in 1497 as the front line between France and Spain. In 1659, when Roussillon became part of France, the border shifted south and the fortress became a prison. Salses is very different from the Cathar castles; it's an early modern fort rather than a medieval castle.

Villefranche-de-Conflent

Getting there 50km from Perpignan on the N116
Tourist office 32 Rue St-Jacques **t** 04 68 96 22 96

As you drive out of Perpignan towards Villefranche and the mountains you'll get a real feel of the Pyrenees. Villefranche itself is a beautiful fortified medieval town. Vauban, who built a number of fine military fortifications for Louis XIV, was responsible for its defences. The ramparts are virtually complete and fun to explore with kids. The highlight of the visit is the massive castle.

Château Fort Liberia

Villefranche-de-Conflent **t** 04 68 96 34 01
Open April–Oct daily 10–8; Oct–Mar 10–6
Adm Adult €5.34, child €3

The castle was built in 1681 and renovated in the 19th century by Napoleon III. To reach it, take the underground passageway (known as the Thousand Steps, though there are actually 734 of them) up to the gate.

The castle houses permanent exhibitions on archaeology and the local caves. In the dungeons there are some scary reconstructions of murders, which might be too much for small children.

In July and August you can visit at night and enjoy a Catalan meal served by waiters in old-fashioned costume.

Fort Lagarde

Prats-de-Mollo, between Villefranche and Perpignan **t** 04 68 39 70 83
Open April–June daily 2–6; July–Aug 10–6; Sept–Nov 2–5; shows July–Aug daily 2.30 and 4
Adm Adult €7, child (6–12 years) €4; tickets for shows adult €6.40, child (6–12) €3.81

Stop in on this 17th-century fort on the way back to Perpignan from Villefranche. During the special military shows attendants dressed as 18th-century soldiers fire canons and muskets from the ramparts and show off their riding skills.

Good to know...

This stretch of coast can be very windy. When the local wind, *la tramontane*, blows it's impossible to stay on the beach, and even before it really gets going it can push sea temperatures down.

A car is a must for exploring along this route, and if you have a baby, you'll need the raincover for the pram to cope with the wind.

Buckets and spades

The coast running south to Spain has been heavily developed in recent years but it still has lots of charm and is beautifully offset by the mountains rising up behind. There are acres upon acres of sandy beaches, all of which are great for kids, and the resorts aren't as built up as, say, Agde or Juan-les-Pins.

For an excellent family beach where the little ones can play safely in the water try Leucate Plage, which is protected from the wind by a cliff. Port-Barcarès is a relatively modern resort (built in the 1970s) and the place to go if you want to sail or windsurf. It is basically a holiday village with bungalow accommodation set between a large lagoon and the beach.

Just 12km from Perpignan is Canet-en-Roussillon (**www**.ot-canet.fr), the busiest resort on this stretch of coast. It has a lovely beach and is great for a family day out or a longer stay. It has three little museums, which are fun if you're in town, but not worth a special trip: one devoted to cars, one to boats, and one to old toys, and all open in the summer season only. There's a small aquarium next to the port as well.

Argelès-sur-Mer is an attractive and lively old town but it's the capital of camping so is fit to burst in July and August. With the exception of Collioure, the resorts don't have much to single them out for recommendation but they are welcoming and packed with families.

The drive south along the zigzag coast road from Collioure features steep coves and vertiginous cliffs with stunning views. At Cap Rederis you can see the Costa Brava stretching out in front of you, which may whet the kids' appetites to travel further. The little ports between Collioure and the borders are nothing to write home about but it's fun to drive to Cerbère to show them the defunct frontier post (although you'll feel your age telling them what it was like crossing European borders when you were a kid). Once you've caught a glimpse of Spain, turn around, as the coves across the border are industrial and none too pleasant. Don't be tempted to drive to the motorway to cross back into France – it's a very long drive.

Town life

Collioure

Getting there **It's 21km from Perpignan off the A9 and there's a large car park by the old port. There are regular train and bus connections from Perpignan and trains from Paris**
Tourist office **Pl du 18 Juin t 00 33 (0)4 68 82 15 47 www.collioure.com**
Special events **Good Friday: Procession of Penitents. July–Aug: Weekly folk dancing in the town centre. Mid-Aug: Town festival with fireworks**

Collioure is one of the best-kept secrets on the coast, familiar to very few outside France. Here the Pyrenees tumble into the sea, creating a series of beautiful bays and rocky headlands, which give this stretch of coast a unique character. Collioure is a great base for a family holiday, with a castle, three little sandy beaches and a shady market square with plenty of cafés. It has a strong Spanish feel so if your kids know France quite well they'll like making comparisons.

There is little development here: you won't find water slides or go-karts and there's none of the hype that has spoilt a lot of the coast along the Riviera. The wind is less likely to be a problem here, either, because it's more sheltered than some of the other coastal towns. Wind, however, was one of the things that first put Collioure on the map: it seemed to make colours especially brilliant and inspired the painters Matisse and Dérain to spend a summer here. None of their paintings are

Can you spot...an anchovy?
Collioure is famous for its anchovies, which are caught at night with the aid of huge searchlights.

Look out for...
Les Sentiers d'Emilie dans les Pyrénées Orientales, a guide to family walks in the area. It's on sale in most bookshops and newsagents, and even if you can't speak French the maps are very useful.

left in Collioure, but the tourist board has put copies on the spots where they set up their easels. Today, Matisse would still recognize the red roofs, the green shutters, and the sailboats bobbing in the harbour in the glittering sunlight. They are all just as they were when he was in town, give or take a few postcard stalls and ice-cream vendors.

Royal Palace

Collioure **t** 04 68 82 06 43
Open 10–7 (6 in winter)
Adm Adult €3, child free

This was originally the summer palace of the kings of Majorca, who ruled the area, but it was rebuilt by Louis XIV's master castle builder Vauban in the 17th century. He ordered a large portion of the old town to be torn down in order to make way for the rebuilt castle, which is almost the same size as the rest of the town. Take a look inside and try to recapture it in sand on the beach afterwards.

Steam power!

Le Train Jaune

Villefranche-de-Conflent **t** 04 68 04 80 62
Getting there 50km from Perpignan on the N116, or by early morning bus from Perpignan station
Tickets: €90 return for a family of 4

This is a fantastic journey in a steam-powered train with bright yellow carriages, some of which are open topped. This is an actual train journey lasting 2hrs 45mins in total, not simply a tourist attraction, but the trip is delightful and gives a flavour of the Pyrenees. The train runs 63km from Villefranche to the Cerdagne Plateau, and rattles through some beautiful gorges and across the precipitous viaduct of Séjourné. If you don't want to go the whole way, get off at Mont Louis, the highest fort in France, built by the ever-busy Vauban. There are some great walks to go on from the train; ask for information in the station.

In low season there's just one train a day but in high season there are eight, although you may need to queue as long as 30mins for a ticket.

Nature lovers

Gorge de Galamus

A visit to the gorge makes a fantastic family outing and shouldn't be missed. The views are spectacular – the gorge is white and rocky, with a river of an incomparable blue-green – and the road is cut out of the rock and weaves along a ledge, which makes for a great adventure. This is an extremely narrow gorge so don't sound the horn as it can cause little rocks to loosen and fall off as you drive along; the kids no doubt will love it, but it's not the best idea for the hire car. You can stop for a gorgeous lunch at Au Vieux Moulin (*see* p.177), a lovely restaurant at the end of the gorge in Cubieres-sur-Cinoble, or picnic by the river and hire kayaks for €15 a day. There are some lovely natural pools for swimming, too. Combine the trip with an outing to Quéribus (*see* p.149) or Tautavel (*see* p.156) for an unforgettable day.

Grottoes and Caves

Grotte de l'Aguzou

Axat **t** 04 68 20 45 38
Getting there On the D118 15km from Axat
Open Daily 9–5, tour takes 8hrs (not suitable for children under 10)

This tour is an extraordinary chance to explore the underground world of stalagmites and stalactites, but is not for the under-10s or for the claustrophobic as the entire day is spent underground. The route itself isn't too strenuous, so you need to be keen rather than fit, and it's best if you

Did you know...?
Stalactites hang down from the ceiling of caves and stalagmites grow upwards. They are made out of the minerals that are carried in the water and accumulate as it drips through the roof.

Good to know...

Nature Activities Côté Soleil – if you have a sporty family you'd do well to get hold of this tourist board booklet, which lists all the sporting activities in the region, many of which are designed specifically for families. If you like riding, look out for the leaflet *Bienvenue à la Ferme*, which lists farms (*les fermes équestres*) where you can ride. Many of them also offer accommodation.

have a working knowledge of French. You'll be kitted out with a helmet and a torch, but you'll need to bring a sweater, a picnic lunch and water.

Grotte des Grandes Canalettes

Villefranche-de-Confluent **t** 04 68 96 23 11
Getting there 1km out of town in the direction of Vernet-les-Bains
Open Daily Mid-June–mid-Sept 10–6; mid-Sept–Oct; April and early June 10–12 noon and 2–5.30; Nov–April Sun and school hols only 2–5. *Son et lumière* show July–Aug 6.30
Adm Adult €10, child (5–12) €5

The tour takes you through some amazing caverns, with names like the White Hall, the Temple of Angkor and the Lake of Atolls. Subtle lighting and classical music enhance the atmosphere and there are special *son et lumière* shows in summer.

Sporty kids

Aqualand

Chemin du Mas des Capellans, Saint-Cyprien Plage
t 04 68 15 21 47
Getting there 20km south of Perpignan on the D81
Open June–Sept daily 10–6; July–Aug 9.30–8
Adm Adult €16.50, child (3–12 years) €14.50

Can you spot...the Pic di Canigou?
In fact you can't miss this mountain. It's sacred to Catalans and on the Feast of St Jean in June torches are lit at the summit and carried to each village. Every town has a bonfire with dancing and fireworks.

Aqualand

Av du Roussillon, Port Leucate **t** 04 68 40 99 98
Open Mid-June–Aug daily 10–6 (7 mid-July–mid-Aug)
Adm Adult €12.50, child (3–12 years) €11.50

Both parks have several huge slides and plenty of small, shallow pools for toddlers.

Argèles Adventure

Plage Nord, Argelès-sur-Mer **t** 04 68 95 41 66
Open Daily 10–5, July–Aug 9–12 midnight; restricted opening hours in winter, so call ahead
Adm Adventure Park: adults €15, child (under 12) €12; Animal Parc: €6

This is a huge adventure playground for the over-5s, arranged in five levels of difficulty. There's also a

Sailing with kids

Children's first encounters with the ocean can often stay with them for life. Some wade right in to the top of their nappy and others set about building a massive fortification to stop the waves from coming anywhere near them. Parents do nothing to help, one minute calling them back from the water's edge, the next dunking them in the sea up to their armpits. So if you're not that confident in the water yourself, getting them into a small boat, especially one manned by only you, can be hard to achieve. However, you don't need to have much experience to try your hand at simple boating with the kids. Start small, with a large, flat-bottomed canoe and paddle around in the shallows until they get the feel of the water. Don't even think about getting in a boat without proper life jackets; check the boat hire shop has a range of children's sizes and that all the straps work. If they don't, go somewhere else.

Some holiday resorts like Mark Warner in Corsica (*see* pp.197 and 214) run specific children's sailing courses, introducing them to the high thrills of water-skiing and windsurfing into the bargain. In this part of the Mediterranean it is best to go for lessons in the morning when the sea tends to be calmer. If you are taking lessons yourself, get the feel of a boat on your own before taking anyone out with you. Choose something that's easy to sail like a Funboat or a canoe for family sailing or take a trip with one of the qualified instructors. Older children who are confident swimmers can learn alongside the adults in their own boats.

snack bar, an animal park and a playground for little ones and it's a good venue for younger teens in the evening.

Look at this!

Musée d'Art Moderne

8 Bd Maréchal Joffre, Céret **t** 04 68 87 27 76
www.musee-ceret.com
Getting there 30km from Perpignan, off the A9 on the D115. There's no train service but you can catch a bus from Perpignan
Open Daily 10–6 (7 summer), Wed–Mon in winter
Adm Adult €5.50

You might feel as though you're in the middle of nowhere but in artistic terms the mountains of Roussillon were once a hub of creativity. Picasso and many other famous cubists settled in Céret at the beginning of the 20th century and later many artists came here during the Second World War to escape the Nazis. This is a really lively modern art museum, which is very accessible for kids. If you are in Roussillon for a while, it is worth looking into the kids' workshops on a Wednesday afternoon.

AGDE

Getting there Agde is just off the A9 motorway. It's 70km from Montpellier airport and there are direct trains from Paris
Getting around There's a little tourist train and a regular shuttle bus from Agde town to Cap d'Agde. The resort is ideal for cycling; hire bikes at Cap Adventure, 19 Av des Serjeants, Le Cap d'Agde, **t** 04 67 26 36 00
Tourist office Place Molière **t** 00 33 (0)4 67 94 29 68 **www**.capdagde.com **www**.agde-ville.fr
Special events There are always lots of activities for kids to try out in Cap d'Agde. April: Kite Festival, with special workshops for kids to make and decorate their own kites. May: Every Sunday there are kids' theatre displays and acrobats at the port

Despite its ancient past this area is swamped in a huge modern development, Cap d'Agde. At times it can make you feel as though you are lost in suburbia, although on the plus side it means there's a huge range of accommodation to choose from. Agde features in many holiday brochures and is a good family resort with lots of campsites, but don't come expecting the glamour of the Riviera or to be bowled over by the beauty of the coast. The kids, however, will love the beaches and there are lots of children's activities throughout the area. The tourist office has an excellent booklet that lists absolutely everything you can do in Adge, and if you have a car it's a good place to use as a base for exploring the region.

The resort is divided into three sections – the old town of Agde, Cap d'Agde and Grau d'Agde. There are bus connections between the three of them, but if you have teenagers it pays to rent bikes so they can get about independently. There are more than enough bars, cafés, kids' clubs and sports activities to make it an attractive destination for older kids and teenagers.

Things to see and do

The **Ile des Loisirs**, or Leisure Island, which actually is a small island is an area dedicated to little amusement parks for kids, has cinemas, mini-golf and karting plus lots of bars, restaurants and a disco. Don't come expecting to find a new Disneyland; this is a small-scale affair and typical of the theme parks you'll find all around the Med.

Dino Park

Ile des Loisirs, Cap d'Agde **t** 04 67 26 65 13
Open Mar–Nov daily 10–6
Adm Adult €6.10, child €14

No, you have not read the prices incorrectly, children are charged more here; perhaps for liking dinosaurs and fairground rides, or perhaps in recognition of the fact that adults are here really as minders. This is a bit different from the usual funfair experience, with 18 model dinosaurs and exhibitions on the origins of the universe, but the emphasis is on recreation rather than learning. In addition to all things dinosaur there are trampolines, badminton, volleyball and playgrounds.

Toon's Land

Ile des Loisirs, Cap d'Agde **t** 04 67 00 04 44
Open Mar–Nov 11–8
Adm Adult €6.10, child (over 9) €14

A family funfair with circus acts and a mini-farm plus a ghost house and numerous rides.

Musée de la Magie

Place Agde Marine Cap d'Agde **t** 04 67 01 54 80
Open April–Oct 3–12 midnight (7 on weekends)
Adm Adult €6, child €4.50

Guided tour through the history of magic, with regular magic shows and special magic courses for kids. There is also a shop where you can pick up tricks to practise at home.

Aquarium du Cap d'Agde

Quartier de l'Avant-Port, 11 Rue des Deux-Freres
t 04 67 26 14 21 **www**.aquariumagde.com
Open Sept–June Mon–Sat 2–6, Sun 11–7; July–Aug 10am–11pm
Adm Adult €6, child (6–12) €4

This aquarium sets out to explain the underwater world to children. There's a new baby shark pool and in the summer months the museum organizes trips to the beach for a hands-on marine experience. There are lots of other kids' activities here, both inside and outside the aquarium.

Can you spot...a volcano?

You're standing on top of one. Agde is at the end of a string of defunct volcanoes that stretch up to the Massif Central, which is why the beaches are black. Take a walk up to Mont Saint-Loup, which has a great view along the coast – it was created in a volcanic eruption millions of years ago. All that volcanic activity put the bubbles in Perrier water – the spring isn't far from here (see p.174).

Did you know...?

The name Agde comes from the Greek work agathos, meaning 'good'. The city was founded by the Phoenicians and is France's oldest city after Marseille.

Museum of Ephèbe

La Clape **t** 04 67 94 69 60
Open Thurs–Tues 10–12 noon and 2–6 (2–7 July–Aug)
Adm Adult €3, child (over 8) €1.52

This museum houses a collection of archaeological finds discovered off the coast and returned to the area from the Louvre in Paris in 1987. Arty kids may enjoy the drawing classes they run here.

Boat trips and beaches

There's a huge marina at Cap d'Agde and numerous trips you can take along the coast from Agde, but probably the most exciting trip is in a glass-bottomed boat. Contact Les Bateaux Blancs et Bleus, from Quai Jean Miquel, Le Cap d'Agde, **t** 04 67 26 28 41. Trips run April–Nov.

There are 14km of sandy beaches in this corner of of France; some are free and some are given over to beach clubs but most of them are child-friendly, with playgrounds and pedalos, although there is a nudist beach too. Swimming is safe along this stretch of coast and most beaches have a beach guard. La Grande Conque beach, which is the end of a chain of dormant volcanoes that stretch up into the Auvergne, is famous for its black volcanic sand. Club Mickey at Plage du Grau d'Agde, is a beach club for 3–15-year-olds. If you have trouble parking try the Centre Plage Richelieu, t 04 67 26 76 93, open daily Jul and Aug 10–6.

Cinemas

Le Festival

Ile des Loisirs, Cap d'Agde **t** 04 67 26 71 66

Le Richlieu

8 Rue Mirabeau, Agde **t** 04 67 26 71 66

Water sports

Agathé Blue

23 Rue de l'Escalade, Cap d'Agde **t** 04 67 00 02 11

Diving for kids over the age of 8.

Centre Nautique du Cap d'Adge

Plage Richelieu Est **t** 04 67 01 46 46

Sailing courses for kids 8 and above; windsurfing from age 13.

Aqualand

Avenue des Iles d'Amériques (between Vias and Marseillan Beach) **t** 04 67 26 85 94
www.aqualand.fr
Open June–Sept daily 10–6; July–Aug 9.30–8
Adm Adult €16.50, child (3–12) €14.50

This massive water park has literally kilometres of slides, a 'kamikaze' river and rapids. There's also a paddling pool for the little ones.

Horse riding

Le Gardian

Rte de Rochelongue, Agde **t** 06 62 01 98 93

Pony treks for the under-8s, from 1–4hrs.

AROUND AGDE

Town life

Pézenas

Getting there Pézenas is just off the A9 autoroute, about 45mins from Montpellier and less than 30mins from Agde.
Tourist office Place Gambetta BP 10 **t** 00 33 (0)4 67 98 36 40 **www**.ville-pezenas.fr
Special events February: Pézenas Carnival includes a procession and dancing in the streets. June: Celebrations commemorating Molière's stay in the town during the 18th century. December: Christmas Market

Pézenas is a real gem of a town, with a delightful medieval centre where you can while away an afternoon shopping or go for an evening meal. It's main claim to fame is through its celebrated former resident, Molière, who holds a place in French hearts that is as dear as Shakespeare is to the English. There are no major sites or historic monuments to tick off the list in Pézenas; it's simply a pleasure to stroll around the old town or to take the kids to the playground in the pretty Parc Sans Souci. While you're exploring take note of the street names, one of which refers to the Jewish ghetto that stood here until the Jews were expelled from France in 1394 by Charles VI.

Can you spot...a boiled sweet?

Suck on a berlingot while you do your sight-seeing in Pézenas, a boiled sweet flavoured with mint and fruit purée and a speciality of the region. You can buy them by the bagful at the factory Boudet on Chemin St-Christol.

North of Pézenas are some lovely villages and the tourist office has a useful leaflet outlining some walking tours in the area.

Shopping

Shopping is one of the main activities here and you'll find plenty to catch your eye along the old streets. Of particular interest to the children will be the branch of La Cure Gourmande on Rue de la Foire and La Maison du Jouet, a good old-fashioned toy shop on Rue St-Jean.

Picnics and snacks

The local delicacies are *petits pâtés*, a pastry made with sweetened lamb, originally cooked up by the servants of Lord Clive, Govenor of India, who took a holiday here in the 1770s. Maison Allary on Rue St-Jean is the place to buy them (*closed Mon*).

Buckets and spades

Sète

There's a huge, if slightly uninspiring, sandy beach at Sète, a popular holiday destination for French tourists but also a working port, the second along the south coast after Marseille. It's a gritty little place, which could do with a slap of paint, but the town is teeming with canals, cafés and beaches and boats. If your children are early risers go to the dockside to watch the fishermen unload their catches and if you visit at the end of August you'll catch the water-jousting contests. Sète is fun to visit, but don't base yourself here for the whole holiday; you'll want to scurry home for the night to somewhere less workaday.

Look at this!

La Plaine des Dinosaures

Mèze **t** 04 67 43 02 80
www.musee-parc-dinosaures.com
Getting there On the N113 north of Mèze, just off the A9, exit Sète
Open Sept–June 2–6; Oct–Jan 2–5; July–Aug 10–7
Adm Adult €6, child (5–12 years) €4.50

This museum is a mini Jurassic park, with huge dinosaur skeletons and models looming over the trees. Follow the path that winds through the pine forest and it will take you back 60 million years, to a time when Mèze was a gigantic tropical plain teeming with dinosaurs. Today, you can see one of the biggest collections of dinosaur eggs in the world and a giant, 80ft-long skeleton of a Brachiosaurus. Little ones will enjoy the sand pit where they can play at being a palaeontologist. The outing takes about 1½ hrs.

MONTPELLIER

Getting there Montpellier is just off the main A9 motorway. The airport, **t** 04 67 20 85 85, is 8km from town and there are direct flights from London (**www**.britishairways.com and **www**.ryanair.com) and Paris. There's an airport shuttle bus to the train station on Place Auguste Gibert, which takes 20mins. TGV trains run from Paris, Lille and Brussels
Getting around The city has one of the best tram systems in Europe – sleek, modern and buggy-friendly. Kids often regard it as one of the attractions and it's probably more exciting to ride than the usual tourist minitrain. More prosaically, there is a taxi rank outside the train station.
Tourist Office 30 Allée Jean Lattre de Tassigny **t** 00 33 (0)4 67 60 60 61 **www**.ot-montpellier.fr **www**.montpellier.mediterranee.org

Montpellier is a strikingly modern and vibrant city, so confident in its importance to the South of France that its tourist board trumpets it as 'The Capital of the South' or 'The Rome of Tomorrow'. Since 1977, this once quiet university town has tripled its population and has enjoyed huge new development projects, such as Antigone. Designed by Catalan architect Ricardo Bofill on a positively palatial scale, it provides moderate-income housing for 100,000 people. With its vast size and decorative arches and columns, its style could best be described as 'futuro-classical' – somehow appropriate for the Rome of Tomorrow. Antigone is great to stroll around with the kids; look out for the fountain in the main square , which has an almost hypnotic effect as it grows and shrinks before you. It's a great place to relax and cool off, and is usually surrounded by hordes of little kids splashing through it.

The other hub of city life is the old Place de la Comédie. It's the place to stop for a drink and people watch, and has a huge paved square where the kids can run around. Nearby there's a lovely park with a good playground.

Montpellier is likely to be a huge hit with anyone over the age of 8, especially if they've travelled in France before. Its lively atmosphere is enhanced by the number of students in town. There has been a university in Montpellier since the 13th century (Nostradamus, the man of predictions , *see* p.119, studied medicine here) and students make up nearly a quarter of the population.

Shopping

The best place to shop is the huge Centre Commercial Polygone in the Antigone. Here you'll find all the main stores, including the Galeries Lafayette department store and FNAC for books and CDs. There's also a branch of Nature et Découvertes, a wonderful toyshop for kids interested in nature and a good place to take junior astronomers. If you are heading out into the country stock up here with essential equipment such as bug viewers and star guides. Teenage girls will find a branch of the excellent-value and ubiquitous Pimkie here, too. There are more good shops in the old town: for stylish clothes Agnès B women's wear is on Rue Petit St-Jean and the men's is on Rue St-Paul. Rue Loge has a branch of Petit Bateau, the kids' clothes shop, and the discount bookshop Maxi Livres. For one-offs and bargains browse among the stalls of the flea market underneath the Aqueduc St-Clément on Saturdays.

Picnics and snacks

Look out for the local sweets, almonds covered in dark or white chocolate coloured black or green to look like olives. They make great gifts and picnic treats and you can buy them at Le Diamant Noir, on Rue St-Guilhem.

There are daily food markets throughout the old town and a Sunday farmers' market in Antigone. Also in Antigone, in the Polygone Shopping Centre, there's an INNO supermarket, one of the most upmarket of the French chains, with a great selection of ready-prepared food perfect for picnicking.

Things to see and do

One of the best ways to see the old town of Montpellier with kids is to hop aboard the Petit Train, **t** 04 67 60 60 60, which leaves from Place de la Comédie and takes three different circuits round the town. Trains run morning and evenings, July–Sept. For something more sedate, jump on board a horse and cart; you'll also find them in Place de la Comédie.

For some greenery and a place for the children to run around, you might want to visit the Jardin des Plantes, on Rue Auguste Broussonnet. There's a small admission charge: adult €3.50, child (5–10) €1.50, and it's closed on Monday.

If you want a more futuristic experience, catch the sleek city tram (tickets are available on the platform) and head for the Odysseum, which really does look like an architectural drawing come to life. Here you'll find the huge Gaumont Multiplex cinema, **t** 0892 696 696 and the Gaumont IMAX, **t** 04 99 52 33 11.

Planétarium Galilée

Odysseum **t** 04 67 13 26 26
Open Performances Wed and Sun 2–7, Fri and Sat 2–10, and Tues and Thurs 2–10 in school hols
Adm Adult €6, child (under 12) €5

There are great shows at this stylish planetarium, although you'll need to speak French to get the best out of the visit. The reclining seats are huge, so if you have a baby or toddler there's plenty of room for them to share a seat with you.

La Patinoire Vegapolis

Odysseum **t** 04 99 52 26 00
www.vegapolis.net
Open Daily, times vary but it's always open in the afternoon
Adm Adult €4.60, child (under 16) €3.50

This huge, state-of-the-art skating rink is right next to the cinema, and is as shiny and high-tech as you would expect in the new improved Montpellier, with massive video screens. It provides skating lessons and is a magnet for the local kids.

Piscine Olympique d'Antigone

195 Av Jacques Cartier, Antigone **t** 04 67 15 63 00
Open 9–7, later at weekends
Adm Adult €4.57, child €2.29

Locals are rightly proud of their gigantic pool so pack your swimsuit and take a dip. A word of warning: many pools in France do not accept boxer-style trunks as swimwear.

Sports

Le Domaine de Grammont

Av Albert Einstein **t** 04 67 64 32 90
Getting there Off the A9, exit Montpellier Est
Open Daily 5am–11pm

This huge sports centre has all kinds of activities, from riding to tennis, plus a large skateboard park. Prices vary depending on what you choose to do.

SPECIAL TRIPS FROM MONTPELLIER

Aigues-Mortes

Getting there South of Montpellier on the D82
Getting around If you are with small children the easiest way to get around is to catch the minitrain from la Porte de la Gardette, **t** 04 66 53 85 20; tickets: adult €3.80, child (4–12) €2.50
Tourist office Porte de la Gardette **t** 00 33 (0)4 66 53 73 00 **www.**ot-aiguesmortes.fr
Special events July: Circus Festival. August: Medieval high jinks at the Fête de St-Louis, where you can meet Louis IX himself. October: Local festival, with lots of Camargue bulls on show

In the 13th century this was the only part of the Mediterranean coast held by France and so, when Louis IX (St Louis) decided to set off for the Crusades and needed a base for his operations, he had no choice but to build his port in the mosquito-infested Camargue. It was a real battle against the elements, and even the street plans

Tell me a story:
What were the Crusades all about?

In its heyday Aigues-Mortes was full of knights about to set sail for the Holy Land, since Jerusalem, and the other places holy to Christians in what is now Israel, had fallen under Muslim control during the 11th century. In 1095, the emperor of Constantinople, who was in charge of the eastern section of the Christian world, asked the pope, who was his counterpart in the west, to send troops to drive out the Muslims. The pope, keen to mend relations with Constantinople, was happy to oblige and turned to the kings and knights of Europe for help.

Pious men like King Louis IX believed that going on a crusade was their holy duty, a sentiment that was encouraged by the Church, who offered redemption for past sins to those who embarked on a crusade. Crusading was also potentially quite a lucrative business, as the victors had their choice of spoils from the sacked towns. Whatever their motivation, thousands of people set off on the Crusades during the Middle Ages. The Seventh Crusade set off from Aigues-Mortes in 1248 and included King Louis, his wife, children and 38,000 men. Louis would never see France again; he died of typhus in North Africa.

Organizing such ventures was a phenomenally ambitious feat, but nonetheless there were numerous Crusades throughout the Middle Ages. The saddest of all was the Children's Crusade of 1212, in which 30,000 children, led by two young boys, set off from Germany and northern France for the Holy Land. Many of the children died crossing the Alps, and the rest were lost at sea when they attempted to sail across the Mediterranean from Marseille.

were devised to stop the wind from racing down the avenues. Although its location was inauspicious, by the late 13th century it had four times the population it does today (helped, no doubt, by Louis' tax incentives to attract residents). Despite this, history has not been kind to Aigues-Mortes, and its ominous-sounding name, 'Dead Waters', proved true. The town went into decline from the mid-14th century when the sea retreated from the harbour. Today, after being virtually forgotten for centuries, Aigues-Mortes makes its livelihood from tourism and salt. However, the efforts of Louis have not been forgotten: this is one of the very few places in France where you'll still see the statue of a king.

Its troubled past aside, today Aigues-Mortes is a great place to visit with kids. It's bustling with French tourists and has lots of charm, upmarket shops and pleasant restaurants. The nicest place to stop for a drink or a meal is in the main square, Place St-Louis; it's safe enough for the kids to run around while you relax for a moment. If you fancy a dip in the sea head for Plage de l'Espiguette, which has beautiful sand dunes stretching as far as the eye can see.

Shopping

The town has a number of upmarket boutiques, especially for women's clothes if you feel like a treat. For sweets and gifts, try La Cure Gourmande on Rue Amiral Courbet.

Picnics and snacks

On the main street, Grande Rue Jean Jaurès, you'll find plenty of small shops selling picnic basics and roast chickens. The Fournil Saint-Louis has a good selection of snacks and makes its own chocolates on site.

Things to see and do

Eglise Notre Dame des Sablons

Rue Jean Jaurès
Open Daily 8.30–12 noon and 2–7
Adm Free

This is the oldest building in Aigues-Mortes, and was where the Crusaders were blessed before setting out for the Holy Land. Some additions have been made since that time: look out for the modern stained-glass windows. Keep an eye out for the modern residents, too: storks often nest on the roof of the church.

Tour de Constance

t 04 66 53 61 55
Open Daily 10–5 (9.30–8 in summer)
Adm Adult €5.50, child free

This tower owes its horrible history to Louis XIV's Edict of Nantes of 1685, with which he tried to end Protestantism in France. Those people who refused to convert to Catholicism were held here, most of whom were women. One prisoner, Marie Durand, was locked up as a young girl and was imprisoned for 38 years. She is supposedly responsible for carving the 'resist' on the round window in the

Look out for...
J'explore Aigues-Mortes, a children's guide to the city produced by the local council. It costs €4.5 and is on sale in newsagents.

upper room. Further on around the ramparts is the Tour de Bourguignons, which has just as grisly a past. It is named for the Burgundians who were killed in such numbers during the Hundred Years' War between England and France that their bodies were salted and stacked in the tower to stop the spread of disease. The bodies have since been buried, but from the ramparts you can see the salt pans where they dug the salt to preserve the bodies. (To visit the salt pans, *see* below.)

Salins du Midi

Getting there Take the Petit Train du Salin, **t** 04 66 73 41 88
Open Daily in season, ring for trip times, takes 1hr
Adm Adult €5.34, child (4–12 years) €3.05, English commentary

Salt has been harvested here since Roman times and now accounts for over half the salt produced in France.

Le Cinema 3D

Place de Verdun **t** 04 66 53 68 50
Open Daily 3–7; shows start on the hour
Adm Adult €5.70, child €3.40

This tiny cinema is on the edge of the huge, marshy area known as the Camargue (*see* p.124). To get a taste of what's around the corner, pop in and watch this 30min film about the area.

Boat trips

L'Aventure

t 04 666 73 74 74
Boats leave 11am daily
Tickets Adult €7, child (3–12 years) €4.50

A 1hr-30min tour of the Petite Camargue.

Le Pescalune

Porte de la Gardette **t** 04 66 53 79 47
www.perscalune-aiguemortes.com
Tickets Adult €10, child €5 for the longer trip

Trips run into the Petite Camargue and last either 1hr 30min or 2hrs 30min. Boats leave daily at 10.30 and 3 for the longer trip. Shorter trips depart Sundays only at 3 and 4.45 in July and August.

AROUND MONTPELLIER

Animal lovers

Parc Zoologique du Lunaret

Montpellier **t** 04 67 54 45 23
Open May–Sept 9–7 (5.30 in winter)
Adm Free

This zoo has a good selection of animals , and has the added bonus of free admission. There's a little train to help you get around the winding paths and a lovely wooded park opposite, le Parc de Montmaur. Bring a picnic and relax.

Mini-Ferme-Zoo

Cessenon-sur-Orb **t** 04 67 89 54 14
Getting there 21 km northwest of Béziers on D14
Open June–Oct daily 10–8; Nov–May, Wed, Sat–Sun, bank hols and school hols only
Adm Adult €7, child (2–16 years) €5

This farm is in the middle of the valley of the Orb on a wooded hillside and has 600 farm animals from around the world. There is also a petting zoo, a kids' playground and picnic area.

Seaquarium

Av du Palais-de-la-Mer, Le Grau-du-Roi
t 04 66 51 57 57
Open May, June and Sept Mon–Sat 9.30–12 noon and 2–6.30, Oct–April Mon–Sat 10–7, July–Aug Mon–Sat 10am–12 midnight, Sun and bank holidays 9.30–8
Adm Adult €8.60, child (5–15) €5.80

The aquarium features a huge fish tank full of sharks that you can walk under by way of a tunnel. There's also a museum of the sea exhibiting some extraordinary shells and a collection of ancient amphora jars found off the coast.

Good to know...**hunting**

Hunting is a big sport in France, and it is not unusual to see posses of men with rifles roaming the countryside. Be prepared: it can be quite alarming for the little ones, and it's not very relaxing to picnic to the sound of gunfire.

Town life

St-Guilhem-le-Désert

www.saint-guilhem-le-desert.com

Hidden away in the Gorges de l'Hérault is the lovely medieval town of St-Guilhem-le-Désert. The name doesn't refer to the surrounding countryside, which is green and shady, but to the fact it is so isolated ('désert' originally meant hidden). The town itself is perfect for a stop for morning coffee, an afternoon's stroll or even to rent a house. The old medieval streets are safe enough for children to play hide-and-seek in, and there's a nice central square with an Italian feel which is perfect for a relaxed lunch.

The village is very much a mini-Pézenas (*see* p.163); there are no particularly important sites to see and it's simply a pleasure to soak up the atmosphere. The surrounding countryside is beautiful and full of things to do, with opportunities for kayaking (*see* p.169) or visiting underground caves (*see* p.169) and the prehistoric site of Cambous (*see* p.170). For details of walks in the area, look for *Les Sentiers d'Emilie autour de Montpellier*, a guide to family walks in the region available from the newsagent in the main square.

Shopping

For sweets, there is a branch of La Cure Gourmande on Rue Cor de Nostra Dona. For toys, try Le Boi Jeux at both 10 Rue Descente du Portal and 12 Place de la Liberté.

Buckets and spades

Montpellier is just a short bus ride from the sea, but the nearest beaches are overdeveloped and can be a bit depressing. Instead, head out to the modernist resort of La Grande Motte (**www**.ot-lagrandemotte.fr), built in 1962 as a French government initiative to stem the number of tourists flocking to Spain instead. The architect Balladur came up with the idea of building a series of pyramids along this unassuming, mosquito-infested stretch of coast, and they are now a symbol of the resort. Whether or not the development is a resounding success is open to interpretation (it is still studied in French schools as an example of the pros and cons of mass tourism), but it has a splendid sandy beach, funfair rides and masses of (mainly pricey) accommodation (*see* p.233).

Theme parks

Amigoland and Babyland

Le Grau-du-Roi **t** 04 66 61 66 74
Open July–mid-Sept 9.30–7; (Jul–Aug 8.30)
Adm Free, rides priced individually

You'll see the big wheel as you drive into town and although you shouldn't go expecting Alton Towers it's a fun evening out at what is essentially a funfair on two sites. Amigoland is for older children, and there are smaller-scale entertainments for the little ones at Babyland.

Nature lovers

Gorges de l'Hérault

This area, although only roughly an hour from Montpellier, feels quite remote and is dotted with tumbledown villages with an authentically French atmosphere (*see* St-Guilhem-le-Désert, left). There are lovely hidden places for walking and picnics, especially around the dramatic peak of Pic St-Loup, which is 30k north of Montpellier. Another good picnic spot is at the Lac de Salagou, southwest of St-Guilhem-le-Désert. It's an artificial lake but very pretty all the same. Heading further north you'll find the magnificent rock formation called the Cirque de Navacelles, which looks like a deep lunar crater and is the place to contemplate just how stunning nature can be. Westwards you'll find the

Going underground

Subterranean Languedoc is as full of holes as a huge Gruyère cheese and around Montpellier you'll find some of the best caves in France. Most were inhabited in prehistoric times and it's fun to visit at least one while you're in the region. Take something warm to wear and pack a copy of Jules Verne's *Journey to the Centre of the Earth* to read afterwards.

wild Parc de Haut Languedoc, which is great riding country. The Maison du Parc, on Rue du Cloître in St-Pons-de-Thomières, **t** 04 67 97 38 22, can advise you on activities suitable for kids.

Grottoes and caves

Grotte de Clamouse

St-Guilhem-le-Désert **t** 04 67 57 71 05
www.clamouse.com
Open Feb–June daily 10–5; Jul and Aug 10–7; Dec–Jan 12 noon–5
Adm Adult €7, child (6–12) €3.50, tour takes 1hr

This is one of the most famous caves in Languedoc, with some of the prettiest and most delicate crystals you can see underground. There are English tours in summer.

Grotte des Demoiselles

St-Bauzille-de-Putois **t** 04 67 73 70 02
www.demoiselles.com
Getting there 38km north of Montpellier
Open Daily July and Aug 9.30–6, Oct–Mar 9.30–4.30, all other times until 5.30pm
Adm Adult €7, child (6–12 years) €7, tour takes 1hr

This cave is easy to access if you have little ones: an underground funicular takes you into the huge cave called the Cathedral, where you can see its famous stalagmite that looks like the Virgin Mary.

Grotte de la Dévèze

St-Pons **t** 04 67 97 03 24
Open April–Sept 2–5; July–Aug 2–6

A beautiful cave on three levels, with some extraordinary coloured rocks.

Grotte de Laroque

Laroque **t** 04 67 73 55 57
Open Easter–Nov 10–6; July–Aug 10–7

A much smaller and less touristy site than the neighbouring Grotte des Demoiselles.

Grotte de Labeil

t 04 67 96 49 47
www.grotte-de-labeil.com
Getting there On the D151 north of Montpellier just before les Rives
Open Daily 11–5 (7 in summer)
Adm Adult €6.40, child (5–12) €3.20

The entrance to this cave was once used for making the famous blue-veined Roquefort cheese. The main visit takes 45mins but you can also go on a cave safari and explore the caverns off the main route; kids must be over the age of 6, however.

Can you spot…a fairy?
According to local legend the Grotte des Demoiselles is inhabited by fairies, and you can spot them at twilight. Shepherds looking for lost sheep say they've seen fairies dancing at the mouth of the cave.

Grottes de Trabuc

Mialet **t** 04 67 85 03 28
www.grottes-de-france.com
Getting there Between Anduze and St-Jean-du-Gard on the D50
Open Daily mid-Mar–Nov 9.30–12 noon and 2–6.30; mid-Oct–mid-Nov Sun only

This grotto's main feature is its lake, the Lac-de-Minuit, which is 25m deep and houses an army of 100,000 stone soldiers made out of stalactites and stalagmites. Guided tours in English.

Sporty kids

This is a fantastic area for water sports, especially kayaking.

Canoë La Vallée des Moulins

St Martin de Londres **t** 04 67 73 12 45

To kayak down the Hérault gorge you'll need to be over 6 and know how to swim. Trips run from 3–32km and all equipment is supplied.

Canoë Rapido

St-Guilhem-le-Désert **t** 04 67 55 75 75

This activity is suitable for children over 4 years. Canoes seat four (two of the passengers must be under 10). If you reserve a place 48hrs in advance there is a 10% reduction; every second child is free.

Canoë Le Moulin

St-Bauzille-de-Putois **t** 04 67 73 30 73

Situated at the foot of the Cévennes, this canoe club runs trips from just 3km in canoes for one or two people. It's possible to pop little people in between two adults in a two-person canoe. Life jackets, paddles and a plastic container to put your towels and picnic in are included. Pack some sun cream and plenty of water.

GARD

***Good to know...*bullfights**

Most bullfights in the South of France aren't the bloody battles you see in Spain and are far more dangerous for the bullfighters than the bulls. Here the aim is for the bullfighter to remove a cockade tied around the bull's horns, which is not as sissy as it sounds. If you see a bullfight advertised as a *corrida* or a *novillada*, it's a traditional Spanish bull-fight, where the bull is put to death.

Look at this!

Cambous

t 04 67 86 34 37
Getting there South of St-Martin on the D32
Open Easter–Hallowe'en Sat and Sun 2–6, Fri–Wed 2–6 school hols only
Adm Adult €3.05, child free

These are the remains of one of the first Iron Age agricultural settlements in France, home to some of Europe's first farmers who lived here 5,000 years ago. Alongside the remains are some reconstructed prehistoric village huts. Be warned that it's a hike from the car park (opposite the turning in front of the château), so be prepared with water and a pushchair if you're bringing little ones. Out of season you can drive part way down the dirt track that leads to the site for a picnic, and although you won't be able to see the settlement it's a delightful spot for a relaxing afternoon.

NÎMES

Getting there There are direct flights from Paris (**www**.airlittoral.com) and London Stansted (**www**.ryanair.com) to Nîmes/Arles/Camargue airport, **t** 00 33 (0)4 66 70 49 49, 8km south of town. There's a regular shuttle bus and TGV services from Paris and Lille, plus train connections from Arles, Carcassonne, Marseille and Montpellier. The station is a 10-min walk from the Arènes. If you're coming by car, Nîmes is just moments from the main A9 and A54 autoroutes. Theft is a problem in the city, so use a proper car park; the best one is just by the Arènes and is open 24hrs, 7 days a week
Getting around Once you're in town you can get everywhere on foot. The tourist minitrain, **t** 04 66 70 26 92, adults €5, child (3–12) €2, which runs April–Oct 9.30–6, July and Aug 9.30am–10pm, is a good way of orientating yourself and seeing the city if you're travelling with toddlers
Tourist office 6 Rue Auguste **t** 04 66 58 38 00 **www**.ot-nimes.fr
Special events February: Carnival. May: Feria, with the first bullfights of the year and dancing in the streets. July: Gypsy Music Festival

Nîmes was once one of the most important Roman cities in the South of France and the old town is still laid out according to the old Roman street plan. The amphitheatre is one of the most complete in the world and the Maison Carrée is one of the best-preserved Roman temples around. The city centre is a living Roman town, which will catch the kids' imaginations, and is a pleasure to stroll around.

Nîme's old town is built from distinctive ivory-coloured stone, which gives the city a surprisingly modern feel and a definite identity of its own. Its streets are largely pedestrianized, which makes it an ideal place to visit with small children, and in the summer there are plenty of outdoor tables in pretty, traffic-free squares, which are perfect for family dining. The little ones will love the merry-go-round by the amphitheatre and older kids and teens will like the way the city mixes old with new,

Good to know...

Nîmes has a crime and drugs problem. Look after your valuables when you are walking around the town and be careful where you park your car.

Can you spot...a crocodile?

A crocodile chained to a palm tree is the symbol of Nîmes and celebrates the Roman victory over Cleopatra. The Roman legion that made Nîmes their headquarters had come direct from conquering Egypt.

even though Norman Foster's modern art gallery, the Carré d'Art, is a bit of a disappointment.

Now that the budget airlines are flying here, Nîmes makes a great destination for a long weekend. If you are staying longer in the region it makes a good city base for exploring further afield, and is a must for a stopover or day trip if you're holidaying elsewhere in the region.

Shopping

You can while away many pleasant hours window shopping round the streets of the old town. All of the main chains have branches here, too: the wonderful sweetshop La Cure Gourmande is on Boulevard Victor Hugo; there's a FNAC in the shopping centre next to the Halles Centrales and the discount bookshop Maxi Livres is on Rue de L'Aspic. Cacharel, which makes stylish baby goods and has revamped its chic women's range, is a local firm with a factory shop on Avenue du Maréchal Juin. There's a flea market on Avenue Jean Jaurès on Sunday morning and on Thursday nights in summer there's an evening market, which is a good place to pick up souvenirs.

Picnics and snacks

You can buy the basics at Monoprix on Boulevard Amiral Courbet or Shoppi on Rue Perrier. For something a bit tastier, don't miss the market (Les Halles), which is close to the Maison Carrée. Villaret at 13 Rue Madeleine is the best *boulangerie* in town and sells a wide range of tasty breads, tarts and the local speciality – biscuits known as *croquants*. There is a food market on Av Jean Jaurès every Tuesday and Friday morning.

Things to see and do

Les Arènes

t 04 66 76 72 77
Open 9–6.30 in summer, closes for lunch in winter
Adm Adult €4.45, child €3.20

The amphitheatre is one of the best preserved in the world and in its heyday up to 24,000 people (which by Roman standards wasn't very many) regularly crowded in here to watch the gladiators fight to the death. Today it still has a rather gloomy atmosphere of foreboding. The arena was shaded by a huge awning and if you look carefully along the top of the building you can still see the sockets that held large masts used to support the awning.

After the Romans the amphitheatre had a chequered history, first as a fortress, which was besieged several times, then as a medieval shanty-town. There were over 200 houses crushed within its walls when restoration work began in the early 19th century. Today the amphitheatre is used for bullfights and rock concerts.

Maison Carrée

t 04 66 36 26 76
Open Daily 9–6.30 (5 in winter)
Adm Free

The Maison Carrée (literally 'Square House') is neither a house, nor is it square, but it is the best-preserved Roman temple in the world. It was built in the 1st century and dedicated to the grandsons of Emperor Augustus who were known as the 'Princes of Youth'. This part of Nîmes was once the heart of the old Roman forum and it was usual to find a temple in such a prime position. After the fall of the Roman Empire the temple was used at different times as a house, a stable and a church, and today it holds exhibitions, most notably a fresco discovered when the Carré d'Art gallery was being built.

Jardin de la Fontaine

This is one of the prettiest and oldest city parks in France and within it is the **Tour Magne** (*open 9–5; 9–7 in summer*) reputedly the oldest Roman monument in the whole of France. It was probably built to commemorate the opening of the Via Domitia, the main road from Rome to Spain, and was also used as a lookout tower.

Near the park on Rue Lapèze is the Castellum, a round basin dating from Roman times that was

Did you know...

The first known residents, a Celtic tribe who lived in Nîmes before the arrival of the Romans, considered the Fontaine, the local spring, sacred. It was dedicated to the god, Nemasus, which is where the name Nîmes comes from.

Did you know...
where denim comes from?
The first people to wear blue jeans were the cowboys of the Camargue. When the heavy cloth was first exported it was known as cloth 'de Nîmes' – meaning 'from Nîmes' – which was corrupted to 'denim'.

used to collect water from the Pont du Gard and then distribute it throughout the city. The only other one of its kind is in Pompeii.

SPECIAL TRIPS FROM NÎMES

Pont du Gard

t 08 20 903 330
Getting there 27km from Nîmes off the N86. Parking costs €4.50 a day, if you can park on the Rive Gauche
Open 7am–1am; museum open daily 10–6, 9.30–7 in summer
Adm Free for the bridge; museum, adult €12.96, child (5–21) €11.43

The Pont du Gard really is a magnificent sight against the clear blue sky of Provence. No matter how many times you've seen it in pictures, the reality won't disappoint – make the time to visit if at all possible.

The aqueduct stands 157ft above the river and is not only the highest but is also one of the best-preserved aqueducts in the world, built by the Romans to carry fresh water to Nîmes from the nearest spring, 30 miles away. You can walk across the bottom tier, which in the 18th century was extended to make a proper road bridge. Look out for the old graffiti on the walls.

The aqueduct has over 2 million visitors a year, so time your visit for early morning or evening, when the tourist buses have gone. At around 10 every evening in July and August the bridge is lit up – a magical sight that is worth missing bedtimes for. There are some good shops and restaurants on site and the café (similar to a motorway service station) has a kids' menu for €5.30. There are opportunists about, unfortunately, so watch your valuables and make sure you lock the car.

If the Pont du Gard has whetted the children's appetites for all things Roman, don't miss the exhibition in the nearby museum, Le Grand Expo. The exhibition is exceptional and the admission worth every penny. Plan for about 1hr 30mins to get the most out of it. There's a stunning film that follows the course of the aqueduct from the source to Nîmes and a fanastic hands-on museum in the Ludo, the children's section. Here they can sniff Roman spices, make a mosaic, try their hands at engineering or see how an archaeologist works. It's a great museum for anyone from 18-months to teenagers, and everything is in English so comprehension won't be a problem. In the summer there are special children's workshops and special shows, including gladiators. Call **t** 08 20 90 33 30 for more information.

The oldest olive tree in the world is on the path down from the museum heading towards the Pont du Gard. It sprouted in Spain in 908 AD and was brought here in 1985.

A trip to the Pont du Gard can be a whole day out, with swimming in the River Gard and a picnic on its banks. If you feel adventurous you can even kayak underneath the bridge. Kayak Vert (**t** 04 66 22 80 76), based at Collias, 6km upstream, hire boats, and it will take you half a day to paddle downstream to the Pont du Gard from there.

The Romans and their baths

Roman towns used a lot of water; every town had a bathhouse and plenty of fountains, every large city had public toilets with running water, and the houses of the wealthy had hot running water. Nîmes particularly needed lots of water because the huge amphitheatre (*see* p.171) was flooded for naval battles. There is a reconstruction of a Roman public loo in the Pont du Gard museum and in Vaison-la-Romaine you can see the real thing (*see* p.94).

Fancy a souvenir...?

This is a great place to pick up something to take home. There are wooden Roman swords for €3, jars of Roman spreads and plenty of plastic models of Julius Caesar, all for under €10.

AROUND NÎMES

Animal lovers

Les Aigles de Beaucaire

Château de Beaucaire **t** 04 66 59 26 72
www.aigles-de-beaucaire.com
Open Mid-Mar–end Oct, closed Weds except in school hols. Shows Mar–June on the hour 2–5, Jul and Aug 3–6, Sept and Oct 2.30–4.30
Adm Adult €7.50, child €5

The only way to get into the castle is to book into one of the hourly bird displays, which take place in the grounds of the old château with falconers dressed in period costume. In summer, choose a late afternoon show as you'll be sitting in the full sun. Beaucaire itself is an odd place; a fascinating, if shabby, old medieval town full of gangs of disaffected youth.

Le Vieux Mas

Rte de Fourques **t** 04 66 59 60 13
Getting there 8km south of Beaucaire, near Arles
Open Daily Mar–Nov 10–7; Dec–Feb Wed, Sat, Sun and school hols only 10–12.30 and 1.30–6
Adm Adult €4, child (over 5) €2.5

Old MacDonald's farm in sunny Provence, this farm shows what it would have been like to till the land 80 years ago, with farmers dressed in traditional costume. There is plenty of livestock to keep the little ones happy, and a children's corner where they can pat the baby animals.

Town life

Uzès

Getting there North of Nîmes on the D982
Tourist office Place Albert 1er **t** 00 33 (0)4 66 22 68 88 **www.**ville-uzes.fr

Uzès is a beautiful medieval hill town with an arcaded market. Large parts of the town centre are virtually pedestrianized, so it's easy to explore with kids. Have a leisurely stroll around town, stop for coffee in the main square – it's a lovely place to unwind and if you are looking for a house to rent, the surrounding villages are ideal.

There's a small cinema, La Capitole, **t** 08 92 68 22 74, a rarity in these parts as most rural cinemas closed down years ago.

The tourist office can advise on walks for families in the surrounding countryside.

Shopping

There's a colourful market on Saturday morning on Place aux Herbes, where you'll also find a branch of the sweetshop La Cure Gourmande and a good toy shop, Au Bois d'Mon Cœur.

Throughout the town you'll find shops selling ready-made food and takeaway pizza. La Boulangerie Uzèsienne sells lovely savoury *fougasse* flatbreads and Nougatine on Boulevard Gambetta is the place to buy *pain au chocolat* or to stop off for a quick lunch (*see* p.178).

Boulevard Gambetta also has a Petit Casino for groceries and a Monoprix, which is the best place to buy kids' clothes. If you need something for the baby, head for Bébécado on Boulevard Libération.

Tell me a story: The Drac of Beaucaire

According to local legend, a terrible dragon, known as the Drac once roamed the river banks around Beaucaire. Although he was invisible to the villagers, he would trick them into falling into the river by making the water look as if it were dotted with rubies and emeralds.

The Drac captured a beautiful young girl to look after his baby. One of her jobs was to rub the baby with the human fat saved from the bodies of the Drac's victims. One day the girl accidentally rubbed her eyes with the fat and from then on she could see the dragon, even when he was being invisible.

The girl kept her new powers secret and when the baby dragon grew up she went back home to her family. Years later, she spotted the baby dragon, who was by then grown up and extremely fierce, walking in the city of Beaucaire. She alone could see him and called out loudly. The dragon was so angry he had been tricked that he scratched her eyes out and fled the city, never to be seen again.

Steam power!

Train à Vapeur des Cévennes

St-Jean-du-Gard, northwest of Nîmes
t 04 66 60 59 00
Trains run June–Aug daily; April–May and Sept Mon–Sat; Oct Tues, Thurs and weekends
Tickets Adult return €9.60, child (4–12) €7

Catch the train at Anduze, La Bambouseraie or St-Jean-du-Gard. It puffs its way through 13km of beautiful countryside and provides the easiest and most entertaining way to see the Cévennes with the kids. Don't be shy about going to inspect the engine, even if your train vocabulary isn't all you wished it might be. In the station at St-Jean-du Gard, there's a souvenir shop, picnic area and café. Break the journey at Générargues.

Nature lovers

La Bambouseraie

Générargues **t** 04 66 61 70 47
www.bambouseraie.fr
Open Daily Mar–1 Nov from 9.30
Adm Adult €6, child €3

This bamboo forest in the heart of the Cévennes was planted in the 19th century by the botanist Eugène Mazel and is the only one of its kind in Europe, with over 150 different types of bamboo. (Bamboo from here is sent to Berlin zoo to feed the pandas.) Kids will love running through the labyrinth of bamboo tunnels or visiting the Laotian village in the middle of the park. The forest rangers organize varying activities throughout the year – there's a cooking week in May when you can taste the bamboo shoots.

Look at this!

Musée du Bonbon Haribo

Pont des Charrettes **t** 04 66 22 74 39
www.haribo.com
Getting there Just outside Uzès
Open Tues–Sun July–Sept 10–7; Oct–June 10–1 and 2–6, closed first 3 weeks of Jan
Adm Adult €3.81, child €2.50, under-5s free

Can you spot...?
Haribo's new Asterix and Obelix sweets? Make sure you buy a bag to munch while you visit the Roman remains in Nîmes.

There has been a sweet factory here since 1862; Haribo, actually a German company, didn't enter the scene until much later, when it bought the original company in the 1960s. Today Haribo is one the world's biggest producers of fruit gums and liquorice products and is probably the most popular children's sweet manufacturer in France.

In the museum you can find out everything you ever needed to know about making jelly sweets, but buying them in the shop is the pinnacle of the visit.

Perrier Factory

t 04 66 87 61 01
Getting there 18km south of Nîmes off the N 113; follow the signs to Vergèze
Open July–Aug Mon–Fri 9.30–10.30 and 1–6, Sat and Sun 1–4.30; rest of the year daily 9.30–4. Tours leave every 30mins
Adm Adult €4.12, child (7–18) €1.50

There are 1,200 different mineral water springs in France; some are famous for their curative powers and some taste absolutely foul. Perrier's claim to fame is its reputed 50 million bubbles in every litre. On the tour, the fizzy stuff flows like – well – like water; you can drink as much as you like for free. Perrier water was put firmly on the map in the 19th century by one Dr Perrier, but its origins are much older – Hannibal is supposed to have stopped off here for a quick swig on the way to Italy.

Le Musée du Train et du Jouet

Moulin de Chalier **t** 04 66 22 58 64
Getting there Arpaillargues, 3km west of Uzès
Open Mar–Oct daily 10–12 noon and 2–7; July–Aug 9–7, Nov–Feb Wed, Sat–Sun only
Adm Adult €5.34, child €3.81, reductions for families of more than 4

Not somewhere to drive miles out of your way to see, but a nice little outing for small children if you are in the area. Thomas fans will love the model railway and there's a good selection of old toys.

All roads lead to Rome

Just outside Lunel you can see a stretch of the old Via Domitia – which was the main Roman road between the Rhône and Spain. In its heyday hundreds of Roman soldiers marched along it and endless carts would have rattled back and forth loaded with goods. If you look carefully you can see the grooves made by the carriages and chariots. They would have had to stop to pay a toll to cross the bridge. To find the Via Domitia from Lunel take the D34 for 2.5km before turning onto the D110 for Villetelle. Just before the bridge over the motorway you'll see a little road leading to the ruins of an old Gaulish settlement called Ambrussum, park here by the old Roman bridge.

Mas Gallo-Romain des Tourelles

4294 Rt de Bellegarde **t** 04 66 59 19 72
www.tourelles.com
Getting there 4km southwest of Beaucaire on the D38
Open May–Oct daily 2–7, July–Aug 10–12 noon and 2–7, Nov–Easter Sat only
Adm Adult €4.60, child €1.50

This vineyard is on the site of a Roman villa and here they still make wine as they did in Roman times. You can see the reconstruction of a Roman wine cellar and the ruins of the villa and you can taste and then buy some wine to bring home. For the kids there are Roman games and grape juice when it comes to the wine tasting. They'll also enjoy tasting and buying the Roman spreads on sale in the shop.

Mine Témoin

Chemin de la Cité Ste-Marie **t** 04 66 30 45 15
Getting there Rochebelle, just outside Alès on the (N106)
Open Daily April–Nov 9–12.30 and 2–5.30, June 9–6.30, July–Aug 10–7.30. Last tour 1hr-30min before closing time. Guided tours in English during July and Aug on Wed at 3
Adm Adult €5.79, child (6–12) €3.20.

More industrial tourism, only this time in an old coal mine. Don your tin hat and explore the 1/2km of tunnels that were dug out of the mountain between 1945 and 1968. An old miner explains what it was like to work underground and the little ones will like the animated model of a mine horse. Don't forget your sweater, as it's chilly down there.

There's a shop and picnic area and some lovely walks in the forest around the museum.

Theme parks

Amazonia

Rte d'Orange, Roquemaure **t** 04 66 82 53 92
Getting there On the RD 976
Open July–Aug daily 10.30–7; Mar–mid-Nov weekends, school hols and bank hols only
Adm Varies according to season, but from €11

Small amusement park with a South American theme aimed at 6–12-year-olds.

Sporty kids

Kayak Vert Gardon

Collias **t** 04 66 22 80 76

Canoes are for one or two people, with room for a little one between two adults in a two-person canoe. The route isn't too challenging and is suitable for over-7s paddling solo depending on how far you plan to go (you can choose routes from 6–29km in length). Jackets, paddles and a plastic container for towels and foodstuffs are included. Bikes are also available for hire, and the surrounding countryside is gently undulating and undemanding.

Carcassonne

L'Arbre de Vie

3 Pl Marcou **t** 04 68 71 45 33

Place Marcou is one of the most pleasant spots to eat in the old town, even if it is a bit touristy. This restaurant serves authentic cassoulet, the local speciality made of beans and goose fat, and some tasty tarts and ice-cream. It's a nice place to enjoy breakfast, too, and there's a small garden. Children's menu €7.32, adult menus from €10.62.

L'Escalier

23 Bd Omer Sarraut **t** 04 68 25 65 66
Open Sun eve–Sat

If it's one of those days when everyone wants to eat something different this Tex-Mex melange of international cooking will save you from a family bust-up. There are Italian, Greek and Texan dishes all on one menu and the restaurant has the kind of decor and upbeat feeling that will appeal to teens especially. Pizza menu €15.24; kids' pizza menu €6.10, with drink and ice cream.

Around Carcassonne

Villerouge-Termenès

La Rôtisserie du Château

Château de Villerouge-Termenès **t** 04 68 70 06 06
Open Tues–Sun lunch Feb–Dec

If the kids have seen the French cult movies *Les Visiteurs*, in which a group of medieval knights are accidentally transported into the modern world, they'll love this 'visiteur' experience in reverse. The restaurant serves up a medieval banquet at long trestle tables. The food is fairly predictable – essentially a meal of roast meats – but with children that's probably a bonus. Menu from €25.

Narbonne

Le Castel

26 Bld Dr Lacroix **t** 04 68 41 35 07

Pizzas, steaks and salads served in a family-style atmosphere.

Perpignan

L'Arago

1 Pl Arago **t** 04 68 51 81 96
Open all year round, every day.

The house speciality here is beef but they also serve up a good selection of reasonably priced pizzas, from €6.10. There's a nice terrace on the first floor and although this is a busy spot you'll never have to wait long for a table.

Bistrot le St-Jean

1 Cité Bartissol **t** 04 68 51 22 25
Open Tues–Sun lunch, Mon lunch and Feb–Dec

This wonderfully atmospheric restaurant has a large terrace, which is actually part of the cathedral next door.It's a good place to try local Catalan specialities with small, restless children, as they can wander about the terrace while you relax. Lunch menu €8.84, evening menus from €14.94.

Chez Luigi

Pl de la Résistance **t** 04 68 35 15 56

This place serves great pizzas made from a whole host of fresh ingredients and salad dressing comes in baby bottles, which kids will find amusing. The staff are very helpful and don't mind keeping the kitchen open when they spot a weary and hungry family late at night. Lots of local families eat here. Pizzas from around €6–8.

Le Petit Moka

Pl République **t** 04 68 34 31 92

This is the best café along the row in the main square and is the most sensible choice to head for with children. It's something of an institution in Perpignan, good for either breakfast or a snack, and is very popular with locals. The crêpes cost from €2 and a *croque-monsieur* will set you back just €2.50. For some, the best bit about munching through a *pain au chocolat* here is that the café is next door to a snail shop where you can watch the slimy critters crawling around in huge trays before there are scooped up and sold in bags. Others may prefer to sit indoors.

Le Voilier des Saveurs

1 Bd Kennedy **t** 04 68 50 25 25
Open all year except 1–22 Aug

One of Perpignan's best restaurants, as popular with families as it is with lunching businessmen.

Everything on the menu is local and seasonal and the atmosphere is cosy. Lunch menu from €13.72, evening menu from €18.29.

Auberge St-Vincent

3km out of Perpignan on the road for Canet t 04 68 50 61 81

Just 5mins out of town in the glorious countryside this restaurant, which serves up traditional Catalan cuisine, is a great place for a relaxing family meal. There's a shady terrace and a special play area for children. Menus from €7.32.

Around Perpignan

Tautavel

Le Petit Gris

Rte d'Estagel t 04 68 29 42 42

Catalan pork, lamb, sausages and wild boar in season grilled at your own table. It's a popular place, especially for lunch on Sunday.

Collioure

La Crêperie Bretonne

10 Quai de l'Amirauté t 04 68 82 54 91

This is a really pleasant place to stop for a snack, just in front of the Château Royal. Open Feb–Oct and during the Christmas holidays.

Gorge de Galamus

Au Vieux Moulin

Cubieres-Cinoble t 04 68 69 81 49

This is in one of the most beautiful settings in the area, and is an ideal place to break for lunch if you've taken a trip to Tautavel or Quéribus. Food is served in the garden of an 11th-century mill on the banks of the river. Dishes are simple – omelettes, paella, salads and sausages – but all of it is outstandingly good quality and service is cheerful. Children's menu is €6.50, adult menus from €12. The place is popular with local families and it's easy to see why – there's also a children's playground, a picnic area if you're not up for the restaurant (€7.60 to use the tables) and a small café. After lunch hire a kayak for €15 and spend the afternoon messing about on the river. If you are camping you can also pitch your tent here for €4 plus €3 per person.

Céret

Le Pied dans le Plat

9 Place des Neuf-Jets t 04 68 87 17 65

This is one of the best places for a quick lunch in the village. Salads cost from €6.10 and you can choose your own filling for your crêpe (from €3.05), so it's ideal for fussy eaters. The menu features other staples like *confit du canard*, and although there's nothing especially outstanding about the food, the staff are friendly, it's very reasonable and there's a pleasant terrace.

Prades

L'Hostal de Nogarols

On the way to St-Michel-de-Cuxa t 04 68 96 24 57

Great pizza and local dishes served in a shady garden.

Agde

La Tamarissière

21 Quai Théophile-Cornu, 5km out of town on the D32 t 04 67 94 20 87

Open Tues–Sun lunch

The restaurant is on the banks of the River Hérault and has a beautiful garden. You'll find a relaxed atmosphere and old-fashioned cooking – try *bourride*, a fish stew and a local speciality. You'll need to book in the busy summer months. Menus from €27.

Around Agde

Cap d'Agde

O Kakaô Beach

Mail de Rochelongue t 04 67 26 52 01

Open April–Sept

This restaurant is set right on the beach and serves up excellent crêpes and ice-cream.

Pézenas

L'Aparte

13 Rue de la Foire t 04 67 98 03 04

Older kids who like books will love the atmosphere in this café-cum-bookshop. Tea and a pastry will set you back about €2.50. However, this is the ultimate example of everything stopping for lunch – the café is closed for a break from 12.30–2.30!

Montpellier

Hippopotamus

Esplanade de l'Europe, Quartier Antigone **t** 04 67 15 96 40

Part of the family-friendly chain, situated in the modern part of town. There are steaks, burgers, kebabs, chips galore and a host of salads. Kids get colouring books and pens. Children's menu €7.50, adult menus from €12.90–€24.20.

La Crêperie des Deux Provinces

7 Rue Jacques Cœur **t** 04 67 60 68 10

Open all day on Sat, lunch only Mon–Fri and Sun

Just off the main square in the old town, this is a good spot for an affordable family lunch. The menu consists of crêpes and salads.

Le César

Pl du Nombre d'Or, Antigone **t** 04 67 64 87 87

Open Mon–Fri

This is a great place to eat with children in the warm weather, as it's near the enormous fountain and the area is virtually car-free. It's a basic brasserie, but the food is good and there are regional specialities available too. Menus from €15.

Toast Tea

7 Rue Vallat **t** 04 67 60 87 87

This café has a terrace on the pretty square in front of the church and is a popular place for Sunday brunch, which costs €10.37. If you don't want to breakfast in your hotel this is a nice place to start the day. Menus start at a reasonable €6.10.

Pizzeria du Palais

22 Rue du Palais **t** 04 67 60 67 97

Italian-run pizza joint serving up good-sized, tasty dishes.

Nîmes

L'Aventure

16 Pl du Marché **t** 04 66 76 04 17

The most family-orientated of the restaurants in the Place du Marché, an ideal location as it's virtually pedestrianized and the kids can run around while you relax. The restaurant is popular with local families and serves a selection of pasta, pizza and salads. For something traditional, try *brandade*, a dish of mashed cod popular with fish-loving kids. Highchairs available and friendly service. Pizzas from €5.50, children's menu €7 and adult menus from €11.

Around Nîmes

Uzès

Le Jardin des Oliviers

Chemin du Pont Romain **t** 04 66 22 60 84

This lovely restaurant is on the road to Nîmes. Meals are served under the trees in summer and in front of a huge log fire in winter. The starter is buffet style and there's one main course, which is usually lamb. Adult meals cost between €15–€20.

Nougatine

25 Bd Gambetta **t** 04 66 22 09 72

Behind the patisserie is a lovely teashop, serving pizza, salads, toasted sandwiches and pastries, ideal for breakfast or lunch.

Corsica

Corse du Sud • Haute-Corse

CORSE DU SUD 184
Ajaccio 184
Special trips from Ajaccio 188
Around Ajaccio 189
Bonifacio 190
Special trips from Bonifacio 192
Around Bonifacio 193

HAUTE-CORSE 195
Bastia 195
Special trips from Bastia 196
Around Bastia 197
Calvi 199
Special trips from Calvi 202
Around Calvi 202
Corte 203
Around Corte 205

WHERE TO EAT 206

07

Corsica

Highlights

The long and winding road around Cap Corse, p.196
Wandering through the chestnut forests of the Castagniccia, p.198
Riding the Chemin de Fer de la Corse – the marvellous mountain train between Ajaccio and Bastia, p.203
An ice-cream in the square at Corte, p.204
Lazing on the beach at Rondinara, p.194
Meeting the menhirs in Filitosa, p.190

Such a perfect day

Morning On the beach or exploring the museums and shops in Ajaccio, p.184
Lunch Taking the train down by the river in the Restonica valley, 205
Afternoon Exploring the Citadel at Corte, p.203

Special events

New Year's Day
Children go from house to house to wish their neighbours well and to try to right any wrongs that have come between them in the last 12 months

Easter
Festivities held in Bonifacio, Calvi, Erbalunga and Sartène. The Greek Orthodox Easter is celebrated in Cargèse

Springtime
Locals head off en masse to hunt for wild asparagus

October
Mushroom-picking season; locals go to Bastelica

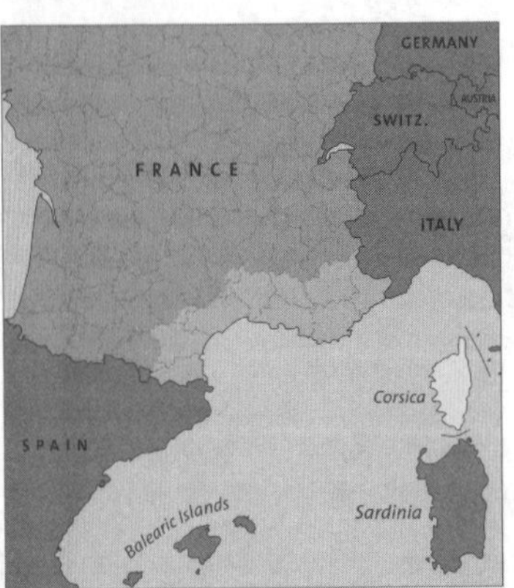

Getting there by air

Corsica has four main airports: Ajaccio, **t** 00 33 (0)4 95 23 56 56, **www**.ajaccio.aeroport.fr Bastia, **t** 00 33 (0)4 95 54 54 54; Calvi, **t** 00 33 (0)4 95 65 88 88; and Figari, **t** 00 33 (0)4 95 71 10 10, **www**.figari.aeroport.fr.

Some British travel companies have direct flights to Corsica as part of their package deals and there are some charter flights in high season, but if you fly independently from the UK or the USA you'll probably have to change planes in Paris, Nice or Marseille. Some cheap flights are starting to appear so it's worth shopping around. If you're already on the Riviera look out for special weekend break deals.

Air Liberté
t 00 33 (0)8 03 80 58 05, **www**.airliberte.fr
Has connections from Marseille, Nice and Paris to Figari.

Air France
t 00 33 (0)8 02 80 28 02, **www**.airfrance.fr
Flies from Paris, Marseille and Nice to Ajaccio, Bastia and Calvi.

Air Littoral
t 00 33 (0)8 25 83 48 34 **www**.air-littoral.fr
Has connections from Montpellier to Ajaccio, Bastia and Figari; from Marseille to Calvi and Figari; from Lille to Ajaccio, Bastia, Calvi and Figari; and from Nice or Toulouse to Calvi and Figari.

Corse Méditerranée
t 00 33 (0)8 36 67 95 20, **www**.corsemed.com.
Flies from Marseille and Nice to Ajaccio, Bastia and Calvi. Routes change seasonally and it's worth asking about fly-drive deals.

Corseair
t 00 33 (0)1 49 79 75 75, **www**.corsair.fr
Flies from Paris, Toulouse, Marseille and Lille to Ajaccio and from Paris to Calvi and Figari.

Ollandini
t 00 33 (0)4 95 23 92 92.
The main Corsican charter company, with flights to most big French cities, and it also organizes coach tours.

Charter Diffusion
t 00 33 (0)5 61 62 86 85
Flies out of Toulouse to Bastia and Ajaccio.

Getting there by sea

Boats sail for Corsica from Marseille, Nice and Toulon to Ajaccio, Bastia, Calvi, Ile-Rousse,

20 km
10 miles
N
Cap Corse
Barcaggio
Rogliano
Macinaggio
Marine de Porticciolo
Sisco
Nonza
Erbalunga
Pietrabugno
Plage de Toga
BASTIA
St Florent
Golfe de St Florent
Plage de Loto
Plage de Saleccia
Plage de Malfalco
Désert des Agriates
Plage d'Ostriconi
Nice/Marseille/Toulon
Genova/Nice
Marseille/Toulon/Savona
Marseille
Nice
L'Ile-Rousse
N197
Calvi
Lavatoggio
Grotte des Veaux Marins
Calvi-Ste Catherine Airport
Bastia-Poretta Airport
N193
N198
Ponte Leccia
Piano
Talasani
San Giovanni-di-Moriani
Moriani-Plage
San Nicolao
Bonifato
Cirque de Bonifato
Forêt de Tartagine
Forêt de Carrozzica
Monte Cinto
Réserve Naturelle de Scandola
Corte
Cascade de Radule
Gorges du Tavignano
Gorges de la Restonica
Plage de Caspio
Golfe de Porto
Porto
Les Calanche
Gorges de Spelunca
Forêt d'Aïtone
Bergerie de Grotelle
Monte Rotondo
Sto Pietro-in-Venaco
Venaco
N200
Tyrrhenian
Bravone
Fort de Pasciolo
Vivario
Plage d'Arone
Forêt de Rospa Sorba
Forêt de Vizzavona
Monte d'Oro
Vizzavona
Etang de Diane
Cargèse
Plage de Pero
Cascades des Anglais
Aléria
Sea
Sagone
Plage du Liamone
Tiuccia
Monte Renoso
Golfe de Sagone
Golfe de la Liscia
Castello de Capraja
Cascade du Voile de la Mariée
Parc A Cupulatta
Bastelica
Cascade d'Aziana
AJACCIO
Campo dell'Oro Airport
Anse de Minaccia
Punta de la Parata
Iles Sanguinaires
Grande Sanguinaire
Porticcio
Tour de Capitellu
Toulon/Genova
Plage de Ruppione
Golfe d'Ajaccio
Marseille/Nice
Forêt de Bavella
Quenza
Monte Bianco
Cala d'Orzu
Filitosa
Pinarellu
Propriano
Ospedale
Casteddu d'Araghju
San Ciprianu
Mediterranean
N196
Sartène
Montagne de Cagna
Grossa
Porto-Vecchio
Marseille
Alignements de Pagliaghju
Plage de Palombaggia
Sea
Tizzano
Mégalithes de Cauria
Roccapina
Corsica-Sud Airport
Santa Giulia
Figari
Rocher du Lion
Plage de Rondinara
Golfe de Figari
Plages de Maora et Santa Manza
Bonifacio
Ile Lavezzi

Propriano and Porto-Vecchio. The main ferry companies are:

Southern Ferries SNCM Ferryterranée, **t** (in France) 0891 701 801, **www**.sncm.fr **t** (in the UK) (020) 7491 4968, **f** (020) 7491 3502;

Corsica Ferries
t (in France) 08 25 095 095, **t** 04 95 50 78 82, **f** 04 95 50 78 83, **www**.corsicaferries.com
In the UK contact Via Mare, **t** (020) 7431 5456, **www**.viamare.com

Crossing times have been speeded up dramatically over the last few years and high-speed ferries (NGV – Navire à Grande Vitesse) from Nice to Calvi take just 2hrs 45mins, but they don't run in bad weather. Winds in this part of the world can be strong, even in summer, so bear this in mind when making travel arrangements. The traditional ferries are more reliable and many have pools on board to help while away the 10-hr crossing time. The new luxury ferry, the *Napoléon Bonaparte*, even has Internet access to keep teen computer buffs happy.

Ferry prices for foot passengers are very competitive, so don't just consider the ferry as an option for drivers. If you're on the Côte d'Azur it's also worth considering driving to Savona in Italy. From Nice it's a 1½ hr drive and high-speed ferries from Savona to Calvi take just 2hrs. In bad weather the traditional ferry takes 6hrs. Ferries also run from Genoa, La Spezia, and Livorno. The crossings from Italy are generally cheaper because it's so much closer than the French coast.

Taking the ferry is a great option with children – it gives a sense of just how isolated Corsica is and is well worth the extra time it takes to get there; the slow night boat is especially romantic. It's important to make your travel arrangements for July and August as early as possible, however, as the ferries get booked up quickly. In case you need to check conditions before you sail, contact the Shipping Forecast, **t** 08 36 68 08 13.

Getting around by car

Driving is really the only option with a family, as buses are infrequent (*see* below), but allow yourself plenty of time to get around the island as the roads are full of twists and potholes. The cheapest place to buy petrol is at supermarkets, but petrol in general is expensive, so fill up before you catch the ferry. Stock up on sick bags while you're on the plane or ferry; Corsica's winding roads and hairpin bends may unsettle stomachs. Car hire can be pricey so it's worth investigating fly-drive packages before you leave home and check that insurance is included in the price.

Car hire The following companies have offices in Corsica:

Avis
In UK **t** 0990 900 500, **f** 0870 6060 100
www.avis.co.uk
In USA **t** 800 331 1084, **f** (516) 222 3000
www.avis.com

Europcar
In UK **t** 0870 607 5000, **f** 01132 429 495
In USA **t** 800 800 6000, **f** (918) 669 2821
www.europcar.com

Hertz
In UK **t** 0990 996 699, **f** (020) 8679 0181
In USA **t** 800 654 3001
www.hertz.com
There's also a Hertz office in the Mark Warner resort at San Lucianu.

Getting around by bus and air

There are no flights between Corsica's four airports and bus travel isn't an ideal option with a family. Buses are few and far between and stiflingly hot in summer – avoid them if you can.

Getting around by train

SNCF **t** 00 33 (0)8 36 35 35 35
Information **t** 00 33 (0)4 95 32 80 57/60/61
The trip from Ajaccio to Bastia is one of Europe's great train rides, with breathtaking views along the coast. From Bastia sit on the right-hand side facing the direction of travel for the best views, though in summer you'd better arrive early and stand right by the platform if you want to get a seat. You'll probably want to avoid the last carriage as it's a smoking one. You can hop on and off along the line, but with only four trains a day you'll need to plot your route carefully in advance. Trains run from Ajaccio to Calvi and Bastia through Corte. There's no rail service in the south of the island (*see* p.203).

Getting around by bike

Corsica is tough cycling country and it's not an easy option with children, but if you are staying close to or in one of the resort towns, it is worth considering hiring a bike to give teens some freedom.

Useful websites
www.allerencorse.com
www.lacorse.com
www.visit-corsica.com
www.internetcom.fr/corsica
www.corsica-isula.com
www.corsicaweb.fr
www.planete-corsica.com

Corsica is a mini-world, with tiny bays, towering cliffs, a fjord, marshes, forests, sand dunes, mountains and even a desert. It's as if a child drew the map of the island and incorporated every geological feature known to man. Swing the car along the tiny mountain road to the beach at Rondinara, way down south near Bonifacio, and you'll think you've arrived in Never-Never Land – the bay looks as though the only thing missing is Captain Hook's ship.

If the glitz and the traffic jams of the Riviera leave you cold, this is the place to go. You won't find a list of theme parks and attractions waiting at the local tourist office, but you will find some of the best beaches in the Mediterranean and some beautiful, wild and unspoilt countryside. Corsica is a huge mountainous outcrop and a natural fortress. If you come by plane you'll get to see why the French call it 'une montagne dans la mer' – a mountain in the sea.

The best way to enjoy a family holiday in Corsica is to spend a week on the beach letting the kids get all that digging and splashing out of their systems before heading off to explore the island. Although villas high up in the mountains feature in all the brochures, they aren't ideal with kids – Corsica's roads are long and narrow and it's a long, hot commute to the beach. If you have teens in need of some independence and nightlife you'll also want to stick close to the big resorts, and consider hiring bikes so they can get around on their own.

Apart from travel and accommodation costs, you'll find that Corsica won't eat too far into the family holiday budget, especially if you bring your own car. It's a place to picnic and unwind in the great outdoors, with minimal commercial attractions. Its cities are small – Corte is about the size of a large English village – and there are plenty of small, inexpensive restaurants. Corsicans have a lot of affection for children and you'll get a warm welcome wherever you go.

Sea breezes keep the island cool in summer, so it's a good destination with babies. You'll only encounter crowds in the main resorts in August, and even then it's possible to escape to the wilderness and the empty bays of Cap Corse. In the more remote areas it pays to book a hotel in advance if you're touring, not because you'll have to beat your way through the crowds for a room but because there are very few places to stay in the wilder parts of the island and B&Bs are virtually nonexistent.

If you think they'll never put down the GameBoy long enough to pay attention to their surroundings, invest in a copy of *Asterix in Corsica*. All the island's characteristic features are in there, from its distinctive smell to the herds of wild pigs. Even the gorgeous girl of the book was modelled on a real beauty from Bonifacio.

Although the best beaches for kids are in the southwest, almost all the beaches in Corsica are lovely, and with 1,000km of coast, you can't really go wrong, wherever you stay. Although the resorts are busy, it's possible to find a villa with a large garden full of cork and cypress trees, just a short walk from a wild, sandy beach with lots of rock pools. Even the busiest beaches are deserted by early evening as holiday-makers head home to stoke up their barbeques. Corsica is truly the Mediterranean at its best – with not a high-rise hotel in sight.

AJACCIO

Getting there Chances are you'll arrive here. The airport is 6km from town. A bus runs hourly to the town centre or there are plenty of taxis; a trip to town costs around €10 by taxi. Ferries arrive conveniently in the town centre. If you're arriving by car it's best to park in Place Charles de Gaulle. In summer the traffic is a nightmare; the streets are so congested that it's quicker to walk than take the bus, so avoid driving around in the town unless you absolutely have to
Tourist office 3 Bd du Roi Jérôme **t** 00 33 (0)4 95 51 53 03 **www**.tourisme.fr/ajaccio
Special events Most of the big festivities here centre on Napoleon, the town's most famous son. June: During the *Journées Napoléoniennes* there are parades, torchlight processions and fireworks. St Erasmus Day on 2 June sees a parade of fishermen in honour of their patron saint, with free grilled sardines at street stalls along the route July: Blues Festival. August: Napoleon's birthday is celebrated with more parades and fireworks

If the kids have heard of anyone from France besides the Marseille footballer Zinedine Zidane, it's likely to be Napoleon. The man who made himself emperor of France and then set out to conquer Europe was born in Ajaccio on 15 August 1769. Napoleon made his home town the capital of Corsica in 1811 and it hasn't looked back since.

English school kids are usually amazed that someone so important could come from such a tiny, far away place. Only 60,000 people live in Ajaccio (and very few of them share the Frenchman's enthusiasm for Napoleon). And although the house where Napoleon's parents lived was large by Corsican standards, it's tucked away in a narrow side street, the front is overrun with vegetation and the interior is surprisingly simple and homely.

Ironically, it was because France took control of Corsica that Napoleon had his first break. When the island came under French rule in 1769 the sons of the Corsican aristocracy were offered places at top military schools to ensure their loyalty, which is how Napoleon came to be in the French army. The plan worked: Napoleon was determined to keep Corsica part of France and ruled it with an iron fist.

Although the locals are proud of their unique heritage, some of them still resent French rule. Claude Erignac, the prefect of Corsica, was shot dead here in 1998.

Politics aside, Ajaccio has lots of charm. It may be a busy port and the capital of the island but it is a small, friendly place. There are palm trees, vast white squares, port-side cafés and Italianate, ochre-hued buildings. The town was built by the Genoese and it doesn't feel remotely French, though the population has a palpable mini-Riviera chic all of its own. You won't want to spend your entire holiday here but it's well worth devoting at least one day to shopping or dining out down by the waterfront.

The town comes to life in the evening during the summer when there are stalls and rides along the Quai Napoléon. Ferries dock just by the main restaurant area and after dinner kids will enjoy

Is it dangerous?

As you travel around the island, you may see the bombed-out remains of holiday houses and discotheques. There are political slogans painted on the roads and walls and many of the French street signs are crossed out or shot to pieces.

After Napoleon nothing much happened in Corsica until the French lost control of Algeria in 1962. Thousands of French, plus the Foreign Legion, flooded in, many of them keen to make money out of tourism. From a growing fear that the traditional way of life was about to be destroyed, a nationalist movement was born. In 1975, it turned nasty, with a bombing campaign that targeted tourist villages and foreign-owned property and by the mid-1990s the nationalist movement had splintered into disparate groups that turned on each other.

Although the politics may look pretty Balkan, there's no need to worry. Most Corsicans don't support the nationalist movement and tourists have never been caught up in the nationalist campaign, which has largely run out of steam. Holiday homes have only ever been attacked while they are empty – and on the plus side, there's very little petty crime on the island.
The only real danger in Corsica are the roads, which are tortuously windy and often blocked by herds of sheep and wild pigs. Even the long flat road that runs between Bastia and the south can be a problem due to traffic congestion. Allow plenty of time for trips and don't drive when you're tired.

watching the ships arrive. It's a very Corsican affair as a large number of the people arriving aren't holiday-makers, but Corsicans who live and work abroad and there's usually a gaggle of relatives ready to welcome them home.

Shopping

The main shopping district runs between Cours Napoléon and the pedestrianized Rue Fesch. Here you'll find the usual jumble of souvenir outlets (Art'Isula is certainly the best of the bunch) plus a number of designer clothes shops for kids. Top of the pile is Chris Line, 52 Rue Fesch, a massive and impressive store which stocks junior ranges of Kenzo, Lacroix, Nike, Elle, DKNY, Timberland and Chevignon, for ages 0–16. Across the road is a specialist kids' shoe shop Bunny, where you'll find a few pretty alternatives to the standard flip-flops

Tell me a story: the Corsicans

The Corsicans have always had a reputation for being suspicious of foreigners: when Odysseus sailed into the bay at Bonifacio he was supposedly attacked by cannibals. It's not all that surprising that the natives were hostile since just about everyone who set foot on the island was out to conquer Corsica; sitting slap-bang in the middle of the western Mediterranean, it's an irresistible prize. The Greeks arrived first, followed by the Romans. After a short break, the Pisans came, then the Genoese and the French. The British even had a go and Nelson lost his eye fighting the French at Calvi. The French arrived in earnest in 1769 and are still there. Ironically it was the island's most famous son, Napoleon Bonaparte, who set out to make Corsica a French province forever. It didn't take the Corsicans long to work out that the best way to avoid invading forces was to hide far away from the coast on top of the mountains. Even today, the Corsicans on the island – all 120,000 of them – tend to avoid tourists by hiding away in their perched villages, like eagles in their nests. The rest of the population are more recent settlers of the last few decades but even so, there are fewer people living on the island than there were a hundred years ago. To get a real feel for the people and the island, head inland. It's a real adventure setting off up into the mountains; the kids will love seeing herds of semi-wild pigs running about, and you'll find tasty food at farm restaurants – look out for signs saying '*ferme auberge*'.

Did you know...?

Corsica may be part of France, but it's 300km south of Marseille and only 80km from Tuscany. Culturally it's closer to Italy – Corsican is an Italian dialect, not a French one. Listen carefully – when you think you hear someone speaking Italian on the island it's probably a Corsican. A lot of Corsican children do their lessons in their native tongue and take their end of school baccalauréat exam in Corsican.

and sandals, while next door is Top Look with Buffalo shoes and Killah Babe tops for fashion-conscious teens. There's even a Corsican equivalent of Claire's Accessories – Vent Sucré at 60 Rue Fesch has scandalously cheap bead jewellery, gauzy bags and ornate handkerchiefs for pocket-money treats. For labels like Diesel Kids, Replay & Sons and Billtornade Enfant, walk to the end of Rue Fesch by Place Foch and head down to Maximom, 6 Rue Stephanopoli, for some boutique heaven. Gamers meanwhile should head over to the Cyber Store at 61 Cours Napoléon or Cours Prince Imperial to stock up on Nintendo, Sega and Sony new releases, plus PC titles and DVDs. Beach babes and boys can also take a look in at Maresias, 22 Cours Napoléon, to stock up on Billabong, MKY, Rusty and Hana Beach summertime staples. For bargains check out the Sunday flea market on Boulevard Lantivy.

Picnics and snacks

The bakery Au Four à Bois on Cours Napoléon is open until late at night and is the best place to buy snacks and picnic basics. Bread is baked several times a day so it's always fresh. Cours Napoléon also has a large Monoprix. The morning market in Place César-Campinchi sells some of the best cheese and cold cuts in Corsica and is open daily until noon. Galéani at 3 Rue Fesch, has Corsican pies ideal for picnics and tasty *canestrelli* biscuits.

Things to see and do

Les Petits Trains

t 04 95 51 13 69/**t** 04 95 51 53 03

Tourist trains run from Place Foch around the old city and pass right by Napoleon's front door. They also run along the Punta de la Parata overlooking the Iles Sanguinaires. The trains only run in the summer months, but are the best way of sight-seeing without tears .

Maison Bonaparte

Rue St Charles **t** 04 95 21 43 89
Open 9–12 noon and 2–6, closed Sun afternoon and Mon morning
Adm Adult €2.60, child free

There's little left from Napoleon's childhood inside the museum but it's still worth a visit. Inside you can see the sedan chair that carried his mother home while she was in labour, the room where he was born and the presents he brought back for his mother from his early campaigns.

The reason there's so little to see in the house is because it was ransacked, first by Corsican nationalists furious that Napoleon had sided against them and later by the British. Napoleon's family were forced to flee in 1793 and although his mother lived here briefly after that, it was never to be a real family home again.

Most guides will tell you the house is a disappointment, but with a few carefully chosen words you can bring it to life for the kids. It's the best place in town to try to kindle some historical interest in children, as the other examples of local Napoleonic memorabilia and the art collection put together by Napoleon's uncle in the Musée Fesch are unlikely to appeal to them. If you've anyone mugging up for a History GCSE, don't miss the Maison Bonaparte.

La Relève de la Garde Impériale

Every Thursday evening in summer you can see the Imperial Guard on parade at 7pm in Place Foch. The display lasts 45mins, and has plenty of pipes, drums and military paraphernalia.

Tour de Capitellu

Just south of Campo dell'Oro airport

This is one of the island's biggest Genoese watchtowers and is another good outing for Napoleon fans. In the revolutionary turmoil of the early 1790s, Corsican nationalists tried to take back control of the island from the French. They seized Ajaccio, and Napoleon, who sided against the nationalist leader, Paoli, planned to attack his home town from here while the French fleet dealt with the English, who were backing Paoli.

For once things didn't go according to plan for Napoleon. Bad weather held up the fleet and Napoleon and his 50 men ended up besieged in the tower, forced to eat their horses in order to survive. Eventually they escaped and some months later Napoleon returned to rescue his family from Paoli and his supporters. Napoleon's actions had put them in great danger, and they were forced to meet secretly, which they did at the tower before fleeing to Toulon. Not surprisingly, Napoleon grew to hate the tower and tried to blow it up; he was unsuccessful, but you can still see the big crack he made in its side.

Fancy a souvenir...?

Art'Isula at 55 Rue Fesch is a real Aladdin's cave of a shop, features authentic Corsican handicrafts such as jewellery, T-shirts, ceramics and hand-woven baskets. At the opposite extreme, you might want to take home a china cup immortalizing Napoleon and Josephine – France's answer to the Charles and Di mug.

Look out for...

P'tite Vadrouille en Corse avec Scopetta by Eve Andréani (La Marge Edition) is a colourful book aimed at the junior end of the family, featuring a small goat. Through Scopetta's adventures little ones can find out everything they need to know about the island and learn French into the bargain. You might also look out for Les Jeux des Sept Familles Corses, a 'happy families' card game with a Corsican theme. Both the book and game are on sale in main newsagents across the island. If your kids are good at languages they'll also enjoy Célia et le petit poney by Rufin Gutierez (Moriani 2001), a story in French and Corsican and colourfully illustrated throughout. French speakers will also enjoy Contes traditionnels de Corse by Jean Muzi (Milan 2000), an interesting collection of local fairytales.

Musée A Bandera

1 Rue Général-Lévie **t** 04 95 51 07 34
Open Daily in summer 9–7
Adm Adult €3.80, child (10–14) €2.30

If you have time, this history and military museum is worth a quick visit. It helps if you can read French, but even if not, children will like the diorama of the Battle of Ponte Nuovo of 1769 at which the French defeated the nationalists. Toy soldier fanatics will be in their element.

Good to know...Pass-musées

This 7-day pass offers access to all the museums in Ajaccio for an all-inclusive price of €10. Passes are on sale in museums and at the tourist office.

The Citadel

For most of the year Ajaccio's stronghold is occupied by the military and closed to the public eye, but in September the doors are flung open to tourists for the *Jours de Patrimoine* (something akin to the UK's National Museums' Week).

If you're there in September you can catch a glimpse of the bloodstained wall where the Corsican Resistance fighter Captain Fred Scamaroni left a final message in his own blood before garrotting himself with a piece of wire from his cell.

Boat trips

There are a number of companies that run trips from the harbour.

Nave Va

t 04 95 21 83 97
www.naveva.com

This company runs trips out to the Iles Sanguinaires (*see* below) plus day or half-day trips to Bonifacio, the Scandola Nature Reserve, Capo Rosso, Girolata and the Calanches de Piana. There are also boats to Porticcio, between Cargèse and Sagone and from Porto.

Corsica Jet Evasion

Plage du Trottel **t** 06 12 04 02 16
www.corsicajet.com

Jet skis and boat hire.

Ajaccio Ship Shop

28 Cours Lucien Bonaparte **t** 04 95 50 59 09
www.ajaccioshipshop.com

Here you can rent a self-drive boat, either by the day or for longer trips.

Cinemas

Foreign-language films are often shown with subtitles. Look out for VO (*version originale*) in the listings – it indicates that the film isn't dubbed.

Note that film classifications aren't as stringent in France as in the UK, so teenagers can see films here that they might be too young to see in the UK.

Aiglon

14 Cours Grandval, **t** 04 95 51 29 46

Cinema Bonaparte

10 Cours Napoléon, **t** 04 95 51 29 46

Empire

30 Cours Napoléon, **t** 04 95 21 21 00

Cinema Laetitia

48 Cours Napoléon, **t** 04 95 21 07 24

***Tell me a story:* Napoleon**

France commandeered Corsica in the same year that Napoleon was born; he would return the favour by going on to command France. A brilliant general, he was able to take control of France in the chaos that followed the French Revolution and then went on to crown himself emperor and to conquer large swathes of Europe. Napoleon's armies spread the ideals of the French Revolution across the continent, lighting fires that would burn long after he was dead.

To the French he's a hero, who not only made Paris the capital of a huge empire but who also organized the country, making it function efficiently after a long line of disastrous kings and years of revolutionary turmoil. The Corsican view is more mixed, ranging from pride through to indifference and contempt.

Napoleon was born in the modest town of Ajaccio on 15 August 1769, just weeks after Corsica was taken over by French rule. His father had been closely allied with the Corsican nationalist Paoli, who had fled to England with the arrival of the French (had Napoleon's father followed suit, the world's greatest Frenchman might have been born in England).

In 1783 Napoleon's brief childhood came to an end. Awarded a place at French military school, he set sail for France and the rest, as they say, is history. Napoleon's feelings about his homeland were mixed; he was mocked for his Corsican accent, and nothing made him angrier than to be described as 'the Corsican', yet he always said he could recognize his native island with his eyes shut. He remained loyal to his family throughout his life and promoted them to top jobs in the empire, but he last visited the island in 1793 and would never return.

Horse riding

Poney Club d'Ajaccio

Rte de Sartène, Campo dell'Oro **t** 04 95 23 03 10

Offers riding from 5 years; 1hr's riding costs €15 and a whole day costs €45.

Parks and playgrounds

Place de Gaulle

This large concrete square is where Corsican mums come with their young to promenade among the palms and watch the fountains at play. At Christmas there's an ice rink too. Tech-heads will want to spend their time flicking through the latest CD-ROMs in the two computer game shops on the square.

If your kids have skateboards with them head for Boulevard Lantivy to the small but perfectly formed skateboard park by the coast. It's worth a look just to watch the locals doing back flips silhouetted against the deep blue of the Med.

Nightlife

You can enjoy the nightlife without a baby-sitter, as kids are welcome in any bar, day or night. You'll see lots of prams on the terraces outside the trendiest nightspots. At night the majority of Ajaccien youth heads down to the café-bar La Taverne, facing the post office. Le Globo on Place de Gaulle is the place for trendy, good music; during the day it's a nice place to stop for a coffee while the kids play in the square.

Town beaches

The city beach is Plage St-Francois below the citadel, a thin strip of fine yellow sand that, sadly, is plagued by ants in summer.

A bit further west, past the roller skaters' paradise of Place Miot, is a horseshoe-shaped beach, Plage Trottel, which is pretty popular with the local youngsters. The sand is coarser here and you'll need to watch out when swimming as the offshore rocks are bristling with sea urchins, but there's a nice shaded café bar and public toilets (*see* also Special Trips below).

SPECIAL TRIPS FROM AJACCIO

Iles Sanguinaires

Getting there Nave Va, **t** 04 95 21 83 97 **www.naveva.com**

Trips out to the Iles Sanguinaires run daily at 3pm from the harbourside in Ajaccio. The journey takes 2hrs and costs around €70 for a family of four

These four small islands get their name from the red rocks that glow blood-red in the sunset – *sanguinaire* means bloody. The biggest island was once a quarantine station and at one time its lighthouse keeper was the writer Alphonse Daudet (*see* p.128); he described his experiences in *Lettres de mon moulin*.

Porto

Getting there Porto is 28km south of Calvi and 32km north of Ajaccio. There's a bus service from Ajaccio, otherwise you'll need a car to get here
Tourist office La Marine **t** 00 33 (0)4 95 26 10 55 **www.porto-tourisme.com**

Porto has some of the most dramatic scenery on the island and is featured in nearly every holiday brochure, and as a result is busy in season. It's a good base for older children, who will enjoy boat trips to the Scandola Nature Reserve and walking in the mountains, and you'll find all the facilities to keep older kids and teens occupied. The village of Cargèse, where Club Med has its base, is the chic place to head for, for shopping or café life. If you are coming with small children or older kids keen on snorkelling, choose your accommodation carefully. Some of the beaches in the Porto area are pebbly and, as the beach drops sharply into the sea, they can be dangerous when the waves are high. Plage de Bussaglia, Plage de Caspio and Plage de Gradelle are pebbly but better for swimming, while the sandy Plage d'Arone shelves away very quickly into the sea.

For safe beaches with sand head south to the Golfe de Sagone. Near Cargèse, Plage de Pero, Plage de Stagnoli and Plage de Chiuni (where Club Med is based) are all sandy and good for kids. At Sagone

Plage de Liamone is a long sandy stretch but Plage de Santana has a dangerous current so should be avoided. Instead try the beach at Tiuccia, which is famous for its golden sand and is ideal for children.

Things to see and do

Aquarium de la Poudrière

Next to the tourist office t 04 95 26 19 24
Open Daily 10–6 (9 in summer)
Adm Adult €5, child €2.25, under-7s free

The aquarium, which gets its name from the old powder house in which it is located, houses an interesting collection of fish and underwater plants from the nearby nature reserve at Scandola.

The Genoese Tower

Open April–Oct 9–9
Adm Adult €1.75, child (under 12) free

Most of the towers on the island are deserted but you can actually get into this one. Inside the tower is a small exhibition, which explains what it was like to be a watchman. On a good day you can see the next tower in the chain at Capo Rosso.

Cinema

There's an open-air cinema in July and August that shows some films in their original language (*v.o.* or *version originale*), **t** 04 95 26 10 49.

Horse riding

Centre de Randonnée Equestre des Deux-Sorru

Letia **t** 04 95 26 69 94
Open all year round

Organizes rides from 1hr to half a day for beginners and up.

AROUND AJACCIO

Animal magic

A Cupulatta Centre

t 04 95 52 82 34 **www.acupulatta.com**
Getting there 21km out of Ajaccio on the N193, the to Corte
Open Daily April–mid-Nov 10–5.30, July–Aug 9–7
Adm Adult €7, child (under 12) €3.50

This is Europe's largest centre for the breeding and preservation of tortoises, and although it is primarily devoted to scientific research, many of the tortoises can be seen by the public. There are some truly enormous tortoises here; the largest is from the Seychelles and is big enough for the keepers to sit on it. The centre houses over 3,000 tortoises from 120 different species, and there's a special breeding programme and a hospital on site. In Corsica, lots of tortoises fall foul of the garden lawnmower and the most fortunate end up here for treatment.

Philippe Magnan, the centre's owner, was an accountant until the day his dog brought a wounded tortoise in from the garden and his life changed for ever. He sometimes takes the guided tours of the site so you might be lucky enough to meet him. If it's hot, visit first thing in the morning when the tortoises are most active. It's a pleasant leafy spot and there's a good souvenir shop.

Did you know...?
The first tortoise appeared on earth almost 200 million years ago. The tortoise was once a common pet in the UK but now it is illegal to keep one.

Buckets and spades

North of Punta de la Parata is Ajaccio's best beach, Anse de Minaccia. You'll need a car to get there, but the dunes and fine sand are worth the effort. There's a nice beachside café and the locals come here to look for little shells called '*œil de Ste-Lucie*' that are supposed to be lucky.

East of the town is the sandy beach of Ricanto and southeast is the little resort of Porticcio, whose main beaches are busy and good for water sports. Just south of Porticcio is the beautiful silvery beach of Ruppione where you can smell the maquis while you sunbathe.

If you really want to get right away from it all, head even further south for Cala d'Orzu near Monte Bianco.

Acqua Cyrne Gliss

Porticcio, 15km south of Ajaccio **t** 04 95 25 17 48
Open Daily 15 June–15 Sept, 10.30–7
Adm Adult €15, child (5–10) €11, (2–5) €7

This is a great place for kids to burn off excess energy, with 600m of waterslides, water games, playgrounds and bars for refreshments. Entry is free if it's your birthday, but otherwise it is quite expensive for what it is.

Nature lovers

Bastelica

Getting there Follow the D3 up into the mountains

This charming village is famous for its semi-wild pigs, which you'll see on the road as you approach, and it is an ideal place to come for a walk as it's cool even in summer. In autumn it's a popular spot among the locals for mushroom picking, an activity best left to the experts.

Look at this!

Filitosa

Petreto-Bicchisano, 17km north of Propriano
t 04 95 74 00 91
Open Easter–Oct 8–8
Adm Adult €3.30, child free

Among the olive trees of Filitosa, one of which is an incredible 1,200 years old, lie some of the most important Neolithic standing stones in Europe. These are no ordinary obelisk-style menhirs, but have been intricately carved with the faces of long-dead warriors, some of which even have hands, feet, ribs and backbones. They look like drawings by Picasso and are among the first portraits ever found in Europe. Nothing is known about who made them or why, and they were discovered only in the 1940s by the farmer Charles-Antoine Cesari, who used to keep his sheep here. The travel writer Dorothy Carrington wrote about their discovery in *Granite Island*, which describes her stay with the family in 1948. A few years later, the site was fully excavated and a whole host of other stones were revealed. Visit as late in the day as you can to catch the atmosphere of this magical setting. Today you'll also find a small museum, bar and souvenir shop but the site still has a lot of charm and the family still run the reception area. The whole visit takes about 1½ hrs.

BONIFACIO

Getting there The nearest airport is at Figari, 10km away. You can visit on a boat trip from Porto-Vecchio or Ajaccio, and ferries sail from Sardinia just across the narrow straits. Otherwise you'll need a car; there's plenty of parking near the old town even in summer
Tourist office 2 Rue Fred Scamaroni **t** 00 33 (0)4 95 73 11 88 **www**.bonifacio.com
Special events March/April: Easter is a big event in Bonifacio. June: Medieval Festival

It' s worth sacrificing a day on the beach for a trip to Bonifacio. It's like no other place in Corsica and will impress even the sulkiest teenager. The old town sits high up on the white jagged cliffs above a dramatic fjord – it's a miracle the Genoese managed to build it at all (and houses do topple off from time to time). To get there you'll need to drive across a wild wooded area of maquis, which makes the outing feel like a real adventure. From Bonifacio's sheer cliffs you'll be able to see Sardinia, only 12km away; ferry crossings take only 1hr, so you may want to make the trip. If you don't want to go that far there's an underground passage, dug during the Second World War, to Gouvernail de la Corse, a rock offshore that looks like a ship's rudder, hence its name.

Picnics and snacks

Boulangerie Faby on Rue St-Jean-Baptiste is the place to buy local pies and biscuits.

Things to see and do

Petit Train

t 04 95 73 15 07

Leaves from Quai Noël-Beretti and is a good option for touring the town with tiny ones.

Can you spot...the monument to the French Foreign Legion?

The French Foreign Legion was based in Bonifacio until 1989. If you park your car on the headland near the old city you'll spot the monument, brought here from Algeria in 1963, as you walk into town. It was the mass influx of settlers from Algeria after its independence that sparked the nationalist movement in Corsica.

Tell me a story: Odysseus

In the *Odyssey*, Homer describes a bay with walls of stone that reached far into the land, with cliffs at the mouth that met like giant gates. Many historians believe he was describing the long fjord-like bay at Bonifacio, where the white cliffs rise up from the water like walls.

In the story, Odysseus's companions sailed straight into the bay while he wisely moored his ship outside. The locals weren't friendly: they threw enormous boulders down onto the ship and then ate the crew for dinner. Odysseus and his shipmates, however, escaped and set off for another adventure.

L'Escalier du Roi-d'Aragon

Open Daily July–Aug 9–8
Adm €1.20

Legend has it that the soldiers of the king of Aragon, who laid siege to the city in 1420, built this staircase in a single night. In fact it's much older than that and was probably used to bring water up to the town. There are a dizzying 187 steps so it's not one to try with a pushchair! Look out for the rock at the bottom in the shape of Corsica.

L'Aquarium de Bonifacio

71 Quai Comparetti **t** 04 95 73 03 69
Open Daily Easter–Oct 10am–12 midnight
Adm Adult €3.35, child €1.50

This small aquarium is housed inside a cave and has 13 different tanks full of local marine life – lobsters, starfish, crabs and much more. You can see them all in about 30mins.

Boat trips

There are some great boat trips from Bonifacio, which children will love. A number of different companies run trips from the port side, all charging the same price (adult fares are around €9 and under-12s usually travel free). Trips run from 9–7. In high season you may want to make a reservation with Les Vedettes Thalassa, **t** 04 95 73 01 17, which goes on a spectacular journey past the huge cliffs. You'll go to to the Grotte de Sdragonato ('Little Dragon Cave'), where you can see the sky through a large hole that's shaped surprisingly like the map of Corsica. Then it's on to the Grotte Napoléon which looks just like the emperor's famous hat. The trip takes about 45mins.

Good to know...?

Bonifacio can be a very windy place, even in the height of summer, so pack a fleece or jumper and a raincover for the buggy.

Boats also run to the largest of the group of islands just offshore – the Ile Lavezzi, which gives its name to the whole chain. The islands are uninhabited but on Ile Lavezzi is a tragic cemetery full of soldiers who drowned when their ship, the *Sémillante*, sank in February 1855 during a freak storm en route to the Crimea. In the weeks that followed, horribly disfigured bodies were washed ashore and of the 750 bodies only the captain was ever identified.

If you fancy a day out on the islands make sure to pack some food and something to drink, as there is nothing to buy when you get there. Be warned – don't even consider taking a boat trip if it's windy. The sea gets extremely rough when the wind blows, even when the sun is shinning. It can be very frightening and will probably make children seasick.

Sailing

Ecole des Glénans

On the Santa Manza road, 300m from the port
t 04 95 73 03 85

Sailing courses for adults and children over 13.

Can you spot...a Genoese watchtower?

It may look peaceful, but Corsica was once one of the most dangerous places to live in the Mediterranean. In the 15th century, Barbary pirates plundered the Corsican coastline and took anything of value, including boatloads of locals to be slaves. The Genoese, who ruled the island at the time, built a string of almost 100 watchtowers along the coast between Cap Corse and Bonifacio. They were manned by watchmen day and night and were always in sight of two neighbouring towers. If something was wrong a fire was lit and within an hour the whole island could be alerted to the danger. The towers were also designed to be places for local people to hide. The door stood 20 ft off the ground and was reached by a ladder that could be pulled up in seconds.

SPECIAL TRIPS FROM BONIFACIO

Sartène

Getting there Sartène is on the N196, about 1hr north of Bonifacio. It takes 1hr 15mins to drive from Ajaccio. To get there with a family you'll need a car
Tourist office 6 Rue Borgo **t** 04 95 77 15 40
Special events March/April: Good Friday Procession. This 3-hr procession through the town is straight out of the Middle Ages. The Grand Pénitent, whose identity is only known to the local priest, follows the Stations of the Cross around the city clad in chains, red robes and a hood. The rest of the year the chains can be seen in the Eglise Ste-Marie. There's a long list of local men keen to play the role of the Grand Pénitent, but since Sartène is famous for its violent history that's probably not a surprise

Sartène has a tumultuous history – not due to invading armies or despotic leaders – but to its own local feuds. It was the town's dubious honour to be renowned for its bloody vendettas. In the 18th century, when the vicious quarrelling was at its peak, the chance of dying in a vendetta was 1 in 150. Family was pitted against family in quarrels that lasted years. Bizarrely, the fear of sparking a vendetta often kept the local community in check: the worry of getting the family embroiled in such a row was a disincentive for young girls to get involved with boys their parents disapproved of and visa versa. However, most vendettas had their origins in the most idiotic of arguments: a row over a chestnut tree led to 36 deaths and an argument about a dog caused the complete annihilation of two families.

By the 19th century, romantic novelists like Dumas, Maupassant and Mérimée were using stories of real-life vendettas as models for their more dramatic literary excesses, which, in turn inspired the Corsicans to model themselves on the novels' heroes; Hollywood filmmakers are not the only ones to inspire ruthless violence. Sartène is peaceful today, but the last vendetta only came to an end in the 1960s. To get a sense of just how horrible it was to live in vendetta-ridden Corsica, have a coffee in Sartène's leafy main square – the surrounding houses are virtual fortresses. That said, the locals are proud of their turbulent history and there is an authenticity about the town that is unspoilt by tourism. Kids will enjoy exploring the narrow alleyways of the old quarter of Santa Anna and you may also be lucky enough to hear some traditional Corsican polyphonic music.

Picnics and snacks

There are lots of cafés in the Place de la Marie, a car-free zone that is safe for children to run around in. Laurent Targetti, 4 Cours du Général de Gaulle, sells bread, Corsican pastries and excellent local biscuits called *canestrelli*.

Things to see and do

Musée de la Préhistoire

Sartène **t** 04 95 77 01 09
Open Mon–Sat 10–12 noon and 2–6 in summer, otherwise times vary
Adm Adult €3, child €1.50

This area is especially rich in prehistoric sites and the museum, situated inside an old prison, has a collection of prehistoric Corsican artefacts. It's not worth a huge detour, though. For more of an insight into prehistory, you are better off donning your walking boots and heading out in search of the real thing in the maquis (*see* below).

Prehistoric Sites

The nearest site to Sartène is at Alo Bisugè on the D21 and is a collection of ruined huts and cut-stone rectangular hearths dating from 2000 BC. To get there, follow the N196 south then take the D48 in the direction of Tizzano. Turn right on to the D21 in the direction of Grossa.

More impressive still are the Mégalithes de Cauria, further south just off the D48. Near the car park is a collection of 25 menhirs, older than those at Filitosa and some of which have roughly shaped heads and features. Some 400 yards further are 45 menhirs laid out in an unusual north–south alignment. Follow the path up from the car park and you'll find Corsica's biggest and best dolmen, known locally as the Devil's Forge.

As you turn back onto the Tizzano road you'll find, standing like a stone army. a collection of 258 menhirs – the biggest in the Mediterranean. Unfortunately you'll have to admire them from a distance; you can't walk on to the land any more.

Porto-Vecchio

Getting there Ferries arrive here from Italy and Marseille. It's 20km from Figari airport, from where you can get a shuttle bus in the summer months or hire a car. By road, it's 28km north of Bonifacio on the highway to Bastia, but be warned that parking in the town is extremely difficult in the height of summer – it's best to travel early in the morning. There are buses from the town to the nearby beaches of Santa Giulia and Palombaggia

Tourist office Rue du Député de Rocca Serra **t** 00 33 (0)4 95 70 09 58 **www**.accueil.portovecchio.com

The southwest of Corsica is flatter and marshier than the rest of the island and if you've just flown over or driven through some of the most breath-taking scenery to get here, it can, at first sight, be a bit disappointing. But just wait until you've seen the beaches – half-moon bays of white sand slip gently into the sea, allowing plenty of space for toddlers to paddle and for big kids to splash about in safety. The gentle waves are perfect for older children and teenagers to learn to snorkel and to try their hands at water sports. The clear blue sea is fantastically clean and there are lots of tiny fish, even in the shallow waters.

The Porto-Vecchio area is the perfect base for a family beach holiday. There's lots of accommodation to suit all budgets, plenty of facilities and some nightlife for teens. Although it's a top tourist centre, if you head out of town you'll find plenty of secluded spots. The old town is a pleasant place to shop, eat an ice-cream and buy a postcard but there's not much sightseeing to distract you from the real point of a holiday here – the beach – so there's no reason at all to feel guilty if you just want to laze about in the sun.

This part of the coast was once rife with malaria and plagued by pirates, so the Corsicans kept away. The last time this area saw as much activity as it does today was in ancient times – you'll find some of Corsica's best prehistoric sites hidden in the maquis, but for sightseeing you'll need to head out of town in a car.

Can you spot...a cork tree ?
The countryside around Porto-Vecchio is covered in cork trees; until the arrival of tourists the main business in town was making corks. The trees are easy to spot, with their low, twisted branches and spongy bark.

Did you know...?
The chestnut tree is known colloquially as the arbre à pain, the bread tree, because it is such a staple foodstuff in much regional cooking. It was the Genoese who brought chestnuts to Corsica and forced the unwilling locals to plant them, but soon most Corsicans couldn't imagine how they had managed without them. They dried the chestnuts and ground them into flour that was then used to make bread, cakes and polenta. The leaves of the chestnut trees were used to stuff mattresses or were whizzed up to make wine. There's a chestnut festival in Evisa in November where you can try chestnuts cooked up in more ways than you can possibly imagine.

AROUND BONIFACIO

Buckets and spades

Bonifacio

The beaches close to Bonifacio are best avoided; they're quite dirty and accessible by flights of steep steps so are difficult to reach with little children. The closest family-friendly beach is Plage de Sperone, 6km east of town, a pearly white cove with calm, shallow water and lovely views of the islands. If parking is a problem, try the Plage de Santa Manza. Other beaches in the area are either close to unpleasant swamps, too busy or too dirty.

The coves around Bonifacio can be very dangerous when it's windy, so keep a close eye on the kids. It does mean that the area is fantastic for windsurfing, especially at Calalonga Plage. When the weather is fine Calalonga, is another good beach for small children as it's gentle and secluded. Don't miss Plage de la Rondinara some 15km to the northeast, which looks like a Pacific lagoon. There's a great, inexpensive café right on the beach.

Sartène

Around Sartène, the best places for swimming are the beautiful sandy beaches at Tizzano or Roccapina. The latter is better for very small children – they'll like the enormous Rocher du Lion, a huge craggy rock looming up on a headland above the beach that actually does look like its namesake. If you look carefully you'll see some rock formations nearby that look like an elephant and a gorilla. There are paths leading up to the top of the rocks but they can be risky as there aren't any safety barriers.

This part of the coast has seen more than its fair share of famous wrecks. In 1887 the luxury steamer *Tasmania* went down with a trunkload of jewels on board, a present from the maharajas of India for Queen Victoria. The trunk was recovered, minus a bag of diamonds. The story has it that a bandit buried them in the maquis, but that he was arrested and never came back to claim his loot.

Porto-Vecchio

Situated 6km south of Porto-Vecchio, Palombaggia is a golden semi-circle of sand fringed by pines and dunes. This is one of the most popular beaches on the island and can get crowded in August, but if you're travelling with little children and want to avoid the midday sun; there's no need to give it a wide berth. Beaches empty early; by six everyone has gone home for dinner so an evening picnic is a beautiful end to the day. Further south still is Santa Giulia, quieter and again perfect for children as it is a wide, shallow bay. There are plenty of opportunities for water sports to keep older children busy here.

North of Porto-Vecchio head for Baie de San Cyprianu, a half-moon bay of white sand with a lagoon behind. Further north, 20km from Porto-Vecchio, is Pinarellu, with clear shallow water and white sand, plenty of water sports, a good beach café and a Genoese watchtower. For real hidden gems it's worth investing in a detailed map and following bumpy tracks that head in the direction of the sea – many of them lead to beaches that are off the tourist track.

Look at this

Casteddu d'Araghju

Getting there On the D759 north of Porto-Vecchio
Open all year round
Adm free

This is the most impressive of Porto-Vecchio's prehistoric sites and the best one to visit with older children. The fortress is perched on a rocky outcrop and it takes about half an hour to reach it from the car park; this is not an outing to attempt with toddlers, and you'll need sturdy footwear. The climb is worth every step, though; from the top there's a fantastic view across the Gulf of Porto-Vecchio. The fort itself is monumental. Its 7ft-thick walls are built into the rock and within there was once a village with a population of 200, which was pretty big by prehistoric standards.

Take some water but reward yourself with a cold fizzy drink at the village snack bar where you can find brochures explaining the site.

Musée de l'Alta Rocca

Lévie **t** 04 95 78 47 98
Open Tues–Sun 9–12 noon and 2–5, daily in summer
Adm Adult €3, child €1.50

If the kids are interested in prehistory it's worth driving to Lévie to see the Granny of all the Corsicans – Bonifacio Woman, who lived 8,500 years ago. She was just 4ft 9in tall and, according to scientists, lived on a diet of fish and small mammals and had terrible rheumatism in her feet. All the same, she lived to what must have been a ripe old age of 35. You can also see the skeleton of the extinct 'rabbit cat'. The museum has just been reopened after a major renovation and also houses a collection of prehistoric pots and tools found in the area.

Sporty kids

Water sports

Ecole de Voile San Cyprianu

t 04 95 70 47 51

Pedal boats and kayaks for hire.

Bike hire

Porto-Vecchio is a good place to hire bikes, as the ground is flatter than in most other areas of Corsica. It's a good option if you're holidaying with teens, as having a bike here will give them more freedom.

Corse Nature Evasion
Baie Santa Giulia **t** 04 95 70 56 75

Années Jeunes
Av Georges Pompidou **t** 04 95 70 36 50

Boat trips

There are a number of different boat companies along the harbour who run trips along the coast to Bonifacio and to the *Pecorella* shipwreck, where experienced older swimmers can snorkel. Be warned that even if the weather is calm in Porto-Vecchio, the sea around Bonifacio can be very choppy, so check the weather conditions before you commit yourself. These trips are better made with older children – toddlers, small boats and deep sea just don't mix. Take water, sunhats and plenty of sun cream.

Unfortunately prices are high: a trip to the *Pecorella* wreck is around €75 and a day trip to Bonifacio will set a family of four back around €150, although the trip usually includes a picnic lunch. Contact Ruscana, **t** 04 95 71 41 50, **www**.croisieres-ruscana.com

You may find it better to hire your own boat so you can decide exactly where you want to go and for how long. You can hire a boat from Marine Location, **t** 04 95 70 58 92, or alternatively take a stroll along the harbour and negotiate the price.

Nature lovers

Forêt de l'Ospédale

This is an ideal spot for a family walk, just behind Porto-Vecchio. The easiest trail starts at Cartalavonu, is mainly flat and leads to a rocky, grassy plain with beautiful views. Follow the signs for the 'sentiers des rochers'. A more energetic and demanding walk leads from l'Ospedale, the old malaria hospital from which the forest gets its name, to the Lac de l'Ospedale. It takes 2hrs and is a bit slippery underfoot, so is not recommended for small children or pregnant mums.

BASTIA

Getting there Trains from Ajaccio, Corte, Calvi and Ile-Rousse arrive at the train station on Av du Maréchal-Sébastiani, **t** 04 95 32 80 61. The airport is 17km south of town and there's a regular bus service to the town centre. Boats arrive from Italy and France at the Gare Maritime, **t** 04 95 55 25 52. For taxis, **t** 04 95 34 07 00
Tourist office Pl St-Nicolas **t** 00 33 (0)4 95 54 20 40 **www**.bastia.tourisme.com
Special events April: Comic Book Festival. July: La Relève des Gouverneurs, a historical festival with lots of pageantry, costumes, flags and drums. July/August: Street theatre and live music throughout the town

Bastia was founded by the Genoese in the 15th century and today it's a bit rough and ready, just like Genoa itself. You'll either love its vibrancy and authenticity or hate its scruffiness. This is Corsica's main city so don't be surprised by the shopping malls and general urban sprawl to the south. During the Second World War it was badly bombed by the Americans; unfortunately the town had just been liberated from the Germans but this news did not reach the US commander in time. This was also where the daredevil pilot and novelist Antoine de

Can you spot...the Moor's Head?
Chances are you'll come home with at least a pencil or rubber bearing the picture of a young black man with a white scarf tied around his head. It's the Corsican national emblem, the Testa Nera or Moor's Head, and is the symbol of SC Bastia, the local football team. The symbol goes much further back, however: the Crusaders put his picture on their shields, as did the kings of Aragon when the pope gave them the island in 1297 to spite the Genoese. They never actually managed to conquer Corsica, but from then on maps always marked Corsica with the symbol of the moor's head. Later in the 18th century, Corsica's nationalist leader Pascal Paoli adopted it as the symbol of the Corsican flag. Don't forget to look out for the Moor's Head when you're in England. The symbol spread to England with the Crusades, but exists only as a popular pub name.

Saint-Exupéry, author of *The Little Prince*, flew his last mission before he disappeared into the sea just off Nice in July 1944 (*see* p.78). Today it's the one town in Corsica junior football fans may have heard of; Bastia has the island's top team.

You're likely to find yourself passing through town on the way to catch a ferry or a plane. It's worth stopping for a drink in the Vieux Port, but steer clear of the gardens around the citadel, which are home to some of Bastia's more dubious inhabitants and not the place to take children. You'll find plenty of cafés on Place St-Nicolas.

If you're looking for somewhere to stay, head north out of Bastia, where there are a number of family-friendly hotels along the twisting coast road to Cap Corse.

If you have a car, drive up to the mountain pass on the road to Patrimonio. Bloodthirsty children will love pointing out the smashed cars on the rocks below you as you negotiate the hairpin bends, but there is a stunning view once you've reached the top, and if you're lucky you'll find the car park full of cows. There's usually a little van serving snacks at the top too.

Shopping

The Boutique Jumanjy sells designer gear for ages 0–teens, including Naff Naff and Elle, and marks the start of the shopping district, which runs from Avenue Emil Sari to Boulevard Général de Gaulle. Le Palais des Bébé on Boulevard Paoli is the place for baby clothes. There is a flea market on Sunday morning for one-offs and bargain hunting.

Picnics and snacks

For snacks head for Place St-Nicolas, where there are endless kiosks selling hot dogs and paninis. For more substantial shopping there's a little daily market on Place du Marché. The best patisserie is Agostini on Place Vincetti and the best ice-cream is at Serge Raugi on Rue Capanelles.

Things to see and do

Terra Nova

The old Genoese citadel sits high above the Vieux Port; on foot it's a steep climb from Quai du Sud or you can drive up as far as the car park on Place Dominique Vincetti. The area is great for exploring and is full of winding streets and Bastia's finest houses, which have recently been restored to their former grandeur. Take time to visit the museum (*see* below) while you're up there:

Le Musée d' Ethnographie

Place du Donjon t 04 95 31 09 12

The museum is due to reopen in the summer of 2003 after extensive renovations and is well worth a visit. It houses some fascinating historical bits and pieces, including one of Napoleon's many death masks and the original Corsican flag of independence. You can also visit the dungeons where Resistance fighters were held by the Nazis during the Second World War, and on the museum terrace you can see the submarine that was used to smuggle weapons and ammunition into occupied Corsica.

Cinemas

Le Regent

Rue César Campinchi t 04 95 31 30 31

Boat trips

Compagnie Saint-Jean

12 Bd Auguste Gandin t 04 95 58 88 52

Organizes various boat trips along the coast of Cap Corse.

SPECIAL TRIPS FROM BASTIA

Cap Corse

Tourist offices Petrabugno **t** 00 33 (0)4 95 32 01 00; St-Florent Rte de Cap Corse **t** 04 95 37 06 04

The northern promontory of Cap Corse is 40km long and 10km wide and is a world of its own. Until the road was built in the 19th century it was only accessible by boat. If you're driving round it today, be prepared; the roads are hair-raising, with 5,000 bends and sheer drops down to the sea, so don't get caught up admiring the view as you negotiate a sharp right-angled bend. It really doesn't help that there are shrines to unfortunate drivers outside every village, but steel your nerves and the rewards will become apparent: the scenery changes as you turn each corner. One minute you pass a rocky beach reminiscent of Cornwall, the next you could be in Liguria and then, just as suddenly, the landscape resembles the wild and windswept Scottish Highlands.

St-Florent

St-Florent at the bottom of Cap Course is a good base for exploring the area. It has good facilities and the shady Place des Portes is a nice spot for an evening stroll or for watching locals playing *boules*.

Erbalunga

The beaches on the eastern side of the Cap are generally better for families; the coast on this side of the island is relatively more gentle than the western side, with mountains sloping into the sea. Erbalunga is a good base or stop-off point, but it only has one hotel so you'll need to book in advance. Once an important port, today Erbalunga is a pretty fishing village and is famous for its Good Friday procession. Fortify yourself for the drive round the Cap with a cool drink beside the harbour.

Further along the coast, the town of Sisco has a good beach and some reasonable hotels. It's a good place to take a family walk: follow the path to the Col St-Jean for some stunning views. Next along the coast is Porticciolo, which has a good sandy beach and a couple of hotels and *chambres d'hôte*.

Plage Taramone at Macinaggio is another good place for a swim. From here you can gaze across to the island of Elba where Napoleon was briefly exiled. The view to the sea beyond is so enticing it's no wonder that Corsicans from this part of the island became intrepid explorers. Many of them set sail to make their fortunes in America and the Caribbean and built huge villas on Cap Corse when they returned.

The tourist office has details of a pleasant walk known locally as the 'sentier des douaniers', which goes past the Genoese tower from the beach at Macinaggio. You won't want to try the whole hike with children, but there are some short walks along the path which they'll enjoy, or you can rent bikes at Cap Corse Location, **t** 04 95 35 45 19.

Good to know...

When planning your holiday on Cap Corse remember that tortuously bendy roads make for long journeys. Come prepared with supplies too: there are few petrol stations, shops and places to stay in the area, and the only cash point is by the post office in Macinaggio. Take sick bags from the plane or ferry, as some bends are enough to turn the toughest of stomachs, and bring a fleece or sweater, as it's windy even in summer.

If walking isn't your thing you can catch boats here for a jaunt along the coast. The trip takes 1hr and costs about €8 head.

Barcaggio

As you drive on to Barcaggio you'll pass the beautiful village of Rogliano perched on the hillside. There is another lovely beach and a little hotel at Barcaggio, and it's another good place for walking with kids as it marks the other end of the 'sentier des douaniers'. Further along in Centuri there's a mini-market and plenty of snack bars along the little harbour fronts.

The road on the western side of Cap Corse really has to be seen to be believed – the mountains plunge straight down into the sea. Along the way, stop in Nonza's leafy square for a cooling drink or to stock up at the mini-market. Admire the black sandy beach from a distance, however: not only is the climb back up the cliffs a killer in the heat, but there's an old asbestos mine just up the coast, which accounts for the beach's strange colour.

AROUND BASTIA

Buckets and spades

The closest beach to Bastia's city centre is the pebbly and none-too-clean Plage de Toga. There's a much better beach for children, with sand, 4km south, at Plage de l'Arinella. Further south, the stretch of coast between the small seaside village of Moriani Plage, 20km from Bastia, and Bravone is referred to in the holiday brochures as the Costa Verde. It certainly lives up to the name, lying as it does along the flank of the chestnut forests (*see* **Castagniccia**, below) and, further south, a phalanx of eucalyptus trees. Along this stretch, the Mark Warner resort of San Lucianu reclines among miles of yellow sand and is conveniently situated for walks, cycling and water sports. The coast can be quite gusty in the afternoons so plan any sailing for the morning and relax after lunch. There are plenty of auberges and pizza joints dotted along the roadway and mile upon mile of low-rise holiday apartments. *See* **Désert des Agriates**, p.198, for more good beaches.

Nature lovers

The Castagniccia

Getting there The chestnut forests are off the N198 near Moriani Plage. Follow the signs to Taglio, San Giovanni-di-Moriani or Cervione

From the coast, near the village of Moriani Plage, it looks like a pleasant enough walk up to the chestnut forests, past lemon and kiwifruit trees and along winding roads. In fact it's a 10-km hike from here to San Nicolao and the roads become more twisted and steep the further you go. The best option is to hire a mountain bike or car and stop off for walks and meals en route. If you're visiting in September be sure to stop in Talasani when the local bars and eateries resound to the strains of salsa and indigenous polyphonic airs. Polyphonic music (consisting of several melodies played together) is a Corsican speciality, somewhat like a Welsh male choir, but with a more gothic edge. It is a very sonorous, beautiful and moving sound and the opportunity to hear it in its native setting shouldn't be missed. In San Giovanni-di-Moriani you'll find the charming little restaurant Cava (*see* p.207) with wonderful views over the coast. Be sure to book in advance.

The Désert des Agriates

Getting there The beaches are all difficult or impossible to reach by road; if you try you'll bounce along some pretty rough tracks. Hardy types do it on foot or by bike but with children in the height of summer that's not a realistic option. The best way to get there is to catch one of the shuttle boats that leave regularly in summer from St-Florent: Le Popeye II, **t** 04 95 37 19 07 and U Saleccia, **t** 04 95 36 90 78 can both supply snorkels and masks to hire on board. If you want more independence it's possible to hire a private boat in St-Florent. Just talk to the fishermen on the port side; with a big family it might be a better deal. If your family are competent riders, Course Escapades in Lama, **t** 04 95 48 22 99, runs horseback trips into the Agriates

This wild stretch of land was once the most important agricultural area on the island (hence '*agriates*' which means arable land) but fires, overfarming and erosion have reduced it to a wilderness of rocks and maquis. It escaped being turned into a nuclear test site in the 1970s and is now protected, hence the lack of roads.

The Agriates' main attractions are its fabulous beaches: Plage de Saleccia is the best beach on the island, it's 1km long and backed by sand dunes and

Tell me a story: Something spooky

Corsica was a wild and lonely place until tourists discovered it in the 1970s. Despite the many invasions by all and sundry out to control the Mediterranean, Corsicans hid up in the hills and had little to do with the newcomers for centuries. As a result, strange customs from Neolithic times have lived on in Corsica, undisturbed by the modern world.

When the travel writer Dorothy Carrington arrived in the late 1940s she found a land where stories of ghostly apparitions and prophetic dreams were widely believed, where Christian and even Greek and Roman ideas didn't push out the old beliefs. The peasants she met recounted tales of how the spirits of the dead lived in the maquis and claimed the souls of the living, calling out the names of those next to die. There were tales of phantom funerals, when the most unfortunate discovered it was their own body lying in the coffin. Predicting when the grim reaper was coming to call was apparently quite common in Corsica. A group of people known as *mazzeri* actually brought death home with them. Ordinary people by day, at night they became bewitched and left their sleeping bodies to go hunting in the maquis. They would kill the first animal they saw and in the animal's face would recognize the next person in the village to die – maybe even someone in their own family. They were then compelled to go back and announce the impending death. Dorothy Carrington describes meeting a *mazzeri* in her book *Granite Island* (Penguin, 1984) – read it after dark if you dare.

With stories like this dominating the conversation, it was not surprising that Corsicans were terrified of the dead. A huge cult of death developed and food and drink would be left on graves to mollify the dead. You can still see evidence of it today in the collections of huge tombs in the cemeteries and the shrines along the road where people have been killed in car accidents.

pine trees; Plage du Lodo is a sheltered cove with a fine sandy beach; and Plage de Malfalco and Plage de l'Ostriconi are equally beautiful and have exceptionally fine sand. Bring a picnic and enjoy a day in the wilderness.

Look at this!

Aleria

Getting there It's on the main coast road, 30km south of Bastia. The only feasible way to get there with kids is by car

The Romans took a great interest in Aleria, and at one time made it the capital of Corsica. Their love of oysters might have had something to do with it – the area is renowned for them and they are still farmed in the huge lagoon to the northeast of town, the Etang de Diane, just as they were in Roman times. Today, there's also a nice restaurant where you can try them. Look out, too, for the nearby Ile des Pêcheurs – an island made entirely out of oyster shells discarded by the Romans when the oysters were salted before being shipped to Rome. Napoleon was so taken with the local oysters that he used to order baskets of them to be shipped over to Elba when he was in exile.

If you want to try the local delicacy, bear in mind that they're are not at their best in summer when they are spawning. This is the origin of the old adage about avoiding oysters unless there is an 'r' in the month – they won't make you ill necessarily, but the flavour might be affected. In August the town has a special Roman festival when you can don your toga, play Roman games and taste Roman food – but maybe avoid the oysters.

If your children have a penchant for Roman ruins, Aleria has lots of sun-bleached foundations and courtyards to explore, plus rows of pillars, walls and drainage and hypocaust heating systems.

The Musée Jérôme Carcopino

Fort de Matra (and excavations) **t** 04 95 57 00 92
Open Daily 8–12 noon and 2–7 (5 in winter)
Adm Adult €1.50, child (under 10) €0.75

The recently designed museum, housed in the Fort itself, is an accessible collection of ancient Roman artefacts, including some fun erotic pots that you may or may not want to point out. The excavations of the Roman city are 300m from the museum, in an atmospheric spot surrounded by cypress trees, and include a forum and the remains of some of the Roman temples. A lot of the city is yet to be excavated, which can make it fun to speculate about what's left to find. After the trip cool off at Plage de Padulone, 3km east.

CALVI

Getting there The airport is 7km south of town and a taxi into town costs around €15. Calvi also links into the train line from Ajaccio to Bastia, or you can catch a direct train to Ile Rousse. Ferries arrive here from France and Italy
Tourist office Port de Plaisance **t** 00 33 (0)4 95 65 16 67 **e** omt.calvi@wanadoo.fr
Special events March/April: Good Friday Procession. July: Fireworks Festival. November: the Festival du Vent features displays of extraordinary kites and lots of street theatre, **www.le-festival-du-vent.com**

This is the trendy corner of Corsica where you can get down to some serious star spotting. Calvi has been a tourist centre since the 1930s and has a real Riviera atmosphere, with loads of facilities and plenty of places to stay. As it's a haunt for the rich and famous, not all the accommodation is suited to the average family budget and it gets very busy in high season. For a day out, however, you can guarantee that you'll find something to keep all the family happy. It's a lovely place to come to stock up on traditional ceramics, local foodstuffs and home-grown fashion and there's a lively café scene in the evening, so it's good for teens. Stop off for a drink at Quai Landry and explore the back streets for places to eat.

Did you know...?
Admiral Horatio Nelson lost his eye during the siege of Calvi when the British sided with the nationalists against Napoleon. Britain wanted to claim Corsica as a naval base but Napoleon wasn't having any of that. He booted out the British and Corsica has been French ever since.

Good to know...

There were once seals along the coast around Calvi, but despite what the local maps might say, it's not worth setting off on a seal-watching walk, as you won't find them here any more. Although Corsica may look wild and unspoilt, its individual Mediterranean environment is under threat even in the most remote parts of the island. Please take especially great care when out walking and do not disturb the natural habitat.

Shopping

Boulevard Wilson is the main shopping street. There's a clothes market near the Super U supermarket on the first and third Thursday of the month. La Maison du Bébé is the place to buy toys.

Picnics and snacks

There's a fruit and vegetable market every morning by the church of Ste-Marie Majeure. Aux Gâteaux Corses on Boulevard Wilson sells traditional biscuits and cakes.

Things to see and do

The Citadel

The Genoese made Calvi their main stronghold and their huge citadel dominates the town. Although you can't get into most of it you can still enjoy a walk along the ramparts to gawp at the expensive boats lining the marina. There's a special sound and light show in mid-July and audio tours are available from the tourist office. If your child speaks French there are special children's tours in the form of a treasure hunt, Citadelle Aventure, aimed at children aged 8–14. To reserve a place call **t** 04 95 65 16 67. Just off Piazza d'Armes is the building Corsicans claim to be where Columbus was born. You'll see the sign

.S.
S.A.S.
.X .M .Y.

all over town, it is Columbus' signature.

Little is known for certain about Columbus' early life: he himself was strangely cagey about signing his name or talking about his past, which has led to plenty of wild speculation. Historians don't think Calvi's claim to be his home town holds much water, but don't tell any Corsicans that.

Cinemas

Open-air cinema

There's an open-air cinema in July and August on the Col de Fogata on the N197 near Ile Rousse, **t** 04 95 60 00 93.

Playground and parks

Scimia Calvese

At the northern end of the beach
Open Daily 10–6
Adm Adult €15, child €12

This is a huge 700-m maze complex made up of bridges, pulleys and ladders. Come here to run off excess energy if you're not going to the beach.

Boat trips

Colombo Line

Quai Landry **t** 04 95 65 32 10

Offers boat trips to the Scandola Nature Reserve (*see* p.202).

Corse Loisirs Location

Port de Plaisance **t** 04 95 65 21 26

Rents boats with or without a captain.

Water sports

Calvi Nautique Club

On the beach **t** 04 95 65 10 65

Hires kayaks and windsurfing kit, etc.

Town beaches

The beach is at the end of Quai Landry and is initially dominated by beach bars and parasols but gives way to a public section further along the bay. It isn't Corsica's best beach but it's rock free and shallow so is fine for kids.

There are two good beaches, Plage de Lozari to the northeast and Plage de Rindara to the southwest. If you want to surf, head for the beach at Algajola.

Can you spot...a member of the Foreign Legion ?

You'll recognize them straight away; just watch out for a band of tall, fit men wearing their famous kepis. The 2e Régiment Étranger de Parachutistes is based just outside town at Camp Raffali.

Twenty thousand leagues under the sea: diving with kids

Corsica is one of the best places to learn to dive. The water is warm and clear, and there's hardly any pollution and very little fishing. As a result, it's easy to see fish and marine life in sheltered outlets just off the coast, and for teenagers with diving experience there are a number of easily accessible wrecks around the east coast.

Most diving clubs are experienced with children and will make a big effort to make them feel at ease. Nearly all the big centres have the necessary equipment suitable for children and are affiliated to the Fédération Française d'Etudes et de Sports Sous-Marine (FFESSM) and there's usually an instructor who speaks English.

Under French law, children over the age of eight can start diving with parental consent, but some clubs and resorts may have a higher age limit. Children will usually only be taken in the sea after they've taken the induction lessons in a pool.

There are lots of diving schools on the island; check what's on offer at your local resort and choose the one that seems best suited to your needs. A few centres offer baby-sitting services if you book ahead. The average price for a dive is €40. Not all clubs take credit cards; so make sure you have plenty of cash.

Although one of the best areas for diving is off the south coast near the Ile Lavezzi, which is famous for its friendly fish, it isn't ideal for children, as it is notoriously windy and there are strong currents. There are still great places for junior divers, however. Among the best are the sheltered inlets near Propriano; the Golfe de Porto; the coast from Calvi to Ile Rousse; near Bastia; and off the beaches around Porto-Vecchio, particularly off the island of Le Toro. The Mark Warner resort at San Lucianu is also good for kids and adults wanting to learn how to dive; advanced divers can take excursions to dive near wrecks (*see* p.214).

Remember, feeding fish damages the environment and it's against the law to remove shells and seaweed. Do not dive with a cold or ear, nose or throat problems, or while pregnant. Never dive the day you arrive or the day before you fly home; it can be dangerous as flying affects the way your body deals with the disposal of nitrogen and puts you at greater risk of decompression sickness.

If diving is a bit adventurous for you, don't despair – Corsica is a snorkeller's paradise and you can see some beautiful underwater sights just a few yards off the coast. It pays to be careful, though, because although the sea may look warm and welcoming you need to be wary of strong winds and fast-flowing currents. Never snorkel alone and never take children who are not strong swimmers far from the beach.

The following clubs offer diving courses for children over the age of eight. Most only operate in summer. For a full list of clubs see **www.**plongee-corse.org or ask at the tourist office.

Ajaccio

Corse Plongée

Le Ratajola, Rte de Molini

Porticcio

t 04 95 25 46 30

Bastia

Thalassa Immersion

Base Nautique de Ville-di-Petrabugno
www.tibastia.free.fr

Calvi

Ecole de Plongée International de Calvi

In the port **t** 04 95 65 43 90

Calvi Citadelle

In the port **t** 04 95 65 33 67

Calvi Castille

In the port **t** 04 95 65 14 05

Ile Rousse

Ecole de Plongée de l'Ile Rousse

On the port side **t** 04 95 60 36 85

Porto

Centre de Plongée du Golfe de Porto

In the port **t** 04 95 26 10 29
www.plongeeporto.com

Generation Bleue

Marina de Porto, Rive Droite **t** 04 95 26 24 88
www.generation-bleue.com

Porto-Vecchio

Hippocampe

Club la Chiappa
t 04 95 70 56 56

SPECIAL TRIPS FROM CALVI

Réserve Naturelle de Scandola

Getting there Two companies in Porto organize trips to the Scandola Nature Reserve and the Calanches de Piana, a series of creeks with some stunning rock formations

Porto Linéna operates out of the Hotel Monte Rosso, **t** 04 95 26 11 50, and has a 12-seater boat, the *Mare Nostrum*, which is small enough to enter the sea grottos. Sailings are from Easter–Oct. Nave Va operate out of the Hotel Cyrnée, **t** 04 95 26 15 16, and runs evening cruises, which is a good option if the weather is hot. These boats seat up to 180 people so they can't get through the narrower openings in the caves. Boats also run from Ajaccio (*see* p.187), Calvi, Cargèse and Sagone. To reserve a seat, in Calvi, contact Colombo Line, Quai Landry, **t** 04 95 65 32 10; in Cargèse contact the tourist office; and in Sagone you need to go to the restaurant L'Ancura, which is right by the port side

A huge volcanic eruption 250 million years ago created this stunning stretch of headland and since then it's been pounded by the sea and beaten by fierce winds to create an extraordinary collection of grottos and rocky pinnacles. It's home to dolphins and seals, rare plants, bats, birds and fish. If you're lucky you'll spot an eagle and there are an amazing 543 different types of fish in the sea here.

You can only view the nature reserve from the sea so it's not an ideal outing with toddlers, but older kids will love it – this wild area is simply breathtaking. Take a picnic lunch along with you, as the restaurants are very expensive in the villages near the reserve. Pack sunhats, sun cream and a fleece as it is windy on the water.

Fôret d'Aitone

This large pine forest is a good place for a family walk and a picnic. The path from Evisa, the orange-marked route called '*mare e monti*' is an easy family walk that leads to the Grottes des Bandits. (This was once Corsican bandit country but the last Corsican bandit handed himself in years ago.) If you go the whole way it's a 2-hr hike, but you can walk as much or as little as you like. For a much quicker stroll, just outside Evisa on the left-hand side of the road is a small natural pool, only 15mins away. The Maison d'Information du Paesolu d'Aitone, **t** 04 95 26 23 62, on the D84 can give you further advice on where to walk.

Good to know...

The Train-tramway de Balagne runs in the summer between Ile Rousse and Calvi and is a fun way to see the coast if you don't have a car. It stops at a number of pretty spots along the way.

Lac de Creno

This glacial lake is another picnic spot. Leave the car in the small car park just after Soccia. It's a 2hr walk to the lake and back, which, as legend has it, was created by a hammer blow from the devil.

AROUND CALVI

Buckets and spades

Ile Rousse

Getting there Boats arrive here from France and Italy. In summer there's a small train that runs from Calvi, otherwise you'll need a car; it's 30km from Bastia and 16km from Calvi

Tourist office Pl Paoli **t** 00 33 (0)4 95 60 04 35

Ile Rousse is a pleasant place for a stroll, to stock up on shopping in the covered market and to have a drink in its leafy main square. However, it's a busy ferry port, so the town itself isn't the ideal base for a family holiday, but it does have three beautiful sandy beaches and some of the warmest weather.

Things to see and do

Musée Océanographique

On the beach **t** 04 95 60 27 81

Open May–Sept

Adm Adult €7, child €3

Guided tours in English. Tour lasts 1hr 45mins.

The museum has a large aquarium full of local fish and is especially fun to visit if the kids like snorkelling, as it will help identify what they see.

CORTE

Getting there Corte is on the main road between Bastia and Ajaccio and is 38km from Bastia and 45km from Ajaccio. You can catch a train from Ajaccio, Bastia, Calvi and Porto-Vecchio. The train station is a 10min walk east of the town. For taxis call **t** 04 95 46 04 88

Tourist Office La Citadelle **t** 00 33 (0)4 95 46 26 70 **www**.corte-tourisme.com

For just over ten years, in the middle of the 18th century, Corsica was independent and Corte was its capital; today this tiny mountain citadel is still a nationalist stronghold. During this brief period of independence, Napoleon's parents lived here, but were forced to flee when the French arrived, because of their nationalist sympathies. They made their escape on donkeys over the mountains with Napoleon's mother heavily pregnant with her famous son. Trekking across the mountains with a small family is just as tricky today and if you're burdened with a double buggy it is best to enjoy the scenery at a leisurely pace in the car or on the train. The road from Ajaccio to Bastia climbs high into the mountains through herds of pigs and on to Corte. Very few people live in Corsica and most tourists stick to the beach, so even in summer the mountains feel wild and remote.

Corte itself is a university town, so it has a lively atmosphere even out of season. Despite this influx of life, however, the houses have a hushed air and Corte's numerous narrow alleyways seem intent on drawing you away from the heart of town. Corte is really a miniature city and you can see everything in a matter of hours. There's a real tumble-down feel to the place, and the trek up from the train station or along the winding mountain passes is an adventure in itself. The area around Corte is perfect for camping or sampling the delights of a friendly *auberge* (*see* p.208).

Shopping

Corte is a lovely place to come shopping as the roads are generally quiet and much of the wares are made locally. Bright and inviting, Ghjoculi Smunevuli (**t** 04 95 47 05 52) in Place Gaffori sells all manner of wooden items.

Picnics and snacks

Stock up on picnic foods including pies, pizzas and cakes at the Boulangerie de la Gare, located

Le Chemin de Fer de Corse: The Mountain Railway

If you don't have a car and aren't up for a walk, you can admire the wild and dramatic mountain scenery from a railway carriage. The train that runs right along the top of the mountains from Ajaccio to Bastia stops at Corte where you can visit the citadel and passes through some of the most dramatic and breathtaking scenery that Corsica has to offer. Wooded valleys, waterfalls, plunging rivers, hilltop villas and châteaux and stone houses by the dozen line the route from coast to coast. (Less attractive sites include the sewage works, scrap yards, glass-recycling depot and factories, made more startling by being placed slap-bang in the middle of such an area of natural beauty.)

The train rattles and occasionally lurches its way through 32 tunnels and across 52 bridges (including the longest, the Pont de Vecchio built by Gustave Eiffel himself) criss-crossing rivers and gorges. The line is higher than the road and there are some dizzying views across the mountains. Highlights down the line for walkers are the Cascade des Anglais and the forests of Vizzavona (*see* above), the craggy views of Vivario and Venaco and a chance to cool off in the natural pools of the River Vecchio.

The line looks almost exactly as it did when it was built in a speedy five years between 1883 and 1888. Although the modern trains are all diesels, minitrain enthusiasts will like spotting the original water towers for the old steam trains. At Vivario Station you'll see two of them. History buffs will be interested in the Ponto Novu bridge near Ponte Leccia, where the French defeated the Corsican nationalists in the 18th century. It is in ruins now after the Nazis did their best to blow it to smithereens in the Second World War.

The trip from Bastia to Ajaccio is 152km and takes just under 4hrs. There are four trains a day, which are usually on time, but you need to fight for a seat in the summer. Be aware that the end carriage is a smoking carriage and that the toilets may not necessarily have running water.

If you're going the full stretch remember to pack the wet wipes, some crayons and colouring books, as well as a picnic basket and plenty of bottled water to stop the kids from staging an all-out mutiny along the way.

The great outdoors: Walking and Hiking

The main hike along the GR20 is one of the toughest hiking routes in Europe and is not suitable for children. The mountains can be dangerous for even the most experienced walkers, especially in bad weather, so don't take any risks but check with the local tourist office that the walk is suitable for you. If they can't advise you ask them to put you in contact with a local guide who can.

There are, however, plenty of short walks and easy hikes you can enjoy with kids, where you should be able to spot the golden eagles and ospreys that nest in the mountains. Keep an eye out too, for mouflons, a type of wild sheep brought to Europe in Neolithic times from the Middle East, now living on the slopes of Monte Cinto. You can follow the paths called 'sentier de pays', which follow the old mule tracks from village to village, or buy one of the many books featuring family walks in the area, such as *52 Balades en Famille en Corse*. You'll find it in most big bookshops. If you're following one of the paths, it's a good idea to book a taxi to take you back to your car when you get to the next village.

If you want to do more serious walking with teenagers, don't plan a holiday in July and August when the temperatures are at their highest; May and September are the best time to go rambling. These types of holidays are very popular, so if you intend to stay in *gîtes d'étape*, make sure you book well in advance.

A few words of caution: the Mediterranean sun can make the countryside look pretty tame but never underestimate how dangerous it can be, especially with kids. The paths can be slippery and in the mountains the weather can change dramatically, even in summer, when freak storms and flash floods can drive hikers into refuges for days on end. If you're hiking with older children or teens make sure they understand the basic rules and don't wander from the path. The weather can be unpredictable, so check the forecast before you set out, **t** 08 92 68 02 20.

When you're taking a stroll, never pick the flowers – most of them are protected. Take rubbish home with you and if you need to go to the toilet dig a hole – don't use streams as toilets as it's a health risk for local wildlife and other walkers.

Wear proper shoes and a waterproof cagoule and pack the following in your backpack:

map and compass
sun cream and hat
mineral water
mobile phone
whistle
insect repellent
first-aid kit
torch, on long walks

The Bureau d'Information du Parc Naturel Régional de Corse, **t** 04 95 51 79 10 **www**.parc-naturel-corse.com has lots of useful information on walking in Corsica. In the summer months, offices are open in Calvi in the main tourist office; in Corte in the citadel; in Porto in La Marine; and in Porto-Vecchio on Rue du Colonel-Quenza.

Ajaccio

Montagne Corse en Liberté

2 Av de la Grande Armée, Ajaccio **t** 04 95 20 53 14 **www**.montagne-corse.com

Saint Pierre de Venaco

Association Grandeur Nature

Saint Pierre de Venaco, N193 **t** 06 03 83 68 36
Open Daily June–Sept 9.30–6

Organizes walks for families in the Verghellu valley in summer.

Bastia

Objective Nature

3 Rue Notre Dame de Lourdes, Bastia **t** 06 13 86 47 47 **www**.obj-nature.ifrance.com

Open all year round and the place to find out everything you need to know about outdoor activities in Corsica, including the tree-bound activities, Acrobranche, that take place in the Restonica valley in summer.

right in the train station. Place Paoli is where you'll find fresh fruit and vegetables, patisseries and restaurants aplenty, including the friendly ice-cream parlour, L'Escapade.

Ange Ricciardi on Rue Professeur Santiaggi is the place to buy sandwiches or grab a snack and Pâtisserie Marie et Jean-Luc on Place Gaffori sells *gâteau au brocciu*, the local goat's cheese pie. If you are in town on Friday don't miss the market on Avenue X Luciani. There's the Cyber Café L'Oriente, 5 Avenue Jean Nicoli, **t** 04 95 61 11 77, which sells sandwiches, ice-creams, drinks and snacks.

Things to see and do

The Citadel and Musée de la Corse

t 04 95 45 25 45 **www.sitec.fr/museu**
Open Daily in summer 10–8
Adm Adult €5.35, child free

Although part of the museum, the citadel is completely unspoilt. It isn't perched as high up on the mountainside as the postcards lead you to expect, but the view from the battlements to the wall of mountains behind the city is still magnificent. The dungeon is atmospheric without the addition of tacky waxworks; look out for the stone bed complete with stone pillow. The museum itself is an interesting collection of bits and pieces of Corsican history and outside among the castle walls there's plenty of space to stage your own mock battles. There are also two sound archive rooms with atmospheric audio and visual displays where you can listen to the indigenous polyphonic music and look at grainy black and white film.

U Trenu

If the trek to the citadel is too much, there's a little train, U Trenu, **t** 06 09 95 70 36, which leaves from the front of the train station and runs up to the citadel, though it's generally pre-booked for parties and old folk in the season. The walk up looks worse than it is, though: the road does not rise up as steeply as it appears and once inside the town distances are much shorter than they look.

AROUND CORTE

Nature lovers

Gorges de la Restonica

The Restonica valley is famous for its crystal-clear river hemmed in by jagged peaks. Although there was a huge fire here a few years ago and the valley is struggling to recover, it's still fantastic scenery and it would be a pity to come all this way and not take time to see it. Of the two stunning gorges near Corte, this is the only one accessible by car, but it's also easy to reach on foot and is only a short walk away from the station. Turn right onto Av du 9 Septembre and then follow the river. If you are driving, the road is very narrow and camper vans are banned. The D623 runs along the gorge, but it's very twisty and can be a problem for those prone to motion sickness. In the height of summer come early or late in the day to avoid the crowds. There's a car park at the Bergerie de Grotelle, where you could stop for a picnic, but walking is tricky. With teens you could make it up to Lac de Melo, a glacial lake about an hour from the car park, but don't attempt it with small children as the steepest paths are fitted with chains.

Vizzavona

Walking is tough in this part of the world but there's a nice family stroll from the car park at La Foce, just 1km below the Col de Vizzavona. It's a 45min walk from the car park to a picnic spot in a forest of pine and beech trees, where you can swim in the pools of the River Agnone and admire the waterfall known as the Cascade des Anglais. There's a refreshment stall in summer.

Horse riding

Riding is a great way to explore the region, and there are plenty of riding schools that supply basic equipment and are experienced with children. Contact Association Régionale pour le Tourisme Equestre, 7 Rue Colonel Ferracci, Corte, **t/f** 04 95 46 31 74 for a list of stables and guided riding trips.

Ferme Equestre L'Albadu

Ancienne Route d'Ajaccio t 04 95 46 24 55

Hire horses by the hour or day. It's about 1km from the station on the heights above Corte.

Sporty kids

Activity centres

Terra Corsa in Ponte Leccia organizes outdoor activities for kids, including hikes, climbing and kayaking, **t** 04 95 47 69 48. If your children speak good French, ask in the local tourist office for a list of outdoor activities in the area.

Kayaks

The best time to kayak is in the summer when the rivers are at their calmest. If you're a beginner choose a company like A Montagnola in Quenza who will supply all the equipment and guides for kayaking in southern Corsica, **t** 04 95 78 65 19, **f** 04 95 78 73 02; **e** a.montagnola@wanadoo.fr.

WHERE TO EAT

Many of Corsica's beautiful beaches have cafés, which are by far the best places to eat lunch with children. Most offer good, basic cuisine with more range than simply chips or chicken nuggets. In towns, you can't go wrong if you take children to one of the many pizzerias. It pays to eat early in busy resorts – you'll get better service. Wherever you eat the food will be good.

Don't expect a warm welcome in the villages near the coast as the locals endure rather than welcome tourists and you may have to search to find a restaurant that can be bothered to cook lunch for you. Higher up in the mountains where fewer tourists venture it's quite a different story; head here for a real Corsican experience.

Corsica is a picnicker's paradise; there are idyllic places all over the island to unwind with the kids. The best places to buy picnic supplies are the road-side stalls that sell local produce – you'll find them all over the island. Supermarkets are geared up for picnics and you'll find a range of tasty specialities that are ready to go, including the local cheese pies made with sheep's or goat's cheese (*brocciu*) served either plain or with vegetables. The village of Piana is one of the best places to taste these pies and they're often sold on the beach in spring.

Ajaccio

There are plenty of pizza restaurants along Quai Napoléon and a few cafés on the Rue Fesch.

A Casa

21 Av Noël-Franchini **t** 04 95 22 34 78
Open daily, closed Sun in low season

It's not the food that draws the crowds here, but the magic show. The owner is a magician, and on Friday and Saturday evening he entertains his guests with a top-class show that is great family entertainment. It's a good option for a big night on your holiday but you'll need to reserve well in advance in high season. Menus from €11.89–€27.44.

Café de Flore

33 Rue Fesch, opposite the museum **t** 04 95 21 13 87

Dine inside or out at this large, friendly establishment specializing in pasta dishes. There are filled varieties with spinach, pesto and cheese or you can choose your type of pasta and add whichever sauce you like. They also do fresh and generous salads and don't bat an eye when the locals come for coffee, bringing cakes from the bakery a few doors down. Lunch for four will cost around €30.

Da Mamma

Passage Guinguette **t** 04 95 21 39 44
Open Tues–Sat and Sun eve

Set on a pleasant terrace, Da Mamma offers good Corsican cooking and a great chocolate cake. Go for lunch rather than dinner since the terrace has a nasty neon light. Children's menus €6.10, adult menus from €9.90.

Pizzeria U Papacionu

16 Rue St-Charles **t** 04 95 21 27 96
Open Mon–Sat

Good pizza and salad served in the open air on a pedestrianized street.

Le Glacier du Port

Quai Napoléon **t** 04 95 21 08 13

The best place for ice-cream.

L'Amirauté

Port de Plaisance, Charles Ornano **t** 04 95 22 48 22

Right on the quayside by the more modern and swanky of Ajaccio's two harbours, L'Amirauté sits cheek by jowl with many other harbour eateries. What sets it apart is a menu that embraces children's tastes with huge pizzas and mouth-watering *moules au roquefort* for their more adventurous parents. It would be rude not to try the ice-cream or *tiramisu* for dessert. You can dine under the awning outside or up by the wood-fired pizza oven. There are several baby-changing mats inside the ladies' toilet area. Dinner for three is around €50 but come early (by 8) in the evening.

L'Ariadne Plage

Rte des Sanguinaires **t** 04 95 52 09 63

Beach shack where you can enjoy fish dishes while listening to salsa. Good for teenagers.

Around Ajaccio

Porticcio

La Plage d'Argent

Verghia Beach, Porticcio **t** 04 95 25 57 54
Open May–Sept

This is an inexpensive and popular bar by the sea, just south of Ajaccio in the resort of Porticcio.

There's pizza, salad and fresh fish from the tank. Pack your swimsuit and take a dip before dinner.

Bastelica

Le Sampiero Bar

t 04 95 28 71 99
Open Dec–Oct daily, except Fri in winter

A friendly place to stop for an omelette filled with *brocciu*, the local cheese. It is named after the nationalist hero Sampiero Corso, who came from here. (His behaviour towards his wife was less heroic – he chopped off her head).

Le Renoso

t 04 95 28 73 30

A favourite with locals for playing cards and the best place to stop for coffee.

Propriano

Ferme Auberge San Ghjuvanu

Plaine Barracci Monaca, Viggianello, 4km east of Propriano **t** 04 95 76 03 31

Here you can sample traditional family cooking on a farm. Shock the kids by ordering snails – the restaurant is famous for them. There's traditional singing on Friday evenings and it's advisable to book in summer. Menus from €13.

Vero

Ferme Auberge U Celavu

Vero **t** 04 95 52 80 64

Vero is a lovely village tucked away in the mountains behind Ajaccio. This farm establishment offers traditional Corsican specialities; try the cold cuts and the strong local cheese.

Bonifacio

Cantina Doria

Rue Doria **t** 04 95 73 50 49
Open in summer

This is a pleasant restaurant with a pretty terrace, and it's a great place to try some Corsican specialities; the chef is happy to adapt his dishes to suit younger palates. It's advisable to book in advance. Menus from €12.96.

Around Bonifacio

Porto-Vecchio

Le Figuier

Rte de Cala Rossa, 6km from Porto-Vecchio
t 04 95 72 08 78

Pizza, salads and grilled meats served at big wooden tables. Good value and fun.

Sartène

La Caramama

Rue Caramama **t** 04 95 73 41 11

Relaxed family-run restaurant serving basic Corsican food and pizzas. You can eat on a shady terrace in summer. Menus from €12.

Bastia

L'Ambada

Vieux Port **t** 04 95 31 00 90

Because of its strong links with Italy, it's no surprise that there is excellent pizza all over the island. This restaurant on the lively harbour side has great views of the citadel.

Serge Raugi Glacier

2 Rue Capanelle **t** 04 95 31 22 31
Open Tues–Sun

Serves the best ice-cream on this side of the island, either to eat in or take away.

Cotton Café

Quai des Martyrs **t** 04 95 32 36 18

A lively place with a Latin atmosphere, playing local pop every night in summer. Popular with a young crowd and good for a nightcap.

Around Bastia

San Giovanni-di-Moriani

Cava

t 04 95 38 51 14
Open Feb–Nov

This tiny restaurant has stunning coastal views and serves up local specialities such as *brocciu* fritters wrapped in chestnut leaves (in season), stewed kid and rich garlicky soups. Be sure to book in advance. Dinner with wine should cost around €15 for an adult.

Calvi

Pizza Capuccino

Quai Landry **t** 04 95 65 11 19
Open April–Oct

The place to come for a good range of pizzas, pastas (try ravioli *au brocciu*) and salad dishes. Make sure you keep space for the desserts, which are excellent. Pizza from €6.90.

A Scola

27 Haute Ville **t** 04 95 65 07 09
Open summer only

Serves up some of the best cakes in town plus a simple lunch menu of omelettes and salad.

Around Calvi

Porto

Les Galets

Plage de Bussagalia **t** 04 93 26 10 49

Moderately priced beachside restaurant with pizzas cooked in a proper wood oven, good pasta and fish dishes.

Lavatoggio

Ferme Auberge Chez Edgard

Lavatoggio, 2km out of town on the D71
t 04 95 61 70 75
Open May–Sept

Excellent restaurant serving Corsican specialities like roast pork and leg of lamb. Cash only.

Corte

U Museu

Rampe Ribanelle , Vieille Ville **t** 04 95 61 08 36

Enjoy decadent al fresco dining at the foot of the citadel. It may be a bit touristy but it's a good place to try local dishes and enjoy the view. Service can be slow in summer. Menus from €11.43.

L'Escapade

3 Pl Paoli, **t** 04 95 46 32 42

The best place for an ice-cream, hot snack or a crêpe. The cones are cavernous and there are lots of flavours to choose from.

Around Corte

Auberge de la Restonica

Vallée du Restonica **t** 04 95 46 09 58
Open April–Sept

Traditional regional cooking served in a delightfully rustic setting. It's pricier than La Refuge (see below), but good if you fancy a treat. Children's menu €9, adult menu €19.

La Refuge

Vallée de la Restonica **t** 04 95 46 09 13
Open April–Nov

This good, simple restaurant is part of the Refuge Hotel. It's in a beautiful spot by the river and has lots of Corsican specialities on the menu.

Sleep

WHERE TO STAY 210
Hotels 210
Hotel chains 211
Privately owned hotels 212
Apartment hotels 212
Bed and breakfast 212
Holiday villages/family resorts 213
Youth hostels 214
Self-catering 215
Villas 215
French Tourist Board 216
Camping and caravans 216

RECOMMENDED ACCOMMODATION 218
The Riviera 218
Northern Provence 224
Western Provence 227
Languedoc/Roussillon 230
Corsica 234

08

WHERE TO STAY

Choosing the right kind of accommodation for your family is a crucial part of making sure your holiday is a success. Once you've set the budget, where you stay depends on the needs of the whole family, so it's time to sit down and ask the kids where they want to stay, not just to take them. Find out what they want from the holiday; if it's touring around and seeing the sights you'll probably have to opt for hotels or B&Bs. If they fancy lazing by the pool then a villa, apartment or a campsite may be better. Self-catering is an especially good option with toddlers who want to be fed long before the hotel restaurant opens and need to make a mess with their toys. It's also a good option with teenagers who can't get out of bed in time for the hotel room to be cleaned. If you're a sporty family and want lots of activities laid on, including kids' clubs for the little ones, you should consider a holiday complex like Mark Warner, Pierre et Vacances or Club Med.

There is a huge choice of accommodation in the South of France but you'll need to book well in advance if you want to be sûre of getting the perfect hotel or the ideal villa; and if you want to visit one of the big events like the Monaco Grand Prix, you need to book at least a year ahead. Needless to say the Riviera is the most expensive destination in the South of France, but the list below includes accommodation to suit all family budgets.

US holiday villa companies

Doorways Ltd

www.villavacations.com

Good-value properties along the south of France.

Hideaways International

www.hideaways.com

Provides all kinds of accommodation in Southern France.

Overseas Connections

www.overseasvillas.com

Villas of Distinction

www.villasofdistinction.com

Interhome

www.interhome.com

If you fancy something different:

Adventure Center

t (US) 1 800 228 8747 **www**.adventurecentre.com

Organizes outdoor-activity holidays for families.

HOTELS

Don't assume that just because you've crossed the Channel every hotel is suitable for families. There are plenty of luxury hotels, especially in the Relais & Châteaux group, that are designed specifically for people who want to travel without children. However, there are also lots of luxury hotels that are out to attract families – the Hermitage in Monaco is a good example – and you'll find many other hotels like it listed in the recommended accommodation section below.

Room rates vary according to the season, making a short break or half-term hotel holiday far more feasible for families. Off-peak reductions can be as much as 30 per cent on the price of a room. Prices vary tremendously within hotels so be sure to check what rooms are available and at what price – if you don't mind a view of the kitchen roof you can get some bargains. The prices given in the recommended accommodation section at the end of the chapter are for high season, but wherever possible we have listed the best family deal.

In French hotels, the price quoted is just for the room itself; this may vary according to the number of occupants. Rates should be displayed clearly outside the hotel or in the reception area. Breakfast will be charged separately and is usually around €8, although up-market hotels with a buffet breakfast will charge more. You'll get just as good a breakfast in a café round the corner for much less money. Always ask to see the room before you book in and check for extras. There's usually a small fee for an extra bed and sometimes for a cot. Small children usually stay for free in their parents' room, though older kids may have to pay a supplement.

There are some really sumptuous family-friendly hotels but you don't have to break the bank to find something pleasant and clean. If you're on a budget you're better off looking for a 2-star hotel: the rooms usually have their own bathrooms and it's easier at night when you don't want children wandering around the hotel looking for the loo.

Remember, hotel stars are given for facilities, not location and service. If a hotel doesn't have any stars it may not necessarily be a dump; it may just be that the owners haven't bothered to go through the bureaucratic process of being graded.

Hotel chains

Don't turn your nose up at hotels that are part of a large chain. They are excellent value for families and because they're all of a similar standard, you'll know what to expect. You don't have to waste time asking to see the room and can guarantee that they'll be clean and well equipped, if a bit impersonal. The staff are also more likely to be used to dealing with children. Facilities usually include a fridge in the room for storing milk, as well as children's meals and highchairs in the restaurant.

When it comes to standards, value for money and points for being child-friendly, the Accor Hotels chain, which owns Mercure, Novotel, Sofitel and Ibis, wins hands down. If you don't have hours to spend driving around to find that perfect little country inn, especially in the high season when you don't have a booking, these hotels are invaluable. They are popular with French families and they often have summer and weekend promotions for families. Chain hotels nearly always have car parks and are often – though not always – found near a supermarket complex out of town.
In Marseille, for example, the Mercure is the best hotel in the Vieux Port and in Avignon it's right next door to the Palais des Papes. They're often in motorway service stations, too, so don't be worried about having to drive for miles to find a bed for the night. If you're planning on touring, pick up the hotel guide from one of the chains and keep it in the car – you'll find a pile of them at the reception desk. There are other hotel chains out to attract families, but none of them offers the same level of service and value for money as those listed here.

Please note: Prices given are for one room for one night unless otherwise stated.

Look out for...the Bon Weekend en Villes promotion

During the winter months, hotels offer two nights for the price of one in Aix-en-Provence, Arles, Avignon, Carcassonne, Marseille and Nîmes. Call the French Tourist Board (see p.273) or check the website for more details: www.bon-week-end-en-villes.com

Ibis

Central reservations in France **t** 01 60 87 91 00;
UK **t** (020) 8283 4550, **www**.hotel-ibis.fr

This is the cheapest of the bunch – expect to pay around €50 for a room. The big advantage is that up to two children under 12 stay free of charge in their parents' room. Ibis are especially good if you are using the train to travel around, as there's often one right next to the train station.

Novotel

Central reservations in France **t** 08 25 88 44 44;
UK **t** (020) 8283 4500, **www**.novotel.com

Novotel are the most child-friendly of all the Accor chain. The restaurants are especially geared up for children, with a good children's menu, plastic cups to take home, gifts and crayons. The kids' meals are also served until the restaurant closes. Up to two children under 16 can stay free of charge in their parents' room and the rooms are generally big enough to accommodate a family of this size. The beds are already made up in the room when you arrive so you can get the kids to bed easily after a long journey. Many hotels have gardens and little playgrounds, and they all have cots, highchairs and baby-changing facilities. There are Novotels all over the South of France. Expect to pay upwards of €80 per night for a room, depending on the location.

Mercure

Central reservations in France **t** 01 69 36 80 80;
UK, **t** (020) 8283 4500, **www**.mercure.com

The more business-orientated end of the market, but Mercure hotels still have children's menus and up to two children usually up to the age of 16 can stay for free in their parents' room.

Sofitel

Central reservations in France **t** 01 69 36 80 80;
UK **t** (020) 8283 4500, **www**.sofitel.com

The luxury end of the market, these are usually 4-star hotels with pools and gyms and are normally situated in city centres.

Other good chain with family-friendly hotels:

Best Western

Central reservations in France **t** 01 49 02 00 00;
UK **t** 08457 74 74 74, **www**.bestwestern.fr

Has hotels across the region.

Holiday Inn

Central reservations in France t 0800 91 08 55; UK t 0800 897121, www.france.sixcontinents hotels.com

These are more expensive than Ibis, Novotel and Mercure and tend to be on the edge of town, but they have facilities like kettles, which are really useful if you are travelling with a baby.

Kyriad Hotels

www.kyriad.fr

Offer advance reservations on-line and have facilities for babies. Under-12s stay free in their parents' room and there's a children's menu.

Privately owned hotels

There are a lot of umbrella organizations that bring together privately owned hotels. The one you're most likely to encounter is **Logis de France**, central reservations in France, **t** 01 45 84 83 84. It has about 5,000 affiliated hotels, which are small, independent and family run, and they're usually 1–3-star setups. They give families a warm welcome and most have decent restaurants. Over 3,500 have facilities for children, including a children's menu for around €8. Under-2s usually stay free of charge in their parents' room. Look out for hotels labelled *famille-enfants* – they usually have rooms sleeping up to four people and offer a baby-sitting service. You can pick up a free guide at the French Tourist Office, or see **www**.logisdefrance.com, an excellent website where you can search specifically for family-friendly logis.

Apartment hotels

A new and fantastic option for travelling with children is the apartment hotel – made up of small studios and apartments – which you can rent on a nightly basis or longer. The more nights you stay the cheaper it gets. The studios and apartments are all fitted with proper kitchens and washing machines. You'll find them based in cities and towns across France. Self-catering generally cuts the cost of the holiday and the apartment hotel option means you can stop where you want without the commitment of a long stay and you can feed the children when you want. The apartments are cleaned once a week, although you can ask for extra cleaning, so you don't have that tricky problem of dragging teens out of bed or being hassled by staff while you feed the baby.

Citadines

Central reservations in France t 08 25 33 33 32; UK t 0800 376 3898, www.citadines.com

This is one of the main companies on the market. The hotels have 1–3-bedroom apartments and you pay for the apartment you choose and not the number of people staying in it, which is good news for larger families. Apartment hotels are also one of the easiest ways of staying in the main towns in the area, especially in Nice, Marseille and Montpellier. The hotels have cots, bottle warmers and changing mats and most can accommodate disabled visitors. There's often a shopping and takeaway meals service.

Bed and breakfast

In France the closest things to bed and breakfast establishments are called *chambres d'hôte*, which literally means 'rooms of the host'. Properties are graded from simple to luxury and some can be very smart indeed, especially along the Riviera. Don't assume that these are poor man's hotels, especially in the South of France; *chambres d'hôte* can be more expensive than a 2-star hotel.

There are many benefits to choosing this type of accommodation; they have a maximum of only six rooms but the rooms are often large enough to sleep the whole family. Many *chambres d'hôte* have kitchen facilities and will always be willing to let you picnic in the garden. Many are on farms, which is especially fun for children, as there is usually some basic outdoor play equipment and the owners may be able to organize activities like horse riding. Some also have *gîtes* on site to rent for longer stays.

A lot of hosts offer an evening meal, which is called *table d'hôte*, and it's a far cry from the cold ham and sliced tomato of the British bed and breakfast supper of yore. The meals are always excellent and even with wine are far cheaper than eating in a restaurant. The owners usually feed all the guests at once and will often join you. Often everyone sits at one big table, so it can be a very social experience. Don't be surprised if they ask you what you want to eat.

The biggest advantage of staying in *chambres d'hôte* is that it gives you a chance to meet French people, and although many owners speak some English it pays to make an effort to speak French.

The price of the room varies according to the number of people, so be specific about how many people are in your family and what kind of sleeping arrangements you need when you negotiate the price. Breakfast should be included in the room rate, and if you have your own cot or an inflatable bed it can keep costs down. As with hotels, you should always ask to see the room before you agree to take it. If you want to try a *chambre d'hôte* for your holiday you'll need to book up at least a few months in advance, especially along the coast. They're a very popular option and you can find them fully occupied at the weekend from Easter onwards. If you haven't booked in advance try not to leave it until early evening to find somewhere, and don't lose heart if most of the *chambres d'hôte* you call are full; you can always ask the owners if they know someone with a room. The French Tourist Board and French bookshops sell the listings guides *Chambres et Tables d'hôtes*, which has over 14,000 entries and *Chambres d'hôte de Prestige*, which lists some luxury options. Both books cover the whole of France and are invaluable when touring. The French Tourist Board also produces two useful leaflets, *Bienvenue au Château'* and *Château Accueil*, if you want to try *chambre d'hôte* accommodation with real style. Smaller regional guides are also available from the local tourist boards. They're usually illustrated and have a more comprehensive listings system. Look out for the baby bottle sign; it's worth noting even if you don't have a baby, as it's an indication that the owners are child-friendly. There's a concentration of these kinds of *chambres d'hôte* in the Var.

Welcome Guides offer a useful UK booking service for *chambres d'hôte*. Their website is especially good and indicates clearly where children are welcome and what families will be charged.

Welcome Guides Bed and Breakfast in France, t UK (01491) 578803 **www.**bedbreak.com

HOLIDAY VILLAGES /FAMILY RESORTS

Choosing a holiday village or family resort is a good option with children. There will be plenty of activities for children that are graded according to age and there's usually a mixture of events for them, from arts and crafts to sports and even outings. You can leave your children to enjoy the clubs while you have some time to yourself. Before you rush off to book, however, ask the kids if that's what they want; if you spend all day at work, five days a week, the kids may want to spend their holiday with you and not in a club.

When you book your holiday check how much of the childcare is included in the package; most kids' clubs and activities are at an additional cost. Confirm exactly which ages the clubs cater for and ask about the level of experience and qualifications of the carers, including whether they speak English. You might think that this is unimportant, and that if the carers only speak French the kids will pick up some of the language, but this can be quite upsetting for little children and you may not get them to settle. Other questions to ask are about the children–carer ratio; will children be with other children of the same age; how are age groups divided and can siblings stay together?

Club Med

t 0700 2585 633 www.clubmed.co.uk

Operates holiday villages in the south during summer and winter months. Le Lavandou is an especially popular site with French families, which is a plus if you want the children to improve their French. They also have a site in Corsica. Kids' clubs are suitable for children from 4 months to 17 years and you don't pay extra for clubs for older children.

Can you spot...a 'Station Kid'?

A number of resorts in France have the name 'Station Kid', which means that the local tourist office consider the resort family friendly. There will be plenty of playgrounds, beaches with lifeguards, and activities organized by the local authority and private companies. Cap d'Agde is a good example of this kind of resort.

Places in the baby clubs go quickly, so reserve a place when you book.

Mark Warner

t 0870 770 4222 **www**.markwarner.co.uk

San Lucianu in Corsica is Mark Warner's sole venue in the South of France, although they have other resorts in Europe. The hotel is situated right on the beach close to the chestnut forests of the Castagniccia, with spectacular mountain views from the front or sea views from the rear. Rooms are clean and attractive but you'll need to bring your own beach towels and toiletries. There's a small shop that has basics like sun cream and beachwear, or you can take a trip to the shops in Moriani Plage just a short walk away.

The biggest plus to the Mark Warner experience is that everyone gets a holiday. The kids (age restrictions apply, diving is from age 8 only) can join in on a whole range of activities, from sailing and windsurfing to water-skiing and scuba diving (*see* also pp.160 and 201). Back on land there's tennis and football coaching, plus volleyball on the beach. Babies and toddlers have their own range of activities both indoors and out, under the supervision of NNEB or equivalent nannies. Meanwhile parents can learn to windsurf, sail, have diving lessons, water-ski, enjoy a massage or simply lie in the sun. Meals and most activities are all-inclusive and dinners alternate between buffets and sit-down three-course dinners. Wine is free with lunch and dinner and there's also a well-stocked beach bar, which is the focus for the quizzes and themed entertainment for adults in the evenings. There's a free baby-listening service if you stay on the premises, otherwise baby-sitting can be arranged should you fancy an evening out. If you want to explore further, there are weekly excursions and mountain bike/car hire on site.

Pierre et Vacances

t 00 33 (0)1 58 21 55 50 **www**.pierreetvacances.com

The villages feature both hotel rooms and apartments and they have first-class children's facilities, catering for children from 3 months to 18 years in a French atmosphere, including crèche facilities and clubs for kids and teens. Most of the staff speak English, but that isn't always the case, so check before you book or it could make activities like tennis lessons tricky. The level of service is high, and there are some good sites, especially along the Riviera; the site in the Estérel, for example, is particularly good for families.

The following companies also organize holidays in holiday villages:

Maeva

t 00 33 (0)1 41 98 70 00 **www**.maeva.fr

VVF

t 00 33 (0)1 60 81 60 60 **www**.vvf-vacances.fr

Renouveau

t 00 33 (0)4 79 75 75 75
www.renouveau-vacances.fr

The following campsites have kids' clubs and organized activities:

Eurocamp

t 08703 338 338 **www**.eurocamp.co.uk

Eurosites

t 0870 751 0000 **www**.eurosites.co.uk

Haven Europe

t 0870 242 7777 **www**.haveneurope.com

Keycamp

t 0870 7000 456 **www**.keycamp.com

YOUTH HOSTELS

There is no age limit on who can stay in a French youth hostel; they are popular with French families and often have family rooms, so don't be surprised if the local tourist board advises you to try the local hostel when you ask for advice on where to stay. To spend the night in a youth hostel you'll need to join the International Youth Hostel Association in the UK, **t** (01629) 581418, **www**.iyhf.org.

If you forget to purchase one before your arrival in France, you can also get hold of a 'Guest Card' at the hostel of your destination. All you will need to do then is buy a 'Welcome Stamp' each night (for €2.90), for your first 6 nights. Once you have purchased 6 stamps (for a total of €17.40), you will be entitled to full membership for 1 year and be given access to all the youth hostels in the world.

Water wings

If you fancy something different, why not consider renting a boat? For holidays afloat for families on the Canal du Midi:

The Barge Company

12 Orchard Close, Felton, Bristol **t** (01275) 474034
t (USA)1 800 688 0245 **www**.bargecompany.com

Headwater

The Old School House, Chester Road, Northwich
t (01606) 720033 **www**.headwater.com

Crown Blue Line

8 Bear St, Norwich, **t** (01603) 630513
www.crown-blueline.com

SELF-CATERING

Self-catering is a brilliant option with kids. It gives you the flexibility to do what you want, when you want, and to make a home away from home. It can cut costs because you don't have to always eat out in restaurants, but don't assume it's just an option for parents on a budget – there are villas that rent for £15,000 near St-Tropez. On a more realistic note, you'll be lucky to get change from £1,000 for a week's stay in a family villa in the South of France if you use an agency. If you look carefully, however, and are prepared to do some homework you could be lucky enough to find something far cheaper (*see* p.217). Sharing the costs of a more expensive villa with another family is an option worth considering, and if you are on a very tight budget, why not consider camping – there are some lovely campsites in the mountains.

Villas

Some agencies that have good family-sized properties in the South of France are:

Azur Villa

t 00 33 (0)4 93 90 00 93 **www**.azurvilla.com

Local company specializing in properties along the Riviera.

Balfour

t (0118) 940 2620 **www**.balfourfrance.com

Especially nice properties around St-Tropez.

Bowhills

t 01489 872 700 **www**.bowhills.co.uk

Big selection of top-quality villas across the region, many with basic baby equipment. Can provide English-speaking baby-sitters on request.

Chapters by Abercrombie & Kent

t 08450 700618, **t** (USA) 1 800 323 7308 **www**.villa-rentals.com

Features villas across Provence but specializes in properties in the St-Tropez area. This is the luxury end of the market but, if you can afford it, the villas are magnificent and extremely child-friendly. You can rent kids' videos and DVDs in English and hire an exclusive baby-sitter. The company will fence in the pool for you, do your shopping – in fact arrange anything you need, including a personal body-guard. Teens will love staying in one of these houses because pop stars like Robbie Williams and Geri Halliwell use them.

Country Cottages in France

t 0870 076 0760 **www**.cottages-in-France.co.uk

Good, reliable agency with family-friendly properties and descriptions to lead you in the right direction when choosing your house. The sales team visit properties in France and can offer good advice over the phone.

Crystal Holidays

t (01235) 824422 **www**.crystalfrance.com

Good selection of villas and apartments in the South of France, some of which have children's clubs and organized activities for families.

Destination Provence

t (01904) 622220 **www**.destinationprovence.co.uk

Offers a range of villas along the coast and inland.

Dominique's Villas

t (020) 7738 8772 **www**.dominiquesvillas.co.uk

Has a selection of attractive properties right across the region.

French Affair

t (020) 7381 8519 **www**.frenchaffair.com

These are good-sized family cottages with bags of character. Many of the houses are big enough for two families.

Frenchlife

t 0870 444 8877 **www**.frenchlife.co.uk

Corsican contacts

Most hotel accommodation is on the coast, but many villas are set back from the sea in the hills. With children it's best to choose a house as close to the beach as possible, as driving backwards and forwards to the sea along hot, winding roads can be miserable. The local tourist board will have a list of rental property available and there's a good selection of flats and houses on the website **www**.clevacances-haute-corse.com.

There are a number of UK agents who deal exclusively with Corsica:

Voyages Ilena

t (020) 7924 4440 **www**.voyagesilena.co.uk
Features stylish, if pricey, villas. Hotels are marked if they are considered family friendly.

Corsican Places

t (01903) 748 180 **www**.corsica.co.uk
The holiday reps answer the phone themselves and if they don't know the properties personally, they can quickly find someone who does, so you can check whether they're suitable for your family. There is a good, comprehensive selection of villas across the island and the company can arrange baby-sitting locally. Good child discounts if you can travel outside the school holidays. Baby prices include car seat, highchair and cot.

Holiday Options

t 0870 013 0450 **www**.holidayoptions.co.uk
The company has hotels, apartments and villas; those that are particularly suitable for children are highlighted in the brochure.

Corsican Affair

t (020) 7385 8438 **www**.corsicanaffair.com
Offers a range of hotels and villas.

Simply Corsica

t (020) 8541 2200 **www**.simply-travel.com
Good selection of villas and hotels. Water sports club and extensive childcare facilities at the Hotel Ruesco in Capicciolo, north of Ajaccio.

Provides an extensive list of villas, campsites, cottages and apartments across the region.

Interhome

t (020) 8891 1294 **www**.interhome.co.uk

Hundreds of apartments and holiday houses to let at affordable prices, in or close to main resorts.

Quality Villas

t (01442) 870 055 **www**.quality-villas.co.uk

Stylish villas that will make you feel like a film star. The company lays on a complete staff, so there are plenty of baby-sitters.

Vacances en Campagne

t 0870 077 1771 **www**.indiv-travellers.com

Plenty of family-sized houses that are good value for money. The brochure states clearly if the property isn't suitable for children, if there are many steps up to the property and whether the pool is fenced. The website is useful and informative.

VFB

t (01242) 240 310 **www**.vfbholidays.co.uk

Competitively priced hotels, villas and apartments across the South of France. The company also produces a special Corsica brochure. Their brochures are especially easy to use, as the symbols at the top of each property highlight the important features, e.g. if the pool is fenced or not and how far it is to the shops.

French Tourist Board

The tourist board in the area you want to visit will be able to give you a list of properties for rent. This will include farms and *chambres d'hôte* with houses and apartments attached. These are often far cheaper than anything you'll see in a holiday brochure but you will have to do all the research yourself.

Gîtes are rural properties inspected by the tourist board and are a cheaper option than renting villas through agencies. The French Tourist Board (*see* p.273) publishes a listing of approved cottages or visit the website: **www**.gites-de-france.com.

Camping and caravans

There's no shortage of campsites in this part of France, many of which have swimming pools and sports facilities. They get very busy in July and

How to keep costs down

If you're shocked at the cost of holiday villas in the South of France don't panic – you can still find a bargain if try the following:

Bertrand Vacances

t 00 33 (0)1 49 25 26 27
www.bertrandvacances.com
This is not a company but a large website and brochure in which individual owners and companies advertise accommodation including villas, campsites and apartments. You can cut the cost of your holiday dramatically by finding a holiday let this way, as prices are a fraction of those quoted by the major British villa companies. But remember, the villas are not inspected, so it's up to you to make sure the property is suitable for children, and as this is a French agency many of the owners won't necessarily speak English. However, the French tend to book their holidays later than the English, so it's often a good last-minute option.

Le Guide Vacances

t 00 33 (0)1 40 56 35 35 **www**.leguidevacances.com
This is another French catalogue where owners, campsites and agents advertise. It's considered more chic than Bertrand Vacances but again, the properties aren't inspected, so you'll need to ask careful questions yourself and the owners won't necessarily speak English.

Chez Nous

t 0870 444 6600 **www**.cheznous.com
This is the English equivalent of Bertrand Vacances, so you'll need to check the property is suitable for children. Most of the owners who advertise in the catalogue are English, so language shouldn't be a problem. The company can organize Channel crossings at competitive prices.

Owners in France

t 0870 901 3400 **www**.ownersinfrance.com
A much smaller brochure of letting advertisements, but they have some good villas.

August, so don't count on just turning up and pitching your tent. Sites are graded by a star system and 4-star establishments tend to have more trees, a pool, several restaurants and a range of sports facilities. Campsites along the coast are large and can get very crowded in summer and some of the beaches near big campsites can be dirty, so check your accommodation against our list of recommended beaches in this guide.

Camping on a farm is a fun option and a good way to learn some French, although the facilities may not be as good as on a big campsite. Wherever you stay, make sure you clarify exactly what the pitch will cost before you set up your tent, as hidden extras have a habit of appearing when you settle up at the end. Municipal or local government-owned sites are cheaper but often lack the facilities you'll find on a private 3- or 4-star site.

Most sites are closed outside the main holiday season; camping outside official sites is usually not permitted and you should never camp in the forest in summer because of the fire risk.

The French Tourist Board publishes a useful booklet, *Accueil à la Campagne*, and local tourist offices in the south publish useful guides to camping and caravanning – contact them directly. Individual companies also have information about camping: both Bertrand Vacances and Le Guide Vacances carry advertisements for campsites, and the holiday company Supersites, **t** (01903) 748 166, has a good selection (*see* **Holiday villages** p.213). www.supersites.uk.com

The Michelin Guide *Camping and Caravanning in France* is also a good investment.

Useful websites

www.sites-et-paysages.com
www.provence-campings.com
www.select-site.com

RECOMMENDED ACCOMMODATION

Please note: Prices listed are for one room for one night unless otherwise indicated. You usually pay for the room and not the number of people in it, but check exactly what the price you have been quoted covers before you book.

THE RIVIERA

Nice

Chain and apartment hotels are your best bet in Nice. Independent hotels tend to have small rooms and be short on facilities.

Citadines Apart'Hôtel Fleurs

17 Av des Fleurs **t** 00 33 (0)4 93 97 78 00
f 00 33 (0)4 93 97 10 93 **e** resa@citadines.com
www.citadines.com
Price studio for two €10; best family deal – three-room apartment for six €190

This hotel has the largest apartments of the three Citadines in Nice, is the best equipped and is close to all the main attractions in the city. There is a selection of studios and apartments sleeping up to six people, all with fully fitted kitchens. The hotel is in a quiet residential area and has a garden, gym, games room and launderette. There is parking and access to a private beach and a small park just minutes from the hotel. Baby cots, changing mats and bottle warmers are available on request. The hotel also offers a shopping service.

Citadines Apart'Hôtel Nice Buffa

21 Rue Meyerbeer **t** 00 33 (0)4 97 03 28 50
f 00 33 (0)4 93 16 18 32
Price studio for two €110; best family deal – studio for four €150

Old building of character close to the pretty Jardin Alsace-Lorraine, which has a lovely play-ground. The hotel is just 1min from the sea with access to a private beach, and all the main attractions are within walking distance.

Citadines Apart'Hôtel Nice Promenade

35 Bd François Grosso **t** 00 33 (0)4 93 97 95 00
f 00 33 (0)4 93 44 93 88
Price studio for two €110; best family deal – apartment for four €150

This is a new apartment building just 5mins from the Jardin Alsace-Lorraine and 2mins from the sea. All the apartments have balconies and facilities include parking, launderette and baby equipment.

Residence Ajoupa

4 Rue Masséna **t** 00 33 (0)4 93 82 10 05
f 00 33 (0)4 93 16 96 76 **e** ajoupa4@aol.com
www.niceresidences.com
Price studio for two €69; apartment for four €91

Nicely decorated apartments with kitchenettes are for rent on a nightly basis close to the sea and the old town.

Hôtel Mercure

Promenade des Anglais, 2 Rue Halevy **t** 00 33 (0)4 93 82 30 88 **f** 00 33 (0)4 93 82 18 20
e HO360@accor-hotels.com **www**.accorhotels.com
Price rooms from €130

The hotel is right on the sea front with a great view of the bay and is well positioned for walking into the old town. It's part of the chain of hotels that belongs to the Accor group where two children under 16 stay free in their parents' room. Bigger families will need to take two rooms. The position is marvellous but rooms that overlook the bay also get a view of the flight path to nearby Nice airport, which can be noisy in the early evening. The hotel is open all year round but gets booked up during conferences.

Hôtel Novotel

8/10 Esplanade du Parvis de l'Europe **t** 00 33 (0)4 93 13 30 93 **f** 00 33 (0)4 93 13 09 04
www.novotel.com
Price rooms from €120
Open all year round

Part of the child-friendly chain. All the rooms can sleep up to four people with two children under 16 staying free in their parents' room. There's a rooftop swimming pool, baby-sitting service and an indoor play area. This is by far the best hotel to stay in with toddlers, who'll love the gifts and free plastic cups.

Le Danemark

3 Ave des Baumettes **t** 00 33 (0)4 93 44 12 04
f 00 33 (0)4 93 44 12 04
www.hotel-danemark.com
Price rooms from €48; best family deal – room for three €72
Open all year round

This is a small and simple hotel in the centre of town, close to the Promenades des Anglais. It has recently been renovated and has friendly owners. Breakfast, €4.50, is served on the terrace.

La Belle Meunière

21 Av Durante **t** 00 33 (0)4 93 88 66 15
f 00 33 (0)4 93 82 51 76
Price rooms from €43.50; best family deal – room for four €68.30
Open Feb–Nov

This small budget hotel has a student-style atmosphere and would suit families with teenagers. It's close to the station but has a garage and a small garden where you can eat breakfast and have a picnic.

Hôtel Normandie

t 00 33 (0)4 93 88 48 83 **f** 00 33 (0)4 93 16 04 33
www.hotel-normandie.com
Price rooms from €64; best family deal – room for four €86

This hotel is a good budget option in the centre of town. The staff speak English, and there are large, air-conditioned rooms and a private garage. Breakfast is €5.50.

Hôtel Régence

21 Rue Masséna **t** 00 33 (0)4 93 87 75 08
f 00 33 (0)4 93 82 41 31 **e** HTLRegence@aol.com
Price rooms from €78; best family deal – room for three with extra bed €90

Small 2-star hotel in the pedestrianized part of this busy shopping street in the heart of Nice. What the building lacks in style it makes up for in charm. The staff are friendly and there are good-sized family rooms. The hotel is conveniently located just minutes from the seafront.

Around Nice

Cap Ferrat

Hôtel Clair Logis

12 Av Centrale St-Jean-Cap-Ferrat
t 00 33 (0)4 93 76 51 81 **f** 00 33 (0)4 93 76 51 82
www.hotel-clair-logis.fr
Price rooms from €95
Open April–mid-Nov and mid-Dec–mid-Jan

This is a beautiful, old-fashioned villa, the epitome of Cap Ferrat chic, set in an exotic garden. The hotel is just 15mins' walk from the beach. Breakfast costs €10 and you'll be charged €25 for an extra bed. The ground-floor annexe is best for families. Booking essential in summer.

La Bastide

3 Av Albert 1er **t/f** 00 33 (0)4 93 76 19 10
Price rooms from €45; best family deal – triple room with extra bed €70
Open Jan–Oct

Good-value hotel in a place where you'd expect to pay a lot more. Some rooms have a sea view. There's a small garden and a good restaurant serving traditional Provençal food with a children's menu for €8.

Eze

Château Eza

Eze Village **t** 00 33 (0)4 93 41 12 24 **f** 00 33 (0)4 93 41 16 64 **reservations t** 1-800 507 8250 **e** eza@slh.com
www.slh.com/eza
Price rooms from €350; best family deal – suite for four plus baby from €600

If you have money to spare this is one of the most exciting hotels to spend a night in with kids, especially if they are into knights and princesses. This 400-year-old castle was once the home of Prince William of Sweden. Some of the rooms have a real medieval feel to them, so be specific about which type of room you want. The hotel has one of the most stunning positions on the Riviera, with breathtaking views across Cap Ferrat. Luggage is collect by porters with donkeys from the car park and taken up to the hotel, since the old village is a pedestrianized zone. Breakfast is included in the room rate. The hotel is very small, so reservations are imperative throughout the year.

Les Terrasses d'Eze

1138 Route de la Turbie Eze **t** 00 33 (0)4 92 41 55 55
f 00 33 (0)4 92 41 55 10
www.hotel-terrasses-eze.com
Price rooms from €190; best family deal – suite €450, extra bed €30
Open all year round

This stylish modern hotel has a stunning view along the coast and is probably better for older kids. There's a gym, swimming pool and tennis courts and meals are served on a lovely terrace.

Villefranche-sur-Mer

Hôtel de la Darse

32 Av du Général de Gaulle **t** 00 33 (0)4 93 01 72 54 **f** 00 33 (0)4 93 01 84 37 **e** hoteldeladarse@ wanadoo.fr

Price rooms from €40; room for three from €60

Open Mar–Sept

This small, friendly hotel by the port is just a short stroll away from the beach and the train station and is very handy if you want to explore Nice. Book a room with a sea view and enjoy breakfast on the little terrace. It's a nice place to stay if you are looking for relaxing hotel break with a new baby. Breakfast €6.

Monaco

It's only worth staying in Monaco if you've got the money to do it in style. The main attraction in the evening is the Casino, but under-21s aren't allowed in. There are a few budget hotels in the town and in the town of Beausoleil.

Hôtel Hermitage

Square Beaumarchais, Monte-Carlo **t** 00 377 92 16 25 **f** 00 377 92 16 26 26

www.montecarloresort.com

Price rooms from €460; best family deal – junior suite €820, depending on season

The top luxury hotels in Monaco belong to the Société des Bains de Mer. The Hermitage is a beautiful *belle époque* building fit for a princess and is famous for its stained-glass windows designed by Gustave Eiffel. It's a good hotel to come to with children of any age and has some of the friendliest porters around. There's a shuttle service to the private Monte-Carlo Beach Club, access to the luxury spa and fitness centre, a huge pool and a terrace with a view of Monaco.

Around Monaco

Menton

Hôtel l'Aiglon

7 Av de la Madone **t** 00 33 (0)4 93 57 55 55 **f** 00 33 (0)4 93 35 92 39

www.hotelaiglon.net

Price rooms from €111; extra bed: under-6s free, under-12s €19.50, otherwise €28.50

An old-fashioned *belle époque* hotel with friendly service, a heated swimming pool and lovely garden with palm trees. Facilities include table tennis and a kids' play area and there's an excellent restaurant. Breakfast costs €8.50.

Roquebrune

Les Deux Frères

Place des Deux Frères **t** 00 33 (0)4 93 28 99 00 **f** 00 33 (0)4 93 28 99 10

www.lesdeuxfreres.com

Price rooms from €65

Open mid-Dec–mid-Nov

A small, stylish hotel with friendly owners and marvellous views, situated on the edge of the village. Each room is decked out in a different style, the cheapest being an Arabian Nights theme, and there's an excellent restaurant. Booking essential.

Cannes

Citadines Apart'Hôtel Cannes Carnot

1 Rue le Poussin **t** 00 33 (0)4 97 06 92 00 **f** 0033 (0)4 93 38 84 09 **e** resa@citadines.com

www.citadines.com

Price studio for two €71; best family deal – apartment for four €102

The apartments are available for one night or longer and the price goes down the longer you stay. The hotel is close to the station and there's parking and access to a private beach about 10mins' walk away. There are bottle-warmers, cots, a laundry room and a small indoor garden.

Noga Hilton

50 Bd de la Croisette **t** 00 33 (0)4 92 99 70 00 **f** 00 33 (0)4 92 99 70 11

www.hiltoncannes.com

Price rooms from €328; best family deal – suite with extra beds €481

This is right on the seafront and is one of the hotels where the rich and famous stay when they come for the film festival but, as with all hotels in the group, it's still geared up for families. There are 48 suites and 120 interconnecting rooms. Baby bottles, highchairs and cots are available; and there's a car park, a lovely rooftop pool and a good private beach. Kosher food can be served on request. Breakfast is served on the large terrace with a view over the bay, which will make you feel like a star. This is Hilton's fourth hotel in France and the only one in the south.

Around Cannes

Cap Estérel Village

Pierre et Vacances **t** 00 33 (0)1 58 21 55 50
www.pierreetvacances.com
Getting there Just outside Cannes

The village is in a large park and has apartments and villas sleeping up to six. There are children's clubs and lots of sporting activities (*see* pp.65–9).

Antibes

Hôtel La Gardiole/La Garoupe

74 Chemin de la Garoupe **t** 00 33 (0)4 92 93 33 33
f 00 33 (0)4 93 67 61 87
www.hotel-lagaroupe-gardiole.com
Price rooms from €90; suite €165; extra bed €25 for under-10s

The hotels are part of the same group and are in a pine forest close to sandy beaches. Of the two, La Gardiole is slightly cheaper. The rooms are traditional and simple and vary in price according to size. There's a large, shady terrace and swimming pool and it's literally moments to the beach. A haven of calm on this busy stretch of coast. Breakfast costs €10, child's breakfast €6.

Hôtel Royal

Bd Maréchal Leclerc **t** 00 33 (0)4 93 34 03 09
f 00 33 (0)4 93 34 23 31
www.hotelroyal-antibes.com
Price rooms from €115; best family deal – room with extra bed €130

This is a simple family hotel with exceptionally friendly staff. It's just on the edge of the old town and opposite the beach, so is in a great location if you want to mix seeing the sights with some time to play about by the sea. Garage available at €8 per day, breakfast costs €10.

La Jabotte

13 Av Max-Maurey Juan-les-Pins **t** 00 33 (0)4 93 61 45 89 **f** 00 33 (0)4 93 61 07 04
Price rooms from €67
Open mid-Dec–mid-Nov

Spotlessly clean and good value for money, this hotel has a relaxed atmosphere with pleasant bungalow-style rooms overlooking the terrace.

St Raphaël/Fréjus

Les Pyramides

77 Av P Doumer **t** 00 33 (0)4 94 95 05 95
Price rooms from €54
Open Mar–Nov

This pleasant hotel in the town centre has a small garden and is a good option if you are touring, but it is not ideal for a longer stay.

Le Relais d'Agay

Bd de la Plage **t** 00 33 (0)4 94 82 78 20 **f** 00 33 (0)4 94 82 78 33 **e** hotel.relaisdagay@wanadoo.fr
www.relaisdagay.com
Price rooms from €59.50; best family deal – room for four €89
Open April–Nov

Simple, basic hotel on the beach at Agay, which has great water sports facilities for kids. The rooms are big but with the beach on the doorstep you won't spend much time indoors. Breakfast costs €6.50, child's breakfast €5.

Sol e Mar

Plage le Dramont **t** 00 33 (0)4 94 95 25 60
f 00 33 (0)4 94 83 83 61
Price rooms from €86; best family deal – room for four €216
Open mid-April–mid-Oct

The hotel is right on the beach, north of St-Raphaël at Agay. There's a saltwater pool, excellent restaurant and secure garage. This is a great place to unwind with the family.

Résidence Mercure Coralia

648 Av de Boulouris Baie de St-Raphaël
t 00 33 (0)4 94 95 21 71 **f** 00 33 (0)4 94 95 85 43
Price rooms from €144; best family deal – apartment for four €959
Open April–Oct

Apartments and rooms for rent set in a lovely leafy garden. Studios for 2–4 people are from €875 per week. Facilities include a swimming pool, tennis, mini-golf, laundry service and parking.

Hôtel l'Oasis

Impasse Jean-Baptiste Charcot, Fréjus
t/f 00 33 (0)4 94 51 50 44

www.hotel-oasis.net
Price rooms from €49; best family deal – room for four €74

Set back from the beach, this small 1950s hotel is excellent value. It's a great place to stop off if you are touring, as there's a large shady car park and a garden.

Arena Hôtel

139/145 Bd Général de Gaulle, Fréjus **t** 00 33 (0)4 94 17 09 40 **f** 00 33 (0)4 94 52 01 52
www.arena-hotel.com
Price rooms from €95; best family deal – room for four €135

A warm, old-fashioned hotel painted in lovely Provençal colours and part of the Logis de France group. There's a pool and garden, plus a restaurant with a children's menu for €12.50. Rooms are on the small side, so you may need two.

St-Tropez

Don't roll into town in mid-summer expecting to find a room. In the unlikely event that you do find one, you'll pay 20 per cent more than on other parts of the coast. This is an excellent place for self-catering options (*see* p.215), but camping canbe a nightmare as many sites are huge and over-crowded. The best places to stay are out of town, where you can get some great bargains.

Mas Bellevue

Rte de Tahiti **t** 00 33 (0)4 94 97 07 21 **f** 00 33 (0)4 94 97 61 07
www.nova.fr/bellevue
Price rooms from €106

This is a lovely hotel near Pampelonne beach with a good-sized pool, beautiful garden and an excellent restaurant. All rooms have a balcony. You'll need a car to get around.

Around St-Tropez

Bormes-les-Mimosas

Le Mirage

38 Rue de la Vue-des-Iles **t** 00 33 (0)4 94 05 32 60 **f** 00 33 (0)4 94 64 93 03
www.bw-mirage.com
Price rooms from €86; best family deal – two inter-connecting rooms €221; apartments from €314–930 per week

Situated just below the village, this hotel has a beautiful view across the bay. As well as conventional hotel rooms there are also apartments, two pools, tennis courts, a play area and nice leafy gardens full, of course, of mimosa.

Cabasson Beach

Les Palmiers

240 Chemin du Petit Fort **t** 00 33 (0)4 94 64 81 94
www.hotel-lespalmiers.com
Price rooms from €80; best family deal – room for four €186

Just minutes from what must be the most beautiful beaches in the south of France, this hotel is in a large shady garden with a pool. It's a great place to stay and there's an excellent restaurant, which is lucky because half-board is obligatory in high season. Half-board for two €167 and for four €350.

Camping Camp du Domaine

La Favière **t** 00 33 (0)4 94 71 03 12

A 4-star site with full facilities, set in a pine forest next to the beach. There are mobile homes and bungalows for €500–€670 per week.

Cogolin

La Mas de Bourru

Campagne le Canadel, east of Cogolin **t** 00 33 (0)4 94 54 62 21
Price around €50 per night for a family of four sharing a room

This is a beautiful *chambre d'hôte* set among the vineyards and it is excellent value for money. The rooms are large, with space for plenty of kids, and the owners have a young family and couldn't make you feel more at home. You can picnic in the garden and play on the swings. Price includes breakfast.

Gassin

Hôtel Bello Visto

Place des Barrys **t** 00 33 (0)4 94 56 17 30
f 00 33 (0)4 94 43 45 36
www.bellovisto.com
Price rooms from €50; best family deal – room for three €80
Open Easter–end Oct

This hotel is amazingly good value; the rooms are simple but stylish and the view from the shady terrace is one of the best in the South of France. You can eat breakfast while gazing at the snow on the top of the Alps and it's just a short drive to the sea. Place des Barrys is a great place for kids as there are no cars. There's a good restaurant and outdoor tables all year round; breakfast costs €8. There are just nine rooms, so you'll need to book ahead in season.

Grimaud

Hôtel la Pierrerie

61 Quartier du Grand Pont **t** 00 33 (0)4 94 43 22 55
f 00 33 (0)4 94 43 24 78
www.lapierrerie.com/fr
Getting there On the D61, 2km from Port-Grimaud
Price rooms from €89; best family deal – room with extra bed €109
Open April–Oct

This hotel is in the style of an old Provençal farmhouse and is set in a large, leafy garden, with a pool. Although it's close to St-Tropez, it feels quite rural. There are 14 big rooms and breakfast costs €8.

St-Clair

Belle Vue

Chemin des Four des Maures **t** 00 33 (0)4 94 00 45 00 **f** 00 33 (04 94 00 45 25
www.lelavandou.com/bellevue
Price rooms from €64

A 3-star Logis de France hotel that certainly lives up to its name – the views are stunning. It's next to a fantastic sandy beach that is excellent for kids. There's a good, basic restaurant with a child's menu for €15. Breakfast costs €11 and the garage is €11 per night.

Iles d'Hyères

Accommodation is pricey, camping is forbidden and you'll need to book in advance, but you couldn't find a more beautiful spot.

Les Medes

Rue de la Douane, Porquerolles **t** 00 33 (0)4 94 124 124 **f** 00 33 (0)4 94 58 32 49
www.hotel-les-medes.fr
Price rooms from €129; best family deal – apartment for five €308

The hotel is in the heart of the village and has a lovely garden and children's play area; it is close to some beautiful beaches. Under-12s stay free if they share their parents' room; over-12s are €20 sharing. Breakfast €9, child's breakfast €5. There are reductions for longer stays in the apartments.

La Croix-Valmer

La Pinede Plage

t 00 33 (0)4 94 54 31 23 **f** 00 33 (0)4 94 79 71 46
e pinedeplage@aol.com
www.pinede-plage.com
Price rooms from €100; best family deal – apartment for three €256, extra bed €50, cot €25
Open May–Oct

The hotel is on the edge of the beach and has both rooms and apartments, a lovely garden and pool. Breakfast costs €16, child's breakfast is €8 and there's a children's menu in the restaurant for €18.

Ramatuelle

Môtel des Selletes

Chemin de l'Ormède, 4km from the village
t 00 33 (0)4 94 79 88 48 **f** 00 33 (0)4 94 79 82 24
Price rooms from €64; best family deal – apartment for six €145

Well-equipped apartments and studios with kitchens for 2–6 people, set in a large garden with a pool. Rooms are for rent on both a nightly and weekly basis. The beach at Pampelonne is just 10mins' walk away.

Les Tournels

Rte de Camarat **t** 00 33 (0)4 94 55 90 90
www.tournels.com

This is a big campsite but is one of the nicest in the area, situated on a hill surrounded by pine trees and with a swimming pool. You can also rent cottage-style bungalows, which sleep six, for €721 per week.

Ste-Maxime

Le Jas Neuf

112 Av du Débarquement **t** 00 33 (0)4 94 55 07 30
f 00 33 (0)4 94 49 09 71 **e** info@hotel-jasneuf.com
www.hotel-jasneuf.com
Price rooms from €86; best family deal – room for four €183
Open Christmas–Oct

This pretty hotel with blue shutters is 1½km from the beach, with a garden and a heated swimming pool. It's next to the golf course and is a good place to escape the crowds in summer. Some double rooms have additional bunk beds set independently from the main room. Facilities include mini-bars and TV, plus most rooms have either a terrace or balcony. There's a children's menu for €9, a baby-sitting service and air conditioning throughout.

Hôtel Le Préconil

t 00 33 (0)4 94 96 01 73 **f** 00 33 (0)4 94 96 05 62
e Hotellepreconil@minitel.net
Price rooms from €46; best family deal – room with three beds and cot €50

This hotel is tucked away in the back streets and has large rooms sleeping up to four people. It's a good budget option if you want to spend a night or two in town. There's a friendly, relaxed welcome from the owner and you can park in front of the hotel.

NORTHERN PROVENCE

Avignon

Avignon Grand Hôtel

Bd St Roch **t** 00 33 (0)4 90 80 98 09 **f** 00 33 (0)4 90 80 98 10 **e** avignongrandhotel@hotmail.com
Price rooms from €88.42; best family deal – apartment with kitchenette for six €1981.83 per week

This brand new hotel has all mod cons – pool, garden, air conditioning and a garage. The big draw for families are the apartments, which are up to 60sq m – big enough to accommodate very large families – and have kitchenettes in the living room.

Hôtel Cloître St-Louis

20 Rue du Portail Boquier **t** 00 33 (0)4 90 27 55 55 **f** 00 33 (0)4 90 82 24 01
e hotel@cloitre-saint-louis.com
Price rooms from €83.84; best family deal – duplex room for four €198.18

The hotel is built into a 16th-century cloister, and the church, which is still in use, is part of the hotel. In stark contrast to the historic setting, the rooms are high-tech and stylish, with everything in black, grey and white and a stairwell reminiscent of the Pompidou Centre in Paris. There's a rooftop pool, a garden and an ancient cloister where the kids can run around. Meals are served in the garden. It's chic but family friendly and a good option if you have toddlers as it is close to a park. Although the hotel is in the city centre it's extremely quiet and restful.

Mercure Palais des Papes

Rue Ferruce Quartier de la Balance **t** 00 33 (0)4 90 80 93 93 **f** 00 33 (0)4 90 80 93 94
www.mercure.com
Price rooms from €88.42

Part of the family-friendly Mercure chain and ideally situated just a few minutes' walk from the main sights. It's excellent value – two children stay free of charge in their parents' room. There is a garden and a locked garage – quite a plus in Avignon where theft is an issue.

Hôtel la Ferme

Chemin des Bois, Ile de la Barthelasse **t** 00 33 (0)4 90 82 57 53 **f** 00 33 (0)4 90 27 15 47
Price rooms from €65.55
Open summer only

Although Avignon is surrounded by some of the worst suburbs in France, the Ile de la Barthelasse is very rural. The hotel has a swimming pool and a simple but good-quality restaurant with a children's menu. The rooms are air-conditioned and the staff speak English. Avignon can get very noisy during the festival and the Ile de la Barthelasse is the perfect place to escape the crowds, with plenty of space for children to run around. Booking essential in summer.

Camping Municipal Pont St-Bénézet

Chemin de la Bathe **t** 00 33 (0)4 90 82 63 50 **f** 00 33 (0)4 90 85 22 12 **e** info@camping-avignon.com
Price rooms from €38.12; best family deal – bungalow for a week €533.57
Open April–Oct

The site has 3 stars and the best view of the town on offer. There's a small shop and pool on site and a ferry across the river so there's no need to use the car to get into town.

La Ferme Jamet

Chemin de Rhodes, Ile de la Barthelasse
t 00 33 (0)4 90 86 88 35 **f** 00 33 (0)4 90 86 17 72
e fermja@club-internet.fr
Price rooms from €90; best family deal – cottage with kitchenette €140

This friendly *chambre d'hôte* is by far the nicest place to stay in Avignon, in an idyllic country setting with a charming rustic atmosphere. You're only minutes from the Palais des Papes though it feels as if you are in the heart of the countryside. There's a massive garden, a pool and a good choice of accommodation including suites and 3 cottages. Suites sleep up to four people and the cottages rent by the night. The owners speak English.

Around Avignon

Le Barroux

Hôtel les Géraniums

Pl de la Croix **t** 00 33 (0)4 90 62 41 08 **f** 00 33 (0)4 90 62 56 48

Price rooms from €42; best family deal – room for two with extra bed €59

Open April–Oct

Tucked away in a tiny hilltop village near Vaison-la-Romaine, this hotel makes a good base for exploring the Roman ruins, Carpentras or hiking on Mont Ventoux. There are two large terraces and meals are served outside in the summer. Children's menus €7.75. The staff speak English.

Gordes

Auberge de Carcarille

Rte d'Apt par D2 **t** 00 33 (0)4 90 72 02 63 **f** 00 33 (0)4 90 72 05 74 **e** carcaril@club-internet.fr

www.auberge-carcarille.com

Price rooms from €62

This hotel has the most fantastic view of the village of Gordes, one of Provence's most famous *villages perchés*. The atmosphere is relaxed and there's a garden and a swimming pool to cool off in. The restaurant has top-class cooking and a children's menu for €9.50. Breakfast costs €8.

Fontaine-de-Vaucluse

Relais des Murets

Chemin des Murets, Velleron **t** 04 90 20 01 53

Price rooms from €40

Good-value family *chambre d'hôte* with a garden and pool, north of Fontaine on the road to Carpentras. There are good-quality evening meals and the owner gives children riding lessons and will take you out exploring.

Forcalquier

Auberge Charembeau

t 00 33 (0)4 92 70 91 70 **f** 00 33 (0)4 92 70 91 83

e contact@charembeau.com

www.charembeau.com

Price rooms from €46; best family deal – room for four with kitchenette €742 a week

This friendly hotel is fantastic for kids. There's a large garden and pool and bikes for rent – the hotel makes a great base for exploring the wilder areas of Provence. Half-board is obligatory in summer.

Malaucène

Domaine des Tilleuls

Rte de Mont Ventoux **t** 00 33 (0)4 90 65 22 31 **f** 00 33 (0)4 90 65 16 77

e arnouldetdom@wanadoo.fr

Price rooms from €69; best family deal – room for four €101

This new B&B has spacious, simply decorated rooms and a large pool. It's great for families, with a play area and games for the kids. Extra bed costs €16; breakfast €7.

L'Isle sur la Sorgue

Hôtel Araxe

Domaine de la Petite Sourgette, Rte d'Apt **t** 00 33 (0)4 90 38 40 00 **f** 00 33 (0)4 90 20 84 74

Price rooms from €88.50; best family deal – apartment for five €152.50

The hotel has an enormous garden with two swimming pools and a tennis court. Recently renovated, the accommodation is ideal for families and provides a good base for exploring the Luberon (*see* p.99). There are rooms, apartments and bungalows, some of which have kitchenettes. The staff speak English and are very helpful.

Orange

Hôtel Arène

Pl de Langes **t** 00 33 (0)4 90 11 40 40 **f** 00 33 (0)4 90 11 40 45

Price rooms for €92; best family deal – suite €183

Open Dec–Oct

There's no restaurant but if you need to stay in Orange this is the place to head for. The hotel has a large duplex suite in a separate building across the square, which is far less kitschy than the main hotel. All the rooms are air-conditioned and have mini-bars if you need to keep milk cold. Breakfast is

€8. There's a private garage (€7 per night) which is good if you're touring and don't want to unpack the car.

Le Mas des Aigras

Chemin des Aigras, Russamp Est t 00 33 (0)4 90 34 05 66 f 00 33 (0)4 90 34 05 66

Price rooms from €64; best family deal – apartment for five €206

Open Jan–Nov

Just north of Orange off the N7, this hotel is popular with families and has some of the friendliest staff around. The gourmet chef is happy to adapt anything on the menu to suit junior taste buds. There's a big family room next to the restaurant, which has French windows that open out onto the terrace, so you can put the kids to bed and enjoy a romantic meal without worrying about a babysitter. There's also a large garden and pool.

Roquemaure

Clement V

Route de Nîmes t 00 33 (0)4 66 82 67 58
f 00 33 (0)4 66 82 84 66
www.hotel-clementv.fr.st

Price rooms from €57; best family deal – room for four €75

Open mid-Mar–mid–Oct

An excellent, moderately priced hotel with a pool, bikes for rent and bunk beds for kids. There is some lovely countryside to explore in the surrounding area and there are outdoor barbecues in summer. The owners have children and are very friendly. Children's menu is €8, breakfast €6.

Roussillon

Camping L'Arc-en-Ciel

Rte de Goult t 00 33 (0)4 90 05 73 96 f 00 33 (0)4 90 05 74 93

Open mid-Mar–Oct

This is one of the best campsites in the area, 3km from the village, with a children's swimming pool.

Castellane

Le Moulin de la Salaou

Rte des Gorges du Verdon t 00 33 (0)4 92 83 78 97

Price rooms from €32; best family deal – Room for four €51

This hotel has been converted from a 17th-century mill, and has a large, leafy coutryard and friendly staff. Some of the rooms could do with a lick of paint but the view, especially from the annexe, is great. At the centre of the town is a huge craggy rock with a church on top, which is lit up at night; it's a nice romantic spot to visit when the kids have gone to bed. The hotel is just outside the town and close to plenty of sporting activities. The restaurant serves good basic food; set meals are from €9 – €22 and there's a children's menu. A good base for exploring the Gorges du Verdon.

Les Canyons du Verdon

Résidence Hôtelière

Rte de Digne t 00 33 (0)4 92 83 76 47 f 00 33 (0)4 94 84 63 36 e info@studi-hotel.com
www.studi-hotel.com

Price studio for 2–4 €464

Fully equipped self-catering accommodation with kitchenette, bunk beds and laundry. It has a pool and is in a great location for exploring.

St-Maximin

Le Domaine de Garrade

2093 Chemin de Garrade, Rte de Bras t 00 33 (0)4 94 59 84 32 f 00 33 (0)4 94 59 83 47
www.provenceweb.fr/83/garrade

Price rooms from €69; best family deal – room for three €84, room for four €135

Open Dec–Oct

This child-friendly *chambre d'hôte* has a swimming pool and is within striking distance of Aix-en-Provence. Cot and highchair provided. Evening meals cost €23.

Valberg

Le Chalet Suisse

4 Av de Valberg t 00 33 (0)4 93 03 62 62 f 00 33 (0)4 93 03 62 64
www.chalet-suisse.com

Price rooms from €83; best family deal – duplex room for four €120

This chalet-style Logis de France is geared up for families and also rents apartments in the town centre. Breakfast is €8; children's menu €9.50. Games room.

Hôtel le Chastellan

Rue St-Jean t 00 33 (0)4 93 02 57 41
f 00 33 (0)4 93 02 61 65

Price rooms from €58; best family deal – suite €88

Most rooms have balconies with a good view and there's a kids' games room and TV corner.

WESTERN PROVENCE

Arles

Hôtel Le Calendal

5 Rue Porte de Laure **t** 00 33 (0)4 90 96 11 89
f 00 33 (0)4 90 96 05 84 **e** contact@lecalendal.com
www.lecalendal.com
Price rooms from €45; best family deal – room for five €90
Open all year except first week in Jan

The moment you walk in the door you'll know this is the hotel for you. Before you've had time to ask for a room, the kids will have found the toys, books, crayons and videos. There's a toy kitchen just next to the restaurant, potties and changing mats in the toilets and in winter you can enjoy the open fireplaces without worrying, as each one is fitted with a fireguard. There's no minibar but you can keep milk in the kitchen. There are rooms to suit all types of families, some with stunning views of the amphitheatre and Roman theatre (*see* p.122), others overlooking a leafy courtyard where there's a giant chess set. Make sure when booking that you state the age of your children, as each room is designed to suit a different type of family. The staff speak English and couldn't be more friendly.

Hôtel Mireille

2 Pl St-Pierre **t** 00 33 (0)4 90 93 70 74 **f** 00 33 (0)4 90 93 87 28
www.hotel-mireille.com
Price rooms from €78; best family deal – room for three €103

This hotel is just a few minutes' walk from the town centre on the other side of the river and is a good place to escape the crowds. All rooms are air-conditioned and have a minibar for the baby's milk. There's a pool, garden and garage, and the hotel is just over the road from a large supermarket.

Hôtel Le Cloître

16 Rue du Cloître **t** 00 33 (0)4 90 96 29 50 **f** 00 33 (0)4 90 96 02 88 **e** hotel_cloitre@hotmail.com
www.members.aol.com/hotelcloitre
Price rooms from €55; best family deal – room for four €66
Open April–Oct

Part of a 12th-century cloister, this is a friendly, well-priced and simply furnished hotel with clean, bright rooms in the town centre. It's very child-friendly, as the owners have a bunch of kids themselves. Breakfast is €5.50.

Hôtel d'Arlatan

26 Rue du Sauvage **t** 00 33 (0)4 90 93 56 66 **f** 00 33 (0)4 90 49 68 45 **e** hotel-arlatan@provnet.fr
www.hotel-arlatan.fr
Price rooms from €85; best family deal – apartment for four €157

This hotel may be elegant but it's also family friendly in a stylish way – the highchair in the breakfast room looks like an antique. Kids will love the glass floor in the main reception area, through which you can see the Roman ruins. Even if you can't get a room it's worth popping in on a quiet day just to see this, as it brings home the way Roman Arles has mutated into a modern town. The hotel has six suites, some of which have terraces. Ask for details before you book, as each one is different. Each room has a minibar, so you can keep milk chilled, and satellite TV. All the suites are air-conditioned and the staff speak English. There's a private garage but no restaurant and picnicking is strictly forbidden, but this shouldn't be a problem as the hotel is just off the main square, La Place du Forum (*see* p.121). Breakfast is €9; parking €12.50.

Hôtel Mercure

1 Av de la 1ère Division **t** 00 33 (0)4 90 93 98 80
f 00 33 (0)4 90 49 92 76
www.mercure.com
Price rooms from €85; best family deal – room for three €103

If you are arriving late at night in Arles this is the best place to head for, as it is moments away from the motorway and has friendly, helpful staff. The restaurant is pleasant and has a children's menu for €7.80. There's a pool and a small garden.

Around Arles

Les Baux-de-Provence

Le Mas de l'Esparou

Rte de St-Rémy **t** 00 33 (0)4 90 54 41 32
f 00 33 (0)4 90 54 41 32

Price rooms from €59; best family deal – two interconnecting rooms with breakfast €118

This pretty *chambre d'hôte* has a large garden and five rooms, four of which are situated on the ground floor and interconnect. Madame Roux serves the evening meal on the terrace overlooking the pool.

Le Mas d'Aigret

t 00 33 (0)4 90 54 20 00 **f** 00 33 (0)4 90 54 44 00 **e** contact@masdaigret.com
www.masdaigret.com
Price rooms from €95; best family deal – suite for €190, extra bed €15

There are some great views from this hotel, which has 16 air-conditioned rooms, some of which are dug out of the rock, with minibars and satellite TV. There's a family apartment with one small and one large room, roomy wardrobes and air conditioning. The hotel doesn't have a children's menu as such, but they are happy to cook up children's meals. Breakfast is €12.

Camargue

Hôtel de Cacharel

Rte de Cacharel **t** 00 33 (0)4 90 97 95 44
f 00 33 (0)4 90 97 87 97 **e** mail@hotel-cacharel.com
www.hotel-cacharel.com
Getting there 5km from Stes-Maries-de-la-Mer on the D85a
Price rooms from €118 including breakfast; best family deal – room for four with breakfast €158

The best places to stay in the Camargue are these small ranch-style hotels, which have riding schools attached. Most of them are bunched together on the road north of Stes-Maries-de-la-Mer; the Mas de Cacharel is the exception. Just to the north of the town, its setting is in keeping with the owner's softly spoken, laid-back approach. Rooms look out over the lakes – the flamingos are just a few feet away from the window. There's no TV as the owner believes children should be outside enjoying the fresh air and you'll see kids on bikes and horses all over the grounds. There's an enclosed pool and, although there's no restaurant, snacks and wine are available from 12 noon till 8. Horse riding costs from €19 per hour and is suitable for children from 7 years up (*see* p.125). Breakfast costs €9. You'll need to book in advance for the summer but don't rely on doing that by email – things work slowly down here and it can take days to receive a reply. Telephone in advance to be sure of a room.

Le Mas des Salicornes

Rte d'Arles 13460 Stes-Maries-de-la-Mer **t** 00 33 (0)4 90 97 83 41 **f** 00 33 (0)4 90 97 85 70
e contact@hotel-salicornes.com
www.hotel-salicornes.com
Price rooms from €48; best family deal – room for four €73 high season/€60 low
Open April–mid-Nov

The hotel is just outside the town of Stes-Maries-de-la-Mer, the main town in the Camargue. The owner of the hotel, Mr Merlin, is a trained chef and serves up excellent local cuisine. There's a children's menu for €10 and if you like the food, you can join one of his cooking classes. There are also Flamenco evenings on the beach and lots of guitar music in the bar. The hotel has its own stables and a swimming pool and the owner also runs the nearby Mas de Colverts, which has self-catering apartments. In low season you can rent the apartments on a nightly basis.

Fontvieille

La Peiriero

Av des Baux **t** 00 33 (0)4 90 54 76 10 **f** 00 33 (0)4 90 54 62 60 **e** info@hotelpeiriero.com
www.hotel-peiriero.com
Price from €75; best family deal – room for four €91
Open April–Oct. Booking essential in summer

La Peiriero and its sister sister hotel Le Calendal (*see* p.227) have got to be the most family-friendly hotels in France. There are rooms to suit all types of families (specifiy the ages of the children when you book, as the duplex has a precipitous staircase). Near the restaurant (*see* p.140) there's a kids' corner with toys and videos in French and English. The hotel has a large garden with swimming pool, table tennis and a giant chess set. It's an ideal base for exploring, just 15mins from St-Rémy (*see* p.135) and 20mins from Arles (*see* p.121).

Aix-en-Provence

Citadines Apart'Hôtel Aix Forbin

15 Cours Gambetta **t** 00 33 (0)4 42 99 16 00
f 00 33 (0)4 42 96 63 44 **e** resa@citadines.com
www.citadines.com

Price studios from €85; best family deal – apartment for four €110

This self-catering hotel is moments from the Cours Mirabeau and since one of the great things to do in Aix is shop in the market, self-catering accommodation is a great option. Apartments are rented on a nightly basis. Facilities include laundry room and baby equipment such as cots and bottle- warmers.

Citadines Apart'Hôtel Aix Jas de Bouffan

4 Av Achille Empéraire **t** 00 33 (0)4 42 52 56 00
f 00 33 (0)4 42 20 22 46
www.citadines.com
Price studios for two €81; best family deal – apartment for five €102

The hotel is on the outskirts of town, which is by no means as pretty as the centre, but is a good option in summer as it has a swimming pool. There's also table tennis, table football and a garden to run around in. The usual baby equipment is at hand as well as the invaluable laundry.

Hôtel Le Concorde

68 Bd du Roi-René **t** 00 33 (0)4 42 26 03 95
f 00 33 (0)4 42 27 38 90
Price rooms from €38.50; best family deal – triple room with extra bed €75.50
Open Jan–Oct

This warm, welcoming hotel has a garage and a small courtyard where you can picnic.

Les Floridianes

24 Bd Charrier, Aix-en-Provence, FR **t/f** 00 33 (0)4 42 37 23 23
Price rooms from €67; best family deal – room for four €79

This small, modern hotel is about 10mins' walk from the old town and is very handy for the station. The suites, although small, can sleep a family of four plus a baby. Cots are available and each suite has a kitchenette so you can enjoy the fantastic food on sale in the market. There's also a launderette, air-conditioning and swimming pool.

La Bastide du Roy René

Av des Infirmeries **t** 00 33 (0)4 42 37 83 00 **f** 00 33 (0)4 42 27 54 40 **e** Bastide.roy.rene@wanadoo.fr
www.mercure.com
Price rooms from €155

Part of the Mercure group, this is a clean, efficient family hotel with pool, moments from the centre.

Around Aix-en-Provence

Salon de Provence

Camping Nostradamus

Rte d'Eyguières **t** 00 33 (0)4 90 56 08 36
f 00 33 (0)4 90 56 65 05
Getting there 5km north of Salon on the D17
Open April–Oct

This campsite is in a shady spot by the canal and has a swimming pool, plus some accommodation in *gîtes*.

Hôtel de la Touloubre

La Barben Pelissanne **t** 00 33 (0)4 90 55 16 85
f 00 33 (0)4 90 55 17 99
Price rooms from €43

Just 5mins from the Zoo de la Barben (*see* p.119), this hotel has a large shady terrace and friendly staff. Breakfast is €5.50.

Marseille

Since Marseille isn't a major tourist destination it isn't any more difficult to find a room here in summer than it is in winter. The best accommodation for families is in the main chain hotels.

Novotel Vieux Port

36 Bd Charles-Livon **t** 00 33 (0)4 96 11 42 11
f 00 33 (0)4 96 11 42 20
www.novotel.com
Price rooms from €150

Part of the family-friendly chain. Two children stay free in their parents' room. There are gifts, a children's menu and play area, plus a swimming pool, a garage and a terrace. The hotel is close to the Jardins du Pharo and within walking distance of the metro.

Citadines Apart'Hôtel Marseille Centre

4 Place Pierre Bertas **t** 00 33 (0)4 96 17 12 00
f 00 33 (0)4 91 91 97 12 **e** resa@citadines.com
www.citadines.com
Price studio for two €61; apartment for six €100

This option is ideal if you are spending the evening in Marseille with small children. The hotel is close to the port and has 1–3-room apartments.

There's a terrace and underground car park, as well as a laundry room and equipment for babies.

Hôtel La Résidence du Vieux Port

18 Quai du Port **t** 00 33 (0)4 91 91 91 22 **f** 00 33 (0)4 91 56 60 88 **e** hotel.residence@wanadoo.fr

Price rooms from €99; suite for five €114

This friendly hotel is on the town hall (Hôtel de Ville) side of the port with a view of Notre Dame. Rooms are big and airy with balconies, so the children can watch the boats in the harbour, and it's handy for eating out, as it's right next door to the town's best restaurants.

Ibis Marseille Gare St Charles

Square Narvick, Esplanade St Charles **t** 00 33 (0)4 91 91 17 63 **f** 00 33 (0)4 96 11 63 64

www.ibis.fr

Getting there Metro St-Charles

Price rooms from €79

This hotel has a good-sized patio garden and rooms with a view of Notre Dame de Garde. It's the usual Ibis setup and is the best place to stay if you have to catch a train – you can even look at the platforms from some rooms, which is ideal for Thomas fans. It's right by the metro and takes minutes to get to the port. Breakfast is €6.

Hôtel Peron

119 Corniche Kennedy **t** 00 33 (0)4 91 31 01 41 **f** 00 33 (0)4 91 59 42 01

Price rooms from €68

An old-fashioned hotel with bright and colourful rooms, well-priced, family owned and with lovely views of the Château d'If. It's good for families with older children, as it's near the *calanques*, which is great for swimming and walking for older kids.

Around Marseille

Cassis

Hôtel Liautaud

2 Rue Victor Hugo **t** 00 33 (0)4 42 01 75 37 **f** 00 33 (0)4 42 01 12 08

Price rooms from €57; room for four €89

The hotel is ideally situated right on the port and is half a minute from the beach. It's a basic 2-star hotel with a garage and good-value, simple accommodation. There is a good selection of room sizes sleeping 2–4 people. Breakfast is €6.

St-Rémy-de-Provence

Auberge Sant Roumierenco

Rte de Noves **t** 00 33 (0)4 90 92 12 53 **f** 00 33 (0)4 90 92 45 83 **e** santroumierenco@net-up.com **www.aubergesantroumierenco.com**

Prices from €70.13; best family deal – duplex room for four €114.34

This hotel is just outside the village and has a pretty, leafy garden, a swimming pool and two tennis courts. There are large duplex family rooms and the hotel has a relaxed atmosphere away from the tourist bustle of the town. Meals are served under the trees in summer.

Le Soleil

35 Av Pasteur **t** 00 33 (0)4 90 92 00 63 **f** 00 33 (0)4 90 92 61 07 **e** contact@hotelsoleil.com

Price rooms from €50; best family deal – apartment €85

Open April–Oct

Tucked away on quiet side street not far from a little playground, the hotel has a garden and swimming pool and free Internet service.

Villa Glanum

46 Av Van Gogh **t** 00 33 (0)4 90 92 03 59 **f** 00 33 (0)4 90 92 00 08 **e** villa.glanum@wanadoo.fr

Price rooms from €72

Open mid-Mar–Oct

This hotel was not only painted by Van Gogh but was also the residence of the writer Daudet (*see* pp.127–8). There's a large garden with a pool and it's just a few minutes' walk to the Roman remains at Glanum (*see* p.136).

LANGUEDOC/ ROUSSILLON

Carcassonne

Hôtel Astoria

18 Rue Tourtel **t** 00 33 (0)4 68 71 34 14 **f** 00 33 (0)4 68 71 34 14 **e** hotel-astoria@wanadoo.fr

Price rooms from €24; best family deal – room for four €54

Situated near the train station, this hotel is a good option for a family on a budget. You'll get a warm welcome and the rooms are all very clean and have their own bathrooms. Also a garage.

Hôtel le Donjon and Les Ramparts

Cité Médiévale 2 Rue du Comte Roger **t** 00 33 (0)4 68 11 23 00 **f** 00 33 (0)4 68 25 06 60
e info@bestwestern-donjon.com
www.hotel-donjon.fr
Price rooms from €74; best family deal – triples from €76

This hotel is in the old city and is the most exciting place to stay for aspiring knights and princesses. A suit of armour greets you as you walk into the hall, which may be a bit kitsch but then, so is the whole town. Kids will love the whole experience of staying in the medieval city. There are lots of large rooms and suites on offer (suite for four costs €215). Buffet breakfast is €9.50 and there's a good restaurant with kids' menus for €7.

Hôtel Montmorency

2 Rue Camille Saint Saëns **t** 00 33 (0)4 68 11 96 70
f 00 33 (0)4 68 11 96 79
e le.montmorency@wanadoo.fr
www.lemontmorency.com
Price rooms from €56; best family deal – room for four €84, extra bed €10

This classically decorated hotel has a family atmosphere and a selection of large rooms suitable for families. There's a garden and lovely terrace with a view of the ramparts. Breakfast costs €6.

Narbonne

Hôtel Le Régent

15 Rue de Suffren **t/f** 00 33 (0)4 68 65 50 43
e leregent@net-up.com
Price rooms from €43; best family deal – room for four €55

A small, clean and unpretentious family hotel. Some rooms have terraces with a view of the city.

Around Narbonne

Gruissan

Hôtel du Casino Le Phoebus

Bd de La Sagne **t** 00 33 (0)4 68 49 03 05 **f** 00 33 (0)4 68 49 07 67 **e** hotel@phoebus-sa.com
www.phoebus-sa.com
Price rooms from €58; best family deal – room with extra bed and cot €74, (extra bed €11, cot €5)

This is a really good family hotel with a children's playground and disco for teens (plus gambling for adults). There are two pools and it's an ideal spot for sailing, rambling, horse riding and mountain bike tours. The hotel is just moments from the sea. Breakfast is €7.50, child's breakfast €4.50.

Perpignan

Hôtel Mercure Perpignan Centre

5 Cours Palmarole **t** 00 33 (0)4 68 35 67 66
f 00 33 (0)4 68 35 58 13
www.mercure.com
Price rooms for two from €79; best family deal – family room for five €115

What it lacks in atmosphere it makes up for in convenience; the hotel is 2mins from the old city centre. Breakfast is not included in the price but it's much more fun to eat in the main square (*see* pp.154–5 and p.176).

Ibis

14 Cours Lazare Escarguel **t** 00 33 (0)4 68 35 62 62
f 00 33 (0)4 68 35 13 38
www.ibis.fr
Price rooms from €56.41

This Ibis is right in the city centre and has a car park. Two kids stay free in their parents' room, so it's excellent value. The rooms may be a bit institutional but you're likely to spend most of the evenings in the old town rather than at the hotel.

Hôtel de la Loge

1 Rue Fabriques d'En Nabot **t** 00 33 (0)4 68 34 41 02
f 00 33 (0)4 68 35 48 18
www.hoteldelaloge.fr
Price rooms from €54.88; best family deal – room for three €64, extra bed €8

This is the best option if you want something with local character but less so if you have a car, as it's in the pedestrianized old town. It's in a charming 16th-century building with a patio and a fountain and may be a bit scruffy round the edges, but is excellent value.

Around Perpignan

Argèles-sur-Mer

Hôtel Les Albères

Chemin de Neguebous **t** 00 33 (0)4 68 95 31 31
f 00 33 (0)4 68 95 32 32
Price rooms from €87, extra bed €19

The hotel is just a short drive from the beach with great views of the Pyrenees. The staff speak English and there are good-sized family rooms, a large pool, children's playground and a kids' club in July and August. Breakfast is €7.

Collioure

Les Mouettes

Rte de Collioure **t** 00 33 (0)4 68 81 21 69
Price rooms from €76; best family deal – suite for four €95
Open April–Sept

Just outside Collioure, this hotel has large, good-value rooms There's a swimming pool and a nice restaurant with children's menu for €10 and great views.

Canet-en-Rousillon

Hôtel St-Georges

45 Promenade de la Côte Vermeille **t** 00 33 (0)4 68 80 33 77 **f** 00 33 (0)4 68 80 65 04
www.hotel-stgeorges.com
Price rooms from €73, extra bed €29

This old-fashioned hotel is right on the seafront and has a good restaurant serving local dishes. There's a terrace and small pool, plus parking. Breakfast costs €6 and the restaurant has a children's menu for €6.10.

Céret

La Terrasse au Soleil

Route de Fontfrède 66400 Céret **t** 00 33 (0)4 68 87 01 94 **f** 00 33 (0)4 68 87 39 24
e terrasse-au-soleil.hotel@wanadoo.fr
Price rooms from €236; best family deal – room for four €316

This hotel offers a large selection of family-sized rooms and apartments in a lovely setting. It's a great base for exploring the mountains and the art museum in Céret.

Cubieres-sur–Cinoble

Camping Au Vieux Moulin

t 00 33 (0)4 68 69 81 49

At the end of the Gorges de Galamus, this medieval mill has a fantastic little restaurant (*see* p.159) and a little field where you can camp for €15. You can also hire kayaks and buy snacks.

Montpellier

Citadines Apart'Hôtel Antigone

120 Rue Jean Jaurès **t** 00 33 (0)4 99 52 37 50
f 00 33 (0)4 67 64 54 64
www.citadines.com
Price studios for two €71, best family deal – apartment for six €110

This is an exceptionally good Citadines with large apartments in the heart of the modern district of the Antigone. There is the usual launderette, plus cots, bottle warmers and changing mats. There's a beautiful covered market just opposite, so self-catering is a real pleasure here. Apartments and studios are rented on a nightly basis but the price goes down the longer you stay.

Hôtel Mercure Montpellier Antigone

285 Bd de l'Aéroport **t** 00 33 (0)4 67 20 63 63
f 00 33 (0)4 67 20 63 64
www.mercure.com
Price rooms from €105

This child-friendly chain has a hotel right in the city centre in the modern Antigone development. One child is accommodated free in their parents' room.

Around Montpellier

Cambous

Château de Cambous

Viols en Laval **t** 00 33 (0)4 67 55 04 31
f 00 33 (0)4 67 55 04 31
Price apartments from €636 per week; best family deal – apartment for six €1536 per week
Open Easter–Sept

This 13th-century château has been converted into apartments that sleep 2–6 people and is ideally situated if you want to explore the wild countryside north of Montpellier. It's next door to the prehistoric site of Cambous (*see* p.170) and is set in 12 acres of woodland. There are indoor and outdoor pools, a gym, games room and playroom. Washing machines are available in all apartments and there's a large communal freezer. The owner is English so language won't be an issue.

Cap d'Agde

Hôtel St-Clair

Pl St-Clair **t** 00 33 (0)4 67 26 36 44 **f** 00 33 (0)4 67 26 31 11
www.hotelsaintclair.fr
Price rooms from €102

In the centre of Cap d'Adge and close to the beach, this hotel has a playground, children's pool and large family rooms on the ground floor that can sleep four plus a baby. There's a free shuttle service to the beach in July and August.

La Grande Motte

Hôtel Mercure

140 Rue du Port **t** 00 33 (0)4 67 56 90 81 **f** 00 33 (0)4 67 56 92 29
www.mercure.com
Price rooms from €125

Right in front of the beach, this hotel has rooms that sleep up to four people with one child staying free of charge. As a chain hotel it suits the modernist atmosphere of La Grande Motte.

Nîmes

Novotel Nîmes Centre

Esplanade Charles de Gaulle 5 Bd de Prague
t 00 33 (0)4 66 76 56 56 **f** 00 33 (0)4 66 76 56 59
www.novotel.com
Price rooms from €106

The family-friendly hotel chain has a place right in the city centre by the amphitheatre and next to a merry-go-round. There's a play area for kids, and toys and games are dished out with the children's menu. Two children say for free in their parents' room.

Le Lisita

2 Bd des Arênes **t** 00 33 (0)4 66 67 66 20
f 00 33 (0)4 66 76 22 30
Price rooms from €48.10

If you've had enough of clinical, modern hotels this is the place for you. It's a really old-fashioned hotel with huge wardrobes and rickety beds. Rooms are large and can easily sleep a family of four. The rooms at the front look on to the old amphitheatre and the hotel is popular with bull-fighters. A traditional atmospheric experience, but be careful when you lock the door, as the locks are so old they can be difficult to open.

Around Nîmes

Collias

Le Castellas

Grand-Rue **t** 00 33 (0)4 66 228 888 **f** 00 33 (0)4 66 228 428 **e** le-castellas@avignon-et-provence.com
Price rooms from €91; best family deal – room for three €125
Open April–Dec

This stylish and elegant hotel has family rooms and a pretty garden, and is located in a 17th-century building in the heart of town. There's an excellent restaurant with a children's menu for €14, adult menus from €38 and breakfast for €14.

Uzès

Mercure Pont du Gard

Route de Nîmes **t** 00 33 (0)4 66 03 32 22 **f** 00 33 (0)4 66 03 32 10 **e** mercure.relaisuzes@wanadoo.fr
www.mercure.com
Price rooms from €63; best family deal – room for four €85

This hotel is just on the edge of Uzès and is unbeatably good value, although the restaurant service leaves something to be desired. There are five family rooms, each with a double and two large single beds. There's a pool, tennis courts and garden, plus an enclosed parking lot. Breakfast is €8.

CORSICA

Corsica is surprisingly underdeveloped, so if you're touring, head for the big towns to find a hotel. For a central hotel reservation service with efficient last-minute availability contact: Destination Corse, Quartier de la Gare Corte, **t** 04 95 45 21 65, **www**.destination-corse.net

The Chambre Régionale d'Agriculture Service Tourisme, 19 Av Noël-Franchini, Ajaccio, **t** 04 95 29 42 00, **t** 04 95 29 42 69 has a list of bed and breakfasts, but if you are touring don't rely on this kind of accommodation being plentiful. At the height of the season you'll find many hotels with a restaurant operate on a half-board (*demi-pension*) basis only and many won't accept single-night bookings. Remember, especially if you're planning a touring holiday, that many hotels featured in holiday brochures rely almost exclusively on the package deal trade and are fully booked for the entire season. You will also need to be specific when you enquire about the price of a room, as the price quoted may be per person rather than per room. Children are usually charged a supplement, so ask about this when you book. For good camping opportunities, head for the valleys around Corte or resorts like Porticcio.

Ajaccio

Hôtel Dolce Vita

Rte des Sanguinaires **t** 00 33 (0)4 95 52 42 42
f 00 33 (0)4 95 52 07 15
Price rooms from €153
Open 16 Mar–Oct

This is a modern hotel with family rooms, water sports, a swimming pool and a stretch of beach. It's 15mins from the city centre. There's a good restaurant run by one of the best chefs in the area. Meals are served on the terrace and there's a large, pretty garden too.

Hôtel Fesch

7 Rue Cardinal Fesch **t** 00 33 (0)4 95 51 62 62
f 00 33 (0)4 95 21 83 36
www.hotel-fesch.com
Price rooms from €56; best family deal – room for five €68

An old-fashioned hotel in the centre of town with huge family rooms. There's air conditioning but otherwise it's not all that up-to-date and rooms looking onto the street can be noisy. The hotel was the scene of a tense standoff in 1980, when Corsican militants who wanted independence held three French Secret Service agents hostage. Sleep peacefully – it all ended without any bloodshed.

L'Eden Roc

Rte des Sanguinaires **t** 00 33 (0)4 95 51 56 00
f 00 33 (0)4 95 52 05 03
Price rooms from €229, cot €18

This is an up-market hotel 10 km out of town, with spacious rooms and a small private beach.

Kallyste

51 Cours Napoléon **t** 00 33 (0)4 95 51 34 45
f 00 33 (0)4 95 21 79 00
Price rooms from €69; best family deal – room for three with extra bed €106

This hotel has studios for up to four people. It's right in the city centre, and has air conditioning and parking close by. Breakfast is €6.50.

Around Ajaccio

Bastelicaccia

L'Hameaux de Botaccina

t/f 00 33 (0)4 20 00 30
Open April–Oct

Bungalows for two from €38 per night; best family deal – bungalow for five €564 per week

The bungalows all have kitchenettes and are excellent value. There's a leafy garden, home to chickens and tortoises.

Cargèse

Hôtel Hélios

t 00 33 (0)4 95 26 41 24 **f** 00 33 (0)4 95 26 41 25
Getting there 3km out of Cargèse on the road to Ajaccio
Price apartments from €747 per week; best family deal – apartment for six €839
Open Mar–Oct

Has apartments sleeping up to ten people with kitchenettes and laundry facilities, plus on-site pool and children's play area.

Porticcio

Studios Rivoli

Plage d'Agosta **t** 00 33 (0)4 95 25 06 02
f 00 33 (0)4 95 20 09 24
Price studio from €557 per week; best family deal – studio for six in high season €1,144

These modern studios are right on a small cliff just above the beach. Each has its own terrace and kitchenette and sleeps 2–6 people.

Sagone

La Funtanella

t 00 33 (0)4 95 28 02 49 **f** 00 33 (0)4 95 28 03 36
Price rooms from €81
Open April–Nov

This is a family motel by the sea with a large lawn and children's play area. The accommodation is in small villas, which have kitchenettes and sleep 2–8 people.

Bastia

Hôtel L'Alvi

Rte du Cap **t** 00 33 (0)4 95 31 61 85 **f** 00 33 (0)4 95 31 03 95
Price rooms from €110; best family deal – room for three from €140

A modern hotel with a pool and great views across the sea, close to a small pebble beach. The restaurant isn't always open but there is a friendly pizzeria just up the road and the hotel staff are friendly and helpful.

Hôtel Cyrnéa

Rte du Cap 2km north of Bastia **t** 00 33 (0)4 95 31 41 71 **f** 00 33 (0)4 95 31 72 65
Price rooms from €65

This is a modern air-conditioned hotel with a large garden that slopes down to a pebbly beach and good views across the sea to Elba. The owner will give you plenty of good advice on where to walk or go riding and there's tennis and volleyball on the beach.

Around Bastia

L'Ile Rousse

Hôtel Santa Maria

Rte du Port **t** 00 33 (0)4 95 63 05 05 **f** 00 33 (0)4 95 60 32 48 **f** 04 95 51 28 29
www.hotelsantamaria.com
Price rooms from €123

A modern hotel with a sailing school and water sports on site. The hotel also rents villas on an adjacent plot.

L'Amiral

Bd Charles-Marie Savelli **t** 00 33 (0)4 95 60 28 05
f 00 33 (0)4 95 60 31 21
www.hotel-amiral.com
Price rooms from €77; best family deal – room for three €85

Seconds from the beach, this is a family hotel with a relaxed atmosphere and good, clean rooms with air conditioning. Rooms in the annexe sleep three.

Le Désert des Agriates

Camping U Paradiso

Plage de Saleccia, 12km off the D81
t 00 33 (0)4 95 37 82 51

The site has shops, a children's playground, bungalows and a restaurant; and it's just 100m from the best beach on the island.

Ferme Auberge Pietra Moneta

Intersection of the D81 and N197, Palasca
t 00 33 (0)4 95 60 24 88
Price rooms from €45
Open May–Sept

This 18th-century post house has four simple rustic rooms and a great restaurant serving traditional dishes. There's live music on Saturday. Half-board obligatory July–Aug.

Ferme Campo di Monte

Murato **t** 00 33 (0)4 95 37 64 39
Price rooms from €50

Just below the town, this is one of the best *fermes auberges* in Corsica. Rooms are cosy, there's a terrace with delightful views and the restaurant is excellent.

Cap Corse

Finding a room here can be tricky. There are very few places to stay and in the main tourist season it can be difficult to find a room – book well in advance if you can.

Castel Brando

Erbalunga t 00 33 (0)4 95 30 10 30
f 00 33 (0)4 95 33 98 18
www.castelbrando.com
Price rooms from €69; best family deal – suite €160 in high season

This hotel is in an elegant 19th-century Corsican mansion surrounded by a garden full of lush palm trees. The rooms in the annexe have small kitchenettes and are best for families. The hotel is close to the sea, with a good beach for toddlers, but you will have to cross the main road. There's a tennis court for guests 200m up the road, a heated swimming pool and the owners can advise on horse riding and walking in the area. Booking is essential.

Hôtel La Giraglia

Barcaggio t 00 33 (0)4 95 35 65 92 f 00 33 (0)4 95 35 60 54
Price rooms from €62; best family deal – room for three €86
Open May–Sept

The hotel itself is nothing special but it is in the most stunning location, right on the edge of the beach in one of Corsica's remotest spots. The ruined villa across the road, destroyed by nationalists, merely adds to the atmosphere. There's no restaurant and although there's a small café nearby, bring supplies, as this is a fairly remote place.

Bonifacio

Hôtel du Centre Nautique

t 00 33 (0)4 95 73 02 11 f 00 33 (0)4 95 73 17 47
Price rooms from €69; best family deal – room with extra bed €92 (further bed €23)

This hotel has 10 duplex rooms with all the facilities, some with sofa beds. The restaurant serves excellent pasta dishes.

Around Bonifacio

Camping U Farniente

t 00 33 (0)4 95 73 05 47
Getting there 5km northeast of Bonifacio on the N198

This campsite offers bungalow and chalet accommodation, plus two pools and plenty of children's activities.

Camping Rondinara

t 00 33 (0)4 95 70 56 79 f 00 33 (0)4 95 70 56 79
Getting there 14km north of Bonifacio
Price Best family deal – mobile home for six €750 per week
Open May–Sept

A well-equipped camp in one of the loveliest bays in the whole of Corsica, this site has a shop, bar and restaurant. There's a large pool, and the beach, which is perfect for little children, is just moments away. A pitch costs around €27.50.

Résidence Marina di Cava

Calalonga t 00 33 (0)4 95 73 14 13 f 00 33 (0)4 95 73 04 82
Price rooms from €220; best family deal – room for four €550

This is a collection of rooms, bungalows and apartments with beautiful views and an excellent restaurant. The site is just 200m from the beach and is set among the olive trees.

Ferme Auberge Pozzo di Mastri

t 00 33 (0)4 95 71 02 65
Getting there On the D859 just outside town Figari
Price rooms from €45 for two

This big stone house also has a restaurant that will cook up a good lamb or a roast boar.

Les Bergeries de Piscia

Findori t/f 0033 (0)4 95 06 71
Getting there 28km from Bonifacio
Price rooms from €112 for two, including evening meal

This is a peaceful *chambre d'hôte* hidden in the maquis, with five rooms and a pool. It's open all year and serves good regional cooking.

Porto-Vecchio

Hôtel San Giovanni

Rte d'Arca **t** 00 33 (0)4 95 70 22 25 **f** 00 33 (0)4 95 70 20 11
Getting there 5km from Porto-Vecchio
Price rooms from €96

A peaceful hideaway set in 7 acres of flowery gardens in the countryside outside Porto-Vecchio. It's a family-run hotel and you're likely to find the owners' grandchildren playing around in the grounds. There's a good family restaurant and simple, no-frills bedrooms and family suites. Facilities include tennis courts, table tennis, bikes, a kids' play area and a swimming pool set well back from the rooms. Some of the rooms are bungalows set off a pretty terrace.

Hôtel Rivière

Rte de Muratello **t** 00 33 (0)4 95 70 10 21 **f** 00 33 (0)4 95 70 56 13
Price rooms from €96; best family deal – room for four from €153

The hotel is 5km from the centre by a small river. Rooms are simple and there's a large garden with green lawns. Under-12s stay free in their parents' room. Facilities include a large pool, sauna and *boules*.

Grand Hôtel Cala Rossa

Cala Rossa Lecci di Porto-Vecchio **t** 00 33 (0)4 95 71 61 51 **f** 00 33 (0)4 95 71 60 11
Price rooms from €425
Open April–Dec

An elegant, chic and child-friendly hotel with one of the best restaurants on the island and plenty of space for the kids to run around. There are huge gardens, an aquarium and a private sandy beach with water sports. Kids can eat early if they're exhausted after the beach. The rooms all have air conditioning and minibars and some of the family rooms open out onto the garden.

U Capu Biancu

Santa Manza **t** 00 33 (0)4 95 73 05 58 **f** 00 33 (0)4 95 73 18 66
Price rooms from €136; best family deal – room for three €220
Open April–Nov

The hotel is hidden away down a dirt track about 7km from town and is completely secluded, yet it's modern, with the mod cons you'll need like air conditioning and a minibar for milk. Water sports and mountain bikes are all on site and there's a minibus service to nearby Bonifacio if you fancy some sightseeing. If you're burdened with pushchairs you might want to give this one a miss, as the beach is down a steep path. The buffet lunch is a good option with kids who will only submit to being dragged off the beach for a few minutes.

Hôtel du Golfe

Pinarellu **t** 00 33 (0)4 95 71 40 70 **f** 00 33 (0)4 95 71 45 30
Getting there 5km from Porto-Vecchio20km to the north of Porto-Vecchio
Price rooms from €45; best family deal – studios for four €854

Pinarellu is a charming village with an excellent beach. All the facilities you need are close at hand but without as many people as you'll find in Porto-Vecchio proper. The hotel has studios with kitchenettes and bunk beds that can be rented on a nightly or weekly basis.

Hôtel de la Plage

Plage de Pinarellu 20144 Ste-Lucie-de-Porto-Vecchio **t** 00 33 (0)4 95 33 99 91 **f** 00 33 (0)4 95 36 85 13 **e** info@hotel-de-plage.com
Price rooms from €130; best family deal – room for four from €170

This modern hotel has all the usual facilities and is right on the beach. In high season you need to book and stay at least four nights.

Camping Santa-Lucia

Ste-Lucie-de-Porto-Vecchio
t/f 00 33 (0)4 95 71 45 28
Getting there on the N198
Open May–Sept

Good-value site under the cork trees, with plenty of facilities for children. A family of four will pay around €30 for a pitch and there are bungalows to rent by the week if you don't have a tent; they cost €365 for four people.

Calvi

Casa Vecchia

Rte de Santore **t** 00 33 (0)4 95 65 09 33 **f** 00 33 (0)4 95 65 37 93
www.hotel-casa-vecchia.com
Price rooms from €30; chalets from €410 per week, extra bed €50 per week, cot €6

This hotel is set in a shady garden with basic chalet-style rooms, some of which have kitchens. It's close to the beach and just 15mins from the city centre. There's a fair set rate for laundry and the evening meal is good value.

Hôtel La Caravelle

Av Christophe Colomb, L'Orée des Pins **t** 00 33 (0)4 95 65 95 50 **f** 00 33 (0)4 95 65 00 03
www.hotel-la-caravelle.com
Price rooms from €212 for two with half-board

Just a short stroll from the centre is this lovely hotel with gardens, beautiful beach and pleasant restaurant. It's kid friendly and good value, with family rooms that sleep three.

Hôtel Corsica

Rte de Pietramaggiore **t** 00 33 (0)4 95 65 03 64 **f** 00 33 (0)4 95 65 00 54 **e** hotelcorsica@wanadoo.fr
www.best-western-corsica.com
Price rooms from €178; best family deal – deluxe room with extra beds from €212

A modern hotel set on the hills above Calvi, with a children's pool and play area. The rooms have minibars to keep milk fresh. Under-16s stay free in a deluxe room and non-smoking rooms are available. There's a large pool and baby-sitting service, plus a free shuttle bus to the town centre.

Hôtel La Villa

Chemin de Notre-Dame-de-la-Serra **t** 00 33 (0)4 95 65 10 10 **f** 00 33 (0)4 95 65 10 50 **e** lavilla@relaischateaux.com
www.relaischateaux.com/lavilla
Price rooms from €175; best family deal – suite €175–€541
Open April–Dec

The stylish Relais & Châteaux chain is usually child-free, but this luxury hotel, just outside Calvi, is the exception and is happy to welcome younger customers. The hotel has to be the best on the island, a complete haven of luxury services catering for all ages, including babysitting services so you can enjoy the excellent restaurant in peace. There are three pools and a huge 7-acre garden and everything is laid on – tennis, sailing and bikes. You can also rent apartments and villas. The hotel organizes boat trips to the marine nature reserve at Scandola (*see* p.202).

Hôtel Le Rocher

Bd Wilson **t** 04 95 65 20 04 **f** 04 95 65 36 71
Price studios from €126; best family deal – weekly rent for four €245
Open May–Sept

This hotel is right in the town centre, just 200m from the beach. There are studios and apartments with kitchenettes and air conditioning for up to four people.

L'Enclos des Lauriers Roses

71 Rue du 14 Juillet **t** 00 33 (0)4 66 75 25 42 **f** 00 33 (0)4 66 75 25 21 **e** hotel-lauriersroses@wanadoo.fr
www.lauriersroses.com
Getting there North of Calvi on the N197 towards L'Ile Rousse
Price rooms from €68.60; best family deal – rooms for four from €84, extra bed €7.60

There are big rooms that can sleep up to 5 people and this hotel is exceptionally good value, with big rooms that can sleep up to five people. Half-board is obligatory in high season but there are three swimming pools, and a small pool for children, as well as a play area. There are also apartments and villas to rent.

Around Calvi

Algajola

Hôtel Beau Rivage

t 00 33 (0)4 95 60 73 99 **f** 00 33 (0)4 95 60 79 51
e beaurivage@hotelscorse.com
Price rooms from €90; best family deal – room for three €112

This hotel is right on the sand, on a beautiful beach just north of Calvi. Prices are fairly reasonable if you take a room in the annexe. The terrace and bar serve nice food and also overlook the beach; there's a relaxed family atmosphere throughout.

St-Florent

Hôtel Maxime

t 00 33 (0)4 95 37 05 30 **f** 00 33 (0)4 95 37 13 07
Price rooms from €62

In the town centre, just 300m from the beach. Rooms are small so large families will need two. All rooms have minibars, and there's a garden and private parking.

Corte

Ferme Auberge L'Albadu

Ancienne Route d'Ajaccio **t** 00 33 (0)4 95 46 24 55 **f** 00 33 (0)4 95 46 24 55
Price rooms from €38 with breakfast

If you don't mind sharing toilet facilities, you'll have a relaxed rural time at this friendly auberge where you can enjoy proper farm cooking and go horse riding. You can pitch your tent if you'd prefer; if you don't have a car the owner will collect you from the station.

Osteria di L'Orta

Casa Guelfucci **t/f** 0033 (0)4 95 61 06 41
Price rooms from €48

Offers farm accommodation and cooking, plus jams, chutneys, meat and wine for sale.

Camping Alivetu

Faubourg St-Antoine **t** 00 33 (0)4 95 46 11 09 **f** 00 33 (0)4 95 46 12 34 **e** camping-alivetu@laposte.net
Open April–mid-Oct

This is a simple site on the edge of a river, just 5mins from the town centre. There's a basic restaurant, and a pitch for a family of four costs around €30.

Around Corte

Auberge de la Restonica

Vallée de Restonica **t** 00 33 (0)4 95 45 25 25 **f** 00 33 (0)4 95 61 15 79
Price rooms from €53

The hotel is 11/2km out of Corte, next to a mountain stream in the beautiful Restonica valley, and is run by a former footballer. It's open all year round and has a garden with a pool. Obligatory half-board in high season, which costs €114 for two adults, but you won't mind because the restaurant serves up good Corsican food.

Hôtel-Auberge Casa Mathea

Rue St-Roch Poggio de Venaco **t/f** 0033 (0)4 95 47 05 27
Price studios from €60.98

This is a selection of five studios in the village, all with kitchenettes. Breakfast costs €4.57.

Le Kyrn Flor

(*Chambres et tables d'hôtes*; contact J Valentini)
t 00 33 (0)4 95 61 02 88 **f** 00 33 (0)4 95 46 08 02
Price rooms from €53.36

Bed and breakfast accommodation 3km from town on the N193. There are five rooms in the main house, but with a family it's best to opt for a studio in the garden, where you won't hear the traffic and can barbecue in the garden in the evening. Half-board for two adults costs €99.10.

Ferme Auberge Peridundellu

Venaco **t** 00 33 (0)4 95 47 09 89
Getting there 4km out of town on the D143

This excellent little campsite by a stream has a restaurant that serves some delicious home-made cooking. Pitch with car €15.20.

Porto

Hotels in Porto have rooms for up to four people.

Hôtel Le Belvedere

t 00 33 (0)4 95 26 12 01 **f** 00 33 (0)4 95 26 11 97
www.hotel-le-belvedere.com
Price rooms from €64; best family deal – room with an extra bed €72

This small hotel is next to the Genoese tower and has a terrace and beautiful views over the sea. Cots are free of charge; an extra bed costs €8.

Le Colombo

t 00 33 (0)4 95 26 10 14 **f** 00 33 (0)4 95 26 12 10
e Colombo@wanadoo.fr
www.porto-tourisme.com/colombo
Price rooms from €74.70; best family deal – room for four €116
Open April–Sept

This hotel is 1km from Porto town on the road to Calvi. It has a pretty garden, serves a good breakfast and has large rooms, some of which sleep up to four people.

Hôtel Eden Park

Serriera t 00 33 (0)4 95 26 10 60 f 00 33 (0)4 95 26 14 74
Price rooms from €176
Open Mar–Dec

The hotel is up in the hills, 4km north of Porto, so you'll get a lovely breeze. There's a children's play area, swimming pool, tennis court and a leafy garden. The food is great, the restaurant has a children's menu and there are regular barbecues in high season. The hotel can organize water sports and riding.

Les Roches Rouges

Piana t 00 33 (0)4 95 27 81 18 f 00 33 (0)4 95 27 81 76
Price rooms from €71; best family deal – room for five €135
Open May–Sept.

This stylish, old-fashioned hotel was built in 1912 and has a lot of character – it's a listed UNESCO building. The rooms are large, some sleeping up to four people, and the views are spectacular. The hotel is south of Porto, just 10mins from a great sandy beach and is an especially good spot for families who like walking. There's a good restaurant with breakfast for €10.

Eat

EATING OUT 242
A matter of taste 242
Children's menus 243
Markets, picnic food and snacks 243
Fast foods 243
Seasonal treats 244
Farm foods 244

SOUTH OF FRANCE ON A PLATE 245
The Riviera 245
Northern Provence 245
Western Provence 246
Languedoc 246
Roussillon 246
Corsica 247

EATING IN 247
Some recipes for kids 247

USEFUL PHRASES 249

09

EATING OUT

The French love of food is passed down to their children; while British babies are munching on jars of macaroni cheese and rice, their French counterparts are enjoying purées of artichoke, *fruits de mer* and chestnuts. Food is a serious business and for French school children learning about where the best cheese, apples and wine come from is just as important as learning times tables. At the school canteen pupils will be served goat's cheese, stewed rabbit and eat plenty of seasonal fruits and vegetables – no piles of chips and endless burgers.

The stuffy British hotel custom of refusing children entry after 6pm is unthinkable in France; French families expect to dine out *en famille*, especially when they're on holiday, and they tend to take their family holidays in France. If your children are interested in cooking or simply want to enjoy good food while on holiday, France, especially the South, is an ideal destination.

You'll get a warm welcome wherever you choose to eat and most restaurants have a children's menu or will be willing to split portions or bring you an extra plate. Don't expect every restaurant to have a highchair – being child-friendly here is all in the attitude; you'll receive a friendly welcome but there may not be all the trappings. In the more up-market restaurants in the South of France the staff may be welcoming but there are a lot of grey heads in this part of the world, and not all of them French. You might find fellow diners are tolerant but not all that enthusiastic for you to linger, and remember that, wherever you go, children are welcome but bad behaviour is not.

If your kids aren't angels, don't lose heart. The good news is that the real taste of the South of France isn't fancy, overdecorated food drenched in sauce. Traditionally life was tough – meat was a rarity and there wasn't any cream. However, in the summer, there was an abundance of fabulous fruit and vegetables and so some of the best dishes are simple and very fresh and can be enjoyed in a simple auberge or village restaurant.

Good to know...opening times

Mealtimes are taken seriously and everything stops for lunch from roughly 12 noon till 2.30. Getting a meal later in the afternoon can be very tricky and even on the motorway you'll find that after 2.30 the service station won't have much left. The evening meal is eaten between 7 and 11 but last orders can be as early as 9.30. It pays to arrive early in a restaurant to be sure of a table and to get better service. Aim to be at the restaurant of your choice by 12.30 for lunch and 7.30 for dinner.

In season most restaurants are open seven days a week; out of season many close for at least a month and may not open every day, and last orders may be as early as 9p. It pays to call in advance to be sure that the restaurant is open.

A matter of taste

There are plenty of local dishes that appeal to kids and if you're not sure what to order most waiters will be happy to tell you what local children tend to choose. Don't hesitate to ask if you can have something simple like scrambled eggs or plain pasta for toddlers – most restaurants are happy to oblige.

Even in gourmet restaurants they'll serve children first and will be happy to cook dishes that are acceptable to tiny palates. In the countryside it's easy to find top restaurants with large gardens and outside seating, so you won't have to rush your meal when the kids get fidgety. The local tourist office can provide a list of restaurants in the area. But beware – the upmarket gourmet experience in the South of France doesn't come cheap, so go on a night when you aren't going to worry about the mounting credit card bills.

You don't have to pay for a top dining experience to enjoy good food; if you're on a budget there are hundreds of restaurants across the region serving up top-notch food from local ingredients at affordable prices. If your kids wrinkle their noses at everything you try to offer them, remember, as you order yet another plate of *beignets de poulet*, alias chicken nuggets and shovel packets of *pommes noisettes* and *poisson grillé* into your shopping trolley, it's not unusual for the hostess at a swish Parisian dinner party to either send the kids out for a McDonald's or serve up a microwave pizza with the *foie gras*.

Some things on the menu that kids will like include:

Poulet aux pignons a roast chicken dish cooked with pine nuts. A winter favourite in Provence.

Omelette au brocciu an omelette made with Corsican goat's cheese.

Gigot d'agneau leg of lamb, a regional speciality.

Compote de marrons baked sugared chestnuts. Another winter favourite.

Gâteau à la brousse Corsican cheesecake.

Tian a mousse-like gratin of vegetables or cheese cooked in a tiny dish. Good for very small children.

Tian de lait an old-fashioned vanilla dessert. Sometimes it contains rum, so check first.

Don't forget that Auguste Escoffier, the great French chef, was born in the South of France and it was he who invented Peach Melba. It's hard to find a better kids' dessert than that.

Children's menus

A growing number of top hotels and restaurants offer a specific children's menu that is likely to include scaled-down versions of adult dishes. One small chain of hotel restaurants in the Bouche-de-Rhône, which includes Le Calendal in Arles (*see* p.140), has an organic gourmet children's menu that changes daily. If there isn't a children's menu, most restaurants will simply serve a smaller portion; all you have to do is ask. Traditionally restaurants have a set menu, which is the best bet if you want to try a selection of local dishes without breaking the bank. This is also a good way of satisfying your kids' desires to try something new without the extra expense of ordering lots of separate dishes. No one will turn a hair if you share the dishes round; just ask for an extra plate.

If you're not sure whether the chef can cater for children it's best to ask before you reserve a table, but phrase your enquiry carefully in order to avoid offence. A lot of French chefs cater for children as a matter of course and will automatically alter the seasoning in dishes they prepare for them.

Markets, picnic food and snacks

In the South of France it is possible to tempt even the fussiest eaters to try something new, but you don't need to rush headlong into the nearest gourmet restaurant to bring about an immediate transformation. The best place to start is in the market. Kids love grazing and that's just what markets were made for. If you're headed that way, start your gourmet adventures on Cours Saleya in Nice (*see* p.49), where you'll find mountains of luminous fruit and vegetables alongside equally tempting trays of marzipan and boiled sweets, and plenty of stalls selling specialities such as the local version of pizza – *pissaladière*.

The ideal picnic

Cavaillon melon
salad niçoise
cold cuts of meat from the Cévennes or Corsican ham
a loaf of flat *fougasse* bread
Roquefort cheese
***navettes* – Marseille's favourite biscuits**
figs from Gard
***calissons* (marzipan sweets) from Aix**

Picnics are a part of French life, so there's no need to feel that you've short-changed the kids, or yourself, if you never set foot in a restaurant for the entire holiday. As you stock up for a picnic lunch on the beach, the market stallholders will give the kids a quick lesson in how to choose a melon or what the different varieties of strawberries taste like and let them try a whole range of cheeses if they can't decide what to choose.

For ready-made sandwiches look no further than the local *boulangerie*; these are almost always made with half a baguette (you'll find the conventional variety of sandwiches in garages and service stations). Different regions of France will have their sweet specialities too and local bakeries will have a range of cakes and pastries unique to the area. Corsican pastries seem to be particularly popular with children and because many Corsicans left their homeland for the mainland, particularly around Marseille, you can sample these even if Corsica isn't on your itinerary.

Fast foods

If you're looking for something in a hurry don't feel depressed if you have to resort to McDonald's. Despite all the hot air about hating McDonald's, the French just can't eat enough Big Macs. You'll find McDonald's everywhere, although French teenagers often take their burgers home and eat them with a knife, fork and a napkin. Some McDonald's, like those in Cannes and Narbonne, are in great locations and are extremely pleasant. Pizza Hut is popular, too, and France has its own burger and steak chain, Hippopotamus, where the waiters dish out crayons to the kids and serve up the chips with Gallic style. In general, though, restaurant chains have a very minor presence in the South of France; most places to eat are still family-owned businesses and even quite ordinary-looking pizza and pasta places will serve up something tasty.

Seasonal treats

Festivals are another good way of sampling local food and tempting kids to try something new. The local tourist board can give you a list of festivals in the area, and you'll also find details of the best ones for kids in the sightseeing chapters of this guide. There are so many across the region that you're bound to find one near you, whatever time of year you visit. Seasonal specialities are still important, so look out for special markets, such as the truffle market in Carpentras in autumn and winter. As well as planning visits to the local vineyards, plan to see a goat farm or enjoy an olive oil tasting. Visits like this are an important part of the French school curriculum and children are welcome. The local tourist office will have a list of local producers.

Farm foods

One of the best places to try regional French cooking is down on the farm. Many farmers run small, family restaurants in the summer months where you can taste excellent local cooking made with the freshest ingredients. The atmosphere is informal and family orientated and there's always plenty of space for the kids to run around in between courses and make friends with the local children.

The tourist board in Hérault in Languedoc produces a good mini-guide, *Bienvenue à la Ferme*, which lists farms where you can enjoy good home cooking at bargain prices, and you can also get details of farms serving food in Corsica from the local tourist office. Look out for the signs *Table d'Hôte*, *Goûter à la Ferme* or *La Ferme Auberge*.

Christmas cooking

Christmas in Provence is a major event and food plays a starring role in the festivities. The Christmas Eve meal, called the *gros souper*, is a simple affair and very symbolic. The table is laid with three cloths to symbolize the trinity and the meal starts with a sage soup, to represent the sage tea that the Virgin Mary and Jesus drank before fleeing to Egypt. This is then followed by a simple fish dish. After the main course sobriety is thrown to the wind with the traditional serving of 13 desserts to represent Jesus and his apostles. Exactly what is served up varies from house to house but on the table you'll usually find:

- dried fruits, including dates and figs
- *la pompe à l'huile* – a brioche made with olive oil
- *pâte des coing* –quince paste
- white nougat
- black nougat
- nuts, especially almonds
- fresh fruit, usually oranges and apples
- *lou mais* – a cornmeal cake
- *panade* – a tart usually made with apples
- cooked fruits

Many people these days also serve *calissons*, the little marzipan sweets from Aix, although they aren't traditional. In the weeks before Christmas you can buy all the different types of desserts in the Christmas markets held across the region. One of the best is in Aix-en-Provence. If you're feeling more adventurous, some of the dishes are very simple to make and are great gifts. One of the simplest is *dattes déguisées*: all you need is a packet of dates, a packet of marzipan and four different food colourings. Divide the marzipan into four and tint each piece with a different colour. Cut open each date, take out the stone and replace it with marzipan. *Et voilà*!

SOUTH OF FRANCE ON A PLATE

However much the French claim that the hexagon-shaped borders of their beloved home are fixed in aspic, the cultural and epicurean boundaries blur a bit at the edges, especially in the south. This is a definite advantage with kids as it provides more choice and thus makes for one of the easiest regions in France to eat out with children. Along the coast from Nice to Menton the cuisine takes on a real Italian feel and in Roussillon the Catalan influence means there are plenty of tapas restaurants where you can order a selection of small dishes for everyone to share.

Whatever you choose you'll find you'll be savouring a little history. The South of France is one of the crossroads of Europe and has been open to foreign influences, both welcome and unwelcome, since ancient times. The Greeks came first and brought olives and grapes, and were then followed by the Romans – those spicy sauces you'll find here are actually Roman, as is *anchoïade*, an anchovy paste. The idea of serving lots of small vegetable dishes was brought by the Moors from Spain, as was saffron, which turns up in lots of dishes.

On the coast, some of the best places to eat are beach cafés. These are a far cry from the fish and chips joints you'll find in Britain and many are first-class restaurants that make divine use of the local seafood, especially along the Riviera. They often have tables right on the sand, so the kids can carry on digging while you enjoy your meal.

The Riviera

Nice is a kids' paradise when it comes to food. Pasta dishes come in all shapes and sizes; *ravioli* and *gnocchi* (potato dumplings) were invented here when Nice was still called Nizza and was a part of Italy. Nice has only actually been French for less than 150 years and the food here is basically what's popular on the other side of the border. With all those Italian influences it's one of the best places to eat out with children.

This is the land of vine-ripened tomatoes and garlic, and dishes described as *à la provençal* feature a sauce made of both. Local specialities are *pistou*, similar to pesto, and the local version of pizza – *pissaladière*. It's delicious but is made with anchovies so may not be a favourite with everyone.

Salade niçoise is the classic starter, and usually contains tomatoes, cucumbers, hard-boiled eggs, black olives, onions, anchovies, artichokes, peppers, croutons, green beans, tuna and potatoes. It is a good option for children as they can easily pick out the bits they don't like. *Pan bagnat* is *salade niçoise* served in bread – usually baguette – as a sandwich; the juices soak into the bread, making it particularly succulent.

Local kids love *chichis* (deep-fried dough sticks), and *socca* (a large chickpea pancake cooked on a wood-burning stove). A tasty addition to your picnic is *tarte aux blettes*, a cheese and Swiss chard pie. If you're in town in February and March look out for *poutine*, a tiny fish caught in the Baie des Anges, which you'll find cooked up in fritters or an omelette. It's only caught in spring, which is also the time of year to eat *ganses*, a thin, sweet fritter cooked during the Carnival.

Olive bread, *pain aux olives*, is good for a filler between meals, as is *fougasse*, which is a special flat bread, often made with bacon, *aux gratons* (*lardons*). Tempt sweet eaters with locally made candied fruit and nougat from Vence or the local cake from St-Tropez, the *tarte tropézienne*, a sponge cake filled with lashings of custard cream. In the Massif des Maures the chestnuts from Collobrières are some of the best. If you're holidaying during autumn half term, don't miss the chestnut festival held at the end of October where you can try chestnuts in an amazing variety of delicacies.

Northern Provence

Away from the coast the food is more rustic. The speciality here is lamb, especially if you are in Sisteron, which is usually served roasted and without trimmings. In summer don't miss the melons from Cavaillon; their praises were sung by none other than Alexandre Dumas, and he was someone who knew a thing or two about food. Autumn sees the mushroom and truffle season.

In this part of France sweets are the main temptation; Apt is famous for its candied fruit and you can smell the sugar in the air as you drive into town. In Avignon the local speciality is *papalines*, which are chocolates flavoured with orange; Carpentras is the home of *berlingots*, tiny, mint-flavoured boiled sweets; and in Sault they make some of the best nougat in France. Honey is another local speciality; buy it at the market.

Western Provence

The marshy Camargue, south of Arles, is a natural paddy field. In the 1980s the wild rice, which the farmers had never been able to harvest before, cross-pollinated by accident with farmed rice and is now a local speciality, *riz rouge*, red rice. It has a nutty, earthy flavour and goes well with meat or eaten cold in a salad with tomatoes.

Marseille is famous for its *bouillabaisse*. Its name comes from *bouillir*, to boil, and it's essentially a lot of fish boiled up together. A real bowl of *bouillabaisse* is expensive, as scorpion fish, a crucial ingredient, is rare. If the children want to try it but aren't sure whether they'll like it they can always sample the cheaper *bourride* first, an almost identical broth but made without saffron and with cheaper, white-fleshed fish.

While you tour the sights you can munch on Marseille's local biscuits, *navettes*, which are shaped like boats, hence their name, and flavoured with orange flower water, or you could try *chichis-fregis*, Marseille doughnuts. Further inland, Aix is the home of little marzipan biscuits called *calissons* and the *brioche, pompe à l'huile*, which is eaten at Christmas.

Marseille has some excellent ethnic cuisine thanks to its large North African population. Try the couscous while you're here; it is to France what chicken tikka is to Britain, but it is a lot more authentic.

Languedoc

Food here is heavier and less inspired than in Provence and might prove trickier for fussy eaters. The local speciality is cassoulet, a hearty casserole of beans and meat that most children find too heavy. Snails are the other local speciality and these are not often top of the children's menu either. Little palates are more likely to go for *rouzoles* – crêpes filled with ham and bacon – and *aligot*, a potato and cheese purée.

Children often enjoy *petites pâtés* from Pézenas, also called *diabolos*. They are tiny lamb pies supposed to have first been baked here by the servants of Lord Clive of India while he was on holiday. They are a French version of the samosa except the lamb filling is sweet rather than spicy.

Meat eaters will find plenty to tempt them. The local lamb is usually a safe bet with children, as is the *jambon cru de la Montagne Noire*, a type of ham from the Black Mountain near Carcassonne. You'll see lots of sausages on the menu; try Toulouse sausages, which are made of a pleasantly mild-tasting pork.

Fish lovers will enjoy a speciality of Nîmes called *brandade*, which is a cod purée mixed with olive oil and milk, as well as the speciality of the port of Sète, a fish pie called *tielle sètoise*.

If you fancy something sweet and are in Narbonne, try *croquettes au miel*, delicious honey tarts, while in Carcassonne nibble the local candied fruit. Nîmes' sweet speciality is the *croquant Villaret*, a dry biscuit made with almonds and lemon. Don't be tempted by the boxes in the supermarkets; you really need to eat these hot from the baker's oven. The sweeties to suck in Montpellier are called *grisettes*, but for a healthier snack try the famous local figs from the Gard.

Roussillon

Local specialities here are less likely to tempt children than in the rest of the south. A stew locally known as *ouillade* and made of beef and beans is high on the menu. A lighter option is *roussillonade* – a dish of mushrooms and sausages grilled over a pine-cone fire. Lamb is again a speciality, as are anchovies from the Collioure. They are served as a spread and are mixed with olive oil and garlic.

The Spanish influence is very strong and you'll see tapas restaurants across the region. These are a good bet with children because you can order lots of small dishes, so you're more likely to find something to tempt them.

When it comes to dessert try Catalan *crème brûlée* and *nougat noir* from Perpignan. The cherries from Céret are the first to ripen in France and arrive as early as the end of April. The local biscuits are called *rousquilles* and are soft, lemon-flavoured treats covered in meringue; you'll also want to try the almond-covered *croquant de St-Paul-Fenouillet* biscuits and *touron*, a special, soft nougat with dried fruit, which has been made since the Middle Ages.

Corsica

Brocciu features in lots of Corsican dishes, and has done so since Neolithic times. It's a cheese made from ewe's or goat's milk and when it's fresh (the season runs from November–early July) it's like ricotta but as it ages it tastes more like cottage cheese. Look out for *beignets au brocciu*, cheese fritters; in the summer they sell them on the beach or at roadside stalls. Outside Corsica *brocciu* is usually made with cow's milk and doesn't taste as good. Other Corsican cheeses are very strong and less likely to appeal to kids (even Asterix was thrown by their strong smell when he visited the island).

Kids will get a taste of Corsica without too much of a challenge if you order *omelette au brocciu* or cannelloni stuffed with *brocciu*. Otherwise local dishes are more suited to Obelix-style palates and include wild boar and kid stew. Lamb is also a local speciality and with all those wild pigs wandering around it's no surprise that there's plenty of smoked ham and sausages. The best sausages are found in the Castagniccia where the pigs are fed on chestnuts. Plates of ham are the main starter on the island and can make a good small meal for a child.

As in the rest of France, Corsicans don't skimp when it comes to the dessert course. Chestnuts are used as a substitute for flour in biscuits and a traditional cake – *pulenta* – which is usually a hit with kids. Other treats to look out for are *fiadone*, a lemon cheesecake, *moustachole* bread, with big sugar crystals on top and *gayshelli*, sugared biscuits. You might also want to try *canestrelli*, soft biscuits also popular in northern Italy, and *beignets* or *fritelli*, chestnut doughnuts. Children might also want to try the gruesome-sounding *paides morts* (bread of the dead), a nut and raisin bread from Bonifacio.

Corsica is famous for its honey but be aware that the honey changes according to season and can be a bit strong if you choose the autumn variety.

Self-catering is an ideal option with children; it gives you flexibility and is the best way of keeping down costs.

There are masses of large supermarkets, small specialist shops and fantastic markets right across the South of France and Corsica, so finding something that everyone can enjoy won't be a problem. French mothers don't spend their holidays slaving over the kitchen range so you'll find plenty of ready-cooked chickens and other prepared food for sale.

It's tempting when you're more interested in the beach than the cooking to fall back on chicken nuggets and dried pasta as a fast option for children, even if you rustle up something a bit more exciting for yourself. However it is possible to get into the French swing of things and not to end up short-changing the kids at mealtimes.

Your rental property may come with a barbecue, but if not you can pick up a disposable one just about anywhere in France (just don't use them on picnics; they're a fire hazard in the region's dry and highly flammable landscape and in certain areas are illegal). Many supermarkets have ready-made kebabs for sale and there is always an abundance of sausages and steaks. Combine these with good bread, local cheeses, seasonal fruit and a few ready-prepared delicacies and you have delicious, hassle-free eating for virtually the whole holiday.

If you want to make your holiday a well-fed one, invest in a copy of Elizabeth David's classic book *French Country Cooking* (Penguin 1959) and, for little chefs, Teresa Fisher's *A Flavour of France* (Hodder 1998).

Some recipes for kids

Here are a few ideas for simple things to whisk up in your holiday house or even when you get back home. The recipes are easy enough to let junior cooks have a whirl.

Aïoli

This is a classic Provençal dish and is basically garlic mayonnaise.

Mash 6 cloves of garlic and mix in an egg yolk. Then slowly add 275ml of olive oil, drop by drop at first until it thickens, then switch to a steady stream, beating constantly.

Once half the oil has been added, mix in the juice of half a lemon and 5ml of tepid water.

Then add the rest of the oil, beating all the time. Season with salt and pepper to taste.

In Provence this is served with lots of raw chopped vegetables, cod and snails (although you can leave the creepy-crawlies out if you want). It's a good dish to serve up with a barbecue and goes well with both cooked and cold meats.

Aligot

This cheesy, mashed potato dish used to be served by monks to hungry travellers in the southwest and is a popular starter with kids.

Mix 1kg of boiled, mashed potatoes with a clove of garlic, salt and pepper.

Add 400g of grated Cantal cheese and 200g of crème fraîche.

Mix like crazy and serve with crusty bread.

Pistou

You'll find this all along the Côte d'Azur, and you'll probably be familiar with it as pesto, which is what they call it just over the border in Liguria.

In a blender put two large bunches of basil, a clove of garlic, 250ml of olive oil (plus a bit more if it's too thick), 200g of pine nuts and a handful of freshly grated Parmesan cheese. Liquidize it all and serve it up on hot pasta.

A real ratatouille

The key to making an authentic ratatouille is to cook each of the vegetables separately.

You'll need: 2 sliced aubergines; 6 sliced courgettes; a red, green and yellow pepper, sliced; 3 chopped onions, 6 large tomatoes, finely chopped; 3 crushed garlic cloves; a bunch of parsley, chopped; 10 basil leaves; a few sprigs of thyme; salt, pepper, pinch of sugar and olive oil.

Cook the aubergines in the oil until brown.

Take them out and leave to cool.

Then cook the courgettes and peppers separately until brown, and add each to the aubergines.

Cook the onions until transparent, though not brown, then add the tomatoes, garlic, herbs, salt and pepper and a pinch of sugar.

Cook slowly for 30mins, add the reserved vegetables and cook for five more minutes.

Salade niçoise

In Nice this dish varies according to taste, so leave out the bits you don't like or add extra favourites.

Fill a salad bowl with a crispy lettuce.

Add 6 sliced and de-seeded tomatoes, 8 anchovy filets, 100g of cooked, cold green beans, sliced red and green peppers, olives, 6 hard-boiled eggs in quarters, olive oil and fresh basil leaves.

Brew up your own *tisane*

Herbal teas are popular all over the South of France and are usually drunk after a meal. Sage is good if the mistral has given you a sore throat and verbena will calm down hyperactive kids. If you fancy some peace and quiet, *tilleul* (limeflower/linden) will send them to sleep.

To make your own, put 6 leaves of your chosen herb into a litre of water, adding honey or orange peel to taste. Bring to the boil and leave it to stand before straining it and reheating.

USEFUL PHRASES

Most waiting staff will speak at least a few words of English, but you're likely to find them more accommodating if you try to speak some French.

Ordering

To attract the attention of a waiter or waitress, say *monsieur*, *madame* or *mademoiselle*. It is considered rude to say *garçon*.

I would like... *Je voudrais...*
Please can I have...? *Pourrai j'avoir...?*
What is this...? *Qu'est-ce que c'est?*
Is there a children's menu...? *Est-ce qu'il y a un menu d'enfant?*
Is it suitable for children...? *Est-ce que c'est bon pour les enfants?*
Do you have...? *Avez-vous...?*
Do you speak English...? *Parlez-vous anglais?*
Is it without...?
without salt *sans sel*
gluten-free *sans gluten*
without milk *sans lait*
without wheat *sans blé*
without sugar *sans sucre*
without yeast *sans levure*
without peanuts *sans cacahouètes*

The basics

bib *un bavoir*
bottle *un biberon*
spoon *une cuillère*
fork *une fourchette*
knife *un couteau*
glass *un verre*
bill *l'addition*
beaker *un gobelet*
children's portion *une ration d'enfant*
cup *une tasse*
plate *une assiette*
another *un/une autre*
small *petit/e*
big/large *grand/e*
hot *chaud*
cold *froid*
menu *la carte*
fixed-price menu *le menu*
high chair *une chaise haute*
straw *une paille*
WC *le WC/les toilettes*
men *hommes*
women *femmes*

Miscellaneous

ail garlic
assiette plate, but also a single-course dish, intended to be ordered on its own
baguette long loaf of bread
beurre butter
brochette meat (or fish) grilled on a skewer
confiture jam
crème cream
cru raw
cuit cooked
au four baked
frais/fraîche fresh/cold (drinks)
frit, frite fried
fromage cheese
fromage de chèvre goat's cheese
fumé smoked
garni with vegetables
(***au***) ***gratin*** topped with crisp browned cheese and breadcrumbs
grillé grilled
hachis minced
huile (d'olive) oil (olive)
libre service self-service
moutarde mustard
nouilles noodles
œufs eggs
pain bread
pâte pastry, pasta
poché poached
poivre pepper
quenelles dumplings of fish or poultry
sel salt
sucre sugar
sucré sweet(ened)
tranche slice
(***à la***) ***vapeur*** steamed
vinaigre vinegar

Snacks

choucroute Alsatian sauerkraut with pork, different sausages and potatoes; actually a pretty heavy meal, but a brasserie standard
crêpes thin wheat pancakes, served with savoury or sweet fillings like fruit, chocolate, cream, etc.
croque-monsieur toasted cheese and ham sandwich
croque-madame *croque-monsieur* with a fried egg on top

galettes thickish, buckwheat pancakes, eaten with mushrooms, cheese and other savoury fillings

omelette (*au jambon, fromage, aux champignons*) omelette with ham, cheese, mushrooms or potentially many other fillings, usually served with salad

pissaladière Provençal pizza

quiche savoury tart

raclette toasted cheese with potatoes, onions and pickles

salade composée mixed salad with a variety of ingredients – meats, anchovies, cheeses, fruit. Salad is a very popular option nowadays for light lunches, and many modern French brasserie-style restaurants offer a list of several *salades composées*, nearly always with vegetarian choices among them

socca chickpea pancake

tartine open sandwich on flat, buttered bread, with cold meats, cheeses or other toppings

Starters and soups

aïoli garlic mayonnaise usually served with cod, beans, eggs and snails

anchoïde anchovy paste

bouillabaisse fish soup

bouillon broth

bourride fish soup

consommé clear soup

crudités raw vegetable platter

potage thick vegetable soup

soupe à l'oignon French onion soup

soupe au pistou vegetable soup with pulses, flavoured with basil

velouté very thick, smooth soup

vol-au-vent puff-pastry case with savoury filling

Fish, shellfish, snails and amphibians

anchois anchovies

bar sea bass

brandade de morue mashed cod with olive oil and garlic

cabillaud fresh cod

calmar squid

carrelet plaice

coquilles St-Jacques scallops

crabe crab

crevettes grises shrimp

crevettes roses prawns

cuisses de grenouilles frogs' legs

daurade sea bream

escargots snails

friture mixed platter of deep-fried fish

fruits de mer seafood

homard lobster

huîtres oysters

langouste crayfish

limande lemon sole

lotte monkfish

loup (***de mer***) sea bass

maquereau mackerel

morue cod

moules mussels

oursin sea urchin

poulpe octopus

raie skate

rascasse scorpion fish

rouget red mullet

saumon salmon

sole (***à la meunière***) sole (with butter, lemon and parsley)

thon tuna

truite trout

Meat and poultry

agneau lamb

ailerons chicken wings

andouillette chitterling (tripe) sausage

assiette anglaise a plate of cold meat

biftek beefsteak

blanc breast or white meat

bœuf beef

boudin blanc sausage of white meat

boudin noir black pudding

caille quail

canard duck

cheval horsemeat

dinde, dindon turkey

estouffade braised meat stew

foie liver

foie gras fattened duck or goose liver

fricadelle meatball

jambon ham

jambon cru air-dried, salt-cured ham

lapin rabbit

lard (lardons) ***bacon*** (diced bacon)

merguez spicy North African sausage, usually lamb

navarin (***d'agneau***) (lamb) stew with vegetables

os bone

porc pork

poulet chicken

poussin spring chicken
rillettes potted meats (of duck, pork, rabbit...)
rognons kidneys
saucisses sausages
saucisson sliced, salami-type sausage, eaten cold
tête de veau head of veal
veau veal

Meat cuts and cooking terms

Burgers and steaks are usually served medium-rare (***à point***); if you want them well done ask for them ***bien cuit***. Alternatively you can have them ***saignant*** (rare) or ***bleu*** (very rare).

carré (***d'agneau***) rack (of lamb)
contre-filet, faux-filet sirloin steak
côte, côtelette chop, cutlet
cuisse thigh or leg
entrecôte rib steak
épaule shoulder
gigot leg of lamb
graisse fat
magret, maigret (***de canard***) breast (of duck)
noisette (***d'agneau***) small round cut (of lamb)
pavé thick, square fillet
rôti roast

Salad and vegetables

artichaut artichoke
asperges asparagus
aubergine aubergine
avocat avocado
betterave beetroot
cèpes large, brown wild mushrooms
champignons mushrooms
chou cabbage
chou-fleur cauliflower
chou-frisé kale
choux de Bruxelles Brussels sprouts
citrouille pumpkin
concombre cucumber
cornichons gherkins, pickles
courgettes courgettes
cresson watercress
échalote shallot
endive chicory
épinards spinach
fenouil fennel
frites chips (French fries). Be aware that 'chips' in French means 'crisps'.
haricots (***rouges, blancs***) (kidney, white) beans
haricots verts green beans
laitue lettuce
lentilles lentils
maïs (***épi de***) sweetcorn (on the cob)
mesclun mixed green salad
morilles morel mushrooms
oignons onions
persil parsley
petits pois peas
poireaux leeks
poivron sweet red or green pepper
pomme de terre potato
riz rice
salade verte green salad
tomate tomato
truffes truffles

Desserts and pastries

biscuit biscuit
bonbons sweets
brioche light sweet bread
calisson marzipan sweets from Aix
clafoutis custard tart with fruit
compôte stewed fruit
coupe ice-cream cup
crème anglaise very light custard
crème chantilly sweet whipped cream
crème fleurette double cream
crème fraîche (slightly) sour cream
crème pâtissière custard filling (in cakes, pastries)
feuilleté (***aux pommes***) (apple) turnover
fougassette orange-flavoured brioche
gâteau cake
glace ice-cream
madeleines small sponge cakes
miel honey
navettes orange-blossom-flavoured biscuits from Marseille
œufs à la neige soft meringues in vanilla custard
pain au chocolat chocolate-filled pastry
palmier heart-shaped flaky pastry biscuit
petits fours tiny cakes and pastries, served with coffee
sablé shortbread
tarte, tartelette tart, little tart
tarte tatin caramelized apple tart, served upside down

Fruit and nuts

abricot apricot
ananas pineapple
banane banana
cacahouètes peanuts
cassis blackcurrant

cerise cherry
citron lemon
figues figs
fraises strawberries
fraises des bois wild strawberries
framboises raspberries
marrons chestnuts
mirabelles small yellow plums
mûres mulberry, blackberry
myrtilles bilberries
noisettes hazelnuts
noix walnuts
pamplemousse grapefruit
pêche peach
poire pear
pomme apple
prune plum
raisins (***sec***) grapes (raisins)

Drinks

French restaurants will provide a jug of water from the tap (***un carafe d'eau***) for no extra charge, on request. Tap water is safe to drink unless you see the label ***Eau Non Potable***.

bière (***à pression***) (draught) beer
un demi 25cl glass, the normal size in which draught beer is served in France
bière blonde standard, light lager
bière brune dark, more ale-like beer
(***demi***) ***bouteille*** (half) bottle
café black coffee
café crème white coffee
la carte des vins the wine list
chocolat (***chaud***) (hot) chocolate
citron pressé freshly squeezed lemon juice
eau (***minérale***) (mineral) water
(***gazeuse*** sparkling, ***plate***, ***non-gazeuse*** still)
glaçons ice cubes
infusion (***or tisane***) herbal tea
jus d'orange orange juice
lait milk
limonade lemonade
orange/citron pressé freshly squeezed orange/lemon juice
sirop d'orange/de citron orange/lemon squash
thé tea
verre glass
vin blanc/rouge/rosé white/red/rosé wine

Shop

FOOD 254
Supermarkets 254
Baby days 254

OTHER SHOPS 255
Markets 255
Small shops 255
Specialist shops 256

CHRISTMAS SHOPPING 258

FOOD

Getting your hands on the basics is easy, but shopping in France is a different experience from the one you'll have in Britain or North America and it certainly isn't confined to the supermarket. French towns and cities are full of small shops, most of them family-run and many of them selling regional produce. There's plenty to tempt kids – there isn't a single French town that doesn't have a cake shop full of mouth-watering goodies. Market day is still the centre of town life in France and kids will love strolling around the colourful markets.

Supermarkets

Drive into any French town and before you arrive you'll be assaulted by billboards announcing the location of the nearest big supermarket. The signs to look out for are Intermarché, Carrefour, Auchan, Darty, Leclerc, Géant, Casino and Mammouth. A *hypermarché* is a really big supermarket. In town centres you're likely to find the smaller Petit Casino or a Monoprix.

The bigger the supermarket the more credit cards they are likely to accept. French credit cards have a code pass that is typed into a device that looks very much like a calculator. In the South of France there are so many British tourists that most supermarket assistants recognize foreign cards and can process them without a code. In a remote place, however, don't be surprised if the assistant is confused and gets a supervisor. You can't get a code for your UK card at the moment and if you do encounter difficulties don't worry, there's usually a cash point in or near the supermarket.

Most supermarkets are open from 9–7 but don't be surprised if they shut for lunch, especially in rural areas. They always shut on public holidays, although some are open on Sunday mornings.

Big supermarkets will sell everything from washing machines to tomato ketchup, so you'll be able to buy everything you need, especially if you are camping and have left something crucial at home like a saucepan or sharp knife. You'll be able to get paper plates or portable barbecues for picnics and they're a good place to buy toys, children's clothes and often books and stationery. All French supermarkets sell regional products, which are often cheaper than in the tourist shops.

The supermarkets are at their busiest on Saturdays. Most French people will do a big weekly shop in the supermarket but buy fruit and vegetables in the market and bread at the local bakery. The fresh vegetables and fruit on sale in the market will be of a better quality and so will the bread and cakes from the small bakeries.

Good to know...disposable bottles

If you use disposable bottles – the ones with the pre-sterilized plastic bag inside – you'll need to bring enough bags to keep you going through the holiday. They are very difficult to find in France and most French parents have never seen them.

The instructions are only printed in French on the boxes because they've been produced for the Canadian market.

Baby days

Milk

French supermarkets sell everything you could need for babies and small children from ready-to-drink formula milk to great value clothes, so travel light. You'll find a lot of new products that aren't on sale in the UK and USA. In fact in really big supermarkets the choice can be quite baffling, even if you do speak French.

There are three different types of formula milk:

Première age (often written *1ère age*), which is suitable for babies from birth to either 4 or 6 months depending on the brand. You'll see this clearly indicated on the front of the packet or tin – the word for month is *mois*.

Deuxième age (often written *2ème age*), which is suitable for babies from 4–10 or 12 months.

Troisième age (often written *3ème age*), which is for older babies up to 3 years old. It's sometimes also called *lait de croissance*.

Most infant formula is available in ready-to-feed cartons and sometimes in sterilized bottles – all you have to do is screw on a teat. If you need soya or rice milk or other special products either bring them with you or ask in the chemist (it might be an idea to bring an empty packet from home to illustrate what you need). If you are buying milk for older children look for *lait frais pasteurisé*. You'll find it in supermarkets but long-life milk is more common, so do shop around.

Baby food

The gourmet experience in France starts early and the baby food is far more luxurious than anything you'll see in the UK. There are purées of artichokes and chestnuts and masses of rich

Did you know...?
In most French towns you'll find a horse butcher's (boucherie chevaline). Eating horsemeat really took off in the lean times after the French Revolution and French doctors often advise children to eat it to make their hearts healthier. You won't find horsemeat for sale in restaurants – it's usually only eaten at home.

chocolate puddings. The jars are clearly labelled with the age they are suitable for, but if you see food described as *croissance* it's for older babies, usually those over 10 months.

The food gets even better when you hit this stage. The Blédichef range includes *Fondue de pommes de terre aux champignons* and *Panaché de legumes à la Bretonne* – you'll have trouble weaning them back onto macaroni cheese after a few of these. A lot of dishes are suitable for the microwave, which is especially useful if you are driving long distances, as all motorway service stations in France have microwaves you can use.

In France a lot of first feeds such as soups and milky cereals are given to babies in bottles (*un biberon*) rather than from a spoon (but see box). A special teat is often used for these feeds – it's called a soup teat (*une tétine soupe*) and it has a large opening. You need to be careful when you're buying teats (*les tétines*) not to grab a soup teat by mistake, as it will cause the baby to choke if it is used with milk, which will gush out at high speed.

On the supermarket shelf you'll see ready-mixed soups and cereals. They are fantastic when travelling, as they are ideal meals on the go and cut down dramatically on the mess. The Blédina range is tasty and is ready mixed and puréed; *blédidej* is a cereal-based milk with honey, chocolate or vanilla and is meant for use at breakfast; *blédigouter* is a snack, which is milk with fruits, and *blédîner* is a complete meal with milk and vegetables.

Note on babies' feeds

Please note that in the UK putting feeds in babies' bottles is not recommended under any circumstances. Lumps in feeds can cause digestive problems, and purées or soups in bottles can cause choking, so if you are in any doubt about how to feed your baby abroad, please ask your health visitor or doctor for advice.

OTHER SHOPS

French shops are fantastic; you'll find everything you need and more. All you need is the money and the inclination to shop, shop, shop! Many town centres in France are pedestrianized, which takes a lot of the hassle out of shopping with small children.

On the high street, although you will recognize some of the stores, there are plenty of French chains where you can pick up stylish clothes at affordable prices. There are thousands of souvenir shops, too, and it's easy to find something fun and original to bring home.

Markets

The South of France, and Provence in particular, has some of the best markets in Europe, which are open year round. All the markets are excellent but perhaps the best of all are in Aix-en-Provence and along the Cours Saleya in Nice. Avignon, too, has a lovely covered market. Some local markets are daily and others happen just once a week; they're listed under the towns in the main part of the book.

Markets are the best place to find local souvenirs. Teenagers will like the clothes stalls, which, especially in Aix-en-Provence, sell some very stylish gear, and for the younger ones there's always a toy stall where you can pick up bags of plastic animals or toy cars for a few euros. Sometimes you'll find a flea market – *marché aux puces* – attached to the main market. These are fun places to pick up interesting souvenirs and one-off gifts that are a bit more personal than the ubiquitous bag of lavender. The market is often the place to buy local specialities, whether linens and tablecloths, cakes and sweets, or even just fruits and vegetables – for example, Cavaillon is famous for its melons and Carpentras for its tomatoes. You'll see plenty of unusual products for sale in the market, too. In spring look out for huge yellow courgette flowers, which taste great fried in batter and in winter, especially in Carpentras, you'll see lots of truffles.

When shopping in the market take your own shopping bag and plenty of change. Keep an eye on small children – it's easy to lose them in a crowd – and be aware of pickpockets.

Small shops

Although it's easier to pick up everything at the supermarket, you'll miss out on a real French experience if you don't make an effort to shop in small shops. Nearly all French towns and villages will have a bread shop (*boulangerie*), a cake shop (*pâtisserie*) and a greengrocer (*marchand de fruits et de légumes*). French bakers bake several times a day (and that goes for Sundays as well). Much of the bread doesn't keep – you'll need to buy it fresh – although some of the more solid *pain de campagne* will last slightly longer. If you want bread for toasting you'll need to go to the supermarket – it's called *pain de mie* or American toasting. In almost every town you'll find that bakers and cake shops have their own delicious speciality breads.

Food in France is far more regionally based than in the UK or USA. In some towns you'll find local products on sale that you can't buy anywhere else. In Pézenas, for example, they make little cylindrical pies filled with sweetened lamb called *petites pâtes* (*see* p.246) that you won't see on sale even in other villages nearby.

Every reasonably sized town will have an array of small specialist shops. For raw meat you'll need to go to a *boucherie* but for cold cuts you'll need to go to a *charcuterie*. Smaller shops tend to close on Sunday and Monday and always close for lunch. In summer you'll need to shop early if you want to find the best cuts of meat and the best vegetables.

The *charcuterie* will sell some *pâtés* as well as cooked meats but for other pre-cooked foods you'll need a *traiteur*, which is a delicatessen. For dry goods you'll need an *épicierie*. A cheesemonger, a *fromagerie*, may well also be a *laiterie*, which is a shop that sells dairy products.

Specialist shops

Books and videos

Books and videos are more expensive in France than in Britain. Foreign-language books for children are difficult to find and again very expensive, so bring as much holiday reading with you as you can carry.

A bookshop is a *librairie*, but one of the best places to buy books is the huge FNAC chain, which sells some English books, as well as CDs, computer games and videos. There are branches in Monaco, Nice, Cannes, Avignon, Marseille and Montpellier.

For children's books in French look out for the discount chain Maxi Livres.

French books for the under-8s are marvellous but novels for pre-teens tend to be translations of English books – Dick King Smith and Roald Dahl are big favourites. Older kids read a lot of classics. There are some very funny cartoon books for this age group, so spend time to hunt around.

Beware that if you buy videos in France they'll play in black and white on a PAL TV as the French use the SECAM TV system. DVDs don't have the same problem, as we are all region 2, Europe.

Chemists

Every town has a chemist (*une pharmacie*) and if you've got a minor ailment they'll be able to help (*see* also **Minor ailments** p.269).

Note, though, that if your child has a cough they may well advise the use of a suppository rather than cough mixture; if either you or your child finds this off-putting explain that you'd rather have an oral medicine and they should be able to oblige.

Department stores

The two big chains are Galeries Lafayette and Monoprix. The larger branches of Monoprix usually have a supermarket and are a good place to buy toys and children's clothes.

Fashion

Fashion is a serious business and in most big towns you'll find designer label shops for babies as well adults. But French fashion doesn't have to cost a fortune. You can find some really stylish and different children's clothes, shoes and accessories at great prices.

Catalogue shops are big in France. Two companies that sell excellent children's clothes and maternity wear are La Redoute (who also do mail order in the UK) and 3 Suisses. When you go into the shop you make a selection from the catalogue and then order and pay for the goods; if they don't fit or you don't like them you can return them.

A lot of the clothing selected in girls' magazines comes from 3 Suisses. There's no school uniform in France, so a lot of girls' fashion is classic and practical, since it will be worn in the classroom and not just at weekends.

The chain Du Pareil au Même is a big favourite with French families and sells some very stylish gear at low prices. You can order online at **www**.dpam.com. Another shop with stylish, affordable kids' clothes is Orchestra, **www**.orchestra.fr; these shops usually have a toilet and play area and there are branches of both in most big towns.

Teenage girls can't wait to go to Pimkie, **www**.pimkie.com, which is a French version of Miss Selfridge and sells unusual, good-quality clothes at affordable prices. Less exciting but a useful substitute is Jennyfer.

If you can afford it, the clothes at Agnès B are cut small enough for teenage girls to wear and they have a beautiful range of unusual baby clothes.

Souvenirs

Children love buying something to take home after the holiday and there are plenty of affordable trinkets on sale in the South of France. Most attractions don't have enormous gift shops attached – the Palais des Papes in Avignon and the castle in Carcassonne are exceptions, but even in these you'll find some pocket-money items.

Chocolates and sweets are great to bring home as gifts, and the best places to buy them are listed in the book. A lot of these products aren't exported so you won't see them outside France. You can also visit many of the factories and watch the sweets being made; if you're in the Gorges du Loup, don't miss Confiserie Florian at Tourrettes-sur-Loup (**www**.confiserieflorian.com). They have an on-line shopping service too.

Nougat is another regional speciality, traditionally served on Christmas Eve and there are a lot of sweets made out of almonds and chestnuts, especially in Corsica and near St-Tropez. Look out for the chain La Cure Gourmande; there are branches in most of the big towns selling exceptionally good chocolates. They also have a mail-order service on line **www**.la-cure-gourmande.com.

You'll see bags of lavender and herbs everywhere, which may be a bit overwhelming when you see hundreds a day, but these are lovely gifts to bring home that don't cost a fortune and won't break. Soap made from olive oil and lavender is another traditional product and most towns have a small soap shop that sells locally made products.

The best place to buy souvenirs is in the market or at regional festivals, like the chestnut festival in Collobrières near St-Tropez. There's always something happening in one of the villages or towns, so it's worth asking in the local tourist office for a list of local festivals.

Sports and camping goods

Most of the big resorts have shops that sell the relevant sporting equipment and camping goods. If you are travelling out of season, you'll need to go to the main towns. The tourist office will be able to advise you where to go.

Stamps

In addition to the post office you can buy stamps in a *tabac*. For newspapers and magazines go to a *maison de presse*. There is a great selection of French children's magazines, many of which are very educational and a good investment if your children are learning French at school.

Look out for the girls' magazines, particularly. They are very different from the teen magazines in the UK and are far more practical, running features on politics and literature alongside the articles on pop stars and fashion.

Toys

In some places in the South you can find traditional wooden toys for sale but on the whole the toys are much the same as in the UK or USA. You will find games based on local cartoon favourites like Asterix and Obelix, and the French version of Risk, the game of world conquest, has a picture of Napoleon on the front, but otherwise you'll be familiar with many of the games.

Most towns will have a toyshop. The chain JouéClub is especially good, otherwise Monoprix always sells toys and most big supermarkets stock basic supplies.

If you have kids who are interested in the natural world, look for the chain Nature et Découvertes, which sells a lot of interesting games and project books – there's a branch in Marseille.

When it comes to toys, one cultural difference that you'll notice is that French games tend to be quite educational and a lot of emphasis is put on sound recognition when little ones are taught to read and write.

Wine

Forget the kids for a minute and treat yourself to a few bottles to bring home. You can buy good value wine everywhere in France. Local wines will be on special promotion in the supermarket but while you're in the south it's really worth taking the time to visit a vineyard. There are hundreds to choose from and there's always one close at hand. The tourist office will have a list of local vineyards, otherwise just look out for the signs: '*vente au public*' means you can go in and buy a bottle.

CHRISTMAS SHOPPING

Christmas may be the last thing on your mind when the temperature is over 30°C but some of the best souvenirs to bring home from the South of France are associated with Christmas.

All over Provence you'll see *santons*, (little saints), diminutive clay figures dressed in 19th-century peasant costume. They may seem a little twee but they have a long historical pedigree. Since the Middle Ages it was traditional for the local church to have a nativity scene at Christmas. When the churches were closed during the French Revolution the tradition was missed, so people started to make their own *crèches* (nativity scenes or cribs) at home and the first *santons* were sold in Marseille in 1803. What makes a Provençal crib different to any other is that the scenes are very elaborate and feature, in addition to the usual nativity figures, a collection of local characters – bakers, farmers and fishermen, even local celebrities like Vincent Van Gogh. Although originally made out of wood, today they are all made out of clay, so be careful not to drop them. You'll see *santons* for sale all over southern France. Look out for the old-fashioned *santon* shops where they make their own models; Aix-en-Provence, Aubagne, Les Baux en Provence and Marseille have particularly well-known shops. Some shops also sell small bits and pieces to accompany the dolls, like tiny rolling pins, baskets, plates, etc; it's worth keeping an eye out for these, as they make great additions to a dolls' house.

Every December there are special Christmas fairs right across the region. The best *santon* fairs are in Aix, Arles, Aubagne and Marseille in December. They're also the place to buy the ingredients for the traditional Christmas Eve meal (*see* p.244).

Did you know...?

Provence has more Christmas traditions than any other part of France. Christmas starts on 4 December – Sainte Barbe's Day – when bowls of wheat and lentils are dampened and put by the fire to sprout green shoots. This will be the grass for the Christmas crib or crèche. How well the sprouts grow is supposed to tell you how prosperous you'll be for the next year.

Travel and Practicalities

TRAVEL 260

PRACTICAL A–Z 266
Babysitters 266
Consulates and embassies 266
Electricity 267
Insurance 267
Internet 267
Laundry 268
Lost property 268
Manners 268
Maps 268
Medical emergencies 268
Money and banks 269
Mosquitoes 270
National and school holidays 270
Opening hours 270
Post offices 270
Racism 270
Safety 271
Smoking 272
Special needs 272
Telephones 272
Tickets 272
Time 273
Tipping 273
Toilets 273
Tourist offices 273

FAMILY FRIENDLY PHRASE BOOK 274

11

GETTING THERE

Getting to the South of France is easy. Intense competition on transatlantic routes and the increase in low-cost airlines flying out of the UK to southern France means the journey doesn't have to break the bank. French motorways are excellent, and the new high-speed rail link from Paris means the Riviera is only hours from the capital and less than a day's journey from London.

By air

Flight times from London are around 2½hrs. Children under the age of two usually travel for just ten per cent of the adult fare, although they will not be entitled to either a seat or baggage allowance; between the ages of three and eleven children cost between a half and two-thirds of the adult fare, but on low-cost airlines they are usually charged the adult fare. Children over 12 are regarded as adults on all airlines and must pay the full fare. The major international airports are:

Nice

t 00 33 (0)4 93 21 30 30, **www**.nice.aeroport.fr

There's a regular bus service to the town centre (7km away) and to resorts along the coast. Don't use the train link as the airport station is a 10min walk from the terminal. A taxi costs about €25.

There are helicopter connections to Monaco, **t** 00 337 92 05 00 50; Cannes, **t** 00 33 (0)4 93 21 34 32; and St-Tropez, **t** 00 33 (0)4 93 21 45 87.

Good to know...
Flying with babies and toddlers

Sucking on a bottle or dummy (a soother) will help ease earache on take-off and landing. Boots and other high street chemists stock 'earplanes', small plastic devices that fit in the ear and are quite effective if you or your child suffers from air pressure problems. Take a car seat so the baby doesn't have to sit on your lap all through the flight and insist that you take your buggy right up to the door of the aeroplane; it's more convenient and it's less likely to get damaged. Some airlines will let you take buggies inside.

Cheap flights on-line

www.cheapflights.com
www.cheaptickets.com
www.farebase.net
www.lastminute.com
www.moments-notice.com
www.thetrip.com
www.travelocity.com

During the summer Air France runs a shuttle boat service fromNice airport to Cannes and St-Tropez, **t** (in France) 0820 820 820

Marseille

t 00 33 (0)4 42 14 14 14, www.marseille.aeroport.fr

There are regular bus connections to the city centre (22km); taxis cost around €35.

Montpellier

t 00 33 (0)4 67 20 85 00, www.montpellier.aeroport.fr (7km from the city centre)

There's a shuttle bus to the city centre (7km); taxis cost around €15.

Toulouse

t 00 33 (0)5 61 42 44 00, www.toulouse.aeroport.fr

There's a shuttle bus service into town (10km); taxis cost around €22.

From the UK

Air France t 0845 0845 111
www.airfrance.com/uk

Daily direct flights from Heathrow to Toulouse and Nice.

British Airways t 0845 77 333 77
www.britishairways.co.uk

Direct flights to Marseille, Montpellier and Toulouse from London Gatwick and to Nice from Heathrow.

BMI – British Midland t 0870 607 0555
www.flybmi.com

Flights to and from Heathrow to Nice and Manchester to Toulouse. This airline offers excellent value and services are reliable.

BMI Baby t 0870 264 2229
www.bmibaby.com

Flights to Nice and Toulouse from the East Midlands and Cardiff.

Easyjet t 0870 600 0000
www.easyjet.com

From Gatwick, Luton and Liverpool to Nice.

***Good to know...*cheap airlines**

A lot of the deals that appear such good value may come at a price. The price you see advertised depends on availability and when you can fly, and might not be the actual fare you'll be quoted. Food and drink on the plane are not included in the ticket price and are phenomenally expensive, and if your flight is cancelled or delayed the airlines give you only minimal assistance or compensation at best.

If you are flying in and out of London Stansted be warned – it's a long way from the city centre. Late-night trains are often cancelled and buses take 1hr 30mins. A taxi to the city centre costs £80 and without a reservation or a paper licence it can be impossible to rent a car. The best option with a family is to drive to the airport and leave your car in the long-stay car park known as 'the Pink Elephant'. There's a free shuttle bus to the terminal that runs 24hrs and takes 15mins. Parking costs £6.50 for the first day and £6.20 for every subsequent day. For reservations call **t** 0800 844 844.

Ryanair t UK 0870 873 0000
www.ryanair.com

Flights to from London Stansted to Montpellier, Nîmes, Carcassonne and Perpignan.

From North America

Delta Airlines toll free, **t** (800) 241 4141
www.delta.com

There are direct flights to Nice from New York JFK, otherwise you'll have to change planes in the UK or in Paris. Many of the larger airlines provide special on-board services for families, such as designated flight attendants, children's TV channels, play packs and seat-back computer games. There's a huge choice of connecting flights to airports across the region.

Other major North American airlines

Air Canada toll free, **t** 888 5247 2262
www.aircanada.com
American Airlines toll free, **t** 800 433 7300
www.americanair.com
British Airways toll free, **t** 800 247 92 97
www.britishairways.com
Continental Airlines toll free, **t** 800 231 0856
www.flycontinental.com
United Airlines toll free, **t** 800 538 2929
www.ual.com
Virgin Atlantic Airways toll free, **t** 800 862 8621
www.virgin-atlantic.com

Consolidators in North America

Air Brokers Travel toll free **t** 800 883 3273
www.airbrokers.com
TFI Tours International toll free **t** 800 745 8000
Travac Tours and Charters toll free **t** 800 872 8800
www.travac.com
Unitravel toll free **t** 800 325 2222

Please note: 'Toll free' numbers are only toll free if called from within the USA or Canada.

From Australia and New Zealand

Air New Zealand Australia, **t** (13) 2476,
New Zealand **t** (09) 357 3000
British Airways Australia **t** (02) 9258 3300,
New Zealand **t** (09) 356 8690
Cathay Pacific Australia **t** (13) 1747
New Zealand **t** (09) 379 0861
Qantas Australia **t** (13) 1211,
New Zealand **t** (09) 357 8900

By car

Taking the car is a good option with a family; it gives you the freedom to pace your journey to suit you and it makes it easier to travel around when you get there (large parts of the South of France are only accessible by car). You can also cram whatever essentials you need into the boot or roof box, so if your companions insist on taking five teddies, endless Barbies and a whole CD collection, a car may be the only answer to your luggage problems.

Taking a car by ferry

Ferries are much faster than they used to be and the crossing can be as quick as 45mins. Ring around for the prices as it's a competitive business and there are good deals to be had, especially out of the main holiday season. Many lines also offer perks for families – under-4s usually travel free and there are discounts for under-14s. The bigger boats have some good family facilities – restaurants, baby-changing rooms, play areas and video rooms.

The ferry is a good option if you are driving alone with kids as it gives you a chance to take a proper break from the driving, eat something and unwind a bit. If you opt for the Channel Tunnel there are no facilities and you need to stay with your car. Remember that in the winter the crossing can be very rough.

Dover–Calais

P&O Stena Line t UK 0870 600 0600
www.posl.com

35 sailings a day in high season, crossing takes 1hr 15mins.

Sea France t UK 08705 711 711
www.seafrance.co.uk

This French-owned company has some of the most competitive rates and has both the largest and fastest boats. The *Rodin*, a large boat that deals well with rough seas, takes 70mins to cross the Channel. There are microwaves in the restaurant to heat baby food and bottles.

Hoverspeed t UK 0870 240 8070
www.hoverspeed.com

The Super Seacat usually crosses from Dover to Calais in 45mins (but is more affected than the larger ferries by bad weather). Boats also run from Newhaven to Dieppe. Facilities on board are poor and the food can run out when the boat is busy.

Other ferry routes

Transmanche Ferries t UK 0800 817 1201
www.transmancheferries.com

Crossings from Portsmouth to Caen and Poole to Cherbourg.

Brittany Ferries t UK 08705 360 360
www.brittany-ferries.com

Crossings from Portsmouth to Le Havre and Portsmouth to Cherbourg

P&O European Ferries t 0870 242 4999
www.poportsmouth.com

P&O also has a night ferry from Hull to Zeebrugge in Belgium, which is just 45mins from the French border.

Taking a car through the Channel Tunnel

Eurotunnel (Folkestone–Calais) **t** 08705 35 35 35
www.eurotunnel.com

This is the fastest route across the Channel, with up to four departures an hour. You can just turn up and go but you will have to wait for a space. In high season and for morning crossings it's advisable to book. Journey time is 35mins. Check in at least 25mins but no more than 2hrs before departure. There are toilets on board but no food, so pack snacks and drinks.

***Good to know...*Tunnel tips**

At the Channel Tunnel British terminal – off junction 11a of the M20 – you can buy emergency supplies of baby basics and sandwiches. At the French terminal – off junction 13 of the A16 – there are limited shopping facilities but you can buy fresh milk at McDonald's. If you need baby supplies, you'll need to budget enough time to pop into the enormous shopping centre, Cité d'Europe, next to the terminal. The nearest motorway service stations are about 20mins from Folkestone and 45mins from Calais.

Driving south

The golden rule to remember about driving in France is that the country is always bigger than you think it is. You'll also find that if you're renting a villa or apartment the owners or agency may underestimate the time it takes to drive there; it takes two days to drive from London to Marseille, for example:

Calais–Nice 1,167km
Calais–Marseille 1,059km
Calais–Avignon 965km
Calais–Carcassonne 1,079km

With children you need to allow at least one night's stop en route – three if you want to take it slowly and take in the sights. Motorway tolls from Calais to Marseille will cost around £50 each way and can be paid with a credit card.

From Calais, if you're heading for western Languedoc or Roussillon, you need to follow the signs for Paris and then take the A10/A20 south to Toulouse. The motorway takes you right into the suburbs of Paris so plan tto avoid the rush hour. For a route planner see **www**.iti.fr and for information on motorways see **www**.autoroutes.fr.

If you're heading for eastern Languedoc, Provence or the Riviera, drive south along the A26 from Calais. Follow the signs for Reims, Troyes, Lyon and Avignon. This is the old Roman route south. Even if you're heading for eastern Provence and the Côte d'Azur stick to this route, especially if the weather is bad, as the alternative route through Grenoble takes you over the Alps and will add to the overall driving time considerably. Check the weather on **www**.meteo.fr.

Be aware that if you are caught in snow you are legally required to use chains on certain routes and generally it is illegal for hire cars to be supplied without them.

South of Reims you'll drive through some of France's emptiest countryside, which means finding a hotel can be very tricky. Troyes is a good place to break the journey and in busy periods you'll need to book a hotel. The Novotel near the airport is a good option, **t** 00 33 (0)3 25 71 74 74; follow signs for the Barberey shopping centre. South of Dijon there are motorway services with hotels.

Once you get down south, the motorway runs east to west along the entire southern coast. You'll need to watch that you take the right branch of the road at Orange as the motorway splits: for Nîmes and Montpellier you'll need to take the road heading west, for Avignon and Provence take the road east.

If you take a car to France it is advisable to organize **breakdown cover** via the AA or RAC, your home insurance company or specialist services such as:

Europ Assistance, t 01 44 44 22 11
www.europ-assistance.co.uk

Any car entering France must have its **registration and insurance papers** with it plus a hazard-warning triangle, which must be displayed 50m behind the vehicle in the event of an accident or breakdown. If you're coming from the UK or Ireland, remember to use headlamp adjusters for driving on the right. Seatbelts must be worn in the front seats of cars and in the back where fitted.

Drivers who hold a valid **licence** from an EU country, North America or Australia do not need an international licence in France. The minimum age to drive in France is 18 and no one is allowed to drive on a provisional licence. Under-10s may not travel in the front of the car unless they are in special seat-facing baby seats.

The **speed limit** in built-up areas is 50kph (around 30mph); on country roads 90kph (55mph) but 80kph when wet; and on motorways (autoroutes) 130kph (80mph), but 110kph (70mph) when wet. At intersections without signals, the car approaching to your right has the right of way.

*Good to know...*Pit stops

If you're planning a touring holiday with the kids you'll need to schedule in lots of breaks. Service stations are extremely good in France. Most of them have children's menus, microwaves to heat up baby food, and children's play areas, both inside and out. Many have books and comics you can read in the restaurant. If you want to cut costs, garages on the motorway usually sell bread and basics for sandwiches. In the summer many service stations lay on special family entertainments (look up details online at www.autoroutes.fr and www.saprr.fr) and an increasing number of service stations have small museums attached. Service stations marked '*Etapes Sportives*' organize sports activities during the main holiday season, from archery to mini-golf.

If you just want to stop for a quick break or the toilet, stop in an *aire*, which is a large lay-by, many of which have children's playgrounds. If you are travelling with a baby, look out for stations marked '*Relais Bébé*'; they're special baby service stations where you can feed and change the baby.

By car on the night train

You can cut the drive time by putting your car on the train in Calais or Paris, although unfortunately the car wagons can't take people-carriers. The service from Calais runs in the summer only to Avignon, Narbonne, Nice and Toulouse, and the Paris route runs all year. It's cheaper because your car travels separately overnight while you take a day train.

French Motorail UK **t** 08702 415 415
USA **t** 08705 848 84.

By rail

Rail Europe is the UK subsidiary of the French rail company SNCF and can deal effectively and efficiently with all questions on rail travel to France.

Rail Europe UK t 08705 848 848
www.raileurope.co.uk
Rail Europe USA t 800 438 7245
www.raileurope.com

SNCF have a baggage service and will collect and deliver bags if you book in advance.

SNCF t 00 33 (0)8 03 84 58 45.

From the UK Eurostar trains run from London Waterloo or Ashford in Kent to Lille-Europe and Paris Gare du Nord. Trains for the South of France leave from Lille-Europe or Gare de Lyon in Paris. With children the best option is to change at Lille to connect with trains travelling south, as you only need to change platforms, whereas in Paris you need to change stations.

In the summer the Eurostar runs a service direct to Avignon from Waterloo, **t** 08705 186 186, **www**.eurostar.com.

Train **tickets** are usually cheaper if you stay a Saturday night. Tickets vary depending on the age of the child; there are youth and child fares and under-4s travel free. It may be worth investing in a rail pass if you're planning to use the railways to travel around. A France Railpass is valid for 3 or 7 days, and you don't have to travel on consecutive days, just so many days in a set period of time. The pass gives a discount on Eurostar and some branch lines. Rail Europe also organizes holiday package deals through the French Travel Service: **t** 08702 41 42 43, **www**.frenchtravelservice.co.uk.

If you have small children the Eurostar staff may put you in a carriage with other families. Food is expensive on the Eurostar, and supplies, especially of chips, tend to run out before you hit the tunnel, so it may be better to pack sandwiches. Wheelchair-users need to inform Rail Europe staff of their requirements when booking.

The French are famous for their high-speed TGV trains and the number of routes they cover keeps on growing. The service is now so speedy there is no need to travel at night on a sleeper and a lot of the new TGV trains are double-deckers.

Most high-speed trains have baby-changing rooms, bottle-warmers and special family compartments in their second-class carriages where you can make as much noise as you want without disturbing the other passengers. Always travel with a drink and snack as not all French trains, even TGVs, have a buffet.

Most big stations have lifts and it isn't usually difficult to find someone to help you to get on and off the train.

In France, if you avoid travelling on the weekend, you'll find most of the trains are deserted – and if you have 30 window seats in each carriage you're unlikely to have a punch up over who gets a seat with a view. It's also possible to hire DVDs on some lines, including the latest Gallic releases.

By bus

Eurolines 52 Grosvenor Gardens, London SW1
t UK 08705 143 219
www.gobycoach.com

It's a long trip from London: Aix and Marseille (21hrs) Avignon (18hrs) and Toulouse (22hrs). It's no longer the cheapest way to get there and it certainly isn't the easiest option with kids, either. There are, however, connections to 1,200 UK cities via National Express.

BORDER FORMALITIES

Visitors from the European Union and North America can enter France for up to 90 days with just a passport or national identity card. If you plan to stay longer, you'll have to apply for a *carte de séjour*. Other nationals should check their particular entry requirements with their embassies.

VAT refund scheme

If you are from a non-EU country and have spent more than €180 in any one shop, you can claim a refund on any VAT (value added tax, currently at 20.6 percent) paid when you leave the country – as long as you don't stay longer than 90 days. Pick up a *détaxe* form at the shop, fill in the details, get the form stamped by customs when you leave France and then send it back to the shop, which will refund the money to your bank or credit card.

GETTING AROUND

By air

The train and road connections are so good in the South of France that flights between the main towns just aren't necessary. Air Littoral and Air Liberté fly to Corsica from Marseille. Be prepared, though: the flight to Corsica can be very bumpy if the mistral wind decides to blow. In Corsica the best way to get around is by car.

By car

Large parts of the South of France are inaccessible without a car and if you want to travel around the countryside you'll either need to bring your own or hire one. There's an excellent road network, but traffic jams can be a problem, especially along the Riviera in summer. If you're touring, it's best to opt for a hotel with a car park, even if it means staying on the edge of town. Theft is a problem in many parts of the South of France and thieves tend to target rented cars in particular.

Car rental rates are some of the highest in Europe, so if you want to tour around it's worth investigating fly-drive or holiday packages. Local firms offer the best rates. Most car rental companies can also supply children's safety seats for a nominal cost but it's better to reserve them when you book the car.

Petrol stations close early outside the main resorts; after 8pm it can be impossible to find one open so don't head off the main road without a full tank. You'll find the cheapest petrol stations are attached to the supermarkets.

Car rental agents in the South of France

Avis USA toll free, **t** 1 800 230 4898, UK **t** 0870 606 0100, France, **t** 0820 05 05 05
www.avis.com, **www**.avis.co.uk

Europcar USA, **t** 1 877 940 6900, UK **t** 0870 607 5000, France t 00 33 (0)8 25 552 352
www.europcar.com, **www**.europcar.co.uk

Hertz USA **t** 800 654 3001, UK **t** 0990 99 66 99, France **t** 00 33 (0)1 39 38 38 38
www.hertz.com, **www**.hertz.co.uk

By ferry

You can catch boats from the main resorts along the coast to visit other towns and the islands. These are for tourist day trips only. The ferry however is a good way of getting to Corsica.

Boats sail for Corsica from Marseille, Nice and Toulon to Ajaccio, Bastia, Calvi, Ile Rousse, Propriano and Porto-Vecchio. The main companies are:

Southern Ferries SNCM Ferryterranée, France **t** 08 36 67 95 00; UK **t** (020) 7491 4968, **f** 7491 3502
www.sncm.fr

Corsica Ferries, France **t** 08 03 095 095/**t** 04 92 00 42 93, **f** 04 92 00 42 94
www.corsicaferries.com

In the UK contact **Via Mare**, Graphic House, 2 Sumatra Rd, London NW6 1PU, **t** (020) 7431 5456,
www.viamare.com

Crossing times have speeded up dramatically over the last few years and high-speed ferries (NGV, *Navires à Grande Vitesse*) from Nice to Calvi take just 2hrs 45mins, but don't run in bad weather. Winds in this part of the world can be strong, even in summer, so bear this in mind when making travel arrangements. The traditional ferries take about 10hrs and are more reliable. Many of the ferries have pools that will help to while away the time and the new luxury ferry, the Napoleon Bonaparte, even has Internet access. Ferry prices for foot passengers are very competitive, so don't just consider the ferry as an option for drivers.

If you're on the Côte d'Azur it's worth considering driving to Savona in Italy, about 1½hrs drive from Nice. Corsica Ferries operates a service from there, and ferries take just 2hrs. If the weather is bad the traditional ferry takes 6hrs. The crossings to Italy are generally cheaper because it's so much closer than the French coast. Ferries run also run from Genoa, La Spezia and Livorno.

By train

Reservations/information, **t** 00 33 (0)8 36 35 35 35, in English **t** 08 36 35 35 39
www.scnf.fr

Most hotels will help you find out train times.

The French are justifiably proud of their trains and if you don't have a car, the train is the best way to get around. Don't assume the train will restrict you to a city-based holiday, either; the French railway system is extensive and can take you to most of the top sites, if you're happy to catch the

***Good to know...* Thomas Rules!**

Thomas the Tank Engine mania has spread to France. In most French supermarkets you can find the latest news from the Ile de Sodor and catch up on the adventures of Euro-Thomas's pals Pierre, Thierry and M. Gédéon Gibus – also known as Percy, Trevor and, of course, the Fat Controller.

occasional bus too. Although whizzing along the rails at 300km an hour is a national passion, there are plenty of small branch lines. The Train des Pignes (Pinecone Railway, *see* p.104) runs from Digne-les-Bains in the north of Provence across the top of the Gorges du Verdon on the way to Nice. Corsica's Bastia–Ajaccio line (*see* p.203) is a train enthusiast's dream.

The train is an excellent option for travelling with kids, especially if you're on your own. Travelling alone with children you can end up tour organizer, entertainments manager, psychiatrist and arbitrator, and if you don't have to worry about driving then at least you can try to do these jobs properly. If you're lucky you might even grab a quick nap.

There's something very relaxing about sticking to the timetable and if you haven't got a car you can't waste hours searching for that perfect B&B. Next to most main train stations you'll find an Ibis hotel – they charge a bargain flat rate for a room, so you can sleep peacefully without sweating over the bill. Many lines pass through some of the most beautiful countryside, so while the train spotters in the family coo at the signals you can enjoy the view. The train from Monaco to Cannes is one of the best ways to see the Riviera and get a close up view of those glitzy villas, and Monaco station has to be the cleanest on the planet. The line runs eastwards from Marseille, though St-Tropez is not accessible.

Always have water and something to eat with you when you make a long-distance train journey. The vending machines are almost always empty and sometimes the restaurant car fails to open.

There are a number of **discounts** available to rail travellers. Ask at the station for information on discounts for frequent travellers, youth passes and children. The schemes to ask about are: **Carte 12–25** and **Carte Découvert 12–25**, **Carte Enfant+** and **Découvert Enfant+**. Don't assume though that these schemes will automatically save you money if you are on holiday. You have to pay money upfront to receive a discount card and there are restrictions on when you can travel.

By bus

It is possible to use the bus to get around along the Riviera, but generally bus travel is arduous and unreliable and isn't a great option with children.

PRACTICAL A–Z

What's the betting the moment you arrive on holiday you discover one of the kids has head lice and the baby's bottle has gone missing? You can take the stress out of travelling with kids by staying calm and knowing what's what.

The language can seem like a barrier, but most people will be willing to help you out and you'll be able deal with any problems that are likely to crop up. Don't panic – this section is here to help.

Babysitters

Lets face it, sometimes all you need is a bit of peace. If you know you'll need a babysitter before you leave home, choose a hotel with a babysitting service or a rental company that can supply a nanny. In the south of France this will mean basing yourself in one of the big cities or resorts in an expensive hotel or villa; *see* pp.209–40 for recommendations and family-friendly tour operators with baby listening services.

Outside the main towns finding a babysitter is tricky. The local tourist office may have a list of babysitters, but don't assume that they are trained or that they speak sufficient English to care for your child. On the positive side, most French families go out in the evening all together when they're on holiday, no matter how young, so your children will be in good company (*see* **Eat**, pp.241–52).

If you're invited out to someone's home, even if you are combining business with pleasure, most French people will expect you to bring the children and are likely to serve up a microwave pizza alongside the *foie gras*.

If you want a romantic meal, one option is to choose a small hotel with a good restaurant and pack a baby listener.

Babysitting agencies

Allô Mary Poppins 35 Rue Pastorelli, Nice **t** 04 93 62 61 30

Covers all of the city of Nice and most of the surrounding area.

Crous 2 Rue Monteil, Montpellier **t** 04 67 41 50 00

Consulates and embassies

Australia 4 Rue Jean Rey, Paris **t** 01 40 59 33 00 **www**.austgov.fr

Canada 64 Av Jean Médecin, Nice **t** 04 93 92 93 22 **e** consulate.Canada@wanadoo.fr

Ireland 'Les Chênes Verts', 152 Bd J.- F. Kennedy, Antibes **t** 04 93 61 60/50 63

UK 26 Av Notre-Dame, Nice **t** 04 93 82 32 04
24 Av du Prado Marseille **t** 04 91 15 72 10
28 Rue G-de-Chauliac, Perpignan **t** 04 68 54 92 03
www.amb-grandebretagne.fr
New Zealand 7 Rue Léonard da Vinci, Paris
t 01 45 01 43 43
USA 31 Rue Maréchel Joffre, Nice **t** 04 93 88 89 55
12 Bd Paul-Peytral, Marseille **t** 04 91 54 92 00
www.amb-usa.fr

Electricity

France's electricity supply runs on a 220-volt current. American visitors bringing 110-volt electrical appliances will need a voltage converter; visitors from the UK need a standard European plug adaptor for round, two-pin plugs. If you're bringing an electric sterilizer as well as a kettle it pays to bring more than one adapter. You'll need to buy them before you leave home and they're on sale at most airports.

Make sure you have a torch and some candles if you're heading for a rural area as winds and summer thunderstorms can cut power supplies. Warn teens, if they are using a computer, that the current may surge if the weather is bad.

Emergency numbers

Ambulance t 15
Fire t 18
Police t 17
European emergency number t 112

Insurance

It's vital that you take out travel insurance before your trip. As a minimum it should cover cancellation due to illness, travel delays, accidents, lost luggage, lost passports, lost or stolen belongings, personal liability, legal expenses, emergency flights and medical cover. Remember you don't have to buy insurance from the same travel company that sold you your holiday, and it's worth shopping around.

Most insurance companies offer free insurance to children under the age of two as part of their parents' policy. When travelling, always keep the insurance company's 24hr emergency number close to hand – if you have a mobile phone, store it in the memory.

Always report stolen or lost items to the police, however trivial, so that you can make a claim when you get back home.

In the UK

Association of British Insurers t (020) 7600 3333
Insurance Ombudsman Bureau t 0845 600 6666
The government-appointed regulators of the insurance industry, who are able help with complaints.
ABC Holiday Extras Travel Insurance
t (toll free) 0800 171 000
Columbus Travel Insurance t (020) 7375 0011
Endsleigh Insurance t (020) 7436 4451
Medicover t 0870 735 3600
World Cover Direct t toll free 0800 365 121

In North America

Access America USA toll free **t** 1 800 284 8300
Canada toll free **t** 1 800 654 1908
Carefree Travel Insurance USA and Canada toll free **t** 1 800 323 3149
Travel Assistance International USA and Canada toll free **t** 1 800 921 2828
MEDEX Assistance Corporation USA **t** (410) 453 6300

Internet

France was for several years much less wired up than Britain and the USA but is catching up fast. Finding somewhere to check your e-mail, however, can be surprisingly difficult, especially in Corsica. The tourist office will be able to give you a list of local Internet cafés.

If getting online is crucial then choose a large chain hotel, as they'll often have Internet access. Remember, if you need to use your mobile to access the Internet, check the reception is good enough in the area you are visiting before you book your accommodation.

You may come across Minitel, a phone line information service accessed through a terminal service. It was all the rage in the 1980s and was at the time the French answer to the Internet, but if you are travelling you're unlikely to ever have to use this system, which has been superseded by the World Wide Web.

There are lots of Internet sites with information about the South of France.

General sites

www.franceguide.com
www.francetourism.com
www.bestofcity.fr
www.parcmania.com (for details of theme parks)

Languedoc-Roussillon

www.sunfrance.com
www.cr-languedocroussillon.fr/tourisme
www.audetourisme.com

Vaucluse and Alpes-Maritimes

www.provenceweb.fr
www.cr-paca.fr
www.rivieraworld.com
www.cote.azur.fr
www.enprovence.com
www.provence-online.com
www.provenceguide.com
www.provenceweb.com
www.visitprovence.com
www.provence.guideweb.com
www.avignon-et-provence.com
www.crt-riviera.fr

Corsica

www.allerencorse.com
www.lacorse.com
www.visit-corsica.com
www.internetcom.fr/corsica
www.corsica-isula.com
www.corsicaweb.fr

Laundry

There are plenty of launderettes across the region. If you choose an apart'hotel they'll have a washing machine in the complex (*see* p.212) and campsites have washing machines as well.

Every French supermarket will sell detergent for hand-washing.

Lost property

If you lose something important such as a passport you'll need to contact your local consulate and for insurance purposes you'll need to tell the police (*see* also 'Crime', p.271).

Some big towns have lost property offices:

Nice 1 Rue de la Terrasse **t** 04 97 13 44 10
Marseille 18 Rue de la Cathedrale **t** 04 91 90 99 37

When to comes to other important items like teddies, keep them in the suitcase when you are moving around or tie them to the pushchair.

Manners

You'll find you'll get a warm welcome wherever you go in France with your children as long as they know how to behave. French parents don't hold back when it comes to discipline and they expect their children to be polite.

French interactions are much more formal than in the UK. Address shopkeepers, receptionists waiters, etc. with a respectful, '*Bonjour, Madame/ Monsieur*', before asking for anything and it's especially important to be polite when dealing with anyone in authority. Even if your French is minimal, people are more likely to warm to you if you try to speak it, however badly.

Maps

The best map to buy if you're driving to the South of France with kids is the Michelin *Mini Atlas France*. It's small enough to pop in the glove compartment, so it won't end up wrecked on the floor of the car, and it marks all the major routes. If you intend to tour around the South of France, it's a good idea to buy one of the Michelin area maps once you reach your destination.

Medical matters

Emergency Medical Service (SAMU) t 15
SOS Médecins (in Provence only) **t** 04 93 85 01 01
24hr call-out doctor.
Anti-Poison Centre Marseille **t** 04 91 75 25 25

In an emergency the best thing is to call an ambulance. Don't try to drive a sick child to hospital if you don't know the city; it could waste valuable time. It may sound over-anxious but if you are staying in rental accommodation make sure that you have either a landline or a working mobile phone. Ask about local doctors and taxis, which sometimes double up as an ambulance service in very rural areas. Check what you should do in a medical emergency with the owners.

The E111

Visitors from the European Union, Iceland, Liechtenstein and Norway are entitled to the same medical treatment as French citizens as long as they carry a validated E111 form, which is free and available at main UK post offices. It will need to be stamped before you leave. It covers families with dependent children up to the age of 16 (or 19, if in full-time education). Medical care, dental treatment and prescriptions (*ordonnances*) must be paid for up-front in France; 75–80 per cent of costs will be reimbursed at a later date if you have the E111 form. This can be a time-consuming and complicated procedure, however, and you're well advised to take out travel insurance with 100 per cent medical cover before you go.

Nationals of non-EU countries should take out full travel insurance with medical cover before leaving home. In the USA and Canada you may find that your existing insurance policies give sufficient medical cover, and you should always check these thoroughly before taking out a new one. Canadians, in particular, are usually covered by their provincial health plans.

For non-emergencies ask either at the hotel reception or see if the owners of your rented property can help you contact a doctor. The police will always have the number of a local doctor on duty and during office hours the tourist office should be able to help. If your child does need medical attention, don't panic – the French health service is one of the best in the world.

See also 'Family-friendly phrase book', pp.274–6.

Minor ailments

There are pharmacies everywhere in France and they always have a large, green neon cross outside. French pharmacists are highly trained and used to giving advice, and a lot them will speak some English. They can prescribe a wide range of drugs and can carry out basic medical services such as dealing with insect bites or cleaning and bandaging wounds (usually for a small fee). They are also trained to identify poisonous plants and mushrooms. If your child eats something you think could be poisonous always try to take a sample of what they've eaten along with you to the pharmacy or doctor.

The pharmacy will be able to direct you to the nearest doctor on duty and supply a list of local doctors. There's usually the address of the nearest late-night pharmacy posted on the door of the local pharmacy; if not, the police will have a list of late-night pharmacies.

Suppositories are quite common in France, especially for kids' medicine. If you think that could be an issue, come with a full medical bag of your own.

Money and banks

France is one of the 12 countries in the EU that use the **euro**. One euro is divided into 100 cents. There are 8 euro coins, for 1, 2, 5, 10, 20 and 50 cents and 1 and 2 euros, and seven notes, for 5, 10, 20, 50, 100, 200 and 500 euros. The notes are entirely uniform throughout the continent, but euro coins have a common design on one side (with the amount, 5, 10 cent and so on) and a design specific to each country on the other. However, all euro coins can be used equally in any of the twelve eurozone countries.

Credit cards

Most shops and restaurants accept all the big name credit and debit cards – Visa, Mastercard, Delta, American Express, Barclaycard, etc. – and nearly all French automatic cash dispensers (known as DABs, *distributeurs automatiques de billets*) will dispense money on foreign credit or bank cards linked to the international Cirrus and Maestro network (for which there will be a handling fee). Your bank's international banking department should be able to advise you on this.

Banks and traveller's cheques

Banks are generally open Mon–Fri, 9–5, although some are also open on Saturday mornings. All are closed on public holidays.

Traveller's cheques can be changed at any bank or *bureau de change* for a commission. The Banque de France usually gives the best rates, and hotels and train stations the worst.

Cash

It's important to always have a good supply of cash with you. There are fewer *bureaux de change* since the introduction of the euro and French credit cards all have a security code that is typed into a machine every time you buy something. If you don't have a code – and at present you can't get a code for a UK card – it can cause confusion in the supermarket and you won't be able to buy petrol at automated petrol pumps.

Be careful when carrying money around with you; pickpockets are rife in big towns and at tourist hot spots. Always keep wallets in trouser pockets, and hold purses and bags close to your body. Do not drape handbags on the back of your chair or buggy and avoid putting valuables into the small front pocket of mini rucksacks.

Lost credit cards

American Express t 01 47 77 72 00 ; lost American Express travellers' cheques **t** 01 47 14 50 00
Visa t 08 36 69 08 80
Mastercard t 01 45 67 84 84
Diners' Club t 01 49 06 17 17

Mosquitoes

Come prepared for mosquitoes; in some places, like the Camargue, they're a problem all year round. Some insect repellents, especially ones containing DEET, aren't suitable for use on children, so look out for Autun Family, one of the commercial brands on sale in France which is suitable for youngsters. Many supermarkets and pharmacies have their own brands for children, which are often cheaper. If you're travelling with a baby, pack a mosquito net for the pram or carrycot.

Look out for after-sun products with a built-in insect repellent; Piz Buin do a very effective one, which is good value for money and covers the skin more easily than roll-ons. Sprays can make children cough so are best avoided.

National and school holidays

Public holidays generally last a lot longer than a day in France. If the holidays fall on Wednesday, you'll find most people '*faire le pont*' and take Thursday and/or Friday off as well, to link it or 'make a bridge' to the weekend. Watch out for this, as it might mean that shops are closed.

The school holidays vary from region to region and don't necessarily coincide with UK and US holidays. The French migrate en masse to the mountains in spring and to the beach in August, when many factories and businesses close. The busiest day on the roads is 1 August, and it really is busy, so it's best to avoid the roads then.

Public holidays

New Year's Day (1 Jan)
Easter Sunday and Monday (Mar/April)
Labour Day (1 May)
VE Day (8 May)
Ascension Day (end May)
Whit Weekend (mid–late May)
Bastille Day (14 July)
Assumption Day (15 August)
All Saints' Day (1 Nov)
Remembrance Day (11 Nov)
Christmas Day (25 Dec).

In Monaco 27 January and 18/19 November are also public holidays.

School holidays

Spring half term: 2 weeks in February
Easter: 2 weeks in April, not necessarily over the Easter weekend
Summer: end of June–early September
Autumn: half term: 2 weeks in late Oct/early Nov.
Christmas: 2 weeks over Christmas and New Year

Opening hours

Shops and businesses are usually open Mon–Sat between 9–7 but will shut for lunch bang on 12 noon and won't open again until 2pm.

Department stores usually open non-stop Mon–Sat 9.30–6.30. Many shops are closed on Monday mornings. Petrol stations and motorway services are a good place to buy supplies out of hours.

Most national **museums** are closed on Tuesdays but municipal museums close on Mondays. Private museums are more erratic and usually close on Sunday or Monday.

Post offices

Most French post offices (*la poste* or *le bureau de poste*) are open Mon–Fri 8–7, and Sat 8–12 noon. You'll find long queues, as they deal with a lot more than just letters and parcels. Often only a couple of windows (*guichets*) are being used for normal postal functions; look for signs saying *Envoi de Lettres et Paquets* or *Toutes Opérations*.

A lot of big post offices have automatic machines with an English translation that will weigh and issue the appropriate stamps for your parcel.

If you just want to send a letter or a postcard, stamps can be bought from any tobacconist (*tabac*) or supermarket. Hotels often sell them too. The tourist office will have a list of all the local post offices in the area.

Racism

Racism and anti-Semitism are an issue in the South of France. In the 2002 presidential election supporters of the extreme right turned out in droves to vote for their candidate, Jean-Marie Le Pen, and since 11 September 2001 racist and anti-Semitic incidents in France have increased dramatically. Little children probably won't notice but it may be an issue with older kids and teens. It's not unknown for bouncers at discos to turn you away if they don't like the colour of your skin and for restaurants to suddenly be fully booked. Jewish cemeteries and synagogues may be surrounded by police and fierce guard dogs. It can make kids feel very vulnerable, angry and frightened. Make time to discuss the issues with children and help them deal with the mixture of emotions they may feel.

Safety

Crime

Petty crime is a problem in the South of France, particularly pickpockets and car thieves. Take extra care with your valuables when in busy shopping districts and markets. Remember, if you are pushing a pushchair, or distracted by little children, you're an easy target. Don't put valuables in a back-pack or on the back of a pushchair, and never leave them in your car.

Burglary is also a problem, so be as careful when locking your holiday home as you would your own house back home.

If you are a victim of a crime, report it to the nearest police station as soon as possible in order to get the form needed for your insurance claim. You will need to make a statement (*procès verbal*) in the town or village where the crime was committed. If your passport has been stolen, you will also need to contact your consulate, which should be able to arrange emergency travel documents to tide you over.

Always carry your passport with you, preferably in a money belt or similar secure device; according to French law, the police can demand to see some ID any time they feel like it. It's a good idea for older teens out alone to carry some form of ID too.

Lost children

It's easy to get separated from your child in busy airports, stations and markets. Make sure your child knows their full name and that if they are lost the best place to go is into a shop and to ask a female assistant for help. Teach your child your mobile phone number (remember you'll need to add in the country code). It isn't just toddlers who get lost – older children and teenagers can easily stray, so make sure they know where to go to make a public announcement at a station or airport and always fix a place to meet if you get separated.

Road safety and awareness

The biggest danger to your child is being in an environment that they don't know. If coming from the UK, make sure they realize that cars drive on the right side of the road. It may sound trivial but it can make crossing the road very dangerous for children unsure where to look for oncoming traffic.

City kids may be streetwise but unused to wild open spaces and therefore unaware of the dangers of climbing precipitous slopes and cliffs, so keep a close eye on them. Remember, just because you are on holiday, the local environment isn't necessarily safe; the dangers are the same as at home.

Safety in the sun

Try to avoid the sun at its strongest, from 11am–3pm. Choose a waterproof sunscreen with a high protection factor specifically designed for children and apply it liberally and often, particularly after swimming. Make sure children wear hats when outdoors and protect babies with sunshades and hats. In hot weather everyone will need to drink plenty of water.

Teen issues

Mobile phone theft is a problem in France. Make sure teens are careful where they use their phone and know that it's not worth a fight if someone tries to steal it.

The drug scene in the South of France is the same as in other parts of Western Europe – soft and hard drugs are widely available. It's illegal to be in possession of drugs and even a small amount of marijuana could land you in jail.

In the UK, look out for the leaflet *Drugs Abroad*. For more information in the UK call:

National Drugs Helpline t 0800 77 66 00

Warn teenagers who are going out in the evening alone of the dangers of drugs and alcohol. They may be unaware of the danger of swimming when drunk or that the risk of dehydrating in nightclubs is greater in the heat.

Water safety

Make sure children are aware of the dangers posed by the sea and by swimming pools and that they never go swimming alone. Wear plastic shoes if the coast is very rocky and watch out for jellyfish and sea urchins.

Seek medical advice if your child gets stung by a jellyfish, and if they are stung by a sea urchin, remove the spikes as quickly as possible. Soak the affected area in warm water with olive oil or lavender oil and remove the spikes with tweezers.

Before you swim, always check that it is safe to do so. Lakes and rivers connected to the hydroelectric system can be lethal when the dams are opened as the water level can rise dramatically. Currents can be stronger than you realize, and seemingly shallow beaches can slope away from the shore dramatically.

Smoking

Far more people smoke in France than in the USA or UK; you can spot the local secondary school by the gaggle of teenagers puffing away on the steps and words like 'ashtray' regularly appear on school spelling lists. Restaurants and cafés will be smokier than you may feel is healthy for your children.

The big hotel chains like Ibis have non-smoking rooms but most restaurants do not. Luckily in the South of France you can eat outside for a large part of the year. Smoking is illegal on public transport (though not on Corsican trains), in cinemas and theatres.

Special needs

The French Ministry of Tourism has recently had a campaign to improve facilities for disabled travellers and several companies offer discounts and special assistance. Always make it clear you are travelling with a disabled child and ask what services are available; most companies will be able to help you.

The French Tourist Office has a list of regional hotels with disabled facilities and a useful booklet on self-catering accommodation, *Gîtes Accessible à Tous*. There isn't a uniform standard of accessibility so check with each individual hotel or house about specifics. Their website has a section on special needs: **www**.franceguide.com.

In France

Association des Paralysés de France 22 Rue du Pere Guérain, 75013 Paris **t** 01 44 16 83 83

Association Valentin Haûy Service des Ventes, AVH 5, Rue Duroc, 75007 Paris **t** 01 44 49 27 27 **f** 01 44 49 27 10

Comité National Français de Liaison pour la Réadaptation des Handicapés (CNRH) Service Publications, 236 bis Rue de Tolbiac, 75013 Paris **t** 01 53 80 66 66

In the UK

Council for Disabled Children t (020) 7843 6000

Information on travel health and further resources.

Holiday Care Service 2nd Floor, Imperial Building, Victoria Road, Horley, Surrey RH6 9HW **t** 01293 774 535

Provides information sheets for families with disabilities. All sites have been visited and assessed by Holiday Care representatives.

RADAR (Royal Association for Disability and Rehabilitation) Unit 12 City Forum, 250 City Road, London EC1V 8AF **t** 020 7250 3222

Open Mon–Fri 8–5

Provides specialist advice and publishes a guide to facilities at airports called 'Getting There'.

Royal National Institute for the Blind 224 Great Portland Street, London W1S 5TB **t** (020) 7388 1266

Advises on travel matters.

In the USA

American Foundation for the Blind 15 West 16th Street, New York, NY 10011 **t** (212) 620 2000; toll free, **t** 800 232 5463

Mobility International PO Box 3551, Eugene, Oregon 97403 **t** (541) 343 1284

SATH (Society for Accessible Travel and Hospitality) 347 Fifth Avenue, Suite 610, New York 10016 **t** (212) 447 7284

In Australia

ACROD (Australian Council for the Rehabilitation of the Disabled) 55 Charles Street, Ryde, New South Wales **t** (02) 9809 448

Telephones

To use public phones you need to buy a *télécarte* (phonecard), available at any tobacconist shop (*tabac*), train station or post office. French phone numbers have 10 digits and you must dial all 10 from anywhere in France. If ringing from abroad, dial the international code for France, 33, and then the local number, but omit the initial 0.

To make an **international call**, dial 00 followed by the country code (UK 44, US and Canada 1, Ireland 353, Australia 61, New Zealand 64), then the local code (minus the 0 for UK numbers) and finally the number. France Télécom has an English-speaking freephone customer information line, **t** 08 00 36 47 75. For **directory enquiries**, call **t** 12.

Monaco numbers have 8 digits and if you call from France you must use the whole code.

Tickets

The family ticket has yet to reach France. If you have a large family (*une grande famille*) it's worth asking if there are concessions; usually one of the children will be admitted free. Don't forget to ask if the town you are visiting has a special ticket that gives entrance to all the monuments and museums, as it is often a cheaper option.

Generally admission prices are lower than in the UK. The website **www.**gratuitpourlesenfants.com lists attractions and museums where the children get in free.

You can book ahead for opera, theatres and concerts with:

Liaisons Abroad Chenil House, 181/183 Kings Road London, SW3 5EB **t** (020) 7376 4020 **f** 7376 4442 **e** info@liaisonsabroad.com **www.**liaisonsabroad.com

For football, rugby, tennis and the Monaco Grand Prix contact:

Mission Impossible 37 Marylebone Lane, London W1M 5FN **t** (020) 486 1666 **f** 7581 4687 **e** info@missionimpossible.co.uk **www.**mitickets.com

Time

The South of France and Corsica are 1hr ahead of London (GMT), 6hrs ahead of New York, 9hrs ahead of California and 9hrs behind Tokyo and Sydney. Many French people use the 24-hour clock when both writing and speaking.

It pays to take account of even the hour's time difference as it can make children very irritable if they don't get their lunch on time in the first few days of the holiday.

Tipping

A 12.5% service charge is usually added to the bill in restaurants and cafés, and you need only tip above this if the service or food was particularly outstanding or if you made a real mess of the table. Taxi drivers will expect a 10% tip.

Toilets

Many public toilets are high-tech and the infamous 'holes in the ground' are thankfully only found in lay-bys now. Most museums, shops and restaurants have decent facilities.

Don't be surprised if in small villages the cafés and restaurants have only one toilet for both men and women.

Tourist offices

In peak holiday times most tourist offices are open, Mon–Sat 9–6, Sun 11–12 noon.

Tourism staff are often multilingual and can provide information about events, museums, restaurants and hotels. Standards vary – some can be exceptionally helpful, others can't even be bothered to acknowledge your existence. Big offices often have a souvenir shop, a *bureau de change* and a hotel reservation service that can book a room for the same day. In a small town the tourist office will often go under the name *Syndicat d'Initiative*.

In the UK

French Tourist Office Maison de la France, 178 Piccadilly, London W1V 0AL **t** 09068 244 123, calls cost 60p per minute **www.**franceguide.com

Monaco Tourist Office The Chambers, Chelsea Harbour, London SW10 OXF **t** 020 7352 9962 **www.**monaco-congress.com

In Ireland

French Tourist Office 10 Suffolk Street, Dublin 1 **t** (1) 679 0813

In the USA

French Tourist Office 444 Madison Avenue, 16th Floor, New York, NY 10022 **t** (212) 990 0040 9454 Wiltshire Boulevard, Beverley Hills, CA 90212 **t** (310) 271 6665 **www.**francetourism.com

Monaco Tourism 565 5th Ave, New York NY 10017 **t** (212) 286 3330

FAMILY-FRIENDLY PHRASE BOOK

If you want to build on the French you've learnt on holiday, consider enrolling the kids in a French class – there are lots of French courses for children. You could also consider sending them on an exchange; the French Cultural Institute is a good place to ask for advice. The website www.info-france.org has a kids' page if you can't get to the cultural centre.

In London

Institute Français 17 Queensbury Place, London SW7 2DY **t** 020 7 073 1350

They have a children's library and organize events for children. The Institute is next to the French Lycée and you can buy French books and other French products in the shops in nearby Bute Street, which is a mini France in South Kensington.

In Washington

La Maison Française 4101 Reservoir Rd, Washington DC 20007 **t** (202) 944 6043

Words and phrases

Baby days

baby *un bébé*
twins *les jumeaux (*boys or mixed sex twins*); les jumelles* two girls
child *un enfant*
boy *un garçon*
girl *une fille*
nappy/diaper *une couche*
pushchair/buggy/stroller *une poussette*
a baby bottle *un biberon*
a dummy/soother *une sucette*
a teat *une tétine*
sterilizing tablets *les comprimés de stérilisation*
breastfeeding *donner le sein au bébé*

Emergencies

policeman *un agent de police*
police station *un commissariat de police*

Medical Words

ambulance *une ambulance*
doctor *un médecin*
medicine *les médicaments*
hospital *un hôpital*
nurse *une infirmière*
pharmacy *une pharmacie*
pharmacist *un pharmacien*
acne *les boutons*
asthma *l'asthme*
allergy *une allergie*
bandage *un pansement*
cough *une toux*
croup *croup*
chicken pox *la varicelle*
diarrhoea *la diarrhée*
fever *une fièvre*
nappy rash *rougeur du couche*
nits *les poux*
worms *les vers*
to vomit *vomir*
I'm pregnant *je suis enceinte*

Bedtime

babysitting *le baby-sitting/la garde d'enfants*
blanket *une couverture*
bunk beds *les lits superposés*
cot *un lit d'enfant*
bed *un lit*
pillow *un oreiller*
extra bed *un lit supplémentaire*
room *une chambre*
twin room *chambre à deux lits*
double room *chambre pour deux personnes*
single room *chambre pour une personne*
interconnecting rooms *les chambres communicantes*
teddy bear *un nounours*

Is that French?

While you're on your travels in the South of France you'll come across a number of regional dialects. Up in the mountains on the border with Italy some people still speak Piedmontese, which is an Italian dialect. In Roussillon you'll see words written in Catalan. Although attempts have been made to revise the local language in Provence, you won't hear anyone actually speaking Provençal but you will see it used on signs and a lot of hotels, shops and restaurants have names in Provençal. If you want to learn more, look out for the little book *Mon Premier Dictionnaire Français-Provençal en Images*. See also Corsica pp.185–6.

Dates and time

What time is it? *Quelle heure est-il?*
month *un mois*
week *une semaine*
day *un jour/une journée*
morning *le matin*
afternoon *l'après-midi*
evening *le soir*
today *aujourd'hui*
yesterday *hier*
tomorrow *demain*
soon *bientôt*
later *plus tard*

Days of the week

Monday *lundi*
Tuesday *mardi*
Wednesday *mercredi*
Thursday *jeudi*
Friday *vendredi*
Saturday *samedi*
Sunday *dimanche*

Months of the year

January *janvier*
February *février*
March *mars*
April *avril*
May *mai*
June *juin*
July *juillet*
August *août*
September *septembre*
October *octobre*
November *novembre*
December *décembre*

Numbers

one *un*
two *deux*
three *trois*
four *quatre*
five *cinq*
six *six*
seven *sept*
eight *huit*
nine *neuf*
ten *dix*
eleven *onze*
twelve *douze*
thirteen *treize*
fourteen *quatorze*
fifteen *quinze*
sixteen *seize*
seventeen *dix-sept*
eighteen *dix-huit*
nineteen *dix-neuf*
twenty *vingt*
twenty-one *vingt et un*
twenty-two *vingt-deux*
thirty *trente*
forty *quarante*
fifty *cinquante*
sixty *soixante*
seventy *soixante-dix*
eighty *quatre-vingts*
ninety *quatre-vingt-dix*
one hundred *cent*
one hundred and one *cent-et-un*
one hundred and two *cent-deux*
one thousand *mille*

Out and about

open *ouvert*
closed *fermé*
cheap *bon marché*
expensive *cher*
bank *une banque*
entrance *entrée (f)*
exit *sortie*
money *l'argent (m)*
post office *la poste*
shop *un magasin*
supermarket *un supermarché*
tobacconist *un tabac*
toilets *les WC* (pronounced vay-say)

Transport

airport *un aéroport*
bicycle *une bicyclette/un vélo*
bus stop *un arrêt d'autobus*
bus *un autobus*
railway station *la gare*
train *un train*
platform *un quai*
car *une voiture*
taxi *un taxi*
ticket office *un guichet*
ticket *un billet*
toll *un péage*
car seat *un siège du bébé*

Playing

games *les jeux*
crayon *un crayon de couleur*
pencil *un crayon*
toys *les jouets*
playground *un jardin d'enfants*
sandpit *un bac de sable*
slide *un toboggan*
swing *une balançoire*
roundabout *un carrousel*

Teen talk

If kids are out chatting with French contempories or reading magazines, it will help if they know some basic slang. It varies according from region to region, but these are some of the words they might hear. They're generally normally acceptable words (they'll have to look the really rude ones up in the dictionary). It's worth noting that in French some swear words are more acceptable than their English equivalents.

broke *á sec*
good *ben (bien)*
that's really great *c'est la bombe*
great *chouette*
shattered/exhausted *crevé/e*
super *d'enfer*
crazy *dingue*
chat up *draguer*
a policeman *un flic*
loaded *friqué/e*
dosh/money *le fric*
guys *les gars*
a kid *un/une gosse*
a test *un interro*
to have a laugh *se marrer*
cool *marrant/marrante*
a bloke *un mec*
damn *mince*
rubbish *moche*
don't pin me down *ne me colle pas*
rubbish *nul/nulle*
boyfriend/girlfriend *un petit/petite copin/copine*
steal *piquer*
a teacher *un prof*
British people *les Rosbifs*
nice, friendly *sympa*
really super *top mortel*
really *vachement*
to chuck out *virer*

Index

Main page references are in **bold**. Page references to maps are in *italics*.

Abbaye de Thoronet 120
accommodation *see* where to stay
Acqua Cyrne Gliss 189–90
Adventure Golf 65
Agay 48, 68
  Wind Club 71
Agde 161–3
  beaches 162
  food and drink 177
Aguilar 149
Aguzou caves 159–60
Aigues-Mortes 165–6
  food and drink 166
airlines 180, 260–1, 264
Aix-en-Provence 116–18
  food and drink 116–17, 139
  where to stay 228–9
Ajaccio 184–8
  beaches 188, 189
  food and drink 185, 206
  where to stay 234
Aleria 199
Alésia 38
Algajola 238
Algeria 43
Alpes-de-Haute-Provence 101–4
Alpes-Maritimes 48–69, 105–9
Amazonia 175
Amigoland 168
amphitheatres 70, 122, 171
amusement parks *see* parks and playgrounds
anchovies 158
Anthéor 84
Antibes 48, **66–8**
  beaches 68
  food and drink 83
  where to stay 221
apartment hotels 212
Apt 101
Aqua-Splash 65
Aquacity 135
Aqualand 160, 163
aquariums
  Bonifacio 191
  Cap d'Agde 162
  Planet Aquarium 134
  Porto 189
  Seaquarium 167
Aquatica 71
Aquavallée 109
Argèles Adventure 160–1
Argelès-sur-Mer 158
  where to stay 232
Arles 121–4
  food and drink 121–2, 140
  where to stay 227
astronomy 105
  Astrorama 55–6
  Haute-Provence observatory 105
  Nice observatory 53
  Planétarium Galilée 165
Astrorama 55–6
Aubagne 135
Audides caves 103
Auron 109
Avignon 88, **89–92**
  food and drink 90, 109–10
  where to stay 224–5

Babar's Travels 75, **79**
babies 31, 32, 33
  babysitters 266
  food 254–5
  useful phrases 274
Babyland 168
Balades en Pays Catalan 155
bamboo forest 174
banks 269
Barbegal 128
Barcaggio 197
Bastelica 190
  food and drink 207
Bastelicaccia 234
Bastia 195–6
  beaches 197
  food and drink 196, 207
  where to stay 235
beaches
  Agde 162
  Ajaccio 188, 189
  Antibes 68
  Bastia 197
  Bonifacio 193–4
  Cabasson 222
  Calvi 200
  Camargue 127
  Cannes 64
  Corsica 183
  Languedoc-Roussillon 158
  Marseille 134
  Menton 61
  Monaco 60
  Montpellier 168
  Narbonne 153
  Nice 49, 53–4
  Porto 188–9
  Porto-Vecchio 194
  Riviera 48, 53–4, 55, 62
  St-Tropez 74, 77
  Sartène 194
Beaucaire 173
Bénézet, Saint 91
berlingots 96, 163
bicycles *see* cycling
Biot 83
birds of prey 149, 157, 173
Black Death 40, 131
Blanquette 127
boat accommodation 215
boat trips
  Agde 162
  Aigues-Mortes 167
  Ajaccio 187
  Antibes 67
  Arles 124
  Avignon 92
  Bastia 196
  Bonifacio 191, 194
  Calvi 200
  Canal du Midi 150
  Cannes 64
  Fontaine-de-Vaucluse 93
  Fréjus/St Raphaël 71
  Le Seascope 75–6
  Menton 61
  Monaco 60
  Nice 53
  Ste-Maxime 79
  Stes-Maries-de-la-Mer 126
Bonifacio 190–1
  beaches 193–4
  food and drink 190, 207
  where to stay 236
Bonifacio Woman 194
Bonnieux 110
books 35–6, 186
  Babar's Travels 75, **79**
  Balades en Pays Catalan 155
  Copain de la Provence 120
  Count of Monte Cristo 133
  Les Sentiers d'Emilie dans les Pyrénées 159
  The Little Prince 78
  Nature Activities Côté Soleil 160
  The Story of Babar 75, **79**
  Thomas the Tank Engine 265
  Visites Contées 155
bookshops 256
bories 101
Bormes-les-Mimosas 76
  food and drink 84
  where to stay 222
Bouches-du-Rhône *see* Western Provence
Bouvines, battle of 40
bowling 53
Breil-sur-Roya 106

Brunhoff, Jean de 79
bullfights 170
buses 264, 266
butterfly centres 65, 157

Cabasson beach 77, 222
Cabrespine 150–1
calanques 133–4
calissons 117
Calvi 199–200
  beaches 200
  food and drink 200, 208
  where to stay 238
Camargue 114, **124–5**
  beaches 127
  climate 114, 124
  food and drink 140
  where to stay 228
Cambous 170
  where to stay 232–3
camping 216–17
  equipment 257
Camus, Albert 98
Canal du Midi 150
Canet-en-Roussillon 158
  where to stay 232
Cannes 48, **62–4**
  beaches 64
  food and drink 63, 83
  where to stay 220–1
canoeing/kayaking 93, 126, 169, 175, 205
canyons *see* gorges
Cap d'Agde 162
  food and drink 177
  where to stay 233
Cap de Brégançon 48
Cap Corse 196–7
  where to stay 236
Cap Estérel Village 221
Cap Ferrat 54, 55
  where to stay 219
Cap Rederis 158
Capet, Hugues 40
caravanning 216–17
Carcassonne 146–9
  food and drink 148, 176
  where to stay 230–1
Cargèse 234
carnivals 49
  see also festivals
Carpentras 96–7
Carrington, Dorothy 198
cars 182, 261–3, 265
  numberplate game 33
  road safety 271
Casino of Monte-Carlo 58
Cassis 133
  where to stay 230
Castagniccia 198
Casteddu d'Araghju 194
Castellane 101–2
  food and drink 111
  where to stay 226
Cathars 40, **147–50**
caves
  Aguzou 159–60
  Audides 103
  Clamouse 169
  Demoiselles 169
  Dévèze 169
  Gouffre de Cabrespine 150–1
  Grandes Canalettes 160
  Labeil 169
  Laroque 169
  Limousis 151
  St-Cézaire 103
  Souterroscope de Baume Obscure 103
  stalactites 159
  Tautavel 156
  Thouzon 100–1
  Trabuc 169
Celts 38, 39, 171
Cerbère 158
Céret 161
  food and drink 177
  where to stay 232
Cessenon-sur-Orb 167
Cézanne, Paul 117
Chalabre 150
chambres d'hôte 212–13
Chanel, Coco 42
Channel Tunnel 262
Charlemagne, Emperor 39
Chartreuse de la Verne 76–7
châteaux and forts
  Aguilar 149
  Beaucaire 173
  Chalabre 150
  Emperi 119
  Entrevaux 103
  Fort Lagarde 157
  Fort Liberia 157
  Fort Royal 65
  Fort St-Roch 106
  If 132–3
  Les Baux-de-Provence 138
  Peyrepertuse 149–50
  Puilaurens 150
  Quéribus 149
  Roquebrune 62
  Salses 157
  Termes 149
chemists 256, 269
chestnuts 76, 193
children's menus 243
Christmas
  cooking 244
  cribs 124
  shopping 258
chronology 44
Cians gorge 108
cinemas
  Agde 162
  Aigues-Mortes 167
  Aix-en-Provence 118
  Ajaccio 187
  Bastia 196
  Calvi 200
  Cannes 64
  Menton 61
  Monaco 60
  Nice 53
  Perpignan 156
  Porto 189
  St-Tropez 74
Clamouse caves 169
Clement V, Pope 90
climate 31, 88
  Camargue 114, 124
clothes shops 256–7
Clovis, king of the Franks 39
Club Med 213–14
coaches/buses 264, 266
coal mine museum 175
Cogolin 222
Col de Vizzavona 205
Collias 233
Colline du Château 51
Collioure 158–9
  food and drink 177
  where to stay 232
Collobrières 76–7
  food and drink 84
Colmars 102
Columbus, Christopher 200
consulates 266–7
Copain de la Provence 120
cork trees 193
Corsica **180–208**, *181*
  beaches 183
  Corse du Sud 184–95
  Corsican people 185
  cult of death 198
  cycling 182, 193
  diving courses 201
  festivals 180
  food and drink 206–8, 247
  getting there and around 180–3
  Haute-Corse 195–205

Corsica (*cont'd*)
horse riding 205
Mountain Railway 203
politics 184
walking 204
where to stay 216, 234–40
Corte 203–5
food and drink 203–4, 208
where to stay 239
Côte d'Azur *see* Riviera
Cotignac 139
Count of Monte Cristo 133
Coursegoules 81
crèche 124
credit cards 269
Creno lake 202
crime 271
Crusades 40, 166
Cubieres-sur-Cinoble 232
Cubism 68
Cuers 84
cycling
Corsica 182, 193
Fréjus 70
Luberon 100
Narbonne 154
Porto-Vecchio 193
Stes-Maries-de-la-Mer 126

dancing 53
Dark Ages 39–40
Daudet, Alphonse 99, 127, 128
de Gaulle, Charles 42
death cult 198
Demoiselles caves 169
denim 172
department stores 256, 270
Désert des Agriates 198–9
where to stay 235
Dévèze caves 169
dinosaurs
Dino Park 162
Dinosauria 151
fossils 117
La Plaine des Dinosaures 164
disabled travellers 272
diving 68, 201
driving in France 182, 261–3, 265
drugs 271

E111 forms 268–9
eating out *see* food and drink
Ecole de l'Air 119
Edward III of England 40
Eldorado City 135
electricity 267
embassies 266–7
emergencies 267, 268–9
useful phrases 274
Emperi 119
Entrevaux 103
Erbalunga 197
Escalier du Roi-d'Aragon 191
Espace Adventure 107–8
euro 33
Eze 54–5
food and drink 81
where to stay 219

fairies 169
farm foods 244
farms 65, 150, 167, 173
fast food 243–4
ferries 180, 181, 261–2, 265
festivals
Agde 161
Aigues-Mortes 165
Aix-en-Provence 116
Ajaccio 184
Antibes 66
Arles 121
Avignon 89
Bastia 195
Bonifacio 190
Calvi 199
Cannes 62
Carcassonne 146
Castellane 101
Corsica 180
Languedoc-Roussillon 144
Marseille 129
Menton 60
Monaco 56
Nîmes 170
Northern Provence 86
Perpignan 154
Pézenas 163
Riviera 47, 48
St-Rémy-de-Provence 135
St-Tropez 72
Sartène 192
Vaison-la-Romaine 94
Western Provence 114
fighter pilot training 119
Filitosa 190
Film Festival (Cannes) 62
Fontaine-de-Vaucluse 92–3
food and drink 110
where to stay 225
Fontvieille 228
food and drink 141
food and drink 242–52
anchovies 158
baby food 254–5
food and drink (*cont'd*)
berlingots 96, 163
calissons 117
chestnuts 76, 193
children's menus 243
Christmas cooking 244
Corsica 206–8, 247
farm foods 244
fast food 243–4
Languedoc-Roussillon 176–8, 246–7
markets 243, 255
navettes 131
Northern Provence 109–12, 245–6
picnics 243
Riviera 80–4, 245
self-catering 247
shopping 254–5
snacks 243
specialities/recipes 242–3, 245, 247
useful phrases 249–52
Western Provence 139–42, 246
football 132
Forcalquier 225
Foreign Legion 190, 200
forest fires 69
Fôret d'Aitone 202
Forêt de l'Ospédale 195
Fort Royal 65
forts *see* châteaux and forts
François Ier 41
Franks 39
Fréjus 48, **70–2**, 83–4
food and drink 83–4
where to stay 221–2
French Revolution 41–2

Galamus gorge 159, 177
games 33–4
Gard 170–5
Gassin 76
food and drink 84
where to stay 222–3
Gauls 38, 39, 118
Genoese 191, 195, 200
gîtes 216
gladiators 123
Glanum 136–7
go-karting
Antibes 68
Cannes 64
Fréjus/St Raphaël 71
Grasse 103
goat farms 150
golf, Adventure Golf 65
Gordes 97
food and drink 110–11
where to stay 225

gorges
Cians 108
Galamus 159, 177
Hérault 168–9
Loup 103
Restonica 205
Verdon 102, 226
Gouffre de Cabrespine 150–1
Grandes Canalettes 160
Grasse 69
Greeks 38, 52, 130
Grimaldi family 57
Grimaud 76
where to stay 223
grottoes *see* caves
Gruissan 153
where to stay 231
witches of 152
Guernica (Picasso) 68
Gypsies 126
Gyptis 130

Hannibal 155
Haribo 174
health 267, 268–9
Henry VI of England 40
Hérault 161–70
history **38–44**
chronology 44
Crusades 40, 166
holiday villages 213–14
horse riding
Agde 163
Ajaccio 188
Camargue 125
Corsica 205
Fréjus 72
Luberon 100
Porto 189
Ste-Maxime 79
hotels 210–12
see also under individual places
Hundred Years' War 40
hunting 167
Hyères 76

I-Spy 33
If, château 132–3
Ile de Levant 75
Ile des Loisirs 161–2
Ile de Porquerolles 48
Ile Rousse 202
where to stay 235
Ile St-Honorat 65
Ile Ste-Marguerite 65
Iles d'Hyères 74–5
where to stay 223
Iles de Lérins 48, **65**
Iles Sanguinaires 188
Institut Océanographique Paul-Ricard 134
insurance 267
Internet 267–8
Isle sur la Sorgue 225
Isola 109
food and drink 112

Jews 40, 43, 94
synagogues 97
Joan of Arc 40
Juan-les-Pins 66
food and drink 83
karting *see* go-karting
kayaking/canoeing 93, 126, 169, 175, 205
Kelly, Grace 57

La Bambouseraie 174
La Cathédrale d'Images 138
La Croix-Valmer 223
La Grande Motte 233
La Jungle des Papillons 65
La Petite Provence du Paradou 127
La Plaine des Dinosaures 164
La Turbie 61–2
Labeil caves 169
Lagarde 157
lakes
Creno 202
Ospédale 195
Verdon 102
language 34
useful phrases 249–52, 274–6
Languedoc-Roussillon **144–78**, *144–5*
beaches 158
festivals 144
food and drink 176–8, 246–7
where to stay 230–3
Laroque caves 169
laundry 268
Lavatoggio 208
Le Barroux 225
Le Lavandou 48, **77**
Le Parc Australien 149
Le Tholonet 139
Le Trayas 68
Le Tropique du Papillon 157
Les Aigles de Beaucaire 173
Les Aigles de la Cité 149
Les Aigles de Valmy 157
Les Baux-de-Provence 137–8
food and drink 142
where to stay 227–8
Les Issambres 68
Leucate Plage 158
Liberia 157
Ligurians 38, 118
Limousis caves 151
The Little Prince 78
lost children 271
lost property 268
Louis XIV 41
Louis XVI 41
Loup gorge 103
Lourmarin 98
Luberon 97–101
food and drink 110–11

Malaucène 225
Man in the Iron Mask 66
manners 268
Manosque 110
maps 268
Marineland 64–5
markets 243, 255
Nice 50, 51
Marseille **129–32**
beaches 134
food and drink 131, 141
where to stay 229–30
Martel, Charles 39
Mas Gallo-Romain des Tourelles 175
Massif d'Esterel 69
Matisse, Henri 52
medical emergencies 267, 268–9
Menton 60–1
beaches 61
food and drink 82
where to stay 220
Mercantour National Park 108
merveilles 106
Michelin man game 33
milk 254
Mireille 126
mistral 88
Mistral, Frédéric 123, 126
Monaco **56–60**, 82
beaches 60
food and drink 58, 82
where to stay 220
money 269
euro game 33
Mont Saint-Loup 162
Mont Ventoux 98–9
Montagne Ste-Victoire 121
Monte Cristo 133
Monte-Carlo 50, 58
see also Monaco
Montpellier 164–5
beaches 168
food and drink 165, 178
where to stay 232

Moor's Head 195
More, Sir Thomas Coventry 51
mosquitoes 270
motion sickness 34
Mountain Railway 203
museums
A Bandera 186
Alta Rocca 194
Angladon 91
Annonciade 73–4
Appel de la Résistance 93
Archéologique 70
Arlaten 123
Arles Antique 123
Art Moderne 161
Automobiliste 69
Bonbon Haribo 174
Castre 63–4
Docks Romains 132
Ephèbe 162
Ethnographie 196
Galerie des Transports 132
Gorges du Verdon 103–4
Granet 118
Grévin de la Provence 119
Histoire Naturelle 117
Jardin des Vestiges 132
Jérôme Carcopino 199
Le Castillet 155
Magie 162
Merveilles 106
Mine Témoin 175
Monaco 57, 58–60
Napoleon 58, 67, 186
Nature en Provence 104
Nice *see* Nice
Nostradamus 119
Océanographique 202
opening hours 270
Picasso 67
Préhistoire Régionale 61
Riz 129
santon museums 93, 127, 138
Spéléologie 93
Train et du Jouet 174
Troupes de Marine 70
Vivant de l'Abeille 96

Nantes, Edict of 41
Napoleon Bonaparte 184, 187
museums 58, 67, 186
Narbonne 151–2
beaches 153
food and drink 176
where to stay 231
national holidays 270
Nature Activities Côté Soleil 160
navettes 131
Nelson, Horatio 199
Nice 43, **48–54**, 80–1
beaches 49, 53–4
boat trips 53
bowling 53
cinemas 53
Colline du Château 51
Cours Saleya 51
dancing 53
food and drink 50, 80–1
markets 50, 51
museums
Archéologique 52
Masséna 49
Matisse 52
Naval 51
passes 49
Terra Amata 51–2
Observatoire de Nice 53
parks and playgrounds 53
Promenade des Anglais 51
Russian Orthodox Cathedral 53–4
shopping 49
train rides 51, 56
Vieux Nice 51
water sports 54
where to stay 218–19
zoo du Cap Ferrat 54
Nîmes 170–2
food and drink 171, 178
where to stay 233
Northern Provence **86–112**, *86–7*
festivals 86
food and drink 109–12, 245–6
where to stay 224–6
Nostradamus 119
Notre-Dame-de-la-Garde 132
Notre Dame du Roc 101
numberplate game 33

observatories *see* astronomy
Océanographique Paul-Ricard 134
Odysseus 191
OK Corral 135
opening hours 270
Oppidum of Entremont 118
Orange 95–6
where to stay 225–6
Orient Express 106
Ornithologique du Pont de Gau 124–5
Ospédale lake 195

packing 32
Pagnol, Marcel 135
Pagode Hong Hien 70
Palais des Rois de Majorque 156
Papal Palace 90–1
parks and playgrounds
Acqua Cyrne Gliss 189–90
Adventure Golf 65
Ajaccio 188
Amazonia 175
Amigoland 168
Aqua-Splash 65
Aquacity 135
Aqualand 160, 163
Aquatica 71
Argèles Adventure 160–1
Astronomie du Soleil et du Cosmos 105
Avignon 92
Babyland 168
Calvi 200
Dino Park 162
Eldorado City 135
Espace Adventure 107–8
Ile des Loisirs 161–2
La Jungle des Papillons 65
Le Parc Australien 149
Le Tropique du Papillon 157
Marineland 64–5
Marseille 132
Menton 61
Monaco 60
Nice 53
OK Corral 135
Ornithologique du Pont de Gau 124–5
Perpignan 156
see also zoos
Peillon 81
Perfumerie Fragonard 69
Perpignan 154–6
food and drink 155, 176–7
where to stay 231
Perrier Factory 174
Peyrepertuse 149–50
Pézenas 163
food and drink 163, 177–8
pharmacies 256, 269
Philippe Auguste 40
Philippe-le-Bel Tower 96
Philippe de Valois 40
Pic di Canigou 160
Picasso, Pablo 67, 68
picnics 243
Pinecone Railway 104
Plage de Cabasson 77, 222
Plage du Pellegrin 77
Planet Aquarium 134
Planétarium Galilée 165
planning a holiday 31
Plantagenets 40

playgrounds *see* parks and playgrounds
politics of Corsica 184
Pont du Gard 172
popes 90
Porquerolles 74–5
Port-Barcarès 158
Port-Cros 75
Port-Grimaud 76
Porticcio
  food and drink 206–7
  where to stay 235
Porto 188–9
  food and drink 208
  where to stay 239–40
Porto-Vecchio 193
  beaches 194
  food and drink 207
  where to stay 237
post offices 257, 270
practical A–Z **266–76**
Prades 177
prehistoric man 38
  Bonifacio Woman 194
  Casteddu d'Araghju 194
  Satène prehistoric sites 192
  Tautavel 156
Propriano 207
Protis 130
public holidays 270
Puilaurens 150

Quéribus 149

racism 270–1
rafting 101–2
railways 263–4, 265–6
  Corsica 182
  see also tourist trains
Ramatuelle 76, 223
religious wars 41
Renaissance 41
Réserve Naturelle de Scandola 202
restaurants *see* food and drink
Restonica gorge 205
Revolution 41–2
Ricard, Paul 134
rice-growing 129
Riviera **46–84**, *46–7*
  beaches 48, 53–4, 55, 62
  festivals 47, 48
  food and drink 80–4, 245
  Massif d'Esterel 69
  tourism 42, **50**
  where to stay 218–24
road safety 271
Roi Soleil 41
Romans 38–9, 94–5, 122–3
  amphitheatres 70, 122, 171
  bathhouses 117–18, 122, 172
  Glanum 136–7
  Mas Gallo-Romain des Tourelles 175
  Pont du Gard 172
  theatre 122
  Via Domitia 175
Roquebrune 62
  food and drink 82
  where to stay 220
Roquemaure 226
Roussillon *see* Languedoc-Roussillon
Roussillon (Provence) 97–8
  food and drink 111
  where to stay 226

safety 271–2
Sagone 235
sailing courses 160, 191
St-Aygulf 48, 68
St-Cézaire caves 103
St-Clair 223
Saint-Exupéry, Antoine 78, 196
St-Florent 197
  where to stay 239
St-Guilhem-le-Désert 168
St-Honorat 65
St-Jean-du-Gard 174
Ste-Marguerite 65
Stes-Maries-de-la-Mer 125–6
  food and drink 125
Ste-Maxime 77–9
  where to stay 223–4
St-Maximin-la-Ste-Baume 120–1
  where to stay 226
St-Paul-de-Vence 55
  food and drink 81
St Raphaël 48, 68, **70–2**, 83–4
  food and drink 83–4
  where to stay 221–2
St-Rémy-de-Provence 135–7
  food and drink 142
  where to stay 230
St-Roch 106
St-Tropez **72–4**
  beaches 74, 77
  food and drink 73, 84
  where to stay 222
Salin-de-Giraud 129
Salon de Provence 118–19
  food and drink 118, 139
  where to stay 229
Salses 157
salt trade 167
San Giovanni-di-Moriani 207–8
santon museums 93, 127, 138
Saorge 111
Sartène 192
  beaches 194
  food and drink 192, 207
Scandola 202
school holidays 132, 270
school-age children 31, 35
scrapbooks 34, 99
seals 200
Seaquarium 167
Second World War 43
self-catering 210, 215–16, 247
Sénanque 100
Sète 163–4
shopping 254–8
  Aigues-Mortes 166
  Aix-en-Provence 116
  Ajaccio 185
  Antibes 66
  Arles 121
  Avignon 89–90
  Bastia 196
  Calvi 200
  Cannes 63
  Carcassonne 147
  Carpentras 97
  Cassis 133
  Corte 203
  Fontaine-de-Vaucluse 92–3
  Fréjus 70
  Marseille 130
  Monaco 57–8
  Montpellier 164
  Narbonne 152
  Nice 49
  Nîmes 171
  opening hours 270
  Perpignan 155
  Pézenas 163
  St-Guilhem-le-Désert 168
  St-Tropez 73
  Salon de Provence 118
  Uzès 173
  VAT refunds 264
sirènes 101
skating 165
skiing 107, 109
smoking 272
Smollett, Tobias 50
snacks 243
Sospel 105–6
  food and drink 111
Souterroscope de Baume Obscure 103
souvenirs 257
special needs travellers 272
sports centres 165
  see also water sports

stalactites 159
stamps 257
stargazing 105
The Story of Babar 75, **79**
supermarkets 254
sweets
  berlingots 96, 163
  museum 174
synagogues 97

Tarascon 128
Tarasque 128
Tartarin de Tarascon 128
Tautavel 156
  food and drink 177
taxes 264
teenagers 31, 35–6
  teen talk phrases 276
telephones 272
  emergency numbers 267
temperature chart 31
Tende 111
tennis
  Narbonne 153
  St-Tropez 74
Termes 149
theatres 92
theme parks *see* parks and playgrounds
Théoule-sur-Mer 68
Thomas the Tank Engine 265
Thoronet 120
Thouzon caves 100–1
tickets 272–3
time 273
  useful phrases 275
tipping 273
toddlers 31, 35
toilets 273
Toon's Land 162
tortoise sanctuaries 75, 189
Tourist Board 216
tourist offices 273
tourist trains
  Ajaccio 185
  Arles 124
  Avignon 91–2
  Balagne 202
  Bonifacio 190
  Cassis 133
  Corsican Mountain Railway 203
  Domaine de Méjanes 125
  Le Train des Alpilles 129
  Le Train des Merveilles 107
  Marseille 131
  Monaco 58
  Narbonne 154

tourist trains (*cont'd*)
  Nice 51, 56
  Pinecone Railway 104
  St-Jean-du-Gard 174
  U Trenu 205
  Villefranche-de-Conflent 159
toy shops 257
Trabuc caves 169
trains 263–4, 265–6
  Corsica 182
  see also tourist trains
travel **260–6**
  with children 32–3
  to Corsica 180–2
  disabled travellers 272
  useful phrases 275
travel sickness 34
travellers' cheques 269
Trencavel, Ramon Roger 148
Trophée des Alpes 61–2

Uzès 173
  food and drink 178
  where to stay 233

Vaison-la-Romaine 94–5
  food and drink 110
Valberg 107–8
  food and drink 112
  where to stay 226
Vallée des Merveilles 106
Van Gogh, Vincent 136
Var 70–9
VAT refunds 264
Vaucluse 88–101
Vercingétorix 38
Verdon gorge and lake 102, 226
Vero 207
Via Domitia 175
Vikings 40
Village des Automates 119
Village des Bories 101
Village des Tortues 75
Villefranche-de-Conflent **157**, 159
Villefranche-sur-Mer 48, 53–4, **55**
  food and drink 81–2
  where to stay 220
Villeneuve-lès-Avignon 96
Villerouge-Termenès 176
Visites Contées 155
Vizzavona 205
volcanoes 162

walking
  Camargue 125
  in Corsica 204
  Corsica 204

walking (*cont'd*)
  Gorges du Verdon 102
  Luberon 100
  Narbonne 154
  websites and guidebooks 108
water sports
  Agde 163
  Antibes 68
  Breil-sur-Roya 106
  Calvi 200
  Cannes 64
  Corsica 194
  diving courses 68, 201
  equipment 257
  Fréjus/St Raphaël 71–2
  kayaking/canoeing 93, 126, 169, 175, 205
  Narbonne 153
  Nice 54
  rafting 101–2
  safety 271–2
  sailing courses 160, 191
  Ste-Maxime 79
Western Provence **114–42**, *114–15*
  festivals 114
  food and drink 139–42, 246
  where to stay 114, 227–30
where to stay **210–40**
  apartment hotels 212
  bed and breakfast 212–13
  boat accommodation 215
  camping 216–17
  caravanning 216–17
  gîtes 216
  holiday villages 213–14
  hotels 210–12
    see also under individual places
  self-catering 210, 215–16
  villa holidays 210, 215–16
  youth hostels 214
wine 258
witches of Gruissan 152
World Wars 42, 43

Zidane, Zinedine 129
zoos
  Barben 119–20
  Cap Ferrat 54
  Cessenon-sur-Orb 167
  Fréjus 71
  La Petite Ferme 65
  Mini-Ferme-Zoo 167
  Monaco 59
  Montpellier 167
  Parc Animalier des Angles 156–7
  Réserve de Sigean 153
  Sanary-sur-Mer 134

Available from Cadogan Guides...

take the kids

take the kids: Paris & Disneyland® Resort Paris
take the kids: South of France
take the kids: England
take the kids: London
take the kids: Short Breaks from London

City Guides

Amsterdam
Barcelona
Bruges
Brussels
Edinburgh
Florence
London
Madrid
Milan
Paris
Prague
Rome
Venice

Italy

Italy
Bay of Naples & Southern Italy
Bologna & Emilia-Romagna
Central Italy
Italian Riviera
Lombardy & the Italian Lakes
Northeast Italy
Rome, Florence, Venice
Sardinia
Sicily
Tuscany, Umbria & the Marches
Tuscany
Umbria

Spain

Spain
Andalucía
Bilbao & the Basque Lands
Northern Spain
Granada, Seville, Cordoba

France

France
Brittany
Corsica
Côte d'Azur
Dordogne & the Lot
Gascony & the Pyrenees
Loire
South of France
Short Breaks in Northern France

Greece

Greece
Greek Islands
Crete

The UK and Ireland

London–Paris
London Markets
Scotland
Scotland's Highlands & Islands
Ireland
Southwest Ireland

Other Europe

Madeira & Porto Santo
Malta, Gozo and Comino
Portugal

Flying Visits

Flying Visits: France
Flying Visits: Italy
Flying Visits: Spain

Buying a Property

Buying a Property: France
Buying a Property: Italy
Buying a Property: Spain

Cadogan Guides are available from good bookshops, or via **Littlehampton Book Services Ltd**, Faraday Close, Durrington, Worthing, West Sussex, BN13 3RB, **t** (01903) 828 503, **f** (01903) 828 802, *mailorder@lbsltd.co.uk*; and **The Globe Pequot Press**, 246 Goose Lane, PO Box 480, Guilford, Connecticut 06437–0480, **t** (800) 458 4500/**f** (203) 458 4500, **t** (203) 458 4603.